ADVANCES IN QUANTITATIVE ANALYSIS OF FINANCE AND ACCOUNTING

Volume 2 • 1993 (Part A)

Editorial Board

ADVANCES IN QUANTITATIVE ANALYSIS OF FINANCE AND ACCOUNTING

Editor: CHENG F. LEE
Department of Finance
Rutgers University—New Brunswick

VOLUME 2 • 1993 (Part A)

JAI PRESS INC.

Greenwich, Connecticut *London, England*

55 Old Post Road, No. 2
Greenwich, Connecticut 06830

JAI PRESS LTD.
The Courtyard
28 High Street
Hampton Hill,
Middlesex TW12 1PD
England

ISBN: 1-55938-564-2 (Part A)
ISBN: 1-55938-431-X (Set)

Manufactured in the United States of America

CONTENTS

PART B

PART A: LIST OF CONTRIBUTORS

Roger W. Bartlett	California State University, Sacramento
Robert Brooks	University of Alabama
Chingfu Chang	Rutgers University—New Brunswick
S. L. Chang	National Taiwan Central University
J. T. Chen	Taiwan Technology Institute
David C. Cheng	University of Alabama
T. Daniel Coggin	Virginia Retirement System
Ramon P. DeGennaro	University of Tennessee—Knoxville
Dan S. Dhaliwal	University of Arizona
Patricia M. Fairfield	Georgetown University
Kenneth R. Ferris	American Graduate School of International Management
John E. Hunter	Michigan State University
Debra C. Jeter	Austin Peay State University
Marvin J. Karson	University of New Hampshire
Myung J. Kim	University of Alabama
Cheng F. Lee	Rutgers University—New Brunswick
Miles Livingston	University of Florida
William Reichenstein	Baylor University
Shekar Shetty	University of South Dakota at Cedar Rapids
Robert Trezevant	University of Southern California
Gili Yen	National Taiwan Central University

THE CORRELATION STRUCTURE OF THE WORLD STOCK MARKET

John E. Hunter and T. Daniel Coggin

I. INTRODUCTION

Now that national stock markets have developed in a number of countries, investors are increasingly attempting to diversify risk by spreading their portfolios across different national stock markets. Recent comprehensive summaries of the growing international portfolio selection literature are given in Adler and Dumas (1983) and Solnik (1988). The extent to which investment risk can be diversified depends upon the degree to which national markets are dependent up one another. If all national markets were completely dominated by a single world market factor (i.e., if all cross-national correlations were 1.00), then international diversification would have no benefit. If all national markets were completely independent (i.e., if all cross-national correlations were zero), then international diversification over an infinite number of countries would completely eliminate the effect of variation in national markets.

Studies of stocks within the United States have found that the correlation structure of returns is largely explained by a "single index" model. That is, there is

Advances in Quantitative Analysis of Finance and Accounting,
Volume 2, Part A, pages 1–37.

ISBN: 1-55938-564-2

one dominant causal agent or "market factor" in the correlation structure of stock returns (see, e.g., Cohen and Pogue, 1967; Elton and Gruber, 1973; King, 1966; and Meyers, 1973). Other factors, such as industry group, were present but found to be of relatively minor importance. In research which has sparked considerable debate, recent multifactor models derived from the arbitrage pricing theory still find a single dominant factor in U.S. and Canadian stock return correlation matrices (see Brown, 1989; Conway and Reinganum, 1988; Kryzanowski and To, 1983; and Trzcinka, 1986). Early evidence of a dominant "world market factor" was presented by Ripley (1973) and Lessard (1974). Bergstrom and Henriksson (1982) also found that a single index (beta model) was superior to the historical and average correlation models in predicting the covariance structure of returns on 165 national stock market indices for the period 1976–1980.

It therefore seems plausible that correlations between stocks in different countries would also be mediated by the market factors of each country. That is, if stock 1 is from country A and stock 2 is from country B, the correlation between stocks 1 and 2 would drop to zero if the two country-level stock factors were partialled out. In technical terms, this is the mathematical assumption of (first order) "confirmatory factor analysis."[1] If this assumption is satisfied, all the information about the world stock correlation structure is captured by the correlations between the national market factors. Now suppose that the correlations between national market factors are in turn explained by their relationship to the world market factor; that is, suppose that the partial correlation between national market factors drops to zero when the world market factor is held constant. If the correlation between stocks 1 and 2 drops to zero when the world factor is partialled out, then the two stocks fit a model called "hierarchical (second order) confirmatory factor analysis" (Hunter and Gerbing, 1982). In any case, the pervasive nature of national market factors means that information about their correlation structure will play an important role in whatever model fits the data in full detail.

Our chapter begins by examining the correlations between national market factors. Our hypothesis was that this correlation matrix would satisfy a single index model. That is, it was our hypothesis that countries relate to the world market in the same way that firms relate to national markets. We tested this model and found that it fit the data except for some problems associated with the correlation matrix for daily returns. We will present the full hierarchical model for the world market, national markets, and national firms. We are currently gathering data on individual firms to directly test this model; however, there are existing studies which report relevant analyses. We will critique the important work of Eun and Resnick (1984) and Cho, Eun, and Senbet (1986) in this regard.

This chapter also seeks an empirical estimate of the correlation between the returns on national stock markets. Six sets of correlations between national stock indices were located: one using daily returns, two using weekly returns, two using monthly returns, and one using quarterly returns. The average correlations were considerably higher for longer time intervals. We show that the conventional random walk model of stock prices from financial economics (Fama, 1970,1976) predicts that such correlations should be *identical* across time intervals. Thus there was a major methodological complication in our results. In order to resolve our finding, we needed a model which would account for the difference in results across time intervals. The second half of our chapter develops such a model.

The model we present is a noncumulative random fluctuation model for *return* derived from a fluctuation model for *price*. This model was adapted from the classic psychometric error of measurement model discussed in Lord and Novick (1968, chap. 3). The random fluctuation model fits the data. It also generates an estimate of the average correlation between national markets that is free of error of measurement and hence free of the artifactual effects associated with short time interval return data. That is, the fluctuation model attributes the *increase* in observed correlations for longer time intervals to a *reduction* in measurement error. In our data this estimate is $r = 0.56$. We also briefly discuss the application of a recent nonrandom walk ("mean reverting") model proposed by Summers (1986) and expanded by Fama and French (1988) and Poterba and Summers (1988).

II. DATA AND METHODOLOGY

A. The Data

Data were gathered from the International Research Departments at four large Wall Street brokerage houses and one academic study. Six national stock index correlation matrices were obtained based on: daily price changes for the 11-year period 1976–1986 from Salomon Brothers ($n = 20$ countries); weekly price changes for the same period from Salomon Brothers ($n = 19$ countries), and for the 10-year period 1963–1972 from Joy et al. (1976, $n = 10$ countries); monthly price changes for the 5-year period 1982–1986 from Goldman Sachs ($n = 18$ countries), and for the 13-year period 1973–1985 from Merrill Lynch ($n = 9$ countries); and quarterly total returns for the 17-year period 1970–1986 ($n = 12$ countries) from Morgan Stanley. In calculating the return data used for each correlation matrix, Salomon Brothers used the Salomon–Russell global and non-U.S. equity indexes, Goldman Sachs used the Financial Times–Actuaries World indices, Merrill Lynch used Datastream International, Morgan Stanley used Morgan Stanley Capital International and Joy et al. (1976) used *Barron's*. As noted in Roll (1988, n. 12) and elsewhere, we do not feel that the use of price change for the daily, weekly, and monthly correlation matrices (as opposed to using total return for the quarterly matrix) has any impact on our basic results. We view our use of several data sources and time periods as adding validity to our results, since our basic findings are replicated across the several different data bases and time periods.

The problem of *nonsynchronous trading* in the international capital market is an issue for studies of the correlations between national stock markets. To date, there is no generally accepted, nonproblematic method for dealing with this problem. Our discussions with analysts at all four brokerage houses revealed that various attempts to adjust for nonsynchronous trading had no material effect on observed correlation data. Furthermore, as one would expect, the impact of nonsynchronous trading is heavily concentrated in daily return data. Because our correlational data are based on daily, weekly, monthly, and quarterly returns, we do not feel that an adjustment for nonsynchronous trading would have a material effect on our results. Hence no correction was applied to our data. See Appendix B for a discussion of nonsynchronous trading and the "intervalling-effect bias" hypothesis of Cohen et al. (1983). Finally, the stock indices included in our study contain only *investable* stocks (stocks which can be purchased by foreign investors), and we do not double-count stocks listed on more than one exchange (only the primary listing is included).

Each correlation matrix was first examined for evidence of multidimensionality. We initially examined correlations based on national index returns expressed in U.S. dollars. Factor analysis (described below) showed that a single index model fit the correlation matrices based on U.S. dollar returns. However, we were concerned that the fluctuations of the dollar during the period might distort the patterns within the correlation matrices. That is, we were afraid that the fluctuations in an arbitrarily chosen baseline currency would distort the true variation in national index returns. So we then examined correlation matrices based upon national index returns expressed in local currencies. The observed correlations were similar to those based on returns in dollars. Only the results for correlations based on returns in local currencies are presented here. For an analysis of the relative performance of hedged versus unhedged international portfolios, see Eun and Resnick (1988). The six correlation matrices are presented in Tables 1A, 1B, 1C, 1D, 1E, and 1F.

B. Fitting a One-Factor (Single Index) Model

Each correlation matrix was analyzed using ordinary least squares confirmatory factor analysis, alternately termed *oblique multiple-group factor analysis* (Gorsuch, 1974; Harmon, 1976; Nunnally, 1978), with a one-factor model. The world factor was defined as that factor which explains the correlations between the countries in the correlation matrix. This unidimensional model was found to fit the data. Communalities were used in the confirmatory factor analysis, hence the definition of the world market factor was not biased due to missing countries. A further discussion of the importance of communalities is given below and in our critique of the Eun and Resnick (1984) study in Section III.D.

1. Index versus Factor

At this juncture it is important to note a terminology problem that runs through the finance literature using factor analysis; namely, a problem with the word *index*.

Table 1A. Daily Price Change Correlations from Salomon Brothers in Local Currency Terms, 1976–1986

Australia	1.00																			
Belgium	0.06	1.00																		
Brazil	0.02	0.01	1.00																	
Denmark	0.01	0.04	0.04	1.00																
France	0.03	0.19	0.00	0.05	1.00															
Hong Kong	0.31	0.06	−0.01	0.04	0.06	1.00														
India	0.06	0.01	0.01	0.01	0.02	0.06	1.00													
Italy	0.03	0.03	0.01	0.04	0.03	0.04	0.02	1.00												
Japan	0.10	0.00	0.03	0.05	0.14	0.13	0.08	0.06	1.00											
Netherlands	0.11	0.25	0.03	0.10	0.26	0.13	0.04	0.07	0.21	1.00										
New Zealand	0.13	0.13	0.04	0.11	0.11	0.16	0.16	0.08	0.19	0.21	1.00									
Philippines	−0.01	0.00	0.01	−0.04	0.01	−0.01	0.00	−0.01	−0.01	0.00	0.01	1.00								
South Korea	0.03	0.00	−0.05	0.00	0.00	−0.02	−0.04	−0.01	0.03	0.00	0.01	0.02	1.00							
Spain	0.04	0.01	−0.03	0.02	0.04	0.03	0.04	0.02	0.04	0.02	0.06	0.01	0.00	1.00						
Sweden	0.07	0.03	0.01	0.07	0.08	0.06	0.05	0.05	0.10	0.15	0.09	−0.01	0.02	0.01	10.00					
Taiwan	0.08	0.06	0.02	0.02	0.05	0.04	0.05	0.04	0.03	0.05	0.05	0.01	0.00	0.01	0.05	1.00				
Thailand	0.04	0.04	0.00	0.05	0.04	0.22	0.03	0.01	0.09	0.06	0.11	−0.01	0.04	0.06	0.04	0.02	1.00			
United Kingdom	0.04	0.10	0.04	0.04	0.11	0.06	0.01	0.02	0.11	0.28	0.09	0.00	−0.02	0.02	0.03	0.03	0.02	1.00		
United States	0.05	0.05	0.02	0.01	0.06	0.08	0.04	0.02	0.08	0.12	0.06	−0.01	−0.03	0.00	0.02	0.03	0.01	0.16	1.00	
West Germany	0.07	0.15	0.03	0.05	0.16	0.13	0.02	0.01	0.18	0.39	0.12	0.01	0.03	0.02	0.07	0.04	0.03	0.13	0.08	1.00

Table 1B. Weekly Price Change Correlations from Salomon Brothers in Local Currency Terms, 1976–1986

Australia	1.00																		
Belgium	0.17	1.00																	
Brazil	0.02	0.05	1.00																
Denmark	0.23	0.10	0.04	1.00															
France	0.08	0.24	0.08	0.06	1.00														
Hong Kong	0.27	0.09	0.00	0.10	0.04	1.00													
India	0.07	–0.12	0.03	0.00	–0.04	–0.02	1.00												
Italy	0.09	0.09	0.07	0.11	0.00	0.09	–0.04	1.00											
Japan	0.25	0.15	0.02	0.15	0.12	0.21	0.01	0.10	1.00										
New Zealand	0.20	0.07	0.12	0.12	0.12	0.09	0.03	0.08	0.07	1.00									
Philippines	0.20	0.00	0.03	0.03	0.07	0.16	0.03	0.12	0.05	0.05	1.00								
South Korea	–0.07	0.00	–0.05	0.01	–0.03	0.02	0.02	–0.03	0.11	0.11	–0.04	1.00							
Spain	0.10	–0.01	0.05	0.03	0.01	0.07	0.05	0.03	0.10	0.09	0.04	0.02	1.00						
Sweden	0.15	0.04	0.04	0.16	0.02	0.11	0.10	0.04	0.11	0.07	0.11	0.04	0.05	1.00					
Taiwan	0.12	0.10	0.07	0.10	0.09	0.13	0.01	0.13	0.17	0.07	0.10	0.05	0.00	0.05	1.00				
Thailand	–0.01	0.02	–0.01	–0.05	0.01	0.00	0.00	–0.04	0.02	–0.02	0.02	–0.03	–0.03	–0.04	0.04	1.00			
United Kingdom	0.30	0.18	0.11	0.13	0.13	0.16	0.03	0.18	0.23	0.09	0.11	0.02	0.11	0.10	0.12	–0.01	1.00		
United States	0.32	0.23	0.00	0.09	0.18	0.21	0.04	0.13	0.30	0.08	0.13	0.00	0.08	0.10	0.12	–0.04	0.28	1.00	
West Germany	0.18	0.16	0.07	0.07	0.15	0.17	0.04	0.05	0.24	0.07	0.04	0.06	0.07	0.08	0.14	0.05	0.22	0.24	1.00

Table 1C. Weekly Price Change Correlations from Joy et al. (1976) in Local Currency Terms, 1963–1972

Australia	1.00									
Austria	–0.02	1.00								
Belgium	0.11	0.04	1.00							
France	0.06	0.06	0.24	1.00						
Italy	0.02	0.05	0.07	0.03	1.00					
Japan	0.06	0.02	0.10	0.08	0.13	1.00				
Netherlands	0.13	0.06	0.27	0.16	0.12	0.18	1.00			
United Kingdom	0.17	0.08	0.13	0.04	0.07	0.08	0.16	1.00		
West Germany	0.09	0.10	0.22	0.18	0.07	0.13	0.34	0.04	1.00	
United States	0.16	0.02	0.23	0.10	0.02	0.08	0.35	0.13	0.17	1.00

Table 1D. Monthly Price Change Correlations from Goldman Sachs in Local Currency Terms, 1982–1986

Australia	1.00																	
Austria	0.15	1.00																
Belgium	0.15	0.14	1.00															
Denmark	0.28	0.02	0.29	1.00														
France	0.22	0.33	0.46	0.30	1.00													
West Germany	0.12	0.34	0.37	0.28	0.42	1.00												
Hong Kong	0.24	0.11	0.15	0.12	0.29	0.30	1.00											
Ireland	0.28	0.20	0.48	0.42	0.45	0.09	0.24	1.00										
Italy	0.12	0.16	0.36	0.23	0.51	0.26	0.24	0.27	1.00									
Japan	0.15	0.10	0.27	0.05	0.39	0.27	0.12	0.18	0.32	1.00								
Netherlands	0.24	0.19	0.37	0.35	0.43	0.46	0.36	0.34	0.34	0.40	1.00							
New Zealand	0.37	0.16	0.23	0.27	0.31	0.22	0.38	0.37	0.14	–0.02	0.22	1.00						
Norway	0.42	–0.02	0.33	0.37	0.23	0.19	0.37	0.32	0.10	0.12	0.43	0.26	1.00					
South Africa	0.30	0.15	0.15	–0.13	0.18	0.05	–0.10	–0.01	–0.01	0.25	0.08	0.06	0.11	1.00				
Spain	0.09	0.01	0.12	–0.09	0.38	0.19	0.10	0.15	0.49	0.31	0.21	0.12	0.06	–0.11	1.00			
Sweden	0.30	0.07	0.15	0.24	0.25	0.13	0.12	0.12	0.41	0.18	0.28	0.06	0.19	0.17	0.24	1.00		
United Kingdom	0.31	0.06	0.58	0.19	0.50	0.37	0.29	0.42	0.28	0.38	0.51	0.10	0.35	0.25	0.17	0.34	1.00	
United States	0.32	0.20	0.34	0.28	0.45	0.30	0.03	0.32	0.29	0.31	0.49	0.14	0.35	0.25	0.19	0.38	0.56	1.00

Table 1E. Monthly Price Change Correlations from Merrill Lynch in Local Currency Terms, 1973–1985

United States	1.00								
Japan	0.28	1.00							
United Kingdom	0.49	0.30	1.00						
West Germany	0.27	0.35	0.27	1.00					
France	0.29	0.13	0.36	0.17	1.00				
Italy	0.21	0.22	0.32	0.19	0.26	1.00			
Australia	0.43	0.32	0.39	0.20	0.23	0.29	1.00		
Sweden	0.40	0.16	0.30	0.13	0.11	0.22	0.26	1.00	
Hong Kong	0.21	0.32	0.25	0.19	0.12	0.19	0.18	0.16	1.00

Table 1F. Quarterly Total Return Correlations from Morgan Stanley in Local Currency Terms, 1970–1986

Australia	1.00											
Belgium	0.38	1.00										
France	0.38	0.69	1.00									
Italy	0.39	0.44	0.52	1.00								
Japan	0.34	0.36	0.31	0.37	1.00							
Netherlands	0.53	0.67	0.54	0.40	0.50	1.00						
Norway	0.32	0.44	0.35	0.21	0.07	0.34	1.00					
Spain	0.24	0.33	0.23	0.43	0.43	0.31	0.08	1.00				
Sweden	0.28	0.41	0.28	0.43	0.38	0.45	0.09	0.33	1.00			
United Kingdom	0.41	0.58	0.44	0.32	0.42	0.67	0.18	0.19	0.34	1.00		
United States	0.57	0.50	0.45	0.33	0.48	0.69	0.30	0.28	0.42	0.60	1.00	
West Germany	0.39	0.49	0.48	0.37	0.37	0.63	0.01	0.27	0.39	0.45	0.51	1.00

Strictly speaking, a stock index is a composite—an artificial creation intended to be a representative portfolio. As such, an index cannot be a causal agent and hence cannot explain anything, including the correlations between stock returns. On the other hand, the *factors* in a factor analysis are variables connected to the observed variables by a model which is assumed to represent causal effects.

At the level of the world market, it is especially important to distinguish between an index and a factor. We do not have data on all countries in the world stock market. Thus a world market index will have considerable error as an estimate of the value of the world market *factor*. That is, at the world market level, a world index is quantitatively as well as substantively different from the world factor. Our factor analyses presented here are done with communalities in the diagonal, hence the world market factor replaces a world market index in the calculations. We will return to this distinction when we critique the analysis of Eun and Resnick (1984) in Section III.D.

III. RESULTS

A. Testing for Unidimensionality

Our primary formal test for unidimensionality was an examination of the one-factor model residuals using partial correlation. The estimated world factor was partialed out of each correlation matrix. The resulting partial correlations are thus standardized residuals from the one-factor model. If a one-factor model fits, then the matrix of residuals should not be significantly different from zero. Since communalities were used in the confirmatory factor analysis, there was no violation of dimensionality constraints. A chi-square test was applied to each matrix of partial correlations. With the exception of the daily correlation matrix from Salomon Brothers, each chi-square value was not significant at the 0.05 level. That is (except for the daily data), once the world market factor was partialed out, all (residual) intercountry correlations are zero. Thus the fit of the single index model is supported by the results of the chi-square tests. While the chi-square value was nominally significant for the daily return partial correlation matrix, the residuals are very small and random in pattern. The mean absolute residual is 0.027. Hence we believe that there are no truly significant departures from the fit of a one-factor model to the daily data as well.

We note that the nominal sample size in time series correlation assumes *perfect temporal independence* of observations. Thus the nominal sample size does not take into account the redundancy in actual temporal trends. That is, the degree of serial correlation in daily returns effectively *reduces* the nominal sample size. If the nominal sample size for the daily data were reduced by about 77% (to approximately the sample size for weekly data), the chi-square value would no longer be significant. We will further discuss the issue of nonindependence and significance tests in our discussion of the study by Cho, Eun, and Senbet (1986) in Section III.D.

B. World Factor Correlations

The fit of the single index (world market factor) model implies that a key question is the extent to which each country is correlated with the world factor. The correlations between the stock market of each country and the world stock market were estimated by the confirmatory factor analysis of each of the correlation matrices presented in Tables 1A–1F. These correlations (sometimes called "factor loadings") are presented in Table 2.

If we were to rank-order the countries within each data set in Table 2 on the basis of how highly each market correlates with the world market, the United States and Japan would not rank highest. The European countries had the highest correlations, with an especially high correlation for the Netherlands. It is our hypothesis that the size of the country-world correlation is determined not by absolute economic size but primarily by the relative proportion of the national economy that is tied to external trade (and, to a lesser extent, by the degree of constraint on domestic stock market investment by foreigners [Eun and Janakiramanan, 1986]). That is, the greater the relative economic dependence on trade, the higher the correlation between the national market and the world market. We do not formally test this hypothesis in the present study.

The completely surprising finding in Table 2 is reflected in the average factor loading across countries (the last row in Table 2). The average factor loading is 0.23 for daily data, 0.31 for weekly data, 0.495 for monthly data, and 0.63 for quarterly data. Some investigators choose the time interval as a matter of convenience under the assumption that serial cross correlations between indices will be the same for different time intervals. In section IV.A, we show this is implied by the conventional random walk model (Fama, 1970, 1976). Our data sharply contradict the random walk model. Much of the following discussion is devoted to the question of which number best represents the extent of correlation among countries. We now believe that it is the higher correlations for quarterly returns that more accurately estimate the true factor loadings.

A closely related issue is the size of the average correlation between countries. The single index model predicts that the average correlation between countries is equal to the square of the average factor loading. If the average factor loading varies by the time interval, the average correlation between countries would be expected to vary even more. The observed average correlations between countries are as follows:

Daily	=	0.05 Salomon Brothers	=	0.05
Weekly	=	0.08 Salomon Brothers; 0.11 Joy et al.	=	0.095
Monthly	=	0.24 Goldman Sachs; 0.25 Merrill Lynch	=	0.245
Quarterly	=	0.39 Morgan Stanley Capital International	=	0.39

Table 2. World Factor Correlations for Individual Countries Based on Daily, Weekly, Monthly, and Quarterly Returns

Country	*Daily Returns*[a]	*Weekly Returns*[b]	*Weekly Returns*[c]	*Monthly Returns*[d]	*Monthly Returns*[e]	*Quarterly Returns*[f]
Australia	0.29	0.55	0.25	0.49	0.58	0.61
Austria	—	—	0.13	0.28	—	—
Belgium	0.27	0.31	0.49	0.60	—	0.79
Brazil	0.05	0.14	—	—	—	—
Denmark	0.16	0.29	—	0.41	—	—
France	0.32	0.26	0.31	0.75	0.40	0.68
Hong Kong	0.37	0.38	—	0.40	0.39	—
India	0.15	0.04	—	—	—	—
Ireland	—	—	—	0.56	—	—
Italy	0.12	0.23	0.18	0.54	0.46	0.61
Japan	0.38	0.49	0.27	0.45	0.51	0.58
Netherlands	0.60	—	0.63	0.70	—	0.86
New Zealand	0.45	0.29	—	0.40	—	—
Norway	—	—	—	0.50	—	0.33
Philippines	−0.01	0.24	—	—	—	—
South Africa	—	—	—	0.19	—	—
South Korea	0.00	0.04	—	—	—	—
Spain	0.09	0.16	—	0.31	—	0.44
Sweden	0.22	0.26	—	0.43	0.42	0.55
Taiwan	0.15	0.31	—	—	—	—
Thailand	0.20	−0.03	—	—	—	—
United Kingdom	0.29	0.51	0.29	0.69	0.69	0.67
United States	0.19	0.51	0.42	0.63	0.66	0.76
West Germany	0.40	0.42	0.45	0.52	0.43	0.63
Mean Correlation	0.23	0.28	0.34	0.49	0.50	0.63

Sources: [a]Salomon Brothers, 1976–1986.
[b]Salomon Brothers, 1976–1986.
[c]Joy et al. (1976), 1963–1972.
[d]Goldman Sachs, 1982–1986.
[e]Merrill Lynch, 1973–1985.
[f]Morgan Stanley, 1970–1986.

The squared mean factor loading (from Table 2) for daily returns is $(0.23)^2 = 0.0529$, which almost exactly equals the average correlation of 0.05 between countries for daily returns The squared mean factor loading for weekly returns is $[(0.28 + 0.34)/2 = 0.31]^2 = 0.0961$, which almost exactly equals the average correlation of 0.095 between countries for weekly returns. The squared mean factor loading for monthly returns is $[(0.49 + 0.50)/2 = 0.495]^2 = 0.2450$, which exactly equals the average correlation of 0.245 between countries for monthly returns. The squared mean factor loading for quarterly returns is $(0.63)^2 = 0.3969$, which almost exactly equals the average correlation of 0.39 between countries for quarterly returns. Thus the fit of the single-index model is supported by a second (although somewhat weaker) statistical test.

C. Hierarchical Structure of the World Correlation Matrix

Figure 1 presents a hierarchical factor structure for the world correlation matrix. This figure has three parts: (a) the top part of the figure depicts the relationship between the world market factor and the individual country factors, (b) the several subfigures relate each national market factor to the firms within that country, and (c) the missing part of the figure; that is, the missing arrows connect individual firms in different nations. Empirical support for the model as a whole will be organized around the three parts of the figure.

1. The World–Country Model

Consider the model for the national markets presented in Figure 1; i.e., the top part of Figure 1. Figure 1 is a causal diagram (sometimes called a path diagram). There is an arrow from the world market to each national market. This causal arrow means that the world market has a causal impact on each national market, and not vice versa. There is no arrow directly connecting any of the countries. Thus this model implies that the world market explains all correlations between national markets. If the world market factor were held constant over time, then all correlations between national markets would drop to zero. Hence, according to this model, the only thing prohibiting perfect diversification of portfolios across countries is variation in the world market factor.

The world–country market model was directly tested in the analysis presented in Section III.A. We computed the partial correlations between national markets with the world market factor held constant for each of the six correlation matrices. Chi-square tests showed that (except for the daily data previously discussed) these partial correlations are collectively zero; that is, none is significantly different from zero. Thus the top part of Figure 1 is strongly supported in five of the six correlation matrices presented here.

2. The Country–Firm Submodels

Consider each submodel along the bottom of Figure 1. Each submodel shows a given country hierarchically related to individual firms within that country. In each model, there are arrows from the national market to each firm and no arrows from one firm to another. These submodels have been consistently supported by the factor analyses of correlations between firms (see Elton and Gruber [1987, chap.

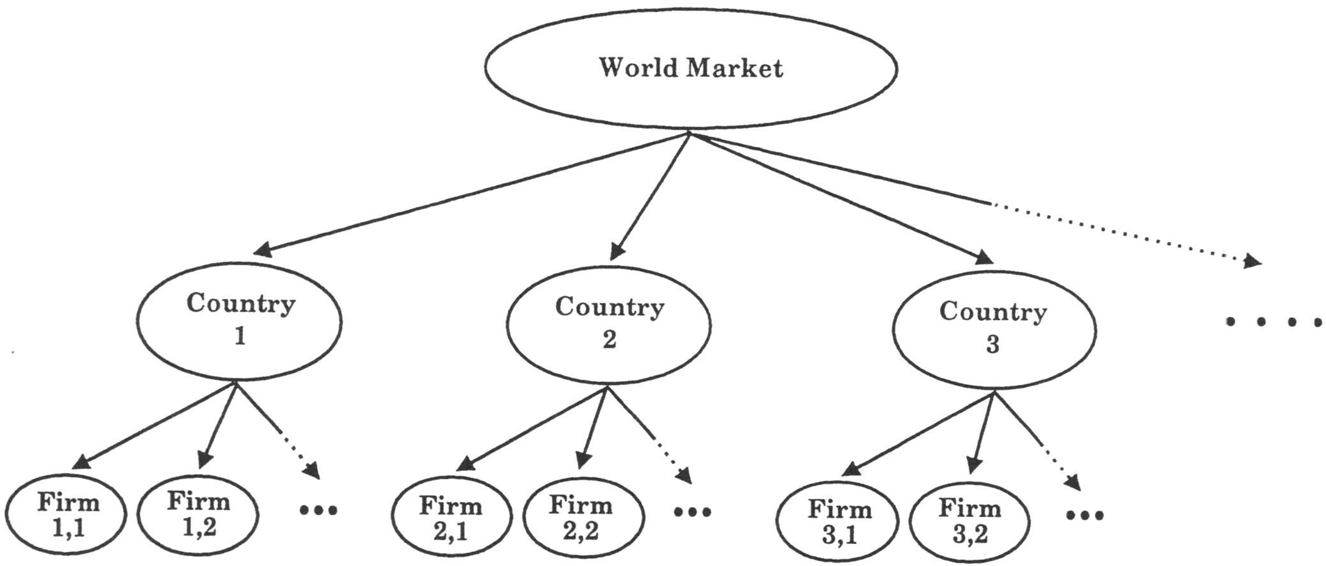

Figure 1. Hierarchical Factor Model for the World Market, for National Markets, and for National Firms

6] for a summary). This submodel is the single-index model of stock return. The single-index model fits the data only if all the partial correlations between firms (with the national market factor held constant) are zero. We do not know if the single-index model has been tried for every country, but the weight of the evidence to date supports its widespread application (including the studies reviewed in Section III.D). A research project we have under way will directly test this relationship.

3. Missing Arrows

In any path (structural equation) model, the most important arrows are those which are not there: the potential relations that are hypothesized to be zero. For each missing arrow, there is a partial correlation which is predicted to be zero. In Figure 1, there are no arrows between individual firms in different countries. The implication is that there is no causal factor other than the national markets that connect firm stock movements. Furthermore, since the national markets are connected only by the world market, the implication of the model is that if the world market were held constant, then the correlation between two firms from different countries would drop to zero.

Consider a stratified firm-level data set in which there is exactly one firm from each country. According to the hierarchical model in Figure 1, the firm correlation matrix would satisfy a single-index model. The general factor for that correlation matrix would be the world market factor. For a nonstratified set of firms, not all the world factor partial correlations would be zero. The partial correlations between firms from different countries would be zero, but the partial correlations between firms within the same country would still be positive.

Because we did not have firm-level data available to us for this study, we could not directly test this part of the hierarchical model. However, there is considerable supporting evidence in a study by Eun and Resnick (1984). In particular, their results suggest there is no tendency for industry factors to go across national boundaries.

D. Related Studies

Eun and Resnick (1984) studied the world correlation structure at the *firm level.* They computed monthly return serial cross correlations ("historical pairwise correlations") for 160 firms in eight countries. The model which best fit their data was the "national mean" model. For this model, the firms are arranged by country and the correlation matrix is correspondingly partitioned into blocks. Within each block are the correlations between all the firms in one given country and all the firms in a second given country. The national mean model assumes that all correlations within such a block are equal.

The fit of the national mean model to the Eun and Resnick data can be considered together with the fit of the single-index model to the national market correlation matrix in our study. The joint fit of these models implies the fit of the hierarchical model. The national mean model also makes an assumption beyond the hierarchical factor model: that, at the firm level, all firms are uniform in the correlation between stock return and the national market factor. This corresponds to the assumption that observed differences in the firm–country factor loadings are solely due to sampling error. However, this assumption was not tested by a formal statistical test. Rather, the national mean model was observed to fit better than other models on the basis of a comparison of mean squared forecast error.

Eun and Resnick also defined a "country index" model in which they thought of countries as "extra-market" factors disturbing a grand single-index model. Their country model would have been equivalent to the hierarchical model except that they did not use communalities in their implicit factor analysis. Thus they replaced each market factor by a market index. For three of the countries, the national market index was based on only ten firms. The world market index was based on only eight countries. Indices using so few representatives will produce noticeable statistical errors of estimation which could be minimized if communalities were used.

Using 349 stocks sorted into 11 country groups, Cho, Eun, and Senbet (1986) presented a test of the "international arbitrage pricing theory" in which they claim that there are three or four "worldwide common factors" (p. 328). If this were true, it would certainly pose problems for the hierarchical model. However, there are three problems with the analysis of Cho, Eun, and Senbet. First, their analysis is an *exploratory* factor analysis rather than a *confirmatory* factor analysis. Therefore their factors are not concretely identified (see our n. 1). Second, they blindly determine the number of factors using a statistical significance test. Thus they are at the mercy of the statistical assumptions made in that test. If an assumption is wrong, they may be overfactoring. We will argue just that. We believe that nonindependence in the serial correlations results in an underestimate of sampling error, which in turn leads to overfactoring. Third, the way in which they applied interbattery factor analysis is not mathematically consistent.

Consider their use of exploratory factor analysis (where factors are not defined a priori) as compared to confirmatory factor analysis (where factors are defined a priori). Cho, Eun, and Senbet use exploratory factor analysis and hence make no attempt to interpret their factors; they only count them. So when they say that there are three or four "worldwide common factors," they make no attempt to define these factors. Therefore we cannot see if the factors make substantive sense, and we cannot bring other data to bear to test their hypothesis. Since the factors are never defined, they must be regarded as potential phantoms. This is a recurring problem for "blind" factor analytic techniques (see, e.g., Elton and Gruber [1987, pp. 348–354] for a discussion).

Consider also their formula for sampling error. They use the conventional formula in which the number of time periods is treated as the number of degrees of freedom. This would be true if the conventional random walk model were true. But we have presented data here suggesting that that model is false in the context of national markets. As we will note in Section IV.E there is mounting evidence that the random walk model does not fit stock return data.

If successive observations are not independent, the nominal number of time points is not equal to the actual degrees of freedom. In the Cho, Eun, and Senbet study, there were 12 monthly returns for each of 11 years; a nominal sample size of 132. However, suppose the serial correlation between observations is not zero. Then the effective sample size might be 100 or 80 or 60 or . . . . This is no minor problem for exploratory factor analysis. The number of factors is determined by a statistical test on the successive eigenvalues. If the sampling error is underestimated, eigenvalues will be accepted as real that are actually the sum of squared sampling errors. Furthermore, the structure is not linear. Spurious roots tend to be equal in size. If sampling error is underestimated, the number of false roots may jump from zero to five in a small interval. We believe this to be a problem in many current exploratory factor analyses done in the context of the APT (arbitrage pricing theory). Other data suggesting that APT methods overfactor have been presented by Conway and Reinganum (1988).

Finally, we note that the particular method of interbattery factor analysis used by Cho, Eun, and Senbet (1986) is not mathematically consistent. They did not consider all countries together. Instead they analyzed countries in pairs. For each pair of countries they attempted to compute the number of common factors. As noted in the previous paragraph, this number is probably overstated in their analysis. But take their numbers at face value. We will show that the numbers that they present in their Table II do not necessarily guarantee even one common factor, much less three or four.

Table 3 presents a hypothetical set of correlations for 12 firms; 4 firms in each of three countries. Panel A of Table 3 presents the serial cross correlations between firms. Panel B presents a factor analysis of the correlation matrix in panel A. Consider interbattery factor analysis as Cho, Eun, and Senbet (1986) used it: by pairs of countries. Interbattery factor analysis will show that countries A and B share two common factors (factors 1 and 2 in panel B). Interbattery factor analysis will show that countries A and C share two common factors (factors 3 and 4 in panel B). Interbattery factor analysis will show that countries B and C share two common factors (factors 5 and 6 in panel B). However, even though the number of common factors is two for each pair of countries, there is not a single worldwide common factor. The two factors "shared" by A and B are different from those "shared" by A and C or those "shared" by B and C.

Thus there are no data in Cho, Eun, and Senbet (1986) that are inconsistent with the hierarchical model. In fact, the average correlations in their Table I fit the hierarchical model quite well.

Table 3. A Hypothetical Example of Correlations between 12 Firms from Three Countries That Contradicts Cho, Eun, and Senbet (1986)[a]

Panel A: Correlations

		A1	*A2*	*A3*	*A4*	*B1*	*B2*	*B3*	*B4*	*C1*	*C2*	*C3*	*C4*
Country A	Firm 1	100	29	0	0	20	20	0	0	0	0	0	0
	Firm 2	29	100	0	0	20	20	0	0	0	0	0	0
	Firm 3	0	0	100	29	0	0	0	0	20	20	0	0
	Firm 4	0	0	29	100	0	0	0	0	20	20	0	0
Country B	Firm 1	20	20	0	0	100	29	0	0	0	0	0	0
	Firm 2	20	20	0	0	29	100	0	0	0	0	0	0
	Firm 3	0	0	0	0	0	0	100	29	0	0	20	20
	Firm 4	0	0	0	0	0	0	29	100	0	0	20	20
Country C	Firm 1	0	0	20	20	0	0	0	0	100	29	0	0
	Firm 2	0	0	20	20	0	0	0	0	29	100	0	0
	Firm 3	0	0	0	0	0	0	20	20	0	0	100	29
	Firm 4	0	0	0	0	0	0	20	20	0	0	29	100

Panel B: Factor Loadings

		1	*2*	*3*	*4*	*5*	*6*
Country A	Firm 1	50	20	0	0	0	0
	Firm 2	50	20	0	0	0	0
	Firm 3	0	0	50	20	0	0
	Firm 4	0	0	50	20	0	0
Country B	Firm 1	20	50	0	0	0	0
	Firm 2	20	50	0	0	0	0
	Firm 3	0	0	0	0	50	20
	Firm 4	0	0	0	0	50	20
Country C	Firm 1	0	0	20	50	0	0
	Firm 2	0	0	20	50	0	0
	Firm 3	0	0	0	0	20	50
	Firm 4	0	0	0	0	20	50

Note: [a]Decimals have been omitted from all data.

IV. THREE MODELS OF ERROR

In our data, the average factor loading went from 0.23 to 0.63 as the return interval went from daily to quarterly. We will show that the conventional random walk model predicts that these correlations should be *identical* across time intervals. Furthermore, we will present a psychometric error model which explains the rise in correlation as being due to a reduction in measurement error. Finally, we will briefly discuss a nonrandom walk model recently derived in response to evidence of autocorrelation in stock returns (Fama and French, 1988; Poterba and Summers, 1988; Summers, 1986). However, this model has not yet been sufficiently well developed to be applied in the present context.

A. The Random Walk Model and the Single-Index Model

The random walk model and the single-index model can be combined. Assume that daily price follows a random walk for the world and national markets. If we let r_i be the daily national market index return (price change) for country i, m be the daily world market factor return, and u_i, be the daily residual for country i from the world market model, then the single index model states:

$$r_i = b_i m + u_i, \tag{1}$$

where m and u_i are each a series of independent identically distributed (i.i.d.) random values from which it follows that r_i is also an i.i.d. random value series; and u_i has a cross correlation of zero with both m and other residuals. If price follows a random walk (as assumed here), then return is modeled as a series of *random shocks*. Thus r_i, m, and u_i are random shocks with zero autocorrelation. We deliberately omit the constant term a_i from Eq. (1) since we are here interested only in covariances between indices.

Consider a week as five (trading) days. The weekly return is the sum of the returns across the five corresponding days.[2] Focus on a single country and use the subscript as the indication of day:

$$r_1 = bm_1 + u_1 \tag{2}$$

$$r_2 = bm_2 + u_2 \tag{3}$$

$$r_3 = bm_3 + u_3 \tag{4}$$

$$r_4 = bm_4 + u_4 \tag{5}$$

$$r_5 = bm_5 + u_5. \tag{6}$$

Use capital letters for the aggregate weekly return. Summing across the five daily returns, we have

$$R = bM + U, \tag{7}$$

where M is the sum of m_i and U is the sum of u_i. If the subscript is now used to indicate different countries, then the weekly equation

$$R_i = b_i M + U_i \tag{8}$$

has the same form as the daily equation. The relative impact of the world market and the residual factor is determined by the variances of the terms. Because the cross correlations between m and u_i are zero, the cross correlation between M and U is zero. Thus:

$$\text{var}(R_i) = b_i^2 \text{ var }(M) + \text{var}(U_i). \tag{9}$$

Because the m's are independent random shocks, the variance of the weekly M is the sum of the variances of the daily m's:

$$\text{var}(M) = 5 \; var(m). \tag{10}$$

Because the u's are independent random shocks, the variance of the weekly U is the sum of the variances of the daily u's:

$$\text{var}(U_i) = 5 \text{ var }(u_i). \tag{11}$$

Since both variances are multiplied by the same factor, the relative variance of M to U is exactly the same as the relative variance of m to u.

Consider now the correlation between two different countries. The covariance is

$$\text{cov}(R_i,R_j) = b_i b_j \text{ var}(M) \tag{12}$$

$$= b_i b_j \, 5 \text{ var}(m) \tag{13}$$

$$= 5 \; b_i b_j \text{ var}(m) \tag{14}$$

$$= 5 \text{ cov }(r_i r_j). \tag{15}$$

Thus the covariance between national markets is multiplied by the same factor as the variances. The correlation is thus unchanged.

We have now shown that the conventional random walk model predicts that the correlation between countries will be the same (and hence the factor loadings on the world market factor will be the same) for weekly as for daily returns. The proof is similar for monthly and quarterly returns. Our proof here used the single-index model to show that the random walk model implies a constant correlation between countries across time intervals. This was done because we previously showed that the single-index model fit our international correlational data. It can be shown that the random walk model alone implies a constant correlation between countries across time intervals.

B. The Fluctuation Model

The random walk model assumes that the independence in stock *return* is caused by independent random change in stock *price* from period to period (e.g., see Fama, 1965 and Granger, 1968). This is the typical model for stock return in financial economics. However, the distinguished econometrician Arthur S. Goldberger (1971) has noted that there is also a psychometric model of error which is in some ways better developed. This so because psychologists more frequently deal with individual-level data, where error is often larger and more visible. The psychometric literature has an alternative to the random walk (Markov) model, which appears to better fit our data.

In psychometric theory, the random walk model is called "real-but-random" change. The psychometric literature would contrast this kind of randomness with *random fluctuations* usually called "error of measurement," and more specifically termed "transient error" (see Tosi et al. [1976] for a discussion). The findings of this study suggest that a substantial part of the randomness in stock returns is better described by *noncumulative* random fluctuation in price similar to error of measurement, rather than by *cumulative* random change in price implied by the random walk model.

The fluctuation, or transient error, model from psychometrics starts with the assumption that there is a baseline, or *true*, value for the variable in question. The *observed* value differs from the true value because of "random error," or transient factors which momentarily deflect the observed value. If P is the observed price of a stock and P^* is the true price, the psychometric model of random fluctuation in stock price is

$$P = P^* + F, \tag{16}$$

where F is the random error factor that deflects the observed value and where the cross correlation between P and F is zero. We further assume here that P^* follows a random walk.[3]

We can derive a fluctuation model for stock *return* (defined here as *price change*) from a fluctuation model for stock *price*. The fluctuation model for stock return is

$$r = r^* + e, \tag{17}$$

where r = observed return, r^* = true return, e = the fluctuation difference; and where the cross correlation between r^* and e is zero. Since true price P^* is assumed to follow a random walk, true return r^* must follow a random shock model. In this model, the observed errors e are *not* independent. Instead, they have a negative (first order) autocorrelation. It can further be shown that all higher-order autocorrelations are zero. This model is fully derived in Appendix A.

C. Aggregation in the Fluctuation Model

Consider a week as the sum of five (trading) days. Then the observed weekly return R is

$$R = R^* + E, \tag{18}$$

where R^* is the sum of the five daily true returns and E is the sum of the five observed daily fluctuation differences. If true price follows a random walk, then the variance of R^* is five times the variance of r^*.

Consider the aggregate sum E. The sum of two days is

$$e_1 = f_1 - f_0 \tag{19}$$

$$e_2 = f_2 - f_1 \tag{20}$$

$$e_1 + e_2 = f_2 - f_0. \tag{21}$$

The intermediate fluctuation f_1 cancels out. Consider three days:

$$e_1 = f_1 - f_0 \tag{22}$$

$$e_2 = f_2 - f_1 \tag{23}$$

$$e_3 = f_3 - f_2 \tag{24}$$

$$e_1 + e_2 + e_3 = f_3 - f_0. \tag{25}$$

The two intermediate fluctuations f_1 and f_2 cancel out. Thus for a week:

$$E = f_5 - f_0. \tag{26}$$

Therefore:

$$\text{var}(E) = 2\ \text{var}(f) = \text{var}(e). \tag{27}$$

Hence the observed error variance for weekly return is no greater than the observed error variance for daily returns.

Consider a month as 20 days and compute the relative error variance of a monthly return. For a random walk, the variance of true monthly return R^* is 20 times the variance of true daily returns. However, the observed monthly error E is just

$$E = f_{20} - f_0, \tag{28}$$

which has the same variance as the observed daily fluctuations. Thus the relative error variance in observed monthly return is 20 times smaller than the relative error variance in observed daily returns. A similar analysis can be applied to quarterly returns.

D. Implications of Measurement Error

Error of measurement can have a large impact on cross correlations such as the correlations between national markets. Psychometric test theory shows that the impact of error of measurement on X is manifested as a reduction in the size of the observed correlation between X and some other variable. The extent of reduction is a multiplicative factor which equals the correlation between perfect and imperfect measurements of T (the true score on X). If Y is the observed score on some other variable, the correlation between T and Y, r_{TY}, is reduced to the observed correlation r_{XY}, where

$$r_{XY} = r_{XT} r_{TY}. \tag{29}$$

The multiplicative term r_{XT} measures the quality of the measurement of T. The square of r_{XT} is called the "reliability" of the measurement in psychometric theory and is usually denoted r_{XX}. The reliability is determined by the relative error of measurement:

$$r_{XX} = 1 - \text{var}(e)/\text{var}(X) \tag{30}$$

$$r = 1/[1 + \text{var}(e)/\text{var}(T)]. \tag{31}$$

Error of measurement in *both* variables causes a *double-sided* reduction in the size of the observed correlation between observations X and Y. If U is the true score for variable Y, then the correlation between T and U, r_{TU}, is reduced to the observed correlation r_{XY}, where

$$r_{XY} = r_{XT} r_{YU} r_{TU}. \tag{32}$$

Hence, the true correlation between two national stock factors T and U will be reduced by the random error in each observed index, X and Y; that is, a double-sided reduction. If each index has the same reliability r_{XX}, the equation for the observed correlation, r_{XY}, is the triple product:

$$r_{XY} = (\sqrt{r_{XX}}\sqrt{r_{XX}})r_{TU} \tag{33}$$

$$= r_{XX} r_{TU}. \tag{34}$$

Thus if national stock market indices are subject to transient error (i.e., fluctuation), then there will be a double-sided reduction in the size of the observed correlation due to the fact that imperfect indices are used to estimate the national market factors. The size of the observed correlation will be reduced by a multiplicative term equal to the reliability coefficient (sometimes referred to as a "stability coefficient" in the case of time series measurement). That is, if r_{XX} is the reliability of national stock market indices, the observed correlation between indices will be less than the true correlation between factors as described by the equation:

$$\text{observed index corr.} = r_{XX}\ (\text{true factor corr.}). \tag{35}$$

The fluctuation model of return predicts that the relative error in observed weekly return will be five times smaller than the relative error in observed daily returns. The relative error in observed monthly return will be four times smaller than the relative error in observed weekly returns. Thus the fluctuation model predicts that the observed correlation between two countries will be larger for weekly than for daily returns, larger yet for monthly returns and larger yet for quarterly returns. This fits the pattern observed in our data.[4]

E. Nonrandom Walk Models of Stock Price

There is increasing doubt about the validity of the random walk model. Fama and French (1988) cite a number of critical studies and add considerable disconfirmatory evidence of their own. Lo and MacKinlay (1988) cite other critics and add further disconfirmatory data. Summers (1986) and Fama and French (1988) have proposed one particular kind of nonrandom walk model. The fluctuation model is another. There are certain similarities between the two models.

The Summers model also assumes that observed stock price is the sum of two components: a ("permanent") random walk component and a "stationary" component. Summers (1986) does not assume that the stationary component is a random error component as in the fluctuation model for price. Instead he assumes that the stationary component has positive autocorrelation with relatively slow decay. The reason for this is that the negative autocorrelation in observed stock return is not nearly as large as predicted by the random error component model. In any case, the data presented by Lo and MacKinlay (1988) do not support the Summers (1986), Fama and French (1988), and Poterba and Summers (1988) "mean-reverting" model.

The weak short-term positive and long-term negative autocorrelation for observed returns was taken by Poterba and Summers (1988) as contradictory evidence for the presence of a random fluctuation (random error) factor. However, their reasoning was based on a further assumption: that the basic (permanent) component of price is a random walk. This is the assumption of the specific fluctuation model presented above. Suppose that assumption is wrong.

Consider the fluctuation model:

$$r = r^* + e. \tag{36}$$

There are two components of observed return: true return r^* and fluctuation difference (error) e. To counterbalance the extreme negative autocorrelation in the errors, suppose that true return has a positive autocorrelation. We are currently exploring this model and it seems to fit both the data of Fama and French (1988) and the data of Lo and MacKinlay (1988), though our findings are very tentative at present.

V. A TEST OF THE RANDOM WALK AND FLUCTUATION MODELS

In this section we will contrast the empirical implications of the random walk model and the random fluctuation model. At present, the only random fluctuation model we have worked out is a model which assumes that true price is a random walk; hence true return is a random shock. This is the model presented as the fluctuation model above. This model will be used for the calculations to follow, although we suspect that a fluctuation model with positive autocorrelation in true return may ultimately prove to be more accurate. We note as an important aside that a positive autocorrelation in true return implies a nonrandom walk model for true price.

The difference between the current fluctuation model and the positive autocorrelation model lies in the specific reliabilities that would be estimated from the data. All fluctuation models imply a large increase in reliability for longer time intervals, but the models differ in the specific ratio by which true return variance is expected to increase as the time interval is increased. The random shock model used here assumes that true return variance is exactly proportional to the time interval. A positive autocorrelation model would predict that true return variance goes up in a more complicated manner.

For this study, we have daily, weekly (5 days), monthly (20 days), and quarterly (60 days) return data. If relative error goes down, reliability goes up. Since the random fluctuation model predicts a large decrease in relative error, it predicts a larger increase in reliability. Thus the random fluctuation model predicts an increase in observed between-index correlations going from daily to weekly returns, an increase from weekly to monthly returns, an increase from monthly to quarterly returns, and a large increase from daily to quarterly returns. The random walk model predicts no difference in these values, The observed correlation increases are

weekly/daily	=	0.095/0.05	=	1.90
monthly/weekly	=	0.245/0.095	=	2.58
quarterly/monthly	=	0.39/0.245	=	1.59
quarterly/daily	=	0.39/0.05	=	7.80.

That is, the observed average between-index correlation nearly doubles from daily to weekly returns and nearly triples from weekly to monthly returns. Overall, the observed average correlation nearly octuples from daily to quarterly returns. This is consistent with the random fluctuation model and does not support the random walk model.

If the ratio of the increase in the correlation between countries is known and if the relative decrease in error variance is known, then it is possible to solve for the reliability of the measurement. The current fluctuation model assumes a zero autocorrelation for true return. For that model, it is possible to calculate the Spearman-Brown reliability (Lord and Novick, 1968) of returns for national indices. It is therefore possible to use this fluctuation model to correct the average correlation between indices for attenuating effect of error of measurement, thus estimating the correlation for perfect measurement. The true average correlation between national stock indices free of random fluctuation (and hence independent of time interval) is estimated to be 0.56. A complete derivation of this result is given in Appendix B.

If true return has a positive autocorrelation (as we suggested earlier), the above calculations would change. The quarterly reliability would be somewhat higher and the corrected value slightly lower. The proper calculations would require knowledge of the autocorrelation. For an autocorrelation of 0.20, the quarterly reliability would be 0.80 and the corrected correlation would be 0.49 instead of 0.56. In any case, the true correlation between national markets must be *larger* than the observed correlation for quarterly returns.

VI. SUMMARY AND CONCLUSION

The primary focus of this study is substantive: an assessment of the extent to which national stock market risk can be diversified by using an international stock portfolio. We found that a single-index (world market factor) model fits correlation data on country-level stock market index returns. However, our finding led to a major methodological digression. The observed average correlation between national stock markets was found to vary dramatically as a function of time interval: from 0.05 for daily returns, to 0.095 for weekly returns, to 0.245 for monthly returns, to 0.39 for quarterly returns. This result does not support the conventional random walk model of stock prices from financial economics. We then presented a random fluctuation model suggested by the classic psychometric error-of-measurement model. The fluctuation model fit the data.

The fit of the world market factor model implies that the limit on the diversification benefit from international equity investment is determined by the degree to which national stock markets are correlated with the world market. If there were perfect correlation, there would be no diversification benefit. If there were zero correlation, specific risk would drop in proportion to the number of countries included.

Reality appears to be in between. In this study, the average correlation between national stock indices free of random fluctuation was estimated to be 0.56, which is greater than zero but less than 1.00. Hence our results suggest that diversification over an infinite number of countries would reduce portfolio return variation by a multiplicative factor of 0.56—but no lower—as that appears to be the true level of variation in the world market factor. That is, our data suggest that international diversification can potentially reduce investment risk (defined by variance of return) down to about 56% of the level that can be achieved using only national diversification.[5] The trick is to find enough stocks of "otherwise equal" quality.

In studies recently published, Roll (1988) found that the world market factor was by far the most significant variable explaining cross-national stock market responses to the October 1987 U.S. stock market crash; while Eun and Shim (1989) found a substantial amount of interdependence amount national stock markets over the period 1980–1985. Hence our finding of a dominant world market factor is supported by other contemporary research.

APPENDIX A: THE FLUCTUATION MODEL FOR STOCK RETURN

In this appendix we derive a fluctuation model for *return* from a fluctuation model for *price*. For simplicity we will state the model at the level of a single stock. We then note that the same model can apply to the country or world market factor as well, though not necessarily with as much variation.

Assume that a given stock on a given day has a *true* price P^*. However, suppose that various transient factors cause the price for that day to randomly fluctuate from the true price. The *observed* price P will then differ from the true price P^* by some amount F:

$$P = P^* + F; \tag{A1}$$

where the cross correlation between P^* and F is zero. Because price fluctuations are usually described as percentage fluctuations, F will be proportion to P^* and hence:

$$P = P^* + fP^* = (1 + f)P^*, \tag{A2}$$

where f is the fluctuation multiplier or percentage fluctuation. The percentage fluctuation f is independent of the true price P^*.

Consider now price change, which we will call return. Return is conventionally assumed to be a random percentage variation in price, say $r^* P^*$, where r^* is the true percent change in price. Thus the true next day price is given by

$$P^*_{t+1} = P^*_t + r^* P^*_t. \tag{A3}$$

The true return r^* is then

$$r^* = (P^*_{t+1} - P^*_t)/P^*_t. \tag{A4}$$

The observed return r is then

$$r = (P_{t+1} - P_t)/P_t. \tag{A5}$$

We will now decompose Eq. (A5) for observed return in order to obtain an approximation for observed return consistent with the psychometric fluctuation model.

$$\text{Since } P_t = (1 + f_t)P_t^*,$$

$$P_{t+1} = (1 + f_{t+1})P_{t+1}^* \tag{A6}$$

$$= (1 = f_{t+1})(1 + r^*)P_t^* \tag{A7}$$

$$= (1 = r^* + f_{t+1} + r^*f_{t+1})P_t^* \tag{A8}$$

Therefore,

$$P_{t+1} - P_t = [(1 + r^* + f_{t+1} + r^*f_{t+1}) - (1 + f_t)]P_t^* \tag{A9}$$

$$= (r^* + f_{t+1} - f_t + r^*f_{t+1})P_t^* \tag{A10}$$

$$= (r^* + e + r^*f_{t+1})P_t^*, \tag{A11}$$

where $e = f_{t+1} - f_t$, the fluctuation difference for observed price. A little more simple algebra shows that we can now rewrite Eq. (A5) as

$$r = (r^* + e + r^*f_{t+1})/(1 + f_t). \tag{A12}$$

Since both r^* and f_{t+1} are very small fractions, the product r^*f_{t+1} is negligible in comparison to either one. Thus there is only trivial loss in precision in approximating the product r^*f_{t+1} by zero. Thus we substitute ($r^*f_{t+1} = 0$) and the approximation ($1 + f_t = 1$) in Eq (A12) and obtain

$$r = r^* + e, \tag{A13}$$

where the cross correlation between r^* and e is zero. This equation is equivalent to the psychometric error of measurement equation.

The conventional random walk model not only makes this approximation but makes a *further* approximation as well, namely $e = 0$. But is e necessarily small in comparison to the very small number r^*? For example, consider two days with 1% fluctuations in price in opposite directions, $f_1 = -0.01$ and $f_2 = +0.01$, and hence $e = 0.01 - (-0.01) = 0.02$. Further consider a return which would be an annual return of 10%. A 10% annual return is a daily return of $r^* = 0.10/250 = 0.0004$. Thus $1 + f = 1 + 0.01 = 1.01$, which differs only trivially from 1; whereas $r^* + e = 0.0004 + 0.02 = 0.0204$ is *51 times* larger than r^*. Thus, as an approximation, we can ignore the f in $1 + f$ but we cannot ignore the e in $r^* + e$. Notice also that

$r^*f_{t+1} = 0.0004(0.01) = 0.000004$, which is negligible in comparison to *any* of the other numbers.

In reality, the fluctuation difference e might be large or small in comparison to true return r^*. This can be estimated from the data. Thus we approximate observed return by

$$r = r^* + e. \tag{A14}$$

In our example, we estimate the actual observed return 0.0206 from Eq. (A12) by the approximate return 0.0204 from Eq. (A14). This difference is trivial in comparison to the difference between $r^* = 0.0004$ and $r = 0.0206$.

We have derived a psychometric fluctuation model for observed return:

$$r = r^* + e, \tag{A15}$$

where the cross correlation between r^* and e is zero. Note that the observed errors e are *not* independent. Rather, they are negatively autocorrelated because adjacent errors contain a common fluctuation:

$$e_1 = f_1 - f_0 \tag{A16}$$

$$e_2 = f_2 - f_1. \tag{A17}$$

That is, the fluctuation f_1 contributes positively to the first fluctuation difference and negatively to the second fluctuation difference. Thus e_1 and e_2 have a (first order) autocorrelation of –0.50. It is easily shown, however, that all higher-order autocorrelations are zero.

It is important to note that the fluctuation model does *not* require a particular model for true stock price. Following the convention in financial economics, the fluctuation model developed in the main text assumes that true price P^* follows a random walk. Any other stochastic process could be substituted. As briefly discussed in the main text, our current belief is that true stock price may in fact have positive autocorrelation.

APPENDIX B: DERIVATION OF THE TRUE CORRELATION BETWEEN NATIONAL STOCK INDICES

The size of the observed average correlation between national markets varies with the time interval:

$$\begin{aligned} \text{Daily } r &= 0.05 \\ \text{Weekly } r &= 0.095 \\ \text{Monthly } r &= 0.245 \\ \text{Quarterly } r &= 0.39. \end{aligned}$$

There is a large increase in the size of the observed correlation as the return horizon lengthens. The average correlation rises from 0.05 to 0.39 (a ratio of 7.80) as the horizon lengthens from one day to one quarter. According to the classic random walk model, there should be no such change. The fluctuation model predicts this large increase.

The specific size predicted for the ratio of correlations depends on the specific fluctuation model used and on the size of the error variance relative to the variance of true return; that is, on the reliability of the return. Appendix C on the correlation ratio and reliability assumes the specific fluctuation model presented earlier, a model which assumes that true price follows a random walk. Appendix C shows that the ratio of correlations for two different time intervals can be used to compute the reliability of return at the shorter time interval. From that reliability, the reliability at each time interval can be computed using the Spearman-Brown formula from psychometric theory (Lord and Novick, 1968; Nunnally, 1978). Given data on four time intervals, there are six pairs from which a ratio can be computed. For each such ratio, there are four reliabilities; one for each time interval. If the classic cumulative change random walk model fits the data, then *all* reliabilities should be 1.00. If the fluctuation model fits the data, there would be *one* reliability for *each* time interval, but that reliability would be *smaller* for shorter time horizons. Consistency of the reliability estimates is an indirect test of the fluctuation model presented earlier. The results of these calculations are given in Table B1.

Not all the reliabilities generated by different starting ratios are the same. The big difference is that between daily return and return for any longer time interval. The first three columns of Table B1, panel B, use daily data in the starting ratio. The reliabilities in these three columns are not consistent with one another and are not consistent with the reliabilities based on longer time horizons. The last three columns of panel B use ratios only for time intervals longer than one day. These three columns are equal to one another and thus fit the consistency prediction of the fluctuation model. According to the classic random walk model, *all* reliabilities should be 1.00. This is disconfirmed in *all* cases.

According to the fluctuation model (which assumes that true price follows a random walk), the reliability estimate should be the *same* for any starting ratio. This is true for ratios using time intervals longer than one day, but false for the ratios using daily data. This would suggest two possibilities: (1) there is a problem with daily data, or (2) true price does not follow a random walk.

Consider the findings for daily returns. According to the data for longer time horizons, the reliability of daily returns is consistently predicted to be 0.04. The daily reliability was estimated to be much higher if the daily return correlation was used in the starting ratio (ranging from 0.41 to 0.11, depending on the length of the longer horizon). This shows that the observed correlation between national markets for the same day is substantially higher than the fluctuation model would predict;

Table B1. Reliability of Measurements for Each Time Interval Starting from Each Possible Ratio of Correlations

Panel A The Six Starting Ratios

Lower Interval	*Upper Interval* Week	Month	Quarter
Day	1.90	4.90	7.80
Week		2.58	4.11
Month			1.59

Panel B Estimated Reliabilities

Time Interval	*Starting Ratio* W/D	M/D	Q/D	M/W	Q/W	Q/M
Daily (D)	0.41	0.16	0.11	0.04	0.04	0.04
Weekly (W)	0.78	0.49	0.38	0.18	0.17	0.16
Monthly (M)	0.93	0.79	0.71	0.47	0.45	1.44
Quarterly (Q)	0.98	0.92	0.88	0.72	0.71	0.70

it was 0.05 when it should have been about 0.02. The other three correlations are in consistent ratios.

We believe that the problem lies with daily returns. In the world market, daily returns for different countries have a problem that is not true for firms within a national market: the *market times* are not simultaneous. The market time for London is 5 hours ahead of the market in New York. Hence the New York market could be directly influenced by the reaction of the London market to events that took place the same day but 5 hours earlier than New York time. The market time for Tokyo is 13 hours ahead of the market in New York. Thus what is nominally the same day in Tokyo is actually the day *after* in New York. Hence national markets in different time zones could be reacting to *one another* on a given day rather than simultaneously reacting to world market forces (see Becker, Finnerty, and Gupta, 1990). This *nonsynchronous trading* may explain the fact that daily correlations are higher than would be predicted from the other time intervals.

Nonsynchronous trading is also included in the "intervalling-effect bias" hypothesis discussed in Cohen et al. (1983). In our study, nonsynchronous trading is the result of different time zones. The problem considered by Cohen et al. is "friction in the trading process," which delays the adjustment of stock price to new information and may induce serial cross correlation in return. In their discussion, they include trading frictions due to (1) thin trading, (2) the actions of specialists seeking to satisfy stabilization obligations or to redress inventory imbalances, and

(3) individual traders who trade only periodically due to information, decision, and transaction costs. These three frictions are not likely to bias national index-level correlations. As noted above, however, nonsynchronous trading (due to different time zones) may upwardly bias observed serial cross correlations between market indices, especially at the daily return level. But a recent study by Lo and MacKinlay (1990) found that nonsynchronous trading was not a major factor in rejecting the random walk hypothesis for daily, weekly, and monthly U.S. stock returns over the period 1963–1987.

We therefore ignore the data for daily return. Consider the last three columns in Table B1, panel B, for weekly, monthly, and quarterly return reliability. In each case there is also a very small secular decrease in the reliability estimate. For example, consider the quarterly data where the reliability estimates drop from 0.72 to 0.71 to 0.70, as data for longer time horizons are used for the starting ratio. This drop is so small that it may not even be statistically significant, but it is perfectly replicated in the drops for weekly and monthly data. Thus the drop suggests that true price does not follow a random walk. At this time, however, we know of no statistical test for the significance of the small drop reliability. Hence, we do not know if it reflects a small or a large problem with the random walk model for true price.

What is the size of the average correlation between nations for true returns? This is obtained by correcting the observed average correlation for attenuation due to random fluctuation error. For each time interval, we use the lowest estimate of reliability from Table B1, panel B, as the operational estimate:

$$\begin{aligned} \text{Weekly} &= 0.095/0.16 &= 0.59 \\ \text{Monthly} &= 0.245/0.44 &= 0.56 \\ \text{Quarterly} &= 0.39/0.70 &= 0.56. \end{aligned}$$

The three estimates are consistent. We therefore estimate the average correlation of true returns between national markets to be 0.56.

APPENDIX C: THE CORRELATION RATIO AND RELIABILITY

The correlation between observed returns differs from the correlation between true returns to the extent that the observed return has a reliability less than 1.00, the extent that price is subject to random error fluctuations. If we assume that true price follows a random walk, the ratio of correlations for two time horizons can be used to compute the reliability of either time horizon. From the reliability of any one time horizon, we can compute the reliability of all other time horizons using the Spearman-Brown formula from psychometric theory (Lord and Novick, 1968; Nunnally, 1978). This appendix briefly outlines the derivation of the two formulas.

Consider the ratio of quarterly to monthly observed average return correlations, a ratio of 0.39//0.245 = 1.59 This is the ratio of quarterly to monthly reliability. Denote the three variances by

VM = variance of monthly true return
VQ = variance of quarterly true return
VE = variance of fluctuation error.

Note that fluctuation error depends on daily fluctuations regardless of the return time horizon and hence has a variance that is independent of the time horizon. If true price follows a random walk, the quarterly true return variance is related to the monthly true return variance by

$$VQ = 3\ VM \tag{C1}$$

Denote the reliabilities by

RM = reliability of monthly return
RQ = reliability of quarterly return.

The reliability ratio RQM is computed by

$$RM = VM/(VM + VE) \tag{C2}$$

$$RQ = VQ/(VQ + VE) \tag{C3}$$

$$RQM = (VQ/VM)\ [(VM + VE)/(VQ + VE)] \tag{C4}$$

$$= (3)\ [(VM/VE + 1)/(VQ/VE + 1)] \tag{C5}$$

If we denote the monthly "signal-to-noise ratio" VM/VE by S, then we have

$$RQM = 3[(S + 1)/(3\ S + 1)] = (3\ S + 3)/(3S + 1). \tag{C6}$$

This equation can be solved for S to yield

$$S = (RQM - 3)/[3(1 - RQM)] \tag{C7}$$

$$= (3 - RQM)/[3(RQM - 1)]\ . \tag{C8}$$

For the observed ratio of $RQM = 1.59$, this yields

$$S = (3 - 1.59)/[3(1.59 - 1) = 0.7966. \tag{C9}$$

The reliability of monthly return can be computed from the monthly signal-to-noise ratio by

$$RM = S/(S + 1) = 0.7966/1.7966 = 0.4434. \quad \text{(C10)}$$

The Spearman-Brown formula says that because the variance ratio of quarterly to monthly is 3, the reliabilities are related by

$$R3 = (3\,R1)/(2\,R1 + 1). \quad \text{(C11)}$$

Hence

$$RQ = [3(0.4434)]/[2(0.4434) + 1] = 0.7050. \quad \text{(C12)}$$

The general Spearman-Brown formula for any ratio of true score variance is

$$Rn = (nR1)/[(n - 1)R1 + 1]. \quad \text{(C13)}$$

This formula works for fractional ratios as well as integers (the Spearman-Brown formula is its own inverse function as a function of the true score variance ratio n). Thus the reliability of weekly and daily return is computed to be

$$RW = R(0.25) = (0.25R1)/[(0.25 - 1)R1 + 1] \quad \text{(C14)}$$

$$= [(0.25)(0.4434)]/[(-0.75)(0.4434) + 1] = 0.1661 \quad \text{(C15)}$$

$$RD = R(0.05) = (0.05R1)/[(0.05 - 1)R1 + 1] \quad \text{(C16)}$$

$$= [(0.05)(0.4434)]/[(-0.95)(0.4434) + 1] = 0.0383. \quad \text{(C17)}$$

To generalize, denote the correlation ratio as RC and denote the time ratio as n. Then the signal-to-noise ratio of the shorter time period is given by

$$S = (n - RC)/[n(RC - 1)]. \quad \text{(C18)}$$

The reliability of the shorter time period is given by

$$R1 = S/(S + 1). \quad \text{(C19)}$$

The reliabilities of all other intervals can be computed by the Spearman-Brown formula.

ACKNOWLEDGMENTS

We thank Gary Bergstrom, Scott Linn, and Robert Haugen for helpful comments and constructive criticism of earlier drafts of this chapter. We also thank Kevin Keane and

Barbara Mueller of Goldman Sachs for invaluable help with the data collection for this project. We alone are responsible for any remaining errors and omissions.

NOTES

1. In an *exploratory* or "blind" factor analysis, no attempt is made a priori to specify what the factors are in a data set. Rather, the factors that emerge are purely the result of a particular statistical manipulation of the data, with no predetermined substantive content. In a *confirmatory* factor analysis, the factors are specified a priori from a substantive theory or model of the process under study. Statistical methods are then used to test the fit of the prespecified model to the correlational data. If the factor analysis is done with ones in the diagonal, then the implicit assumption is that all variables are perfectly measured and there are therefore no attenuating effects due to measurement error. If the factor analysis is done with *communalities* in the diagonal, then the assumption is that there is the possibility of less than perfect measurement. There is a corresponding correction for the attenuating effects of imperfect measurement. Our study used confirmatory factor analysis with communalities in the diagonal to test the fit of the single-index (world market factor) model.

2. Some prefer to work with the natural logarithm of price (to get continuously compounded return) instead of actual (raw) return. It makes virtually no difference which one is used in our analysis. A mathematical appendix is available from the first author to those desiring a derivation of this result.

3. It is important to note that the fluctuation model does *not* require a particular model for true stock price. Following the convention in financial economics, we assume here that true price P^* follows a random walk. Any other stochastic process could be substituted. As we briefly discuss later, our current belief is that true stock price may in fact have positive autocorrelation.

4. Grubel and Fadner (1971) also hypothesized that correlations between groups of stocks from different countries are an *increasing* function of the holding period. They argued that the increase is largely due to the diminishing impact of "random" versus "real" factors over time. Their data on the United States, the United Kingdom, and West Germany for the period 1965–1967 support their hypothesis. Average correlations increased over weekly, monthly, and quarterly holding periods. A similar argument was presented in Pogue and Solnik (1974).

5. The pattern of correlations between national stock indices is analogous to the pattern of correlations between parallel tests in psychometric theory (Nunnally [1978], chap. 6). A key theorem from this theory is that the ratio of the variance of the world market to the variance of a national market is equal to the average correlation between national markets. We found this correlation to be 0.56, suggesting that a well-diversified international stock portfolio can potentially reduce investment risk (defined by variance of return) down to about 56% of the level of a well-diversified national stock portfolio.

REFERENCES

Adler, M. and Dumas, B. (1983). "International Portfolio Choice and Corporation Finance: A Synthesis." *Journal of Finance* 38, 925–984.

Becker, K. G., Finnerty, J. E., and Gupta, M. (1990). "The Intertemporal Relation between the U.S and Japanese Stock Markets." *Journal of Finance* 45, 1297–1306.

Bergstrom, G. L., and Henriksson, R. D. (1982). "Prediction of the International Equity Market Covariance Structure." Center for Research in Security Prices, University of Chicago.

Brown, S. J. (1989). "The Number of Factors in Security Returns." Journal of Finance 44, 1247–1262.

Cho, D. C., Eun, C. S., and Senbet, L. (1986). "International Arbitrage Pricing Theory: An Empirical Investigation." *Journal of Finance* 41, 313–329.

Cohen, K. J., Hawawini, H. S., Maier, S. F., Schwartz, R. A., and Whitcomb, D. K. (1983). "Friction in the Trading Process and the Estimation of Systematic Risk." *Journal of Financial Economics* 12, 263–278.

Cohen, K., and Pogue, J. (1967). "An Empirical Evaluation of Alternative Portfolio Selection Models." *Journal of Business* 46, 166–193.

Conway, D. A., and Reinganum, M. R. (1988). "Stable Factors in Security Returns: Identification Using Cross Validation." *Journal of Business & Economic Statistics* 6, 1–15.

Elton, E. J., and Gruber, M. J. (1973). "Estimating the Dependence Structure of Share Prices—Implications for Portfolio Selection." *Journal of Finance* 28, 1203–1232.

———. (1987). *Modern Portfolio Theory and Investment Analysis*, 3d ed. New York: John Wiley.

Eun, C. S., and Janakiramanan, S. (1986). "A Model of International Asset Pricing with a Constraint on the Foreign Equity Ownership." *Journal of Finance* 41, 897–914.

Eun, C. S., and Resnick, B. G. (1984). "Estimating the Correlation Structure of International Share Prices." *Journal of Finance* 39, 1311–1324.

———. (1988). "Exchange Rate Uncertainty, Forward Contracts, and International Portfolio Selection." *Journal of Finance* 43, 197–215.

Eun, C. S., and Shim, S. (1989). "International Transmission of Stock Market Movements." *Journal of Financial and Quantitative Analysis* 24, 241–256.

Fama, E. F. (1965). "The Behavior of Stock Market Prices." *Journal of Business* 38, 34–105.

———. (1970). "Efficient Capital Markets: A Review of Theory and Empirical Work." *Journal of Finance* 25, 383–417.

———. (1967). *Foundations of Finance*. New York: Basic Books.

Fama, E. F., and French, K. R. (1988). "Permanent and Temporary Components of Stock Prices." *Journal of Political Economy* 96, 246–273.

Goldberger, A. S. (1971). "Econometrics and Psychometrics: A Survey of Communalities." *Psychometrika* 36, 83–107.

Gorsuch, R. L. (1974). *Factor Analysis*. Philadelphia: W. B. Saunders.

Granger, C. W. J. (1968). "Some Aspects of the Random Walk Model of Stock Market Prices." *International Economic Review* 9, 252–257.

Grubel, H. G., and Fadner, K. (1971). "The Interdependence of International Equity Markets." *Journal of Finance* 26, 89–94.

Harmon, H. H. (1976). *Modern Factor Analysis*, 3d ed. Chicago: University of Chicago Press.

Hunter, J. E., and Gerbing, D. W. (1982). "Unidimensional Measurement, Second-Order Factor Analysis and Causal Models." In B. M. Staw and L. L. Cummings, eds., *Research in Organizational Psychology*, Volume 4. Greenwich: JAI Press, 267–320.

Joy, O. M., Panton, D. B., Reilly, F. K., and Martin, S. A. (1976). "Comovements of Major International Equity Markets." *Financial Review* 1, 1–20.

King, B. F. (1966). "Market and Industry Factors in Stock Price Behavior." *Journal of Business* 39, 139–190.

Kryzanowski, L., and To, M. C. (1983). "General Factor Models and the Structure of Security Returns." *Journal of Financial and Quantitative Analysis* 18, 31–52.

Lessard, D R. (1974). "World, National and Industry Factors in Equity Returns." *Journal of Finance* 29, 379–391.

Lo, A. W., and MacKinlay, A. C. (1988). "Stock Market Prices Do Not Follow Random Walks: Evidence from a Simple Specification Test." *Review of Financial Studies* 1, 41–66.

———. (1990). "An Econometric Analysis of Nonsynchronous Trading." *Journal of Econometrics* 45, 181–211.

Lord, F. M., and Novick, M. R. (1968). *Statistical Theories of Mental Test Scores*. Reading, MA: Addison-Wesley.

Meyers, S. L. (1973). "A Re-examination of Market and Industry Factors in Stock Price Behavior." *Journal of Finance* 28, 695–705.

Nunnally, J C. (1978). *Psychometric Theory*, 2d ed. New York: McGraw-Hill.

Pogue, G. A., and Solnik, B. H. (1974). "The Market Model Applied to European Common Stocks." *Journal of Financial and Quantitative Analysis* 9, 917–944.

Poterba, J. M., and Summers, J. H. (1988). "Mean Reversion Stock Prices: Evidence and Implications." *Journal of Financial Economics* 22, 27–59.

Ripley, D. M. (1973). "Systematic Elements in the Linkage of National Stock Market Indices." *Review of Economics and Statistics* 55, 356–361.

Roll, R. (1988). "The International Crash of October 1987." *Financial Analysts Journal* 44 (September/October), 19–35.

Solnik, B. (1988). *International Investments*. Reading, MA: Addison-Wesley.

Summers, L. H. (1986). "Does the Stock Market Rationally Reflect Fundamental Values?" *Journal of Finance* 41, 591–601.

Tosi, H., Hunter, J., Chesser, R., Tarter, J. R., and Carroll, S. (1976). "How Real Are Changes Induced by Management by Objectives." *Administrative Science Quarterly* 21, 276–306.

Trzcinka, C. (1986). "On the Number of Factors in the Arbitrage Pricing Model." *Journal of Finance* 41, 347–368.

INFORMATIONAL EFFICIENCY OF CAPITAL MARKET REVISITED:

ANOMALOUS EVIDENCE FROM A REFINED TEST

Cheng F. Lee, Gili Yen, and Chingfu Chang

ABSTRACT

To turn the hypothesis of semistrong informational efficiency into a refutable one, we examine in this paper the stock price movements around the Chinese Lunar New Year since both "real" and "financial" transactions are virtually suspended in its neighborhood. Using the return associated with the buy-and-hold strategy as the benchmark, we found a profit-making rule by buying stocks before the arrival of the New Year festival and selling them off some time after was seen to exist persistently over the period from 1975 to 1984. Moreover, the conclusion remains intact after the transaction costs have been taken into account. Findings of such kind cast doubt on the validity of the hypothesis of semistrong efficiency.

Advances in Quantitative Analysis of Finance and Accounting,
Volume 2, Part A, pages 39–65.

ISBN: 1-55938-564-2

I. OBJECTIVE AND OUTLINES

Recently, there has been a renewed interest in the issue of stock market informational efficiency. (See, e.g., Ball, 1989, or LeRoy, 1989.) On the empirical front, we have witnessed a two-pronged development.

On the one hand, there now exists a body of events or time-frame-related studies. In this regard, three new sets of findings are noteworthy. First, there now exists a body of literature that reexamines whether a nominal event such as stock dividends/splits possess informational content (e.g., Penman, 1983) or the possibility of its carrying signaling value (e.g., Edes, 1982). Alternatively, LeRoy (1984) and Shiller (1981a,b, 1986) have examined this issue by probing whether the variance bounds of stocks exceed what is deemed reasonable within the capital- asset-pricing model (CAPM) framework. Still, some others are exploring the issue of market efficiency by examining specific phenomena such as the "price-earnings effect" (e.g., Basu, 1983), the size effect (e.g., Reinganum, 1981, or Stoll and Whaley, 1983), or by examining stock price behavior over a particular period, the so-called weekend effect (e.g., Jaffe and Westerfield, 1985), seasonality effect (e.g., Kato and Schallheim, 1985), or year-end effect (Branch, 1977, or Haugen and Lakonishok, 1988).

On the other hand, a number of scholars have attacked the issue of capital market efficiency by investigating the existence/nonexistence of profit-making trading schemes. Malkiel, after reviewing earlier empirical studies, has argued strongly for the efficient-market hypothesis. He has written: "Any regularity in the stock market that can be discovered and acted upon profitably is bound to destroy itself. This is the fundamental reason why I am convinced that no one will be successful in employing technical methods to get above-average returns in the stock market."[1] In contrast, Sweeney (1988) raised serious doubt about the validity of the aforementioned conclusion. He found that among the fifteen profitable stocks in Fama and Blume (1966), "the surviving fourteen show statistically significant profits for 1970–1983 for transaction costs obtainable by floor traders."

Apparently, a consensus on market efficiency has yet to be reached. The present one is a hybrid study. Similar to studies falling in the former category, a chosen event, namely, the Chinese Lunar New Year is used to test the market efficiency hypothesis. At the same time, the present study shares the eminent feature of the studies of the second type by examining whether a profit-making rule exists. Before we move on to carry out the empirical tests, a brief discussion of the weakness of previous event studies and the feature of the present study is in order.

A fundamental difficulty presents itself with regard to previous event studies because in these studies the so-called nominal events such as stock dividends/splits or dividends/ earnings announcements have been used. The difficulty under review is that a proponent of efficient capital market always stands to win. When there are no associative price movements, he or she can argue it is rightly so since stock prices in an efficient capital market should be unresponsive to an event free of informational content. However, if price movements do occur, he or she can still legitimately claim that the efficient capital market hypothesis cannot thereby be rejected since the events chosen are "seemingly" nominal rather than "truly" nominal. Put differently, what appears to be nominal may nevertheless exert real effects. As for the empirical studies of the second type, critics point out the observed profitability should be compared with the return associated with the buy-and-hold strategy (e.g., Malkiel, 1981). Critics also mention that the transaction costs should be explicitly taken into account (e.g., Fama and Blume, 1966). Otherwise, a trading rule which apparently earns the investors excess profits, when properly adjusted for the buy-and-hold return and/or transaction costs, may earn the investors nothing but normal profits.

To turn the hypothesis of market efficiency into a refutable one, we propose to examine the stock price movements around the Chinese Lunar New Year since both "real" and "financial" transactions are virtually suspended during this six-day or so period.[2] However, transaction costs will be taken into account to take care of the interpretational problem mentioned above. Moreover, the return of the buy-and-hold policy will be used as a benchmark to judge whether excess profit exists. Using longitudinal data starting with 1975 and ending with 1984, we have found that shrewd investors, buying stocks before the arrival of the Chinese Lunar New Year and selling them off some time after, could earn themselves returns greater than what can be obtained from a buy-and-hold policy after the transaction costs have been taken into account.[3] Such findings cast serious doubt on the validity of the efficient market hypothesis.

The balance of the paper is organized as follows. Section II explains the rationale for the chosen method in calculating returns and the specification of the base and observation periods. Section III describes our sampling procedure and data set. The empirical results are then presented and discussed in Section IV. Section V concludes the paper.

II. EMPIRICAL METHODOLOGY

In this section, we discuss the computational method, the base period, and the observation period in order.

A. Returns on Stocks

Several methods for calculating returns are available. In the present study, it is inappropriate to adopt methods designed for a specific portfolio such as market-adjusted returns, for example, Clark and Weinstein (1983), or market- and risk-adjusted returns, for example, Brown and Warner (1985), since the New Year exerts a market-wide influence. In addition, no adjustment for risk is necessary because we are interested in returns of identical stocks.[4] All considered, we decided to apply the raw return formula to each stock in the calculation of daily returns. In formal terms, returns of the jth stock earned on date t, $R_{j,t}$ can be defined as follows:

$$R_{j,t} = \frac{P_{j,t} - P_{j,t-1}}{P_{j,0}}$$

where

- t is the tth trading date following the market suspension;
- P_{jt} is the closing price of the jth stock on date t;
- $P_{j,0}$ is the arithmetic mean of the closing price of the jth stock over the base period.

Accordingly, cumulative returns (CR) of the jth stock and the arithmetic mean of cumulative returns of the n sampled firms can be defined, respectively, as follows:

$$CR_{j,t} = \sum_{t=1}^{\tau} R_{j,t}$$

$$\overline{CR}_{n,t} = \frac{1}{n} \sum_{j=1}^{n} CR_{j,t},$$

where $1 \leq \tau \leq 30$.

B. The Base and the Observation Periods

Supposedly, stock prices will adjust against newly released information. The pattern of adjustment, however, varies from case to case. It came to us as no surprise, then, that the types of the adjustment which in turn determine the appropriate specification of base or observation period have been widely studied.[5]

According to Hillmer and Yu (1979), patterns of adjustment can be classified into three major categories. Our study belongs to class I ($b < 0 < e$), in which the beginning of the adjustment, b, takes place in advance of the arrival of the event, 0, whereas the ending of the adjustment, e, lags behind the announcement of the event.[6] Under such circumstances, a base period too close to the event would underestimate the cumulative returns; on the other hand, a base period too distant from the event would increase the likelihood of mistakenly capturing information arising from other events.

To start, we calculate CR on the basis of three possible beginning dates, Sb-15, Sb-10, Sb-5, where Sb-x denotes the stock price on the xth date prior to Lunar New Year's Eve. Fortunately, the results show little difference. Thus, the choice of the beginning date of the base period becomes a less severe problem than it first might appear. Choosing Sb-15 as the beginning date, however, has the advantage of making the base price less susceptible to outliers. As for the ending date of the base period, we arbitrarily choose the sixth day prior to Lunar New Year's Eve, Sb-6, to take care of possible informational leakage. Therefore, in the ensuing analysis, the period starting with Sb-15 and ending with Sb-6—to be denoted by (Sb-15~Sb-6) and be referred to as S4—therefore will constitute our primary base period. Relatedly, cumulative returns calculated on the basis of S1(Sb-5~Sb-1), S2(Sb-10~Sb-1), S3(Sb-15~Sb-1), S4(Sb-15~Sb-6), and S5(Sb15~Sb-11) will be hereafter called $\overline{CR}1$, $\overline{CR}2$, $\overline{CR}3$, $\overline{CR}4$, and $\overline{CR}5$, respectively. For robustness check and readers' reference, all $\overline{CR}$'s will be reported.

Similar considerations arise in the choice of the observation period. On the one hand, most will agree that the stock price adjustments against newly released information can hardly occur simultaneously no matter how efficient the capital market is. Therefore, only under very rare occasions can we expect *e* to coincide with 0. On the other hand, an extended observation period enhances the possibility of incorrectly capturing information associated with other events. All considered, we decided to report the *CR*'s of all stocks traded on the market over a 30-day period, that is, Se + 1 ~ Se + 30 where Se + *D* denotes the stock price on the *D*th day following the reopening of the stock market.

III. SAMPLE

Since the daily stock prices are readily retrievable from the financial press, only the years and the characteristics of the sampled firms need description.

To start with, we need not worry much about market-wide and industry-specific factors because our sample contains all listed companies. As for the firm-specific factors, the following five variables are most often mentioned: (1) earnings, (2) cash dividends, (3) stock dividend, or stock split, (4) new listings, and (5) speculative operation.

Table 1. Breakdown of the Sample

	1975	*1976*	*1977*	*1978*	*1979*	*1980*	*1981*	*1982*	*1983*	*1984*	*Subtotal(%)*
Number of											
listed stocks	76	83	88	95	103	109	114	117	123	127	1,035 (100)
Number of											
unusable stocks	42	31	61	54	50	64	58	42	50	63	515 (49.76)
insufficient data	25	14	31	30	33	27	33	25	29	34	281
stock split	—	—	—	—	—	—	1	—	—	—	1
new listing	—	—	—	—	—	—	—	—	1	—	1
stock dividends	1	6	1	4	1	3	1	3	3	12	35
cash dividends	16	11	29	20	16	34	23	14	17	17	197
Number of											
usable stocks	34	52	27	41	53	45	56	75	73	64	520 (50.24)

Among them, the speculative factor is akin to a market-wide factor since we are not examining a subset of traded stocks. We leave out earnings announcement because previous studies suggest that its effect can go either way. With regard to stock splitting and new listing, there is one exceptional case for each taking place in 1981 and 1983, respectively. These two cases are automatically dropped from the sample. Attention is therefore focused on the elimination of cases in which cash dividends or stock dividends are involved. Our sample does not include such cases, owing to the difficulties in interpreting the association between these two types of events and their associative price movement. (See Section I, second paragraph.) After deleting stocks with insufficient information as well, our final sample contains 520 stocks (see Table 1 for a breakdown).

IV. EMPIRICAL ANALYSIS

The excess returns associated with each usable stock for a period ranging from 1 day immediately after the reopening of the market up to 30 days are calculated. As discussed in the previous section, the excess returns are calculated on the basis of S1(Sb-5~Sb-1), S2(Sb-10~Sb-1), S3(Sb-15~Sb-1), S4(Sb-15~Sb-6), and S5(Sb-15~Sb-11) in turn and are labeled $\overline{CR}1$, $\overline{CR}2$, $\overline{CR}3$, $\overline{CR}4$, and $\overline{CR}5$ accordingly. We graph the pattern of stock price movements in Figure 1. Figure 1 reveals that information leakage does occur during the period (Sb-5~Sb-1). As we mentioned in Section II, that is the very reason that (Sb-5~Sb-1) is picked up as the primary base period on which the ensuing analysis is based. For readers' reference, $\overline{CR}$'s for each year starting with 1975 and ending with 1984 are serially numbered from Table 2 through Table 11. Their graphical counterparts are correspondingly labeled Figures 2–11.

Though more rigorous statistical analyses are conducted below, one point is noteworthy from the tables just mentioned. Using the longitudinal data from 1975 to 1984, we found that shrewd investors can benefit by buying stocks before the arrival of the New Year and selling them off some time after in 8 out of 10 observed years. These amazing, yet consistent, empirical findings suggest that the stock market in Taiwan does not meet the requirements of semistrong form efficiency in the sense that an excess-return-earning trading rule is seen to exist for an extended period of time.[7] We then move on to carry out statistical tests for the 8 years which earn the shrewd investors excess profits. The results are summarized in Table 12.

In Table 12, we find that one $\overline{CR}4$ in 1980 and a few $\overline{CR}4$'s in either 1976 or 1979 fall in the acceptance region. Other than those few exceptional cases, at the 0.01 level of significance, all $\overline{CR}4$'s in the years of 1975, 1978, 1981, 1983, and 1984 point to the rejection of the null hypothesis that cumulative return equals to zero on the *D*th transaction day after the reopening of the stock market. Based on such findings, we therefore tentatively conclude that the hypothesis that the Taiwanese stock market is informationally inefficient cannot be rejected.

Table 2. Returns for 1975

D	$\overline{CR1}$	$\overline{CR2}$	$\overline{CR3}$	$\overline{CR4}$	$\overline{CR5}$	D	$\overline{CR1}$	$\overline{CR2}$	$\overline{CR3}$	$\overline{CR4}$	$\overline{CR5}$
1	3.75	4.08	6.73	8.38	12.71	16	7.96	8.30	11.00	12.68	17.10
	(4.6*)	(4.3*)	(6.0*)	(6.0*)	(7.1*)		(4.3*)	(4.3*)	(5.7*)	(6.1*)	(7.6*)
2	3.96	4.29	6.90	8.53	12.81	17	6.93	7.26	9.94	11.60	15.97
	(2.9*)	(3.0*)	(4.7*)	(5.2*)	(6.8*)		(3.9*)	(4.0*)	(5.3*)	(5.8*)	(7.4*)
3	5.17	5.48	8.10	9.72	14.00	18	5.26	5.57	8.20	9.83	14.13
	(3.2*)	(3.3*)	(5.0*)	(5.6*)	(7.4*)		(2.9*)	(3.0*)	(4.4*)	(5.0*)	(6.6*)
4	10.22	10.54	13.29	14.99	19.48	19	7.69	8.01	10.71	12.38	16.79
	(6.0*)	(6.1*)	(7.8*)	(8.2*)	(9.8*)		(4.4*)	(4.5*)	(5.9*)	(6.3*)	(7.9*)
5	11.42	11.76	14.54	16.28	20.83	20	5.63	5.95	8.59	10.23	14.55
	(7.0*)	(7.0*)	(8.6*)	(8.8*)	(9.2*)		(3.3*)	(3.4*)	(4.8*)	(5.3*)	(7.0*)
6	11.07	11.42	14.20	15.93	20.48	21	5.63	5.95	8.60	10.24	14.56
	(6.2*)	(6.2*)	(7.6*)	(7.8*)	(9.2*)		(3.4*)	(3.5*)	(5.0*)	(5.5*)	(7.1*)
7	10.67	11.01	13.77	15.49	20.00	22	3.28	3.59	6.17	7.77	11.98
	(5.8*)	(5.9*)	(7.3*)	(7.6*)	(9.1*)		(2.0)	(2.1)	(3.6*)	(4.3*)	(6.0*)
8	6.76	7.08	9.74	11.40	15.75	23	3.46	3.77	6.36	7.96	12.19
	(3.8*)	(3.9*)	(5.3*)	(5.8*)	(7.5*)		(2.1)	(2.3*)	(3.8*)	(4.4*)	(6.2*)
9	7.24	7.56	10.23	11.89	16.25	24	2.44	2.74	5.30	6.88	11.06
	(3.7*)	(3.8*)	(5.2*)	(5.7*)	(7.3*)		(1.5)	(1.7)	(3.2*)	(3.9*)	(5.8*)
10	8.18	8.52	11.21	12.89	17.28	25	5.02	5.34	7.96	9.59	13.87
	(4.2*)	(4.2*)	(5.5*)	(6.0*)	(7.6*)		(3.0*)	(3.1*)	(4.7*)	(5.2*)	(7.0*)
11	4.80	5.12	7.72	9.33	13.58	26	3.81	4.13	6.72	8.33	12.56
	(2.5*)	(2.6*)	(3.9*)	(4.5*)	(6.2*)		(2.3*)	(2.4*)	(3.9*)	(4.6*)	(6.3*)
12	5.15	5.47	8.09	9.73	14.01	27	3.49	3.80	6.38	7.98	12.20
	(2.7*)	(2.8*)	(4.1*)	(4.6*)	(6.2*)		(2.1)	(2.2)	(3.7*)	(4.4*)	(6.1*)
13	3.77	4.08	6.67	8.28	12.51	28	4.12	4.43	7.03	8.64	12.89
	(1.9)	(2.1)	(3.3*)	(3.9*)	(5.5*)		(2.4*)	(2.6*)	(4.1*)	(4.7*)	(6.5*)
14	3.47	3.79	6.38	7.99	12.21	29	3.21	3.53	6.10	7.70	11.91
	(1.7)	(1.8)	(3.0*)	(3.5*)	(5.1*)		(1.9)	(2.1)	(3.5*)	(4.2*)	(5.9*)
15	5.72	6.05	8.69	10.34	14.66	30	4.01	4.33	6.92	8.53	12.77
	(2.9*)	(3.0*)	(4.3*)	(4.8*)	(6.3*)		(2.3*)	(2.5*)	(3.9*)	(4.6*)	(6.3*)

Notes: *z-statistic is significant at 1% level of significance. D represents the Dth transaction date after the reopening of the market. $\overline{CR_i}$ refers to arithmetic mean of cumulative returns calculated on the basis of the ith base period, $i = 1, 2, 3, 4, 5$. H_0: $\overline{CR_i} = 0$; H_1: $\overline{CR_i} > 0$. z ($\alpha = 0.01$) = 2.237. z-statistics are in parentheses.

Table 3. Returns for 1976

D	$\overline{CR1}$	$\overline{CR2}$	$\overline{CR3}$	$\overline{CR4}$	$\overline{CR5}$	D	$\overline{CR1}$	$\overline{CR2}$	$\overline{CR3}$	$\overline{CR4}$	$\overline{CR5}$
1	−0.06	2.22	3.49	5.40	6.19	16	−0.51	1.78	3.06	4.98	5.80
	(−0.1)	(4.1*)	(5.2*)	(6.3*)	(6.0*)		(−0.6)	(1.9)	(2.8*)	(3.9*)	(3.9*)
2	2.96	5.32	6.63	8.61	9.44	17	−3.21	−0.99	0.25	2.11	2.89
	(6.7*)	(8.9*)	(8.6*)	(8.8*)	(8.0*)		(−4.5)	(−1.2)	(0.3)	(1.8)	(2.2)
3	2.60	4.96	6.27	8.25	9.09	18	−2.84	−0.61	0.64	2.51	3.30
	(3.9*)	(6.0*)	(6.3*)	(6.9*)	(6.5*)		(−3.3)	(−0.6)	(0.6)	(1.9)	(2.2)
4	0.01	2.30	3.58	5.50	6.31	19	−2.41	−0.17	1.09	2.97	3.77
	(0.0)	(3.2*)	(4.1*)	(5.1*)	(5.0*)		(−2.5)	(−0.2)	(0.9)	(2.1)	(2.4*)
5	−2.79	−0.56	0.67	2.53	3.30	20	−1.53	0.74	2.01	3.91	4.72
	(−5.3)	(−0.8)	(0.9)	(2.6*)	(2.9*)		(−1.6)	(0.7)	(1.6)	(2.7*)	(2.9*)
6	−3.30	−1.08	0.14	1.99	2.75	21	−1.04	1.24	2.52	4.43	5.25
	(−6.1)	(−1.6)	(0.2)	(2.1)	(2.6*)		(−0.9)	(1.0)	(1.8)	(2.8*)	(2.9*)
7	−1.82	0.43	1.68	3.57	4.35	22	−1.74	0.53	1.80	3.70	4.51
	(−2.8)	(0.5)	(1.8)	(3.2*)	(3.5*)		(−1.4)	(0.4)	(1.2)	(2.2)	(2.4*)
8	−2.56	−0.32	0.92	2.79	3.56	23	−3.35	−1.11	0.14	2.01	2.80
	(−4.0)	(−0.4)	(1.0)	(2.6*)	(2.9*)		(−2.3)	(−0.7)	(0.1)	(1.1)	(1.4)
9	−0.96	1.31	2.58	4.49	5.29	24	−2.95	−0.71	0.54	2.43	3.23
	(−1.3)	(1.5)	(2.5*)	(3.7*)	(3.8*)		(−2.1)	(−0.5)	(0.3)	(1.3)	(1.6)
10	−1.70	0.56	1.82	3.71	4.50	25	−0.01	2.31	3.60	5.54	6.37
	(−2.2)	(0.6)	(1.8)	(3.0*)	(3.3*)		(−0.0)	(1.6)	(2.3*)	(3.1*)	(3.3*)
11	−0.63	1.66	2.94	4.86	5.68	26	−0.25	2.06	3.36	5.29	6.13
	(−0.7)	(1.6)	(2.5*)	(3.5*)	(3.6*)		(−0.2)	(1.4)	(2.0)	(2.9*)	(3.0*)
12	−0.25	2.05	3.34	5.27	6.09	27	−0.22	2.10	3.40	5.34	6.18
	(−0.3)	(1.9)	(2.7*)	(3.7*)	(3.8*)		(−0.1)	(1.3)	(1.9)	(2.7*)	(2.8*)
13	−0.66	1.63	2.91	4.83	5.64	28	1.37	3.73	5.06	7.04	7.89
	(−0.8)	(1.7)	(2.6*)	(3.6*)	(3.7*)		(0.9)	(2.2)	(2.7*)	(3.4*)	(3.5*)
14	−0.17	2.13	3.41	5.34	6.16	29	3.97	6.39	7.75	9.79	10.68
	(−0.2)	(2.2)	(3.0*)	(4.0*)	(4.1*)		(2.6*)	(3.7*)	(4.1*)	(4.6*)	(4.6*)
15	0.07	2.37	3.66	5.59	6.42	30	4.26	6.70	8.07	0.13	11.02
	(0.1*)	(2.5*)	(3.3*)	(4.2*)	(4.2*)		(2.5*)	(3.6*)	(3.9*)	(4.4*)	(4.4*)

Notes: See Table 2.

Table 4. Returns for 1977

D	$\overline{CR1}$	$\overline{CR2}$	$\overline{CR3}$	$\overline{CR4}$	$\overline{CR5}$	D	$\overline{CR1}$	$\overline{CR2}$	$\overline{CR3}$	$\overline{CR4}$	$\overline{CR5}$
1	–3.73	–3.52	–5.10	–5.75	–8.06	16	–9.99	–9.78	–11.23	–11.82	–13.96
	(–7.9)	(–6.4)	(–7.7)	(–7.5)	(–9.0)		(–7.9)	(–7.2)	(–7.9)	(–7.8)	(–8.8)
2	–5.47	–5.26	–6.80	–7.43	–9.69	17	–8.41	–8.20	–9.69	–10.30	–12.48
	(–6.9)	(–6.1)	(–7.1)	(–7.0)	(–8.3)		(–7.2)	(–6.6)	(–7.3)	(–7.3)	(–8.5)
3	–5.10	–4.89	–6.43	–7.06	–9.32	18	–9.19	–8.98	–10.45	–11.05	–13.21
	(–5.3)	(–4.7)	(–5.7)	(–5.9)	(–7.2)		(–7.9)	(–7.3)	(–7.9)	(–7.9)	(–8.9)
4	–4.21	–4.00	–5.56	–6.21	–8.50	19	–10.36	–10.15	–11.60	–12.19	–14.31
	(–5.2)	(–4.6)	(–5.8)	(–5.9)	(–7.4)		(–7.9)	(–7.3)	(–7.9)	(–7.9)	(–8.8)
5	–7.01	–6.80	–8.31	–8.93	–11.14	20	–9.67	–9.46	–10.91	–11.51	–13.65
	(–7.0)	(–6.3)	(–7.2)	(–7.1)	(–8.3)		(–7.4)	(–6.9)	(–7.5)	(–7.5)	(–8.4)
6	–8.21	–8.00	–9.48	–10.08	–12.26	21	–9.61	–9.40	–10.85	–11.45	–13.59
	(–6.7)	(–6.1)	(–6.9)	(–6.9)	(–8.0)		(–7.4)	(–6.8)	(–7.4)	(–7.4)	(–8.4)
7	–9.23	–9.02	–10.48	–11.08	–13.23	22	–10.91	–10.70	–12.13	–12.71	–14.81
	(–6.9)	(–6.4)	(–7.1)	(–7.1)	(–8.1)		(–7.6)	(–7.1)	(–7.6)	(–7.6)	(–8.4)
8	–6.29	–6.07	–7.59	–8.22	–10.45	23	–10.63	–10.42	–11.85	–12.43	–14.54
	(–5.4)	(–4.9)	(–5.8)	(–5.9)	(–7.2)		(–7.5)	(–7.0)	(–7.5)	(–7.5)	(–8.4)
9	–9.68	–9.47	–10.93	–11.53	–13.67	24	–12.87	–12.66	–14.05	–14.62	–16.67
	(–7.5)	(–7.0)	(–7.6)	(–7.6)	(–8.6)		(–8.2)	(–7.7)	(–8.2)	(–8.1)	(–8.9)
10	–7.94	–7.74	–9.23	–9.84	–12.04	25	–12.21	–12.01	–13.41	–13.98	–16.04
	(–7.2)	(–6.6)	(–7.5)	(–7.5)	(–8.7)		(–7.8)	(–7.4)	(–7.8)	(–7.8)	(–8.6)
11	–6.18	–5.97	–7.50	–8.13	–10.38	26	–9.43	–9.23	–10.68	–11.27	–13.40
	(–6.7)	(–6.0)	(–7.1)	(–7.2)	(–8.6)		(–6.4)	(–6.1)	(–6.6)	(–6.7)	(–7.5)
12	–7.24	–7.04	–8.55	–9.18	–11.39	27	–9.91	–9.71	–11.15	–11.74	–13.87
	(–7.4)	(–6.8)	(–7.7)	(–7.8)	(–9.1)		(–7.0)	(–6.7)	(–7.2)	(–7.2)	(–8.1)
13	–9.24	–9.04	–10.51	–11.11	–13.27	28	–7.92	–7.72	–9.21	–9.82	–12.00
	(–7.5)	(–6.9)	(–7.6)	(–7.6)	(–8.7)		(–6.3)	(–5.9)	(–6.6)	(–6.7)	(–7.7)
14	–8.98	–8.77	–10.24	–10.84	–13.01	29	–7.71	–7.51	–9.00	–9.62	–11.81
	(–7.3)	(–6.7)	(–7.4)	(–7.4)	(–8.5)		(–6.2)	(–5.9)	(–6.6)	(–6.7)	(–7.8)
15	–11.18	–10.97	–12.40	–12.98	–15.09	30	–7.83	–7.64	–9.13	–9.75	–11.94
	(–8.3)	(–7.7)	(–8.3)	(–8.2)	(–9.1)		(–6.5)	(–6.2)	(–7.0)	(–7.1)	(–8.1)

Notes: See Table 2.

Table 5. Returns for 1978

D	$\overline{CR1}$	$\overline{CR2}$	$\overline{CR3}$	$\overline{CR4}$	$\overline{CR5}$	*D*	$\overline{CR1}$	$\overline{CR2}$	$\overline{CR3}$	$\overline{CR4}$	$\overline{CR5}$
1	3.35	6.18	7.29	9.46	9.70	16	2.45	5.24	6.31	8.43	8.63
	(5.6*)	(7.6*)	(7.6*)	(7.6*)	(7.1*)		(1.5)	(3.0*)	(3.6*)	(4.4*)	(4.5*)
2	5.69	8.59	9.72	11.95	12.19	17	2.97	5.79	6.87	9.02	9.21
	(6.9*)	(8.2*)	(8.3*)	(8.3*)	(7.9*)		(1.7)	(3.1*)	(3.6*)	(4.3*)	(4.4*)
3	5.65	8.55	9.68	11.91	12.14	18	3.73	6.57	7.65	9.82	10.02
	(5.6*)	(7.0*)	(7.3*)	(7.5*)	(7.3*)		(2.1)	(3.5*)	(4.0*)	(4.7*)	(4.8*)
4	3.23	6.06	7.15	9.32	9.55	19	3.89	6.74	7.83	10.00	10.20
	(3.7*)	(5.6*)	(6.1*)	(6.6*)	(6.4*)		(2.4*)	(3.8*)	(4.3*)	(5.0*)	(5.0*)
5	0.89	3.64	4.69	6.79	6.99	20	2.19	4.97	6.04	8.17	8.37
	(0.9)	(3.4*)	(4.1*)	(5.1*)	(5.1*)		(1.4)	(3.0*)	(3.5*)	(4.4*)	(4.4*)
6	2.05	4.84	5.92	8.05	8.26	21	2.28	5.07	6.14	8.27	8.47
	(1.8)	(3.7*)	(4.3*)	(5.1*)	(5.1*)		(1.4)	(2.9*)	(3.5*)	(4.3*)	(4.4*)
7	0.66	3.39	4.44	6.53	6.72	22	–0.25	2.46	3.50	5.56	5.75
	(0.5)	(2.6*)	(3.3*)	(4.3*)	(4.4*)		(–0.2)	(1.5)	(2.1)	(3.1*)	(3.2*)
8	–1.42	1.24	2.26	4.29	4.47	23	–0.14	2.58	3.62	5.69	5.88
	(–0.2)	(1.0)	(1.7)	(3.0*)	(3.1*)		(–0.1)	(1.6)	(2.2*)	(3.2*)	(3.3*)
9	0.56	3.30	4.35	6.44	6.64	24	–0.44	2.27	3.31	5.38	5.57
	(0.4)	(2.3*)	(2.9*)	(3.9*)	(3.9*)		(–0.3)	(1.4)	(2.1)	(3.1*)	(3.1*)
10	2.33	5.14	6.21	8.35	8.56	25	–1.12	1.56	2.58	4.63	4.82
	(1.7)	(3.3*)	(3.9*)	(4.7*)	(4.7*)		(–0.7)	(1.0)	(1.6)	(2.6*)	(2.7*)
11	2.39	5.20	6.28	8.43	8.63	26	–0.27	2.44	3.48	5.54	5.73
	(1.7)	(3.3*)	(3.8*)	(4.6*)	(4.6*)		(–0.2)	(1.4)	(2.0)	(2.9*)	(3.0*)
12	2.44	5.25	6.33	8.48	8.69	27	1.07	3.82	4.87	6.97	7.16
	(1.6)	(3.1*)	(3.6*)	(4.4*)	(4.4*)		(0.7)	(2.2)	(2.8*)	(3.7*)	(3.7*)
13	4.05	6.90	8.00	10.18	10.38	28	1.09	3.83	4.88	6.97	7.16
	(2.5*)	(3.9*)	(4.4*)	(5.1*)	(5.1*)		(0.7)	(2.4*)	(3.0*)	(4.0*)	(4.0*)
14	4.11	6.96	8.05	10.23	10.42	29	1.75	4.51	5.56	7.67	7.86
	(2.4*)	(3.7*)	(4.2*)	(4.9*)	(5.0*)		(1.2)	(2.8*)	(3.4*)	(4.3*)	(4.4*)
15	2.70	5.48	6.55	8.68	8.87	30	2.42	5.20	6.26	8.39	8.58
	(1.7)	(3.2*)	(3.7*)	(4.6*)	(4.7*)		(1.6)	(3.2*)	(3.8*)	(4.6*)	(4.7*)

Notes: See Table 2.

Table 6. Returns for 1979

D	$\overline{CR1}$	$\overline{CR2}$	$\overline{CR3}$	$\overline{CR4}$	$\overline{CR5}$	D	$\overline{CR1}$	$\overline{CR2}$	$\overline{CR3}$	$\overline{CR4}$	$\overline{CR5}$
1	5.19	6.64	4.54	4.24	0.63	16	0.26	1.62	−0.39	−0.69	−4.11
	(13.4*)	(14.0*)	(10.4*)	(8.2*)	(1.2)		(0.5)	(3.1*)	(−0.8)	(−1.3)	(−7.2)
2	7.29	8.77	6.62	6.31	2.62	17	0.48	1.84	−0.18	−0.48	−3.91
	(16.3*)	(16.1*)	(13.9*)	(11.4*)	(5.1*)		(0.9)	(3.5*)	(−0.4)	(−0.9)	(−7.0)
3	5.50	6.95	4.83	4.53	0.91	18	2.21	3.60	1.55	1.25	−2.25
	(12.6*)	(14.0*)	(10.9*)	(9.0*)	(1.8)		(4.2*)	(6.8*)	(3.2*)	(2.4*)	(−4.1)
4	3.53	4.95	2.88	2.58	−0.97	19	2.95	4.36	2.29	1.98	−1.54
	(8.2*)	(10.4*)	(6.4*)	(5.1*)	(−1.8)		(5.3*)	(7.7*)	(4.4*)	(3.7*)	(−2.8)
5	7.11	8.58	6.43	6.12	2.44	20	4.27	5.70	3.60	3.29	−0.29
	(13.5*)	(14.8*)	(12.5*)	(10.8*)	(4.5*)		(7.3*)	(9.4*)	(6.7*)	(5.9*)	(−0.5)
6	6.22	7.68	5.54	5.23	1.58	21	5.06	6.49	4.38	4.06	0.46
	(10.1*)	(11.5*)	(9.1*)	(8.0*)	(2.6*)		(8.5*)	(10.7*)	(8.3*)	(7.4*)	(0.9)
7	3.46	4.87	2.80	2.49	−1.05	22	5.75	7.19	5.06	4.74	1.11
	(5.8*)	(7.8*)	(4.8*)	(4.0*)	(−1.7)		(9.2*)	(11.3*)	(9.2*)	(8.4*)	(2.1)
8	1.61	3.00	0.96	0.67	−2.81	23	4.62	6.05	3.94	3.63	0.04
	(2.8*)	(4.9*)	(1.6)	(1.1)	(−4.4)		(7.6*)	(9.9*)	(7.3*)	(6.5*)	(0.1)
9	2.21	3.61	1.56	1.26	−2.24	24	2.50	3.90	1.84	1.54	−1.97
	(4.1*)	(6.4*)	(3.0*)	(2.2)	(−3.9)		(1.1)	(1.7*)	(0.8)	(0.7)	(−0.9)
10	2.84	4.24	2.18	1.88	−1.64	25	3.57	4.98	2.90	2.59	−0.96
	(5.1*)	(7.4*)	(4.1*)	(3.3*)	(−2.8)		(5.8*)	(8.1*)	(5.2*)	(4.6*)	(−1.7)
11	1.88	3.27	1.23	0.93	−2.56	26	2.75	4.15	2.08	1.78	−1.74
	(3.4*)	(6.0*)	(2.4*)	(1.7)	(−4.6)		(4.3*)	(6.6*)	(3.6*)	(3.0*)	(−3.0)
12	3.05	4.46	2.39	2.08	−1.44	27	3.01	4.41	2.34	2.03	−1.50
	(5.6*)	(8.1*)	(4.8*)	(4.0*)	(−2.7)		(4.4*)	(6.5*)	(3.8*)	(3.2*)	(−2.4)
13	3.61	5.02	2.94	2.63	−0.92	28	4.14	5.55	3.45	3.14	−0.44
	(6.5*)	(9.1*)	(6.0*)	(5.1*)	(−1.8)		(5.8*)	(7.8*)	(5.5*)	(5.0*)	(−0.7)
14	2.00	3.38	1.33	1.03	−2.46	29	3.85	5.26	3.16	2.85	−0.72
	(3.5*)	(6.2*)	(2.7*)	(2.0)	(−4.5)		(5.3*)	(7.3*)	(4.9*)	(4.4*)	(−1.2)
15	0.41	1.77	−0.24	−0.54	−3.97	30	3.91	5.32	3.22	2.90	−0.67
	(0.8)	(3.4*)	(−0.5)	(−1.1)	(−7.2)		(4.8*)	(6.7*)	(4.5*)	(4.2*)	(−1.0)

Notes: See Table 2.

Table 7. Returns for 1980

D	$\overline{CR1}$	$\overline{CR2}$	$\overline{CR3}$	$\overline{CR4}$	$\overline{CR5}$	*D*	$\overline{CR1}$	$\overline{CR2}$	$\overline{CR3}$	$\overline{CR4}$	$\overline{CR5}$
1	1.73	1.09	1.93	2.05	3.72	16	12.82	12.12	13.04	13.17	15.01
	(5.0*)	(2.6*)	(3.9*)	(3.4*)	(4.8*)		(10.2*)	(9.5*)	(10.0*)	(9.7*)	(10.5*)
2	1.40	0.76	1.60	1.72	3.39	17	12.34	11.64	12.56	12.68	14.51
	(3.1*)	(1.5)	(2.8*)	(2.6*)	(4.1*)		(10.3*)	(9.5*)	(10.2*)	(9.9*)	(10.7*)
3	2.73	2.08	2.93	3.05	4.74	18	10.78	10.09	10.99	11.12	12.93
	(6.0*)	(4.2*)	(5.1*)	(4.6*)	(5.7*)		(9.1*)	(8.3*)	(8.9*)	(8.6*)	(9.4*)
4	2.57	1.92	2.77	2.88	4.57	19	11.72	11.02	11.94	12.07	13.89
	(5.9*)	(4.3*)	(5.3*)	(4.8*)	(5.9*)		(9.4*)	(8.7*)	(9.2*)	(8.9*)	(9.6*)
5	2.10	1.46	2.30	2.42	4.11	20	8.39	7.71	8.60	8.73	10.50
	(4.2*)	(2.7*)	(3.8*)	(3.5*)	(4.7*)		(7.4*)	(6.7*)	(7.2*)	(7.0*)	(7.9*)
6	2.99	2.34	3.20	3.32	5.03	21	8.42	7.75	8.64	8.77	10.54
	(5.1*)	(3.7*)	(4.5*)	(4.2*)	(5.2*)		(7.3*)	(6.5*)	(7.0*)	(6.8*)	(7.7*)
7	3.10	2.46	3.32	3.44	5.14	22	7.16	6.50	7.38	7.51	9.26
	(4.9*)	(3.6*)	(4.4*)	(4.1*)	(5.3*)		(6.1*)	(5.3*)	(5.9*)	(5.7*)	(6.6*)
8	5.41	4.75	5.62	5.75	7.49	23	6.59	5.94	6.81	6.94	8.67
	(7.8*)	(6.5*)	(7.0*)	(6.6*)	(7.3*)		(5.5*)	(4.7*)	(5.3*)	(5.2*)	(6.1*)
9	6.65	5.98	6.86	6.98	8.73	24	4.08	3.44	4.29	4.41	6.10
	(9.9*)	(8.6*)	(9.2*)	(8.7*)	(9.3*)		(3.2*)	(2.6*)	(3.2*)	(3.2*)	(4.2*)
10	7.16	6.49	7.37	7.49	9.24	25	3.37	2.74	3.58	3.71	5.38
	(8.9*)	(7.9*)	(8.6*)	(8.2*)	(9.0*)		(2.8*)	(2.2)	(2.8*)	(2.8*)	(3.9*)
11	10.48	9.79	10.69	10.82	12.63	26	5.11	4.46	5.32	5.44	7.14
	(11.4*)	(10.4*)	(11.1*)	(10.7*)	(11.3*)		(4.0*)	(3.4*)	(4.0*)	(3.9*)	(5.0*)
12	11.69	10.98	11.88	11.99	13.80	27	4.57	3.92	4.76	4.88	6.57
	(0.8*)	(10.2*)	(11.1*)	(11.1*)	(12.1*)		(3.8*)	(3.2*)	(3.8*)	(3.8*)	(5.0*)
13	12.74	12.03	12.93	13.05	14.86	28	3.43	2.79	3.63	3.74	5.41
	(10.2*)	(9.6*)	(10.5*)	(10.5*)	(11.6*)		(3.1*)	(2.4*)	(3.2*)	(3.2*)	(4.4*)
14	13.13	12.42	13.33	13.44	15.26	29	1.84	1.21	2.03	2.14	3.78
	(9.2*)	(8.6*)	(9.4*)	(9.4*)	(10.5*)		(1.7)	(1.1)	(1.8)	(1.8)	(3.2*)
15	13.48	12.77	13.69	13.81	15.65	30	3.79	3.14	3.98	4.09	5.76
	(10.3*)	(9.6*)	(10.2*)	(10.1*)	(11.0*)		(3.1*)	(2.5*)	(3.2*)	(3.3*)	(4.5*)

Notes: See Table 2.

Table 8. Returns for 1981

D	$\overline{CR1}$	$\overline{CR2}$	$\overline{CR3}$	$\overline{CR4}$	$\overline{CR5}$	D	$\overline{CR1}$	$\overline{CR2}$	$\overline{CR3}$	$\overline{CR4}$	$\overline{CR5}$
1	0.71	0.81	1.20	1.47	2.13	16	8.19	8.30	8.72	9.01	9.71
	(3.2*)	(3.0*)	(3.5*)	(3.2*)	(3.0*)		(8.5*)	(8.5*)	(8.7*)	(8.5*)	(8.1*)
2	0.79	0.88	1.28	1.55	2.21	17	8.14	8.24	8.67	8.96	9.67
	(3.7*)	(3.6*)	(3.9*)	(3.5*)	(3.1*)		(8.6*)	(8.6*)	(8.7*)	(8.6*)	(8.0*)
3	1.36	1.46	1.86	2.13	2.80	18	7.94	8.05	8.47	8.76	9.47
	(4.9*)	(5.1*)	(4.8*)	(4.4*)	(3.7*)		(8.6*)	(8.6*)	(8.7*)	(8.5*)	(8.0*)
4	3.05	3.15	3.55	3.83	4.51	19	7.41	7.52	7.94	8.24	8.94
	(8.1*)	(8.2*)	(7.7*)	(7.0*)	(5.6*)		(7.6*)	(7.6*)	(7.7*)	(7.6*)	(7.2*)
5	4.62	4.72	5.12	5.40	6.07	20	6.86	6.96	7.38	7.67	8.37
	(11.4*)	(11.4*)	(11.3*)	(10.3*)	(8.0*)		(6.9*)	(7.0*)	(7.1*)	(7.1*)	(6.7*)
6	6.00	6.10	6.51	6.80	7.48	21	6.97	7.06	7.49	7.78	8.49
	(12.1*)	(12.3*)	(12.0*)	(11.1*)	(8.8*)		(6.6*)	(6.7*)	(6.8*)	(6.8*)	(6.4*)
7	5.84	5.94	6.35	6.63	7.31	22	7.69	7.79	8.22	8.51	9.22
	(10.4*)	(10.6*)	(10.6*)	(10.1*)	(8.3*)		(6.9*)	(7.0*)	(7.1*)	(7.1*)	(6.8*)
8	7.16	7.25	7.67	7.95	8.65	23	6.83	6.93	7.35	7.64	8.35
	(11.3*)	(11.7*)	(11.6*)	(11.1*)	(9.2*)		(6.0*)	(6.1*)	(6.2*)	(6.2*)	(6.1*)
9	7.40	7.49	7.90	8.19	8.88	24	6.27	6.37	6.79	7.08	7.78
	(11.0*)	(11.3*)	(11.5*)	(11.2*)	(9.7*)		(5.5*)	(5.6*)	(5.8*)	(5.8*)	(5.7*)
10	7.13	7.22	7.64	7.93	8.63	25	5.63	5.73	6.14	6.43	7.12
	(9.4*)	(9.7*)	(9.7*)	(9.5*)	(8.4*)		(5.0*)	(5.1*)	(5.3*)	(5.4*)	(5.3*)
11	6.80	6.89	7.31	7.60	8.30	26	5.07	5.17	5.58	5.86	6.53
	(8.7*)	(9.0*)	(9.0*)	(8.9*)	(7.9*)		(4.4*)	(4.5*)	(4.7*)	(4.8*)	(4.9*)
12	9.31	9.40	9.84	10.13	10.85	27	5.53	5.63	6.04	6.32	7.00
	(9.8*)	(10.1*)	(10.1*)	(10.0*)	(9.0*)		(5.0*)	(5.1*)	(5.3*)	(5.4*)	(5.4*)
13	11.14	11.23	11.67	11.96	12.69	28	6.56	6.66	7.07	7.36	8.04
	(9.5*)	(9.7*)	(9.8*)	(9.9*)	(9.3*)		(5.8*)	(5.9*)	(6.1*)	(6.2*)	(6.1*)
14	9.31	9.41	9.83	10.12	10.83	29	5.15	5.24	5.66	5.93	6.62
	(8.6*)	(8.7*)	(8.9*)	(8.9*)	(8.4*)		(4.9*)	(5.0*)	(5.2*)	(5.3*)	(5.3*)
15	10.29	10.39	10.82	11.11	11.82	30	2.91	3.00	3.40	3.68	4.34
	(9.4*)	(9.5*)	(9.7*)	(9.7*)	(9.2*)		(2.9*)	(3.0*)	(3.3*)	(3.5*)	(3.6*)

Notes: See Table 2.

Table 9. Returns for 1982

D	$\overline{CR1}$	$\overline{CR2}$	$\overline{CR3}$	$\overline{CR4}$	$\overline{CR5}$
1	0.68	0.88	0.16	–0.05	–1.13
	(3.1*)	(2.5*)	(0.4)	(–0.1)	(–1.6)
2	0.64	0.84	0.13	–0.08	1.16
	(2.7*)	(2.2*)	(0.3)	(–0.1)	(–1.6)
3	1.40	1.60	0.87	0.66	–0.43
	(4.6*)	(3.9*)	(1.8)	(1.1)	(–0.6)
4	0.99	1.19	0.47	0.26	–0.82
	(3.1*)	(2.7*)	(0.9)	(0.4)	(–1.1)
5	0.82	1.02	0.30	0.10	–0.99
	(2.5*)	(2.3*)	(0.6)	(0.2)	(–1.3)
6	1.32	1.53	0.81	0.60	–0.49
	(3.3*)	(2.9*)	(1.4)	(0.8)	(–0.6)
7	1.81	2.02	1.29	1.08	–0.02
	(4.2*)	(3.7*)	(2.2)	(1.5)	(–0.0)
8	2.03	2.24	1.51	1.30	0.19
	(4.6*)	(4.0*)	(2.5*)	(1.8)	(0.2)
9	1.01	1.22	0.49	0.28	–0.82
	(2.4*)	(2.3*)	(0.8)	(0.4)	(–1.1)
10	0.91	1.12	0.39	0.18	–0.91
	(2.0)	(2.0)	(0.6)	(0.3)	(–1.2)
11	0.65	0.86	0.13	–0.07	–1.17
	(1.3)	(1.4)	(0.2)	(–0.1)	(–1.4)
12	0.63	0.84	0.11	–0.10	–1.20
	(1.1)	(1.3)	(0.2)	(–0.1)	(–1.4)
13	0.60	0.81	0.09	–0.11	–1.20
	(1.1)	(1.2)	(0.1)	(–0.1)	(–1.4)
14	–0.01	0.20	–0.51	–0.71	–1.80
	(–0.0)	(0.3)	(–0.7)	(–0.9)	(–2.0)
15	–1.71	–1.50	–2.21	–2.40	–3.46
	(–3.0)	(–2.2)	(–3.0)	(–2.9)	(–3.9)
16	–2.59	–2.39	–3.08	–3.27	–4.32
	(–4.6)	(–3.6)	(–4.3)	(–4.0)	(–4.9)
17	–2.18	–1.98	–2.66	–2.85	–3.89
	(–3.7)	(–2.9)	(–3.6)	(–3.4)	(–4.2)
18	–2.17	–1.97	–2.66	–2.85	–3.88
	(–4.0)	(–3.1)	(–3.8)	(–3.5)	(–4.3)
19	–3.49	–3.30	–3.97	–4.16	–5.17
	(–6.2)	(–5.3)	(–5.6)	(–5.2)	(–5.7)
20	–3.04	–2.85	–3.52	–3.71	–4.73
	(–5.7)	(–4.6)	(–5.0)	(–4.6)	(–5.2)
21	–3.90	–3.70	–4.36	–4.55	–5.56
	(–6.5)	(–5.5)	(–5.8)	(–5.4)	(–5.9)
22	–2.62	–2.43	–3.11	–3.30	–4.33
	(–4.1)	(–3.5)	(–4.0)	(–3.9)	(–4.6)
23	–3.26	–3.07	–3.75	–3.94	–4.96
	(–5.2)	(–4.5)	(–5.0)	(–4.7)	(–5.3)
24	–2.88	–2.69	–3.37	–3.56	–4.59
	(–4.6)	(–3.9)	(–4.5)	(–4.2)	(–4.9)
25	–3.54	–3.35	–4.02	–4.21	–5.22
	(–5.3)	(–4.6)	(–5.0)	(–4.7)	(–5.3)
26	–3.65	–3.45	–4.12	–4.30	–5.32
	(–5.3)	(–4.5)	(–5.0)	(–4.7)	(–5.3)
27	–4.72	–4.52	–5.19	–5.37	–6.38
	(–6.6)	(–5.9)	(–6.2)	(–5.9)	(–6.4)
28	–6.73	–6.54	–7.19	–7.37	–8.35
	(–9.3)	(–8.3)	(–8.5)	(–8.0)	(–8.3)
29	–6.83	–6.64	–7.29	–7.47	–8.45
	(–9.3)	(–8.5)	(–8.7)	(–8.2)	(–8.5)
30	–5.97	–5.79	–6.45	–6.64	–7.63
	(–8.4)	(–7.7)	(–8.0)	(–7.6)	(–8.0)

Notes: See Table 2.

Table 10. Returns for 1983

D	$\overline{CR1}$	$\overline{CR2}$	$\overline{CR3}$	$\overline{CR4}$	$\overline{CR5}$	*D*	$\overline{CR1}$	$\overline{CR2}$	$\overline{CR3}$	$\overline{CR4}$	$\overline{CR5}$
1	3.84	4.39	4.14	4.45	4.01	16	25.20	25.85	25.51	25.86	25.27
	(10.5*)	(8.6*)	(5.5*)	(4.5*)	(3.3*)		(13.9*)	(13.8*)	(13.1*)	(12.5*)	(11.5*)
2	4.22	4.76	4.50	4.81	4.36	17	28.84	29.49	29.13	29.47	28.84
	(10.3*)	(9.3*)	(6.1*)	(5.0*)	(3.6*)		(14.2*)	(14.2*)	(13.7*)	(13.2*)	(12.2*)
3	6.55	7.11	6.85	7.17	6.71	18	29.20	29.85	29.48	29.83	29.19
	(13.2*)	(11.8*)	(8.3*)	(6.9*)	(5.2*)		(13.3*)	(13.4*)	(13.0*)	(12.6*)	(11.8*)
4	10.63	11.21	10.95	11.28	10.81	19	26.65	27.28	26.90	27.23	26.60
	(18.3*)	(16.1*)	(12.0*)	(10.0*)	(7.8*)		(13.5*)	(13.8*)	(13.3*)	(12.9*)	(12.0*)
5	11.72	12.34	12.10	12.46	12.01	20	29.04	29.68	29.31	29.65	29.03
	(15.0*)	(13.4*)	(10.7)	(9.3*)	(7.6*)		(16.5*)	(16.6*)	(15.9*)	(15.1*)	(13.8*)
6	9.81	10.43	10.20	10.57	10.13	21	28.69	29.35	28.98	29.33	28.70
	(11.6*)	(10.6*)	(8.6*)	(7.6*)	(6.2*)		(16.2*)	(16.3*)	(15.5*)	(14.7*)	(13.5*)
7	11.73	12.36	12.12	12.48	12.03	22	31.05	31.71	31.35	31.70	31.07
	(14.4*)	(12.9*)	(10.5*)	(9.1*)	(7.5*)		(17.2*)	(17.2*)	(16.4*)	(15.5*)	(14.3*)
8	12.45	13.07	12.82	13.19	12.72	23	29.76	30.43	30.09	30.45	29.85
	(16.4*)	(14.5*)	(11.6*)	(10.0*)	(8.2*)		(16.4*)	(16.3*)	(15.4*)	(14.6*)	(13.3*)
9	15.47	16.11	15.86	16.23	15.76	24	25.45	26.11	25.79	26.15	25.59
	(18.7*)	(16.6*)	(13.5*)	(11.7*)	(9.7*)		(14.8*)	(14.8*)	(13.8*)	(13.0*)	(11.8*)
10	17.39	18.04	17.78	18.16	17.66	25	26.14	26.80	26.48	26.84	26.27
	(19.1*)	(17.3*)	(14.5*)	(12.7*)	(10.7*)		(16.1*)	(15.9*)	(14.8*)	(13.9*)	(12.5*)
11	16.15	16.78	16.50	16.85	16.35	26	29.97	30.66	30.33	30.71	30.13
	(16.7*)	(15.7*)	(13.4*)	(11.8*)	(10.0*)		(17.3*)	(17.0*)	(15.9*)	(15.0*)	(13.6*)
12	19.34	19.98	19.69	20.04	19.52	27	31.79	32.49	32.16	32.54	31.94
	(17.6*)	(16.8*)	(14.7*)	(13.2*)	(11.3*)		(17.3*)	(17.0*)	(16.0*)	(15.1*)	(13.8*)
13	20.68	21.32	21.01	21.36	20.82	28	29.85	30.55	30.24	30.64	30.08
	(16.5*)	(16.1*)	(14.5*)	(13.3*)	(11.6*)		(16.3*)	(16.0*)	(14.9*)	(14.1*)	(12.8*)
14	20.91	21.55	21.24	21.59	21.04	29	31.59	32.30	32.01	32.42	31.86
	(14.5*)	(14.3*)	(13.2*)	(12.3*)	(11.0*)		(16.8*)	(16.4*)	(15.2*)	(14.3*)	(13.0*)
15	21.83	22.47	22.16	22.51	21.95	30	34.35	35.09	34.80	35.23	34.67
	(13.5*)	(13.4*)	(12.6*)	(11.9*)	(10.8*)		(17.5*)	(17.1*)	(15.8*)	(14.9*)	(13.5*)

Notes: See Table 2.

Table 11. Returns for 1984

D	$\overline{CR1}$	$\overline{CR2}$	$\overline{CR3}$	$\overline{CR4}$	$\overline{CR5}$	D	$\overline{CR1}$	$\overline{CR2}$	$\overline{CR3}$	$\overline{CR4}$	$\overline{CR5}$
1	2.89	4.40	5.47	6.87	7.75	16	7.16	8.71	9.82	11.26	12.20
	(11.6*)	(11.6*)	(11.5*)	(10.6*)	(10.5*)		(10.0*)	(11.9*)	(12.4*)	(12.6*)	(12.3*)
2	4.12	5.64	6.72	8.14	9.03	17	7.18	8.72	9.83	11.27	12.21
	(13.3*)	(3.2*)	(13.0*)	(11.9*)	(11.8*)		(9.2*)	(11.1*)	(11.7*)	(12.1*)	(11.9*)
3	4.43	5.96	7.05	8.47	9.38	18	9.07	10.65	11.78	13.25	14.21
	(11.9*)	(12.4*)	(12.3*)	(11.5*)	(11.3*)		(10.9*)	(12.5*)	(12.9*)	(13.0*)	(12.8*)
4	5.43	6.98	8.08	9.52	10.43	19	9.73	11.31	12.44	13.92	14.87
	(11.3*)	(12.3*)	(12.4*)	(11.8*)	(11.6*)		(10.6*)	(12.1*)	(12.6*)	(13.0*)	(12.9*)
5	7.86	9.45	10.59	12.07	13.01	20	8.23	9.78	10.90	12.35	13.29
	(13.2*)	(13.4*)	(13.3*)	(12.6*)	(12.4*)		(8.7*)	(10.2*)	(10.8*)	(11.3*)	(11.3*)
6	8.26	9.87	11.01	12.51	13.45	21	4.68	6.17	7.25	8.64	9.55
	(12.0*)	(12.3*)	(12.3*)	(11.9*)	(11.8*)		(5.1*)	(6.8*)	(7.6*)	(8.5*)	(8.7*)
7	5.65	7.21	8.32	9.77	10.69	22	4.78	6.26	7.33	8.71	9.62
	(9.6*)	(10.4*)	(10.6*)	(10.3*)	(10.3*)		(5.2*)	(7.0*)	(7.9*)	(8.9*)	(9.1*)
8	7.21	8.79	9.91	11.38	12.32	23	5.24	6.73	7.81	9.19	10.10
	(13.8*)	(14.0*)	(13.7*)	(12.9*)	(12.5*)		(5.2*)	(6.7*)	(7.6*)	(8.5*)	(8.8*)
9	7.01	8.57	9.69	11.15	12.08	24	4.96	6.45	7.52	8.91	9.82
	(13.4*)	(14.3*)	(14.1*)	(13.3*)	(12.9*)		(5.0*)	(6.6*)	(7.4*)	(8.3*)	(8.6*)
10	5.09	6.61	7.70	9.12	10.03	25	3.23	4.68	5.73	7.09	7.97
	(10.4*)	(12.6*)	(12.8*)	(12.5*)	(12.1*)		(3.2*)	(4.8*)	(5.8*)	(6.9*)	(7.3*)
11	4.11	5.60	6.67	8.06	8.96	26	1.53	2.94	3.96	5.28	6.15
	(8.3*)	(11.5*)	(12.3*)	(12.4*)	(12.0*)		(1.5)	(2.9*)	(3.9*)	(5.1*)	(5.7*)
12	5.60	7.12	8.20	9.62	10.53	27	4.53	5.99	7.04	8.40	9.30
	(9.9*)	(12.5*)	(13.1*)	(13.1*)	(12.7*)		(4.2*)	(5.7*)	(6.6*)	(7.7*)	(8.1*)
13	7.06	8.61	9.72	11.16	12.09	28	3.94	5.38	6.43	7.79	8.68
	(11.3*)	(13.2*)	(13.6*)	(13.4*)	(13.1*)		(3.5*)	(4.9*)	(5.8*)	(6.8*)	(7.2*)
14	7.91	9.47	10.59	12.04	12.98	29	5.87	7.34	8.41	9.79	10.70
	(11.9*)	(13.8*)	(14.1*)	(14.0*)	(13.5*)		(5.0*)	(6.3*)	(7.1*)	(8.1*)	(8.4*)
15	7.40	8.94	10.06	11.50	12.44	30	6.69	8.17	9.25	10.64	11.56
	(10.6*)	(12.7*)	(13.0*)	(13.2*)	(12.8*)		(5.4*)	(6.8*)	(7.6*)	(8.5*)	(8.8*)

Notes: See Table 2.

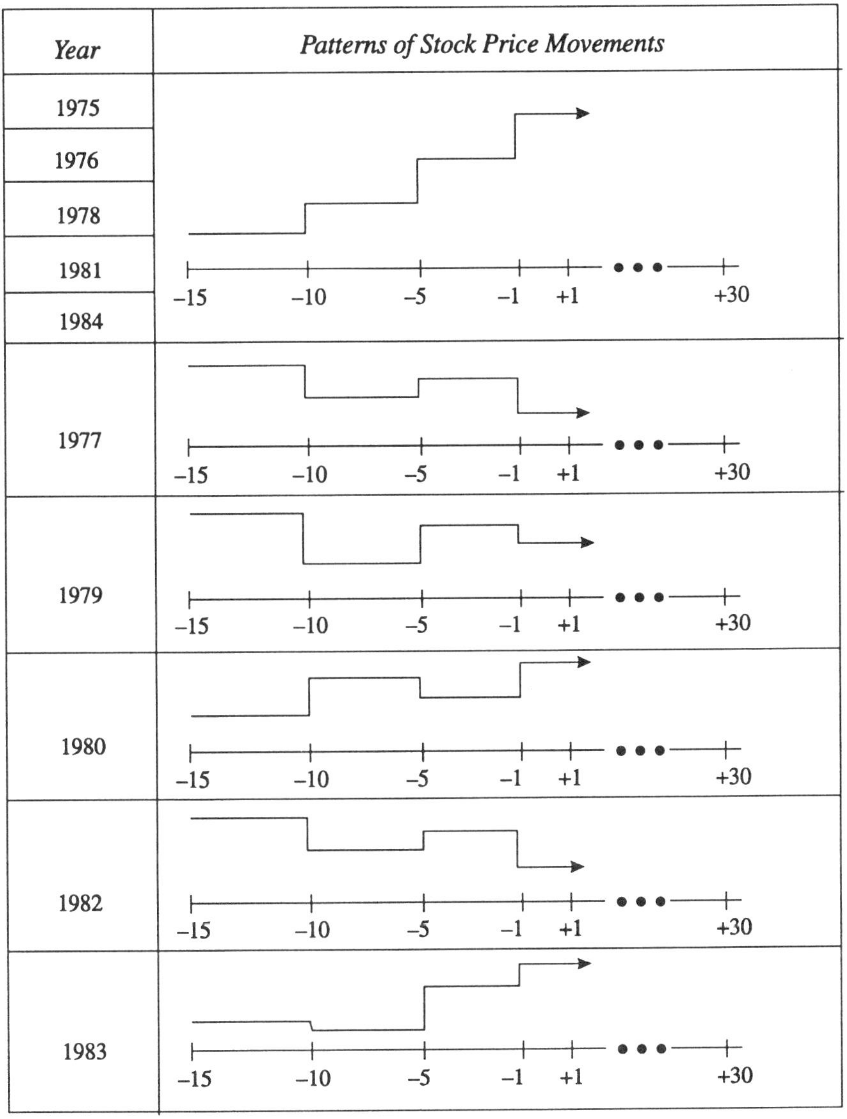

Figure 1. Patterns of Stock Price Movements in Sample Years

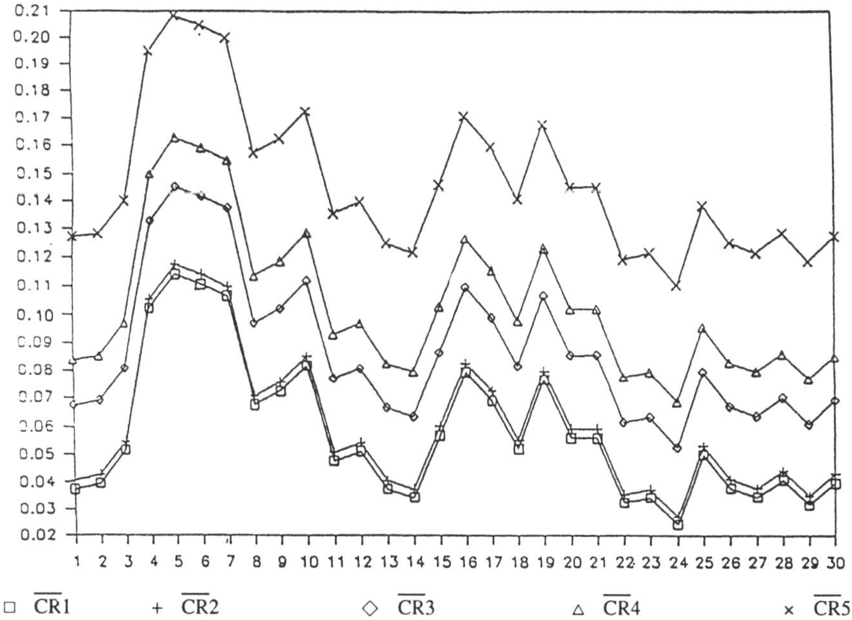

Figure 2. $\overline{CR}$'s for 1975

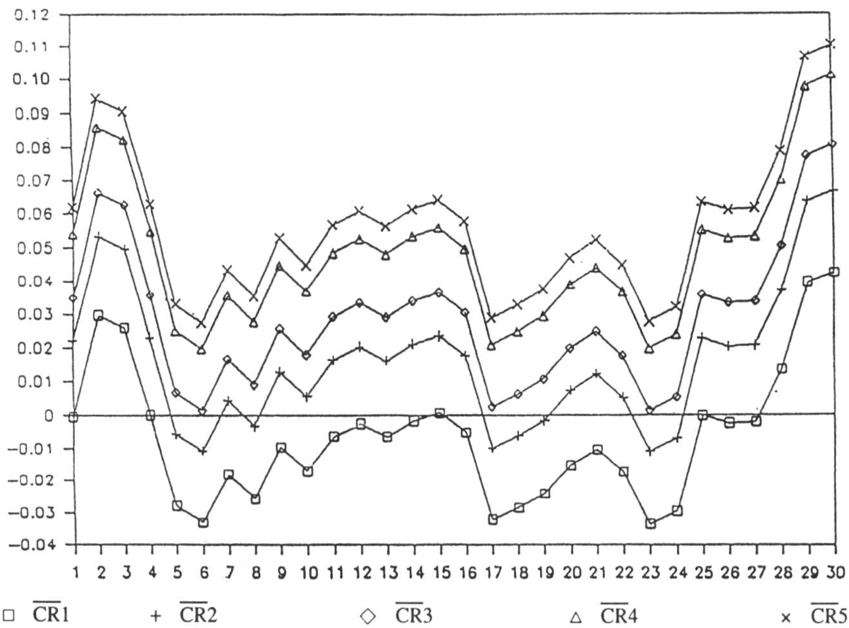

Figure 3. $\overline{CR}$'s for 1976

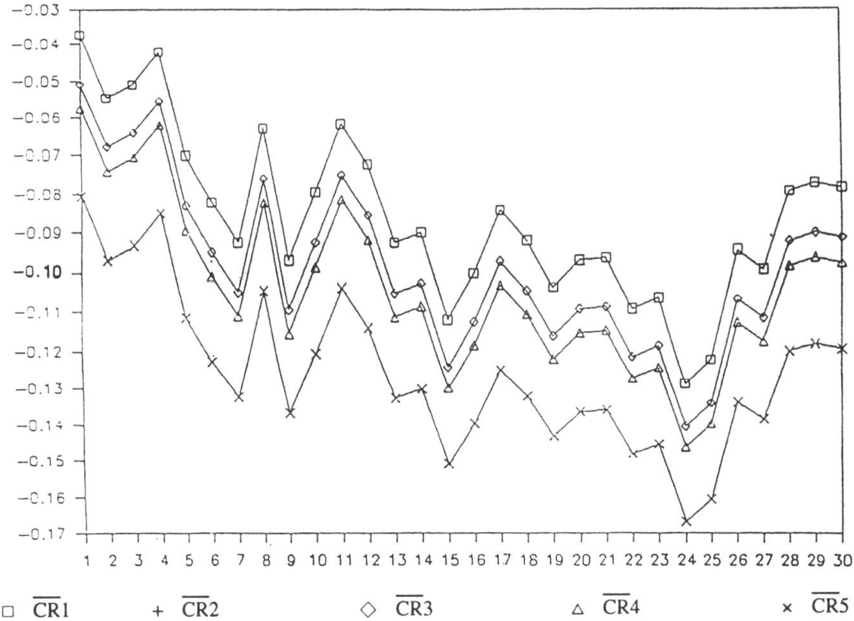

Figure 4. $\overline{CR}$'s for 1977

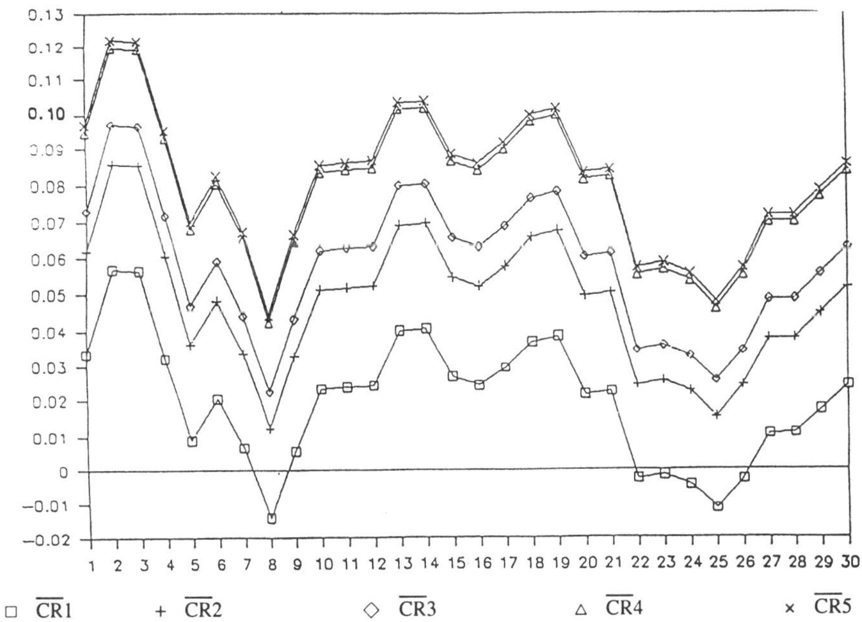

Figure 5. $\overline{CR}$'s for 1978

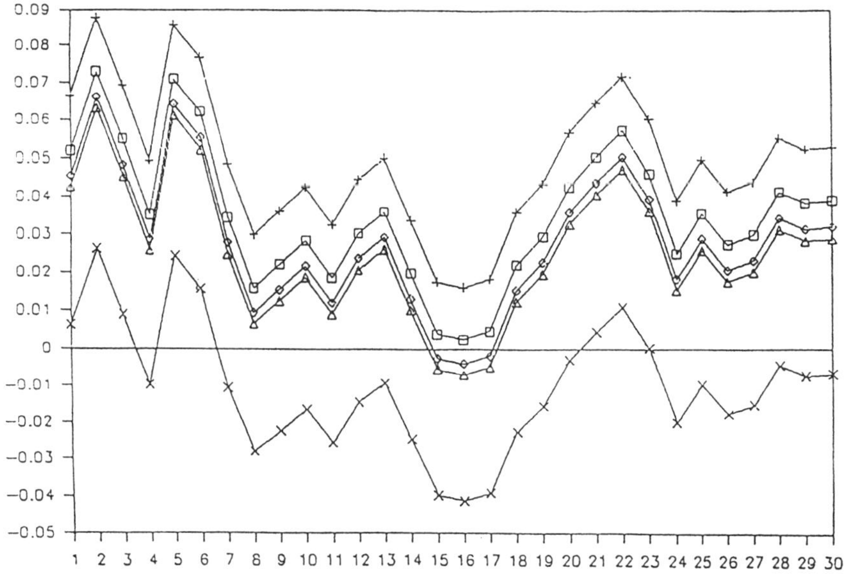

Figure 6. $\overline{CR}$'s for 1979

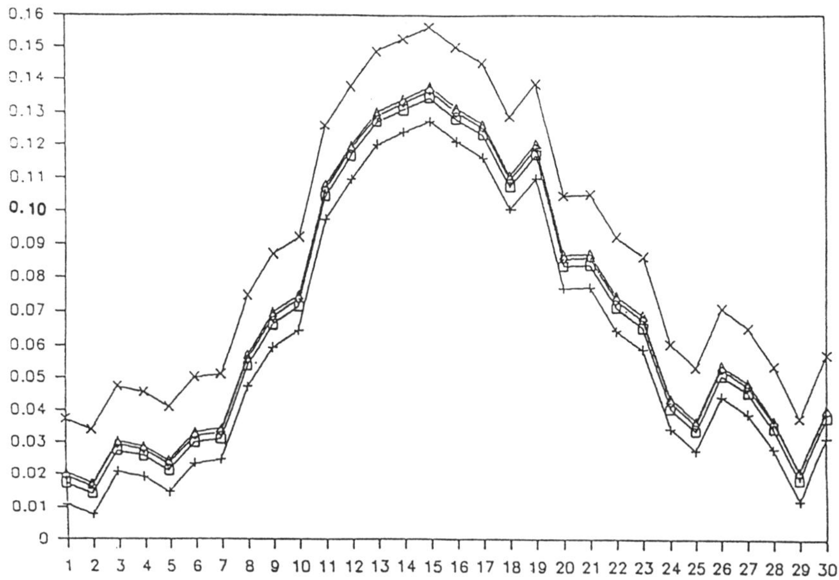

Figure 7. $\overline{CR}$'s for 1980

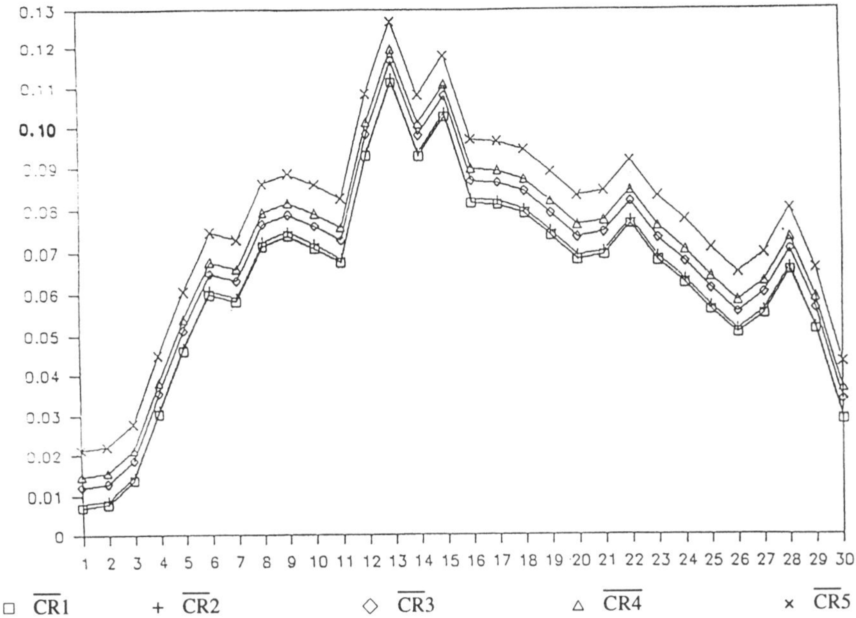

Figure 8. CR's for 1981

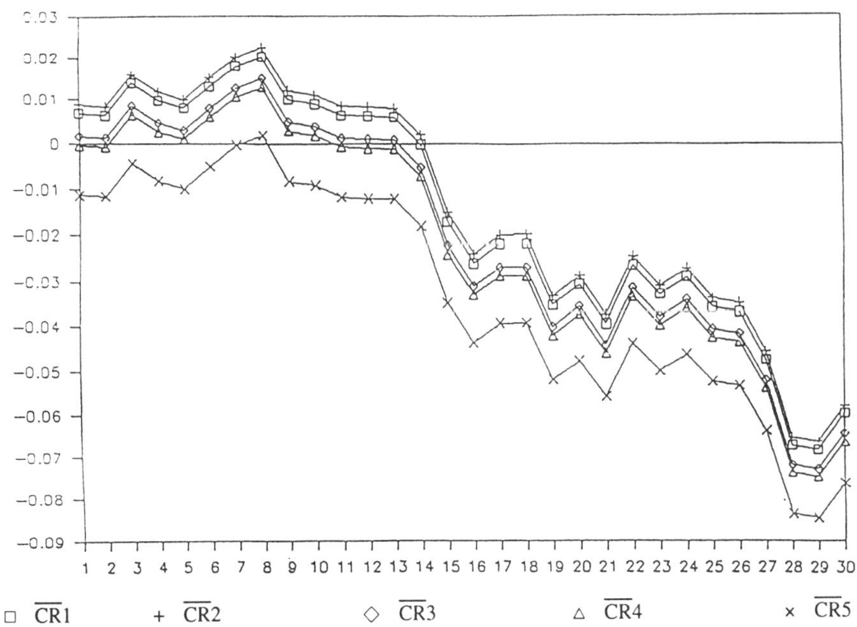

Figure 9. $\overline{CR}$'s for 1982

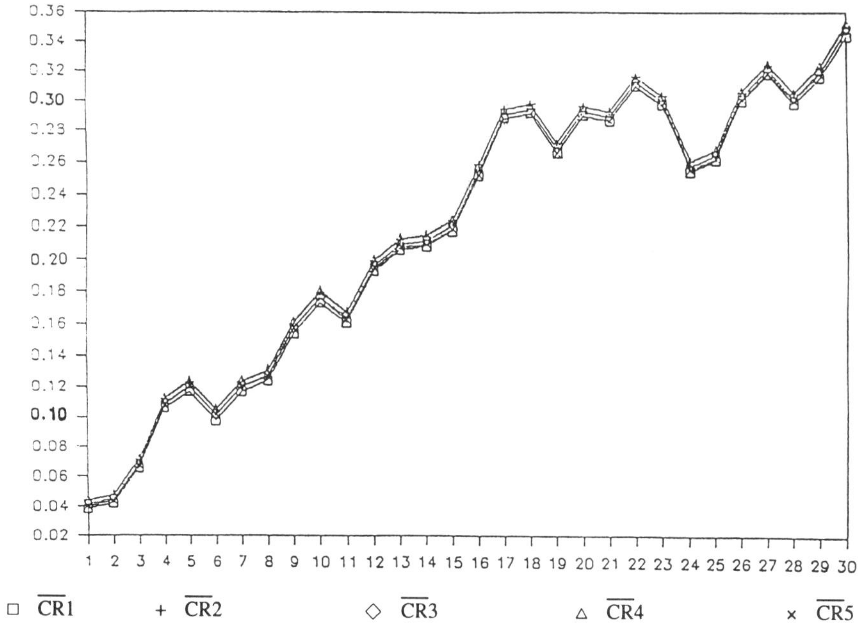

Figure 10. $\overline{CR}$'s for 1983

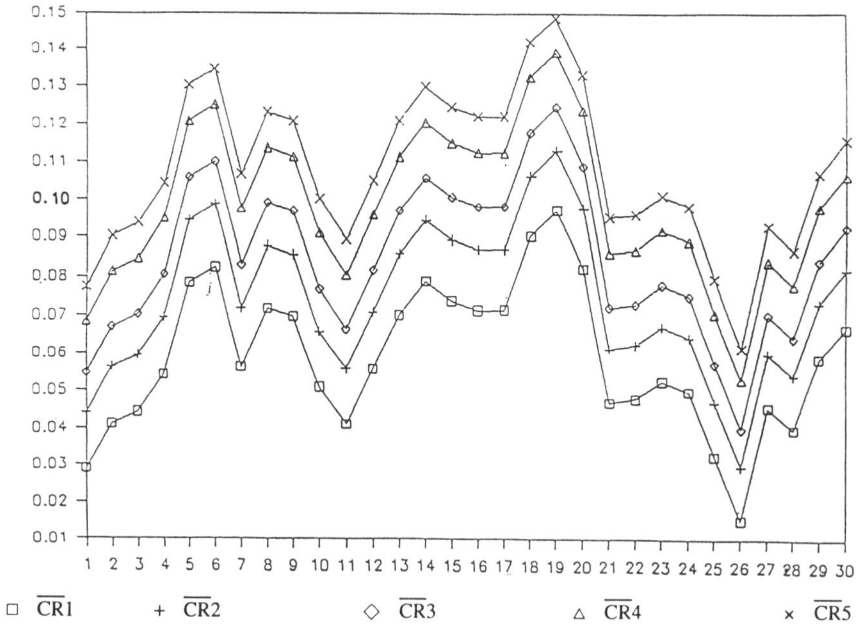

Figure 11. $\overline{CR}$'s for 1984

Table 12. $\overline{CR}4$'s for the Period 1975–1984

D	*1975*	*1976*	*1977*	*1978*	*1979*	*1980*	*1981*	*1982*	*1983*	*1984*
1	8.38	5.40	–5.75	9.46	4.24	2.05	1.47	–0.05	4.45	6.87
	(6.0*)	(6.3*)	(–7.5)	(7.6*)	(8.2*)	(3.4*)	(3.2*)	(–0.1)	(4.5*)	(10.6*)
2	8.53	8.61	–7.43	11.95	6.31	1.72	1.55	–0.08	4.81	8.14
	(5.2*)	(8.8*)	(–7.0)	(8.3*)	(11.4*)	(2.6*)	(3.5*)	(–0.1)	(5.0*)	(11.9*)
3	9.72	8.25	–7.06	11.91	4.53	3.05	2.13	0.66	7.17	8.47
	(5.6*)	(6.9*)	(–5.9)	(7.5*)	(9.0*)	(4.6*)	(4.4*)	(1.1)	(6.9*)	(11.5*)
4	14.99	5.50	–6.21	9.32	2.58	2.88	3.83	0.26	11.28	9.52
	(8.2*)	(5.1*)	(–5.9)	(6.6*)	(5.1*)	(4.8*)	(7.0*)	(0.4)	(10.0*)	(11.8*)
5	16.28	2.53	–8.93	6.79	6.12	2.42	5.40	0.10	12.46	12.07
	(8.8*)	(2.6*)	(–7.1)	(5.1*)	(10.8*)	(3.5*)	(10.3*)	(0.2)	(9.3*)	(12.6*)
6	15.93	1.99	–10.08	8.05	5.23	3.32	6.80	0.60	10.57	12.51
	(7.8*)	(2.1*)	(–6.9)	(5.1*)	(8.0*)	(4.2*)	(11.1*)	(0.8)	(7.6*)	(11.9*)
7	15.49	3.57	–11.08	6.53	2.49	3.44	6.63	1.08	12.48	9.77
	(7.6*)	(3.2*)	(–7.1)	(4.3*)	(4.0*)	(4.1*)	(10.1*)	(1.5)	(9.1*)	(10.3*)
8	11.40	2.79	–8.22	4.29	0.67	5.75	7.95	1.30	13.19	11.38
	(5.8*)	(2.6*)	(–5.9)	(3.0*)	(1.1)	(6.6*)	(11.1*)	(1.8)	(10.0*)	(12.9*)
9	11.89	4.49	–11.53	6.44	1.26	6.98	8.19	0.28	16.23	11.15
	(5.7*)	(3.7*)	(–7.6)	(3.9*)	(2.2)	(8.7*)	(11.2*)	(0.4)	(11.7*)	(13.3*)
10	12.89	3.71	–9.84	8.35	1.88	7.49	7.93	0.18	18.16	9.12
	(6.0*)	(3.0*)	(–7.5)	(4.7*)	(3.3*)	(8.2*)	(9.5*)	(0.3)	(12.7*)	(12.5*)
11	9.33	4.86	–8.13	8.43	0.93	10.82	7.60	–0.07	16.85	8.06
	(4.5*)	(3.5*)	(–7.2)	(4.6*)	(1.7)	(10.7*)	(8.9*)	(–0.1)	(11.8*)	(12.4*)
12	9.73	5.27	–9.18	8.48	2.08	11.99	10.13	–0.10	20.04	9.62
	(4.6*)	(3.7*)	(–7.8)	(4.4*)	(4.0*)	(11.1*)	(10.0*)	(–0.1)	(13.2*)	(13.1*)
13	8.28	4.83	–11.11	10.18	2.63	13.05	11.96	–0.11	21.36	11.16
	(3.9*)	(3.6*)	(–7.6)	(5.1*)	(5.1*)	(10.5*)	(9.9*)	(–0.1)	(13.3*)	(13.4*)
14	7.99	5.34	–10.84	10.23	1.03	13.44	10.12	–0.71	21.59	12.04
	(3.5*)	(4.0*)	(–7.4)	(4.9*)	(2.0)	(9.4*)	(8.9*)	(–0.9)	(12.3*)	(14.0*)
15	10.34	5.59	–12.98	8.68	–0.54	13.81	11.11	–2.40	22.51	11.50
	(4.8*)	(4.2*)	(–8.2)	(4.6*)	(–1.1)	(10.1*)	(9.7*)	(–2.9)	(11.9*)	(13.2*)
16	12.68	4.98	–11.82	8.43	–0.69	13.17	9.01	–3.27	25.86	11.26
	(6.1*)	(3.9*)	(–7.8)	(4.4*)	(–1.3)	(9.7*)	(8.5*)	(–4.0)	(12.5*)	(12.6*)
17	11.60	2.11	–10.30	9.02	–0.48	12.68	8.96	–2.85	29.47	11.27
	(5.8*)	(1.8)	(–7.3)	(4.3*)	(–0.9)	(9.9*)	(8.6*)	(–3.4)	(13.2*)	(12.1*)
18	9.83	2.51	–11.05	9.82	1.25	11.12	8.76	–2.85	29.83	13.25
	(5.0*)	(1.9)	(–7.9)	(4.7*)	(2.4*)	(8.6*)	(8.5*)	(–3.5)	(12.6*)	(13.0*)
19	12.38	2.97	–12.19	10.00	1.98	12.07	8.24	–4.16	27.23	13.92
	(6.3*)	(2.1*)	(–7.9)	(5.0*)	(3.7*)	(8.9*)	(7.6*)	(–5.2)	(12.9*)	(13.0*)
20	10.23	3.91	–11.51	8.17	3.29	8.73	7.67	–3.71	29.65	12.35
	(5.3*)	(2.7*)	(–7.5)	(4.4*)	(5.9*)	(7.0*)	(7.1*)	(–4.6)	(15.1*)	(11.3*)
21	10.24	4.43	–11.45	8.27	4.06	8.77	7.78	–4.55	29.33	8.64
	(5.5)	(2.8*)	(–7.4)	(4.3*)	(7.4*)	(6.8*)	(6.8*)	(–5.4)	(14.7*)	(8.5*)

Table 12. (*continued*)

D	*1975*	*1976*	*1977*	*1978*	*1979*	*1980*	*1981*	*1982*	*1983*	*1984*
22	7.77	3.70	−12.71	5.56	4.74	7.51	8.51	−3.30	31.70	8.71
	(4.3*)	(2.2*)	(−7.6)	(3.1*)	(8.4*)	(5.7*)	(7.1*)	(−3.9)	(15.5*)	(8.9*)
23	7.96	2.01	−12.43	5.69	3.63	6.94	7.64	−3.94	30.45	9.19
	(4.4*)	(1.1)	(−7.5)	(3.2*)	(6.5*)	(5.2*)	(6.2*)	(−4.7)	(14.6*)	(8.5*)
24	6.88	2.43	−14.62	5.38	1.54	4.41	7.08	−3.56	26.15	8.91
	(3.9*)	(1.3)	(−8.1)	(3.1*)	(0.7)	(3.2*)	(5.8*)	(−4.2)	(13.0*)	(8.3*)
25	9.59	5.54	−13.98	4.63	2.59	3.71	6.43	−4.21	26.84	7.09
	(5.2*)	(3.1*)	(−7.8)	(2.6*)	(4.6*)	(2.8*)	(5.4*)	(−4.7)	(13.9*)	(6.9*)
26	8.33	5.29	−11.27	5.54	1.78	5.44	5.86	−4.30	30.71	5.28
	(4.6*)	(2.9*)	(−6.7)	(2.9*)	(3.0*)	(3.9*)	(4.8*)	(−4.7)	(15.0*)	(5.1*)
27	7.98	5.34	−11.74	6.97	2.03	4.88	6.32	−5.37	32.54	8.40
	(4.4*)	(2.7*)	(−7.2)	(3.7*)	(3.2*)	(3.8*)	(5.4*)	(−5.9)	(15.1*)	(7.7*)
28	8.64	7.04	−9.82	6.97	3.14	3.74	7.36	−7.37	30.64	7.79
	(4.7*)	(3.4*)	(−6.7)	(4.0*)	(5.0*)	(3.2*)	(6.2*)	(−8.0)	(14.1*)	(6.8*)
29	7.70	9.79	−9.62	7.67	2.85	2.14	5.93	−7.47	32.42	9.79
	(4.2*)	(4.6*)	(−6.7)	(4.3*)	(4.4*)	(1.8)	(5.3*)	(−8.2)	(14.3*)	(8.1*)
30	8.53	10.13	−9.75	8.39	2.90	4.09	3.68	−6.64	35.23	10.64
	(4.6*)	(4.4*)	(−7.1)	(4.6*)	(4.2*)	(3.3*)	(3.5*)	(−7.6)	(14.9*)	(8.5*)

Notes: *z–statistic or t-statistic is significant at 1% level of significance. D represents the Dth transaction date after the reopening of the market. $\overline{CR_4}$ refers to arithmetic mean of cumulative returns calculated on the basis of the 4th base period. H_0: = $\overline{CR4}$ = 0; H_1: $\overline{CR4} > 0$. $z(\alpha = 0.01) = 2.237$. $t(\alpha = 0.01) = 2.479$. z- or t-statistics are in parentheses.

V. SOME FURTHER ANALYSIS

Before we jump to the conclusion that a trading rule superior to the buy-and-hold strategy exists, however, two complications need to be taken into account. First, whether the average returns generated by the trading rule we discovered in the previous section are indeed greater than buy-and-hold strategy returns remains to be examined. Otherwise, a proponent for an efficient capital market can legitimately argue that the returns observed are consistent with market efficiency because they merely reflect the "normal" returns of a buy-and-hold strategy. At this juncture, a proponent for an efficient capital market can also argue that a profit-making trading rule may exist for January. So, what we observed is nothing but a monthly effect.

Let us deal with the issue of the buy-and-hold strategy first. On the basis of a portfolio containing 33 stocks, Lee (1985) calculated the average rate of return arising from a buy-and-hold strategy as follows: {[(the selling price/the purchasing price) / 1.002] − 1} × 100%, where the product of 0.002 and the purchasing price represents the service surcharges. Over the period from 1977 to 1984, which, incidentally, corresponds closely to the period used in the present study, it is found that the annual rate of return amounts to 11.23%. When restated in monthly terms, the rate of return turns out to be 1.1%. Based on this result, it is safe to conclude that trading around the Chinese Lunar New Year can earn investors a return greater than what can be obtained through a buy-and-hold strategy.

As for the January effect, other than the possible explanation that the Chinese Lunar New Year per se has caused a noticeable upward movement in the stock prices, it can be argued that the phenomenon in question is caused by an abnormally higher stock price in the month of January or by the same token an abnormally lower stock price in December. We now explore these two possibilities. In the first place, the authors ran the regression of price index on a dummy variable representing lunar January and have found its coefficient negative and significant at the 0.01 level. Results of this kind indicate that lunar January returns on the average are not higher than those of other months. To examine returns in late December, we run another regression using again a dummy variable representing late December as the regressor. We have found that the coefficient of the December dummy this time is positive although not statistically significant. These results indicate that excess returns in lunar December on the average are greater than those of other months. These two sets of reinforcing regression results suggest that the excess returns we observed after the reopening of the market are caused by neither abnormally higher prices in lunar January nor abnormally lower prices in lunar December.

Those two further analyses strengthen our earlier position that the returns are attributable to the market suspension in the neighborhood of the Lunar Chinese New Year.

VI. CONCLUSION

In observing stock price movements in company with chosen nominal events, a researcher can interpret the selected nominal events as being only "seemingly nominal"; hence, they are able to exert real effects. Alternatively, the researcher can view the changes in stock prices associated with the selected nominal effect as a piece of evidence against market efficiency. To escape from this interpretational quagmire, we examined stock price movements around the Chinese Lunar New Year, a period in which both real and financial transactions came to a halt.

Using the longitudinal data from 1975 to 1984, we have found a profit-making rule. Moreover, the conclusion remains intact when the buy-and-hold return and monthly effect are taken into account. Findings of such kind cast doubt on the validity of the efficient market hypothesis.

ACKNOWLEDGMENTS

The authors are indebted to Lee K. Benham, Lawrence R. Klein, and numerous individuals for comments and/or encouragement. Stylistic advice generously provided by Dann Isbell is gratefully acknowledged.

NOTES

1. See Malkiel, 1981, p. 146.
2. In 1975 and 1978, the suspension lasted for seven days owing to the presence of Sunday during the interval under examination.
3. The average excess returns range from 1.1 to 16% for various years. In contrast, the transaction costs, composed of three elements, namely, broker's fee for buying, broker's fee for selling, and transaction surcharge, are 0.2, 0.2, and 0.3%, respectively.
4. As Copeland and Weston point out, "Because each security is compared with itself, there is no need to adjust for risk." See Copeland and Weston, 1983, p. 304.
5. For example, see Ball and Brown (1968), Carey (1977), Dann, Mayers, and Raab (1977), Fama et al. (1969), Hillmer and Yu (1979), and Joy, Litzenberger, and McEnally (1977).
6. A preliminary analysis made on historical price indices in Taiwan reveals that stock prices around the Chinese Lunar New Year moved upward in almost every year pending market suspension and continued to rise after the resumption of the transaction. The other two types are $b \le e \le 0$ and $0 < b \le e$.
7. Table 12 shows that *CR4*'s in all sample years with the exceptional years of 1977 and 1982 carry positive numerical values. For both years, 1977 and 1982, prior to the eve of the New Year, the stock price index nosedived on the fourteenth and the nineteenth days, respectively. It seems quite possible that the observed anomalous patterns of these two years are caused by trend factors.

REFERENCES

Ball, R. (1989). "What Do We Know About Stock Market Efficiency?" Keynote Speech at the Inaugural International Conference on Asian-Pacific Financial Markets, November, National University of Singapore.

Ball, R., and Brown, P. (1968). "An Empirical Evaluation of Accounting Income Numbers." *Journal of Accounting Research* (August) 159–178.

Basu S. (1983). "The Relationship between Earning Yield, Market Value and the Return for NYSE Stocks: Further Evidence." *Journal of Financial Economics* (March), 129–156.

Branch, B. (1977). "A Tax Loss Trading Rule." *Journal of Business* (April), 198–207.

Brown, S. J., and Warner, J. B. (1985). "Measuring Security Pricing Performance." *Journal of Financial Economics* 14, 3–31.

Carey, K. J. (1977). "Nonrandom Price Changes in Association with Trading in Large Blocks: Evidence of Market Efficiency in Behavior of Investor's Returns." *Journal of Business* 50, 407–444.

Clark T. A., and Weinstein, M. I. (1983). "The Behavior of the Common Stock of Bankrupt Firms." *Journal of Finance* 38 (May), 489–504.

Copeland, T. E., and Weston, J. F. (1983). *Financial Theory and Corporate Policy*. Reading, MA: Addison-Wesley.

Dann, L. Y., Mayers, D., and Raab, R. J., Jr. (1977). "Trading Rules, Large Blocks and the Speed of Price Adjustment." *Journal of Economics* 4 (March) 3–22.

Edes K. M. (1982). "Empirical Evidence on Dividends as a Signal of Firm Value." *Journal of Financial and Quantitative Analysis* 17 (November), 471–500.

Fama, E. F., and Blume, M. (1966). "Filter Rules and Stock Market Trading Profits." *Journal of Business* 39 (January) 226–241.

Fama E. F., Fisher, L., Jensen, M. C., and Roll, R. (1969). "The Adjustment of Stock Prices to New Information." *International Economic Review* (February), 1–21.

Haugen R., and Lakoniskok, J. (1988). *The Incredible January Effect: The Stock Market's Unsolved Mystery.* Chicago: Dow-Jones Irwin.

Hillmer S. C., and Yu, P. L. (1979). "The Market Speed of Adjustment to New Information." *Journal of Financial Economics* (December), 321–345.

Jaffe J., and Westerfield, R. (1985). "The Week-End Effect in Common Stock Returns: The International Evidence." *Journal of Finance* 40 (June), 433–454.

Joy, O. M., Litzenberger, R. N., and McEnally, R. W. (1977). "The Adjustment of Stock Prices to Announcement of Unanticipated Changes in Quarterly Earnings." *Journal of Accounting Research* 15, 207–255.

Kato, K., and Schallheim, J. S. (1985). "Seasonal and Size Anomalies in the Japanese Stock Market." *Journal of Financial and Quantitative Analysis*, 20, 243–260.

Lee, W. H. (1985). "Taiwanese Stock Market: An Empirical Analysis." Master's Thesis, June, National Taiwan University.

LeRoy S. F. (1984). "Efficiency and the Variability of Asset Prices." *American Economic Review* 74 (May), 183–187.

LeRoy, S. F. (1989). "Efficient Capital Markets and Martingales." *Journal of Economic Literature* (December), 1583–1621.

Malkiel B. G. (1981). *A Random Walk Down Wall Street.* New York: W. W. Norton.

Penman S. H. (1983). "The Predictive Content of Earnings Forecasts and Dividends." *Journal of Finance* 38, 1181–1199.

Reinganum M. R. (1981). "Misspecification of Capital Asset Pricing: Empirical Anomalies Based on Earnings Yields and Market Values." *Journal of Financial Economics* 8 (March), 13–32.

Shiller R. J. (1981a). "Do Stock Prices Move Too Much to Be Justified by Subsequent Changes in Dividends?" *American Economic Review* 71, 421–436.

Shiller R. J. (1981b). "The Use of Volatility Measures in Assessing Market Efficiency." *Journal of Finance* 36, 291–304.

Shiller R. J. (1986). "The Marsh–Merton Model of Manager's Smoothing of Dividends." *American Economic Review* 76, 499–503.

Stoll H. R., and Whaley, R. E. (1983). "Transaction Costs and the Small Firm Effect." *Journal of Financial Economics* 12 (June), 57–80.

Sweeney R. J. (1988). "Some New Filter Rule Tests: Methods and Results," *Journal of Financial and Quantitative Analysis* 23 (September), 285–300.

IMPACTS OF INVESTMENT HORIZON ON RELATIVE RISK AVERSION PARAMETER ESTIMATES:

THEORY AND EMPIRICAL RESULTS

Marvin J. Karson, David C. Cheng, and Cheng F. Lee

I. INTRODUCTION

Recently, Brown and Gibbons (1985) made a landmark contribution to the empirical study of utility-based asset pricing models, which had been neglected for a long time. They presented two estimators for the relative risk aversion in a particular equilibrium model for asset pricing, which is a special case of the general models in Hansen and Singleton (1982). The first estimator is a parametric one; namely, a maximum likelihood estimator based on the assumption of a lognormal distribution of the excessive returns. The second estimator is nonparametric, which is robust to departures from any particular distribution and is more consistent with the spirit underlying utility-based asset pricing models.

In our paper, we extended the Brown and Gibbons' work by introducing a minimum variance unbiased estimator (MVUE) in order for the parametric ap-

Advances in Quantitative Analysis of Finance and Accounting,
Volume 2, Part A, pages 67–92.

ISBN: 1-55938-564-2

proach to show its best when the distribution assumption is correct. Then we recognized the empirical studies by Blume (1970), Fama (1965), Lee (1967), and Lintner (1983), which showed that return distributions are closely related to investment horizon. For instance, Lintner (1983) provided extensive empirical evidence that returns on individual stocks and portfolios are lognormally distributed as the differencing intervals are lengthened more than six months. This implies that the parametric approach may be more appropriate for a longer investment horizon. We experimented with twelve investment horizons, from one month to one year, in comparing the parametric and nonparametric estimators of the utility-based asset pricing model using data from 1926 to 1983. We found that the relative performance of these two approaches varies over investment horizons.

The properties of Brown and Gibbons' (1985) RRA estimators are analyzed in Section II. Our new estimator, MVUE, is developed in Section III and is shown to be superior to Brown and Gibbons' maximum likelihood estimator in the parametric case. Section IV presents empirical results in terms of different investment horizons. Section V summarizes the results of this paper.

II. PROPERTIES OF BROWN AND GIBBONS' ESTIMATORS

Brown and Gibbons (1985) relied on the well-known Euler condition for the dynamic consumption-portfolio problem faced by a representative individual under uncertainty:

$$E[(X_t - 1)X_t^{-B}] = 0, \tag{1}$$

where $X_t = (1 + R_{mt})/(1 + R_{ft})$, a discrete time "excess return"—the return in the market portfolio over the risk-free rate—and B the relative risk aversion. They used both parametric and nonparametric estimation methods to estimate the relative risk aversion (RRA) parameter, B. In this section we will investigate the properties of Brown and Gibbons' estimators.

A. The Parametric Estimator of RRA

On the assumption of a lognormal distribution of the excess returns [i.e., $\ln X_t \sim N(\mu, \sigma^2)$], Brown and Gibbons suggested an adjusted maximum likelihood (ML) estimator for RRA. As derived by Rubinstein (1976), the RRA parameter can be written as

$$B = \frac{\mu}{\sigma^2} + \frac{1}{2}. \tag{2}$$

The ML estimator is

$$\hat{b} = \frac{\overline{\ln X}}{S^2} + \frac{1}{2}, \tag{3}$$

where $\overline{\ln X} = \sum_{t=1}^{T} \ln X_t/T$, $S^2 = \sum_{t=1}^{T} (\ln X_t - \overline{\ln X})^2/(T-1)$.

Note that the ML estimator of B is $[\overline{\ln X}/\frac{(T-1)S^2}{T}] + \frac{1}{2}$. We will refer to $\hat{b}$ as the ML estimator.

While the ML estimator has nice asymptotic properties, it is biased for finite samples. This has important implications when the investment horizon becomes large, as we will show in Section IV. The finite sample bias of the ML estimator can be shown to be

$$\frac{2B-1}{T-3}. \tag{4}$$

Proof:

$$E(\hat{b}) = E(\frac{\overline{\ln X}}{S^2} + \frac{1}{2}) = E(\overline{\ln X})E(\frac{1}{S^2}) + \frac{1}{2}, \text{ since } \overline{\ln X} \text{ and } S^2$$

are statistically independent. Therefore,

$$E(\hat{b}) = \mu\frac{(T-1)}{(T-3)}\frac{1}{\sigma^2} + \frac{1}{2},$$

and after some algebra,

$$E(b) = \frac{(T-1)B-1}{(T-3)}. \tag{5}$$

Therefore, $E(\hat{b}) - B = \frac{(T-1)B-1-(T-3)B}{T-3} = \frac{2B-1}{T-3}$ Q.E.D.

We can also derive the finite sample variance of the ML estimator as follows:

$$\text{var}(\hat{b}) = \frac{(T-1)^2}{(T-3)(T-5)\sigma^4}(\frac{\sigma^2}{T} + \frac{2\mu^2}{(T-3)}). \tag{6}$$

Proof:

$$\text{var}(\hat{b}) = \text{var}\,(\frac{\overline{\ln X}}{S^2} + \frac{1}{2})$$

$$= \text{var}\,(\frac{\overline{\ln X}}{S^2}) = E(\frac{\overline{\ln X}}{S^2})^2 - (E\frac{\overline{\ln X}}{S^2})^2$$

$$= E(\frac{\overline{\ln X}}{S^2})^2 - (\frac{T-1}{T-3})^2 \frac{\mu^2}{\sigma^4},$$

$$\text{and } E(\frac{\overline{\ln X}}{S^2})^2 = E(\overline{\ln X})^2\, E(\frac{1}{S^4}), \text{ by independence,}$$

$$\text{and } E(\overline{\ln X})^2 = \frac{\sigma^2}{T} + \mu^2; \text{ and } E(\frac{1}{S^4}) = \frac{(T-1)^2}{(T-3)(T-5)}\frac{1}{\sigma^4},$$

$$\text{therefore } \operatorname{var}(\hat{b}) = (\frac{\sigma^2}{T} + \mu^2)\,\frac{(T-1)^2}{(T-3)(T-5)\sigma^4} - \frac{(T-1)^2}{(T-3)^2}\frac{\mu^2}{\sigma^4}$$

$$= \frac{(T-1)^2}{(T-3)(T-5)\sigma^4}(\frac{\sigma^2}{T} + \mu^2 - \frac{T-5}{T-3}\mu^2)$$

$$= \frac{(T-1)^2}{(T-3)(T-5)\sigma^4}\left(\frac{\sigma^2}{T} + \frac{2\mu^2}{T-3}\right) \quad \text{Q.E.D.}$$

From Eq. (6), we note that the sample size T should be greater than five for var $(\hat{b})$ to exist, and that as the sample size increases to infinity, var$(\hat{b})$ approaches 0, which together with Eq. (5), implies that $\hat{b}$ is a consistent estimator of B.

Besides,

$$\operatorname{var}(\sqrt{T}\,\hat{b}) = T\operatorname{var}(\hat{b}) = \frac{(T-1)^2}{(T-3)(T-5)\sigma^4}(\sigma^2 + 2\,\mu^2\frac{T}{T-3}),$$

and as T increase to infinity,

$$\operatorname{var}(\sqrt{T}\,\hat{b}) = \frac{\sigma^2 + 2\,\mu^2}{\sigma^4}, \tag{7}$$

which is the variance of the asymptotic distribution of $\hat{b}$ as pointed out by Brown and Gibbons.

B. The Nonparametric Estimator of RRA

Brown and Gibbons' second estimator is nonparametric, which is robust to departures from any particular distribution. They used a simple gradient search algorithm to find the estimator b such that

$$f(b) = \frac{1}{T}\sum_t (X_t - 1)X_t^{-b} = 0, \text{ where } b\,\varepsilon(0, +\infty). \tag{8}$$

This nonparametric estimator is also called the method of moments (MM) estimator. While the MM estimator requires no distributional assumptions, it is also impossible to determine analytically any of its properties. It is surely biased for B and its variance cannot be explicitly determined. Brown and Gibbons derived the variance of the asymptotic distribution of b, in terms of expected values, as

$$\text{var}\,(\sqrt{T}\,b) = \frac{E\{[(x_t - 1)x_t^{-B}]^2\}}{[E\{(x_t - 1)x_t^{-B}\ln x_t\}]^2}, \tag{9}$$

which is correct only asymptotically. Its derivation is based on a first-order Taylor series approximation (see Appendix).

III. THE MINIMUM VARIANCE UNBIASED ESTIMATOR

When the excess return on the market portfolio has a lognormal distribution, a better, in the mean square error sense, method of estimation for the relative risk aversion parameter is minimum variance unbiased estimation (MVUE) rather than the maximum likelihood estimation as proposed by Brown and Gibbons (1985). The minimum variance unbiased estimator (MVUE) for B is

$$\hat{B} = \frac{(T-3)\left(\dfrac{\overline{\ln X}}{S^2} + \dfrac{1}{2}\right) + 1}{(T-1)} = \left(\frac{T-3}{T-1}\right)\frac{\overline{\ln X}}{S^2} + \frac{1}{2} \tag{10}$$

with

$$\text{var}\,(\hat{B}) = \frac{(T-3)}{(T-5)\sigma^4}\left(\frac{\sigma^2}{T} + \frac{2\mu^2}{T-3}\right). \tag{11}$$

Proof:

Since $\overline{\ln X}$ and S^2 are complete, sufficient statistics for μ and σ^2, an unbiased estimator of B that is a function of $\overline{\ln X}$ and S^2 is MVUE.

Since $\hat{b} = \dfrac{\overline{\ln X}}{S^2} + \dfrac{1}{2}$ is a function of $\overline{\ln X}$ and S^2, and since

$E(\hat{b}) = \dfrac{(T-1)B - 1}{T-3}$, $\hat{B} = \dfrac{(T-3)\hat{b} + 1}{T-1} = \left(\dfrac{T-3}{T-1}\right)\left(\dfrac{\overline{\ln X}}{S^2}\right) + \dfrac{1}{2}$ is MVUE and

$$\text{(i)}\quad E(\hat{B}) = \frac{(T-3)E(\hat{b}) + 1}{T-1} = B$$

$$\text{(ii)}\quad \text{var}\,(\hat{B}) = \left(\frac{T-3}{T-1}\right)^2 \text{var}(\hat{b})$$

$$= \frac{(T-3)^2}{(T-1)^2} \frac{(T-1)^2}{(T-3)(T-5)\sigma^4} \left(\frac{\sigma^2}{T} + \frac{2\mu^2}{(T-3)}\right)$$

$$= \frac{(T-3)}{(T-5)\sigma^4} \left(\frac{\sigma^2}{T} + \frac{2\mu^2}{(T-3)}\right).$$

The exact finite sampling distribution of $\hat{B}$ is very complicated and will be derived in another paper. It should be noted that

$$\text{var}(\hat{B}) < \text{var}(\hat{b}), \text{ and bias } (\hat{B}) = 0.$$

Therefore if X_t is distributed lognormally, on the criteria of bias, variance, and mean-squared error (MSE), $\hat{b}$ would never be used to estimate B. And any other estimator should be compared to $\hat{B}$, not $\hat{b}$. We can analytically declare $\hat{b}$ inadmissible. And it is only "at $T = \infty$" that $\hat{b}$ and $\hat{B}$ are equivalent estimators.

IV. INVESTMENT HORIZON AND RRA ESTIMATORS: SOME EMPIRICAL RESULTS

Levy (1972) and Levhari and Levy (1977) have shown that both Sharpe and Trynor measure estimators are not independent of the investment horizon. The Sharpe measure estimator, in our notation, is nothing but $\overline{\ln X}/S$, which is a function of either the ML estimator in Eq. (3) or the MVUE in Eq. (10). Therefore, it is interesting to investigate whether $\hat{b}$ and $\hat{B}$ are independent of the investment horizon.

For empirical studies, both value-weighted and equal-weighted indexes of the New York Stock Exchange for the period from 1925 to 1983 are collected from the Center for Research in Security Prices at the University of Chicago and used as proxies for the rates of return on the market portfolio. The risk-free rate proxies from 1926 to 1952 are the monthly returns on U.S. Treasury bills in Ibbotson and Sinquefield (1979). For the period from 1953 to 1983, risk-free rates are approximated by the yields on 30-day bills from the Center for Research in Security Prices (CRSP) Government Bond File. Although our whole sample is a little longer than that of Brown and Gibbons (1985), the subperiods chosen are almost exactly like theirs for better comparison. We have experimented with twelve investment horizons, from one month to one year, in comparing the ML and the MVUE estimator of the utility-based asset pricing model using data from 1926–1983. The criterion of the estimated MSE is used to compare the ML estimator and the MVUE estimator over different finite time horizons.

The results of the experiments can be summarized as follows. Table 1 presents the definitions of twelve holding periods and seven time periods. In Tables 2–8 the MVUE and ML estimates of the relative risk aversion parameters as well as their

Table 1. Various Holding Periods and Time Periods[a]

Holding Period	*58 Years 1/1926–12/1983*	*27 Years 1/1926–12/1952*	*31 Years 1/1953–12/1983*
1M	$T = 696$	$T = 324$	$T = 372$ (From 325 to 696)
2M	$T = 348$	$T = 162$	$T = 186$ (From 163 to 348)
3M	$T = 232$	$T = 108$	$T = 124$ (From 109 to 232)
4M	$T = 174$	$T = 81$	$T = 93$ (From 82 to 174)
5M	$T = 139$	$T = 64$	$T = 75$ (From 65 to 139)
6M	$T = 116$	$T = 54$	$T = 62$ (From 55 to 116)
7M	$T = 99$	$T = 46$	$T = 53$ (From 47 to 99)
8M	$T = 87$	$T = 40$	$T = 47$ (From 41 to 87)
9M	$T = 77$	$T = 36$	$T = 41$ (From 37 to 77)
10M	$T = 69$	$T = 32$	$T = 37$ (From 33 to 69)
11M	$T = 63$	$T = 29$	$T = 34$ (From 30 to 63)
12M	$T = 58$	$T = 27$	$T = 31$ (From 28 to 58)

Holding Period	13½ *Years 1/1926–6/1939*	13½ *Years 7/1939–12/1952*
1M	$T = 162$	$T = 162$ (From 163 to 324)
2M	$T = 81$	$T = 81$ (From 82 to 162)
3M	$T = 54$	$T = 54$ (From 55 to 108)
4M	$T = 40$	$T = 41$ (From 41 to 81)
5M	$T = 32$	$T = 32$ (From 33 to 64)
6M	$T = 27$	$T = 27$ (From 28 to 54)
7M	$T = 23$	$T = 23$ (From 24 to 46)
8M	$T = 20$	$T = 20$ (From 21 to 40)
9M	$T = 18$	$T = 18$ (From 19 to 36)
10M	$T = 16$	$T = 16$ (From 17 to 32)
11M	$T = 14$	$T = 15$ (From 15 to 29)
12M	$T = 13$	$T = 14$ (From 14 to 27)

Holding Period	15½ *Years 1/1953–6/1968*	15½ *Years 7/1968–12/1983*
1M	$T = 186$ (From 325 to 510)	$T = 186$ (From 511 to 696)
2M	$T = 93$ (From 163 to 255)	$T = 93$ (From 256 to 348)
3M	$T = 62$ (From 109 to 170)	$T = 62$ (From 171 to 232)
4M	$T = 46$ (From 82 to 127)	$T = 47$ (From 128 to 174)
5M	$T = 37$ (From 65 to 101)	$T = 38$ (From 102 to 139)
6M	$T = 31$ (From 55 to 85)	$T = 31$ (From 86 to 116)
7M	$T = 26$ (From 47 to 72)	$T = 27$ (From 73 to 99)
8M	$T = 23$ (From 41 to 63)	$T = 24$ (From 64 to 87)
9M	$T = 20$ (From 37 to 56)	$T = 21$ From 57 to 77)
10M	$T = 18$ (From 33 to 50)	$T = 19$ (From 51 to 69)
11M	$T = 17$ (From 30 to 46)	$T = 17$ (From 47 to 63)
12M	$T = 15$ (From 28 to 42)	$T = 16$ (From 43 to 58)

Note: [a]Because of varying lengths of the holding periods, the number of observations (i.e., T) of a time period might not cover the time span exactly. Care has been taken to maintain the continuity of the data series.

Table 2. Value Weighted: 58 Years (1/1926–12/1983)

Holding Period	*T*	$\overline{\ln X}$	S^2	$\hat{b}$	*var* ($\hat{b}$)	$\hat{B}$	*var*($\hat{B}$)*	*MSE*($\hat{b}$)†	$\frac{var(\hat{B})}{MSE(\hat{b})}$
1M	696	0.004727	0.003273	1.9444	0.4489	1.9402	0.4463	0.4489	99.4
2M	348	0.009430	0.007267	1.7976	0.4123	1.7901	0.4075	0.4123	98.8
3M	232	0.014140	0.013040	1.5845	0.3498	1.5751	0.3437	0.3499	98.2
4M	174	0.018860	0.013590	1.8876	0.4612	1.8715	0.4506	0.4615	97.6
5M	139	0.023710	0.016380	1.9470	0.4911	1.9261	0.4769	0.4915	97.0
6M	116	0.028290	0.025540	1.6074	0.3787	1.5881	0.3656	0.3791	96.4
7M	99	0.033360	0.034270	1.4735	0.3347	1.4536	0.3212	0.3351	95.9
8M	87	0.037720	0.025540	1.9767	0.5389	1.9423	0.5142	0.5402	95.2
9M	77	0.042890	0.035910	1.6945	0.4339	1.6631	0.4130	0.4349	95.0
10M	69	0.048190	0.029110	2.1557	0.6360	2.1070	0.5992	0.6385	93.8
11M	63	0.052420	0.060270	1.3698	0.3187	1.3417	0.2985	0.3196	93.4
12M	58	0.056580	0.045040	1.7563	0.4907	1.7122	0.4568	0.4927	92.7

Notes: *MSE($\hat{B}$) = var($\hat{B}$).

†$MSE(\hat{b}) = \left(\frac{2\hat{b}-1}{t-3}\right)^2 + \text{var}(\hat{b})$.

Table 3. Value Weighted: 27 Years (1/1926–12/1952)

Holding Period	*T*	$\overline{\ln X}$	S^2	$\hat{b}$	*var* ($\hat{b}$)	$\hat{B}$	*var*($\hat{B}$)*	*MSE*($\hat{b}$)†	$\frac{var(\hat{B})}{MSE(\hat{b})}$
1M	324 (1 to 324)	0.005342	0.005129	1.5416	0.6200	1.5351	0.6123	0.6200	98.8
2M	162 (1 to 162)	0.001063	0.01158	1.4181	0.5646	1.4067	0.5507	0.5647	97.5
3M	108 (1 to 108)	0.01595	0.02054	1.2763	0.4894	1.2618	0.4712	0.4896	96.2
4M	81 (1 to 81)	0.02126	0.02131	1.4975	0.6529	1.4726	0.6207	0.6535	95.0
5M	64 (1 to 64)	0.02601	0.02432	1.5694	0.7499	1.5355	0.7031	0.7511	93.6
6M	54 (1 to 54)	0.03189	0.03760	1.3481	0.5853	1.3161	0.5419	0.5864	92.4
7M	46 (1 to 46)	0.03559	0.05589	1.1368	0.4685	1.1085	0.4277	0.4693	91.1
8M	40 (1 to 40)	0.04161	0.03524	1.6809	0.9218	1.6203	0.8297	0.9259	89.6
9M	36 (1 to 36)	0.04784	0.05032	1.4501	0.7265	1.3962	0.6459	0.7298	88.5
10M	32 (1 to 32)	0.05201	0.04356	1.6942	1.0013	1.6172	0.8763	1.0081	86.9
11M	29 (1 to 29)	0.0577	0.1089	1.0296	0.4248	0.9917	0.3663	0.4265	85.9
12M	27 (1 to 27)	0.06378	0.0625	1.5205	0.8698	1.4420	0.7411	0.8770	84.5

Notes: See Table 2.

Table 4. Value Weighted: 31 Years (1/1953–12/1983)

Holding Period	T	$\overline{\ln X}$	S^2	$\hat{b}$	$var(\hat{b})$	$\hat{B}$	$var(\hat{B})$*	$MSE(\hat{b})^{\dagger}$	$\frac{var(\hat{B})}{MSE(\hat{b})}$
1M	372 (325 to 696)	0.003177	0.001665	3.0173	1.6756	3.0037	1.6576	1.6758	98.9
2M	186 (163 to 348)	0.008384	0.003552	2.8602	1.6268	2.8346	1.5918	1.6274	97.8
3M	124 (109 to 232)	0.01258	0.006622	2.3992	1.3423	2.3683	1.2990	1.3433	97.7
4M	93 (82 to 174)	0.01677	0.007015	2.8904	1.7739	2.8384	1.6976	1.7767	95.5
5M	75 (65 to 139)	0.02175	0.009841	2.7097	1.6195	2.6500	1.5331	1.6232	94.4
6M	62 (55 to 116)	0.02515	0.01547	2.1262	1.2530	2.0729	1.1722	1.2561	93.3
7M	53 (47 to 99)	0.03143	0.01622	2.4381	1.4801	2.3636	1.3685	1.4861	92.1
8M	47 (41 to 87)	0.03441	0.01786	2.4270	1.5577	2.3432	1.4252	1.5654	91.0
9M	41 (37 to 77)	0.03855	0.02415	2.0963	1.3380	2.0165	1.2076	1.3451	89.8
10M	37 (33 to 69)	0.04489	0.01745	3.0725	2.3088	2.9296	2.0594	2.3317	88.3
11M	34 (30 to 63)	0.04794	0.02077	2.8079	2.1315	2.6681	1.8810	2.1537	87.3
12M	31 (28 to 58)	0.05030	0.03131	2.1064	1.5014	1.9993	1.3079	1.5145	86.4

Notes: See Table 2.

Table 5. Value Weighted: 13½ Years (1/1926–6/1939)

Holding Period	T	$\overline{\ln X}$	S^2	$\hat{b}$	$var(\hat{b})$	$\hat{B}$	$var(\hat{B})$*	$MSE(\hat{b})^{\dagger}$	$\frac{var(\hat{B})}{MSE(\hat{b})}$
1M	162 (1 to 162)	0.001013	0.008260	0.6227	0.7762	0.6211	0.7570	0.7762	97.5
2M	81 (1 to 81)	0.001935	0.01949	0.5993	0.6840	0.5968	0.6503	0.6841	95.1
3M	54 (1 to 54)	0.002903	0.03563	0.5815	0.5846	0.5784	0.5413	0.5846	92.6
4M	40 (1 to 40)	0.003626	0.03617	0.6002	0.8124	0.5951	0.7312	0.8125	90.0
5M	32 (1 to 32)	0.004532	0.03587	0.6263	1.0705	0.6182	0.9369	1.0706	87.5
6M	27 (1 to 27)	0.005805	0.06237	0.5931	0.7613	0.5859	0.6486	0.7613	85.2
7M	23 (1 to 23)	0.009194	0.09307	0.5988	0.6294	0.5898	0.5201	0.6295	82.6
8M	20 (1 to 20)	0.007252	0.05528	0.6312	1.2834	0.6174	1.0274	1.2837	80.0
9M	18 (1 to 18)	0.008708	0.08073	0.6079	1.0222	0.5952	0.7958	1.0224	77.8
10M	16 (1 to 16)	0.009065	0.06352	0.6427	1.5530	0.6237	1.1665	1.5535	75.1
11M	14 (1 to 14)	0.02020	0.20211	0.5999	0.6064	0.5846	0.4342	0.6067	71.6
12M	13 (1 to 13)	0.02323	0.1124	0.7065	1.2467	0.6721	0.8658	1.2484	69.4

Notes: See Table 2.

Table 6. Value Weighted: 13½ Years (7/1939–12/1952)

Holding Period	T	$\overline{\ln X}$	S^2	$\hat{b}$	$var(\hat{b})$	$\hat{B}$	$var(\hat{B})$*	$MSE(\hat{b})^{\dagger}$	$\frac{var(\hat{B})}{MSE(\hat{b})}$
1M	162 (163 to 324)	0.002451	0.001992	5.3550	3.5254	5.2947	3.4384	3.5292	97.4
2M	81 (82 to 162)	0.01933	0.003656	5.7863	4.4195	5.6542	4.2012	4.4378	94.7
3M	54 (55 to 108)	0.02899	0.005495	5.7755	5.0149	5.5765	4.6436	5.0578	91.8
4M	41 (41 to 81)	0.03847	0.006748	6.2007	6.2282	5.9157	5.6209	6.3182	88.9
5M	32 (33 to 64)	0.04748	0.01260	4.2691	4.2471	4.0260	3.7168	4.3147	86.1
6M	27 (28 to 54)	0.05798	0.01287	5.0035	5.8472	4.6571	4.9822	5.9880	83.2
7M	23 (24 to 46)	0.06198	0.01978	3.6330	4.2745	3.3481	3.5326	4.3726	80.8
8M	20 (21 to 40)	0.07597	0.01457	5.7151	9.3888	5.1661	7.5162	9.7652	76.9
9M	18 (19 to 36)	0.08697	0.01964	4.9282	8.0672	4.4072	6.2807	8.4158	74.6
10M	16 (17 to 32)	0.09496	0.02256	4.7102	8.6506	4.1488	6.4976	9.0702	71.6
11M	15 (15 to 29)	0.09267	0.02747	3.8733	7.0614	3.3914	5.1880	7.3775	70.3
12M	14 (14 to 27)	0.1014	0.01803	6.1251	16.5823	5.2597	11.8725	17.6283	67.3

Notes: Table 2.

Table 7. Value Weighted: $15\frac{1}{2}$ Years (1/1953–1966/1968)

Holding Period	T	$\overline{\ln X}$	S^2	$\hat{b}$	$var(\hat{b})$	$\hat{B}$	$var(\hat{B})$ *	$MSE(\hat{b})^{\dagger}$	$\frac{var(\hat{B})}{MSE(\hat{b})}$
1M	186 (325 to 510)	0.008003	0.001151	7.4533	5.3728	7.3781	5.2573	5.3786	97.7
2M	93 (163 to 255)	0.01601	0.002756	6.3065	4.9697	6.1803	4.7559	4.9863	95.4
3M	62 (109 to 170)	0.02401	0.004644	5.6693	4.8448	5.4998	4.5323	4.8755	93.0
4M	46 (82 to 127)	0.03179	0.005470	6.3112	6.3688	6.0530	5.8152	6.4418	90.3
5M	37 (65 to 101)	0.03975	0.005735	7.4315	8.9798	7.0464	8.0097	9.1460	87.6
6M	31 (55 to 85)	0.04802	0.01107	4.8378	5.2644	4.5486	4.5859	5.3604	85.5
7M	26 (47 to 72)	0.05931	0.01167	5.5838	7.1738	5.1771	6.0719	7.3693	82.4
8M	23 (41 to 63)	0.06585	0.01515	4.8464	6.3977	4.4512	5.2874	6.5866	80.3
9M	20 (37 to 56)	0.07285	0.01762	4.6337	6.8624	4.1985	5.4938	7.0989	77.4
10M	18 (33 to 50)	0.08254	0.01555	5.8071	10.8595	5.1827	8.4546	11.3602	74.4
11M	17 (30 to 46)	0.08394	0.01887	4.9489	9.0597	4.3928	6.9363	9.4636	73.3
12M	15 (28 to 42)	0.09713	0.02788	3.9840	7.2100	3.4863	5.2972	7.5472	70.2

Notes: See Table 2.

Table 8. Value Weighted: 15½ Years (7/1968–12/1983)

Holding Period	T	$\overline{\ln X}$	S^2	$\hat{b}$	$var(\hat{b})$	$\hat{B}$	$var(\hat{B})$*	$MSE(\hat{b})^{\dagger}$	$\frac{var(\hat{B})}{MSE(\hat{b})}$
1M	186 (511 to 696)	0.000381	0.002159	0.6766	2.5729	0.6747	2.5176	2.5729	97.9
2M	93 (256 to 348)	0.000763	0.004269	0.6786	2.6924	0.6748	2.5766	2.6924	95.7
3M	62 (171 to 232)	0.001144	0.008442	0.6355	2.1147	0.6311	1.9783	2.1147	93.5
4M	47 (128 to 174)	0.002066	0.008232	0.7510	2.9629	0.7401	2.7109	2.9630	91.5
5M	38 (102 to 139)	0.004210	0.01346	0.8128	2.3237	0.7959	2.0793	2.3241	89.5
6M	31 (86 to 116)	0.002288	0.01930	0.6186	2.0676	0.6107	1.8011	2.0677	87.1
7M	27 (73 to 99)	0.004580	0.01969	0.7326	2.4141	0.7147	2.0570	2.4145	85.2
8M	24 (64 to 87)	0.004269	0.01928	0.7214	2.8713	0.7021	2.3937	2.8718	83.3
9M	21 (57 to 77)	0.005888	0.02926	0.7012	2.2663	0.6811	1.8357	2.2668	80.1
10M	19 (51 to 69)	0.009212	0.01745	1.0280	4.4141	0.9694	3.4876	4.4184	78.9
11M	17 (47 to 63)	0.01194	0.02122	1.0626	4.2931	0.9923	3.2869	4.2996	76.4
12M	16 (43 to 58)	0.006403	0.03236	0.6979	3.0483	0.6715	2.2896	3.0493	95.1

Notes: See Table 2.

estimated MSE are shown when market rates of return are value weighted. For the whole period of 58 years, the relative estimated MSE, MVUE versus ML, declines steadily from 99.4 to 92.7% as the time horizon lengthens from one month to twelve months. This pattern holds consistently for other time periods. The same pattern can be observed in Tables 9–15, where the market rates of return are equal weighted. This evidence supports our conjecture that the MVUE will outperform ML as investment horizons are lengthened because the excess rates of return tend to distribute lognormally.

The major shortcoming of the method of maximum likelihood or MVUE is the statistical inconsistency when the assumption of lognormality of the excess return is violated. In order to achieve robustness in estimation, Brown and Gibbons (1985) used a nonparametric method-of-moments estimator for the relative risk aversion parameter. In Table 16 (value weighted) and Table 17 (equal weighted) we present the estimates of the relative risk aversion parameter using the method of moments and their estimated standard errors based on Eq. (12) of Brown and Gibbons (1985). However, the formula in their Eq. (12) is true only for the asymptotic distribution of b. It is not valid when sample size is small, as in the case of longer investment horizons. As an alternative, we have experimented with the bootstrap estimates of the bias, variance, and MSE of the method of moments estimator (MME) of the relative risk aversion parameter. The procedures are as follows (see Efron, 1979 and 1986).

For a given realized sample, say $X_1, X_2, \ldots, X_T$, we let $\hat{f}$ denote the empirical probability distribution (epd) of $X_1, X_2, \ldots, X_T$. That is, $\hat{f} = \frac{1}{T}$ on $X_1, X_2, \ldots, X_T$. We then behave as if $\hat{f}$ is the probability distribution of X_t. Define a bootstrap sample as either T-independent selection from $\hat{f}$ or a random sample of size T selected with replacement from $X_1, X_2, \ldots, X_T$. Let $(X_{11}^*, X_{21}^*, \ldots, X_{T1}^*) = X^*(1)$ be the first bootstrap sample, $(X_{12}^*, X_{22}^* \ldots, X_{T2}^*) = X^*(2)$ be the second, ..., $(X_{1M}^*, X_{2M}^*, \ldots, X_{TM}^*) = X^*(M)$ the Mth. (M is usually used to denote the number of bootstrap samples; also $M = 800$ seems to be large enough). For each bootstrap sample, compute b, where b denotes the estimator being studied (in this case the MM estimator); say $b^*(m)$ = the value of b computed from the mth bootstrap sample, giving M values of b. The procedure can be summarized as follows:

(a) The bootstrap estimate of B is $\sum_{m=1}^{M} b^*(m)/M = \bar{b}^*$

(b) The bootstrap estimate of B based on the original sample $X_1, X_2, \ldots, X_T$ is b; that is, the solution to $f(b) = 0$ of Equation (8).

(c) The bootstrap estimate of the bias of b is the difference between (a) and (b):

$$\frac{\sum_{m=1}^{M} b^*(m)}{M} - b = \text{est. bias} = \bar{b}^* - b$$

Table 9. Equal Weighted: 58 Years (1/1926–12/1983)

Holding Period	*T*	$\overline{\ln X}$	s^2	$\hat{b}$	*var* $(\hat{b})$	$\hat{B}$	*var*$(\hat{B})$*	*MSE*$(\hat{b})^\dagger$	$\frac{var(\hat{B})}{MSE(\hat{b})}$
1M	696	0.007532	0.005771	1.8051	0.2561	1.8014	0.2546	0.2561	99.4
2M	348	0.01504	0.01372	1.5958	0.2202	1.5895	0.2176	0.2202	98.8
3M	232	0.02255	0.02499	1.4027	0.1844	1.3949	0.1812	0.1844	98.3
4M	174	0.03007	0.02729	1.6021	0.2328	1.5893	0.2275	0.2330	97.6
5M	139	0.03778	0.03397	1.6121	0.2403	1.5959	0.2334	0.2406	97.0
6M	116	0.04511	0.04797	1.4404	0.2060	1.4241	0.1989	0.2063	96.4
7M	99	0.05307	0.06160	1.3615	0.1910	1.3440	0.1833	0.1913	95.8
8M	87	0.06014	0.04719	1.7746	0.3031	1.7449	0.289	0.3040	95.1
9M	77	0.06824	0.06151	1.6094	0.2650	1.5802	0.2512	0.2659	94.5
10M	69	0.07653	0.05364	1.9267	0.3633	1.8847	0.3422	0.3751	93.7
11M	63	0.08340	0.09708	1.3591	0.2078	1.3313	0.1946	0.2086	93.3
12M	58	0.09022	0.08300	1.5869	0.2794	1.5488	0.2601	0.2810	92.6

Notes: See Table 2.

Table 10. Equal Weighted: 27 Years (1/1926–12/1952)

Holding Period	*T*	$\overline{\ln X}$	s^2	$\hat{b}$	*var* $(\hat{b})$	$\hat{B}$	*var*$(\hat{B})$*	*MSE*$(\hat{b})^\dagger$	$\frac{var(\hat{B})}{MSE(\hat{b})}$
1M	324 (1 to 324)	0.008569	0.009513	1.4008	0.3357	1.3952	0.3316	0.3357	98.8
2M	162 (1 to 162)	0.01708	0.02267	1.2535	0.2902	1.2442	0.2830	0.2903	97.5
3M	108 (1 to 108)	0.02562	0.04134	1.1198	0.2448	1.1082	0.2358	0.2450	96.2
4M	81 (1 to 81)	0.03416	0.04489	1.2611	0.3130	1.2420	0.2975	0.3133	94.4
5M	64 (1 to 64)	0.04255	0.05596	1.2604	0.3288	1.2363	0.3083	0.3294	93.6
6M	54 (1 to 54)	0.05125	0.07509	1.1825	0.2978	1.1567	0.2757	0.2985	92.4
7M	46 (1 to 46)	0.05855	0.1023	1.0724	0.2616	1.0470	0.2389	0.2623	91.1
8M	40 (1 to 40)	0.06809	0.07208	1.4446	0.4640	1.3961	0.4176	0.4666	89.5
9M	36 (1 to 36)	0.07687	0.0999	1.2687	0.3755	1.2248	0.3338	0.3777	88.4
10M	32 (1 to 32)	0.08511	0.08582	1.4917	0.5302	1.4278	0.4640	0.5349	86.7
11M	29 (1 to 29)	0.09397	0.1808	1.0196	0.2657	0.9825	0.2291	0.2673	85.7
12M	27 (1 to 27)	0.1025	0.1234	1.3305	0.4578	1.2666	0.3901	0.4626	84.3

Notes: See Table 2.

Table 11. Equal Weighted: 31 Years (1/1953–12/1983)

Holding Period	T	$\overline{\ln X}$	S^2	$\hat{b}$	$var\,(\hat{b})$	$\hat{B}$	$var(\hat{B})$*	$MSE(\hat{b})^{\dagger}$	$\frac{var(\hat{B})}{MSE(\hat{b})}$
1M	372 (325 to 696)	0.006628	0.002527	3.1231	1.1192	3.1089	1.1072	1.1194	98.9
2M	186 (163 to 348)	0.01325	0.006003	2.7080	0.9805	2.6841	0.9594	0.9811	97.9
3M	124 (109 to 232)	0.01988	0.01095	2.3162	0.8314	2.2867	0.8045	0.8323	96.7
4M	93 (82 to 174)	0.02651	0.01225	2.6640	1.0493	2.6170	1.0042	1.0516	95.5
5M	75 (65 to 139)	0.03370	0.01567	2.6505	1.0641	2.5924	1.0073	1.0676	94.3
6M	62 (55 to 116)	0.03976	0.02513	2.0824	0.8042	2.0306	0.7523	0.8070	93.2
7M	53 (47 to 99)	0.04832	0.02753	2.2551	0.9109	2.1876	0.8422	0.9159	91.2
8M	47 (41 to 87)	0.05339	0.02701	2.4767	1.1054	2.3908	1.0114	1.1135	90.8
9M	41 (37 to 77)	0.06066	0.02924	2.5746	1.2406	2.4709	1.1197	1.2525	89.4
10M	37 (33 to 69)	0.06912	0.02731	3.0309	1.6277	2.8903	1.5538	1.6498	88.0
11M	34 (30 to 63)	0.07438	0.02877	3.0854	1.7607	2.9287	1.5338	1.7886	86.9
12M	31 (28 to 58)	0.07952	0.05049	2.0750	1.0089	1.9700	0.8788	1.0215	86.0

Notes: See Table 2.

Table 12. Equal Weighted: 13½ Years (1/1926–6/1939)

Holding Period	*T*	$\overline{\ln X}$	s^2	$\hat{b}$	*var* $(\hat{b})$	$\hat{B}$	*var*$(\hat{B})$*	*MSE*$(\hat{b})^{\dagger}$	$\frac{var(\hat{B})}{MSE(\hat{b})}$
1M	162 (1 to 162)	0.003182	0.01507	0.7111	0.4259	0.7085	0.4154	0.4259	97.5
2M	81 (1 to 81)	0.00627	0.03772	0.6663	0.3541	0.6621	0.3366	0.3541	95.1
3M	54 (1 to 54)	0.00941	0.07069	0.6331	0.2952	0.6280	0.2734	0.2952	92.6
4M	40 (1 to 40)	0.01285	0.07666	0.6676	0.3848	0.6590	0.3464	0.3849	89.9
5M	32 (1 to 32)	0.01606	0.08823	0.6820	0.4375	0.6703	0.3829	0.4377	87.5
6M	27 (1 to 27)	0.01881	0.1233	0.6526	0.3872	0.6409	0.3299	0.3873	81.2
7M	23 (1 to 23)	0.02593	0.1723	0.6505	0.3423	0.6368	0.2829	0.3425	82.6
8M	20 (1 to 20)	0.02570	0.1116	0.7303	0.6432	0.7061	0.5149	0.6439	79.9
9M	18 (1 to 18)	0.02822	0.1606	0.6757	0.5188	0.6551	0.4039	0.5194	77.8
10M	16 (1 to 16)	0.03212	0.1232	0.7608	0.8148	0.7260	0.6119	0.8164	75.0
11M	14 (1 to 14)	0.05327	0.3120	0.6665	0.3897	0.6409	0.2790	0.3906	71.4
12M	13 (1 to 13)	0.05693	0.2177	0.7616	0.6608	0.7178	0.4589	0.6635	69.2

Notes: See Table 2.

Table 13. Equal Weighted: 13½ Years (7/1939–12/1952)

Holding Period	*T*	$\overline{\ln X}$	S^2	$\hat{b}$	*var* ($\hat{b}$)	$\hat{B}$	*var*($\hat{B}$)*	*MSE*($\hat{b}$)†	$\frac{var(\hat{B})}{MSE(\hat{b})}$
1M	162 (163 to 324)	0.01396	0.003957	4.0272	1.7824	3.9834	1.7384	1.7844	97.4
2M	81 (82 to 162)	0.02789	0.007664	4.1392	2.1057	4.0483	2.0017	2.1144	94.7
3M	54 (55 to 108)	0.04184	0.01223	3.9209	2.2178	3.7918	2.0536	2.2358	91.9
4M	41 (41 to 81)	0.05496	0.01414	4.3874	2.9480	4.1931	2.6606	2.9899	88.9
5M	32 (33 to 64)	0.06905	0.02405	3.3711	2.2926	3.1859	2.0063	2.3318	86.0
6M	27 (28 to 54)	0.08368	0.02761	3.5310	2.6979	3.2979	2.2988	2.7617	83.2
7M	23 (24 to 46)	0.09117	0.03468	3.1285	2.6142	2.8896	2.1605	2.6833	80.5
8M	20 (21 to 40)	0.1105	0.03259	3.8901	4.0862	3.5332	3.2713	4.2453	77.1
9M	18 (19 to 36)	0.1255	0.04027	3.6166	3.9638	3.2499	3.0860	4.1365	74.6
10M	16 (17 to 32)	0.1381	0.04818	3.3662	4.0297	2.9841	3.0268	4.2242	71.7
11M	15 (15 to 29)	0.1320	0.06137	2.6502	3.0328	2.3430	2.2282	3.1613	70.5
12M	14 (14 to 27)	0.1448	0.04191	3.9552	6.6149	3.4236	4.7361	7.0095	67.6

Notes: See Table 2.

Table 14. Equal Weighted: 15½ Years (1/1953–6/1968)

Holding Period	T	$\overline{\ln X}$	S^2	$\hat{b}$	$var(\hat{b})$	$\hat{B}$	$var(\hat{B})$*	$MSE(\hat{b})^{\dagger}$	$\frac{var(\hat{B})}{MSE(\hat{b})}$
1M	186 (325 to 510)	0.01003	0.001454	7.3993	4.3571	7.3247	4.2634	4.3628	97.7
2M	93 (163 to 255)	0.02007	0.003592	6.0868	3.9407	5.9654	3.7712	3.9561	95.3
3M	62 (109 to 170)	0.03010	0.006337	5.2495	3.6620	5.0937	3.4258	3.6880	92.9
4M	46 (82 to 127)	0.03910	0.007840	5.4874	4.5137	5.2658	4.1214	4.5675	90.2
5M	37 (65 to 101)	0.04840	0.009146	5.7927	5.4828	5.4986	4.8906	5.5798	87.6
6M	31 (55 to 85)	0.06020	0.01512	4.4813	4.0372	4.2159	3.5168	4.1180	85.4
7M	26 (47 to 72)	0.07033	0.01757	4.5028	4.6354	4.1826	3.9234	4.7566	82.5
8M	23 (41 to 63)	0.07819	0.02046	4.3209	4.8192	3.9736	3.9828	4.9652	80.2
9M	20 (37 to 56)	0.08773	0.01906	5.1037	7.2444	4.6191	5.7995	7.5377	76.9
10M	18 (33 to 50)	0.09727	0.02358	4.6243	6.8524	4.1391	5.3349	7.1548	74.6
11M	17 (30 to 46)	0.1025	0.02019	5.5790	10.0557	4.9442	7.6989	10.5821	72.8
12M	15 (28 to 42)	0.1170	0.04233	3.2631	4.6505	2.8684	3.4167	4.8626	70.3

Notes: See Table 2.

Table 15. Equal Weighted: 15½ Years (7/1968–12/1983)

Holding Period	T	$\overline{\ln X}$	S^2	$\hat{b}$	$var(\hat{b})$	$\hat{B}$	$var(\hat{B})$*	$MSE(\hat{b})^{\dagger}$	$\frac{var(\hat{B})}{MSE(\hat{b})}$
1M	186 (511 to 696)	0.004384	0.003589	1.3975	1.5567	1.3878	1.5232	1.5568	97.8
2M	93 (256 to 348)	0.006442	0.008385	1.2683	1.3844	1.2516	1.3249	1.3847	95.7
3M	62 (171 to 232)	0.009663	0.01552	1.1225	1.1642	1.1021	1.0891	1.1647	93.5
4M	47 (128 to 174)	0.01418	0.01652	1.3587	1.5135	1.3214	1.3848	1.5150	91.4
5M	38 (102 to 139)	0.01938	0.02202	1.3803	1.4693	1.3327	1.3148	1.4719	89.3
6M	31 (86 to 116)	0.01933	0.03511	1.0505	1.1627	1.0138	1.0128	1.1642	86.9
7M	27 (73 to 99)	0.02712	0.03722	1.2288	1.3308	1.1727	1.1340	1.3345	84.9
8M	24 (64 to 87)	0.02961	0.03324	1.3910	1.7624	1.3135	1.4692	1.7696	83.0
9M	21 (57 to 77)	0.03487	0.03894	1.3955	1.8222	1.3060	1.4760	1.8321	80.6
10M	19 (51 to 69)	0.04245	0.03080	1.8782	2.8149	1.7250	2.2241	2.8445	78.2
11M	17 (47 to 63)	0.04623	0.03747	1.7339	2.7238	1.5796	2.0854	2.7549	75.7
12M	16 (43 to 58)	0.04442	0.05876	1.2560	1.8120	1.1552	1.3610	1.8255	74.6

Notes: See Table 2.

Table 16. Value Weighted: Method of Moments (Standard Error in Parentheses)

Holding Period	*1/1926–12/1983*	*1/1926–12/1952*	*1/1953–12/1983*	*1/1926–5/1939*
1M	1.91336	1.152466	2.98717	0.62292
	(0.68117)	(0.79090)	(1.28976)	(0.86739)
2M	1.80815	1.43662	2.80373	0.60433
	(0.65663)	(0.75453)	(1.25738)	(0.80110)
3M	1.58724	1.29576	2.28390	0.58810
	(0.60733)	(0.70074)	(1.14382)	(0.72806)
4M	1.77531	1.42636	2.85713	0.59617
	(0.68399)	(0.78598)	(1.30442)	(0.84225)
5M	1.89010	1.55560	2.53671	0.63083
	(0.69609)	(0.83196)	(1.26307)	(0.94884)
6M	1.54182	1.30329	2.11017	0.51164
	(0.61449)	(0.73393)	(1.06898)	(0.78511)
7M	1.38029	1.08916	2.42033	0.59214
	(0.57636)	(0.64661)	(1.14410)	(0.69941)
8M	1.82163	1.55320	2.38769	0.62635
	(0.72399)	(0.89232)	(1.17288)	(0.97650)
9M	1.55134	1.34066	2.00662	0.59979
	(0.64312)	(0.78133)	(1.10575)	(0.85413)
10M	2.12606	1.68914	3.20687	0.65135
	(0.77058)	(0.90155)	(1.35657)	(1.02518)
11M	1.23203	0.96832	2.78459	0.58785
	(0.56615)	(0.59464)	(1.33211)	(0.61815)
12M	1.65958	1.44892	2.08162	0.71454
	(0.66291)	(0.81702)	(1.09833)	(0.86250)

Holding Period	*7/1939–12/1952*	*1/1953–6/1968*	*7/1968–12/1983*
1M	4.68658	7.17938	0.67729
	(2.02139)	(2.27688)	(1.58229)
2M	5.33430	5.78014	0.68000
	(2.04470)	(2.20176)	(1.59581)
3M	5.09998	4.87412	0.63471
	(2.11111)	(2.16128)	(1.39384)
4M	5.87357	5.87812	0.75688
	(2.21503)	(2.31010)	(1.62621)
5M	3.91259	7.03532	0.81409
	(1.77735)	(2.69225)	(1.41986)
6M	4.97174	4.15953	0.62443
	(2.00070)	(1.98587)	(1.31456)
7M	3.51312	5.03260	0.74324
	(1.69223)	(2.18706)	(1.39912)
8M	6.42646	4.53612	0.73041
	(2.45920)	(1.94699)	(1.50352)
9M	5.27702	4.45068	0.70602
	(2.08873)	(2.10568)	(1.31006)
10M	5.88227	5.93045	1.06832
	(2.13164)	(2.42953)	(1.79232)
11M	4.67414	6.11330	1.07943
	(2.08607)	(2.25463)	(1.72395)
12M	7.26125	4.60768	0.70369
	(2.59263)	(1.91919)	(1.43638)

Table 17. Equal Weighted: Method of Moments (Standard Error in Parentheses)

Holding Period	*1/1926–12/1983*	*1/1926–12/1952*	*1/1953–12/1983*	*1/1926–6/1939*
1M	1.82451	1.41982	3.08989	0.71731
	(0.52192)	(0.58602)	(1.06922)	(0.64304)
2M	1.67445	1.31718	2.66036	0.68282
	(0.49074)	(0.54767)	(0.98070)	(0.57695)
3M	1.48162	1.18758	2.24973	0.65464
	(0.45264)	(0.50257)	(0.90183)	(0.51779)
4M	1.57934	1.25560	2.67444	0.67299
	(0.49661)	(0.55174)	(1.00860)	(0.57979)
5M	1.66422	1.31999	2.51179	0.70446
	(0.50801)	(0.56763)	(1.00269)	(0.60730)
6M	1.46053	1.21226	2.07767	0.66870
	(0.46661)	(0.53528)	(0.86534)	(0.56074)
7M	1.33767	1.06885	2.28197	0.65806
	(0.44502)	(0.48907)	(0.89465)	(0.51559)
8M	1.67431	1.38009	2.49428	0.73014
	(0.54428)	(0.63106)	(0.95464)	(0.68937)
9M	1.49831	1.21185	2.52230	0.67432
	(0.51470)	(0.56709)	(1.02585)	(0.60757)
10M	1.92436	1.51498	3.11428	0.78050
	(0.61173)	(0.67097)	(1.20284)	(0.74068)
11M	1.28577	1.00180	2.93371	0.67181
	(0.47050)	(0.47398)	(1.13260)	(0.49409)
12M	1.53993	1.31508	2.03643	0.78107
	(0.49788)	(0.59046)	(0.87843)	(0.62259)

Holding Period	*7/1939–12/1952*	*1/1953–6/1968*	*7/1968–12/1983*
1M	3.80663	7.19589	1.40134
	(1.48889)	(2.09444)	(1.23373)
2M	4.14290	5.53111	1.27566
	(1.49154)	(1.96346)	(1.14444)
3M	3.87197	4.62168	1.12786
	(1.51121)	(1.92219)	(1.03483)
4M	4.64502	5.18950	1.39150
	(1.66184)	(1.99922)	(1.16420)
5M	3.32232	5.96657	1.37042
	(1.39060)	(2.25400)	(1.12412)
6M	3.84174	4.08283	1.07733
	(1.44949)	(1.76940)	(0.98647)
7M	3.40150	4.17801	1.27787
	(1.42763)	(1.77187)	(1.03416)
8M	4.80548	4.27375	1.44124
	(1.86681)	(1.72886)	(1.16351)
9M	4.52968	4.77528	1.43913
	(1.63381)	(2.17021)	(1.16757)
10M	4.84361	5.44144	1.95717
	(1.81271)	(2.20528)	(1.43482)
11M	3.61756	6.60011	1.73619
	(1.50795)	(2.37156)	(1.31825)
12M	5.81688	3.83417	1.26366
	(1.91293)	(1.55496)	(1.08210)

Table 18. Simulated MSE of the Bootstrap MM Estimates (Value Weighted: 58 years, January 1926 to December 1983)

Holding Period	$\bar{b}^*$	$MSE(b^*)$	$\frac{var(\hat{B})}{MSE(b^*)}$
		800 Samples	%
1M	2.20	0.3108	143.6
2M	2.72	0.4925	82.7
3M	1.94	0.4386	78.4
4M	2.15	0.6359	70.9
5M	2.17	0.6803	70.1
6M	1.80	0.5730	63.8
7M	1.65	0.5214	61.6
8M	2.10	0.8758	58.7
9M	1.79	0.6683	61.8
10M	2.39	0.9953	60.2
11M	1.59	0.7298	40.9
12M	1.86	0.9989	45.7

(d) The bootstrap estimate of the variance of b is

$$\frac{1}{M-1}\sum_{m-1}^{M}(b^*(m)-\bar{b}^*)^2 = \text{est. var.}$$

(e) The bootstrap estimate of MSE is

$$(\text{est. bias})^2 + \text{est. var} = \text{est. MSE}.$$

The bootstrap simulation results are shown in Table 18 for the whole period of 58 years. It is clear that the estimated MSEs are mostly larger than that of the MVUE and exhibit an increasing trend as the investment horizon is lengthened. As a result the relative estimated MSE, MVUE versus MME, declines steadily as the excess rates of return are more lognormally distributed.

V. CONCLUDING REMARKS

In this study we have provided strong evidence that the estimation of utility-based models of asset pricing should take into account the investment horizon. Brown and Gibbons (1985) found that the nonparametric method-of-moments estimator and the parametric maximum likelihood estimator yielded basically similar results, even though their Hausman tests rejected the assumption of lognormality in all but two subperiods for each index. However, the investment horizon in their study is only one month. Many empirical studies have shown that the excess return is distributed lognormally as the investment horizon is lengthened beyond six months. But when the investment horizon is lengthened by using annual or even quarterly data for empirical studies, the sample size tends to be small and as a result the asymptotic assumption might not hold. Thus even if the market rates of return are lognormally distributed, the asymptotic variance formula of Brown and Gibbons' (1985) ML estimator is biased in the case of finite samples. Instead, formula (6) in our paper should be used in the experiments with different investment horizons. But for the case of lognormality, we derived a minimum variance unbiased estimator, which is more powerful than the maximum likelihood estimator. In the absence of distributional assumptions, Brown and Gibbons proposed a nonparametric MM estimator. However, the variance formula of their MM estimator is correct only asymptotically. Thus for the case of nonlognormality, we proposed the bootstrapping method for computing the variance of the method-of-moments estimator and provided additional evidence that lognormality properties should be taken advantage of in estimating utility-based models of capital asset pricing when the investment horizon is lengthened.

Finally, it is worth emphasizing that Brown and Gibbons' (1985) empirical findings that the parametric and nonparametric estimates of the RRA are strikingly similar and that the log utility specification of the aggregate utility function cannot be rejected were all based on the asymptotic assumption. Brown and Gibbons admitted that their empirical results are open to question and that further empirical work is needed to investigate the implications of utility-based theories of asset pricing. In particular, when investment horizon is being lengthened, lognormality of the market rates of return cannot be rejected; also, the available sample tends to be finite. Statistical inference should be based on the MVUE as developed in this paper. Our empirical study indicates that taking into account the effect of investment horizon on the distribution of market rate of return will enhance the descriptive power of the utility-based asset pricing models.

APPENDIX

The first order Taylor series expansion of $f(b)$, at B, is

$$f(b) = f(B) + f'(B)\,(b - B),$$

where $b \neq B$, b and B are in some closed interval, and $f'(B) = \frac{df(b)}{db}\Big|_{b=B}$ is finite inside the interval. Furthermore,

$$f(b) = \frac{1}{T}\sum_{t=1}^{T} (X_t - 1)X_t^{-b} = 0$$

and

$$f(B) = \frac{1}{T}\sum_{t=1}^{T} (X_t - 1)X_t^{-B} \neq 0$$

and

$$f'(B) = \frac{1}{T}\sum_{t=1}^{T} (X_t - 1)X_t^{-B}\ln X_t \neq 0.$$

Therefore, the approximate bias of b is

$$\text{approx. bias} = -E\left[\frac{f(B)}{f'(B)}\right] = -E\left[\frac{\sum_{t=1}^{T} (X_t - 1)\, X_t^{-B}}{\sum_{t=1}^{T} (X_t - 1)\, X_t^{-B}\ln X_t}\right].$$

As for the approximate variance of b, this is

$$\text{var}\,(b) = \text{var}\,\left(\frac{f(B)}{f'(B)}\right) \cong \text{var}\left[\frac{\sum_{t=1}^{T} (X_t - 1)\, X_t^{-B}}{\sum_{t=1}^{T} (X_t - 1)\, X_t^{-B}\ln X_t}\right].$$

The *approximate* bias and variance are a function of the ratio

$$\sum_{t=1}^{T} (X_t - 1)\, X_t^{-B} / \sum_{t=1}^{T} (X_t - 1)X_t^{-B}\ln X_t = \frac{f(B)}{f'(B)}.$$

The asymptotic results depend on what happens, for large T, to the ratio. Let $f(B) = W_T$ and $f'(B) = Z_t$.

1. Since W_T is a sum of i.i.d. random variables $(X_t - 1)X_t^{-B}$,

$$(W_T/T) \sim AN\,(0, \frac{\text{var}\,(X_t - 1)X_t^{-B}}{T}),$$

where AN denotes asymptotic normality.

Note: $\text{var}(X_t - 1)X_t^{-B} = E[(X_t - 1)\,X_t^{-B}]^2$ = numerator of Eq. (12) in Brown and Gibbons (1985).

2. Similarly, Z_t is a sum of i.i.d. random variables

$$(X_t - 1)X_t^{-B}\ln X_t$$

and

$$(Z_T/T) \sim AN\,(E[(X_t - 1)X_t^{-B}\ln X_t],\ \text{var}\,(X_t - 1)X_t^{-B}\ln X_t).$$

Brown and Gibbons, in their Appendix A, assume that Z_T/T converges in probability to the constant $E[(X_t - 1)X_t^{-B}\ln X_t]$, and hence is not asymptotically normal but asymptotically the constant. Therefore, they argue, var $(\sqrt{T}b)$ = Eq. (12) in Brown and Gibbons (1985), where the denominator is the square of the constant: $(E[(X_t - 1)X_t^{-B}\ln X_t])^2$.

REFERENCES

Blume, M. E. (1970). "Portfolio Theory: A Step Towards Its Practical Application." *Journal of Business* 43, 152–173.

Brown, D. P., and Gibbons, M. R. (1985). "A Simple Econometric Approach for Utility-Based Asset Pricing Models." *Journal of Finance* 40, No. 2, 359–381.

Efron, B. (1979). "Computers and the Theory of Statistics: Thinking the Unthinkable." *SIAM* 21, 460–480.

Efron, B. (1986). "Bootstrap Methods for Standard Errors, Confidence Interval, and Other Measures of Statistical Accuracy." *Statistical Science* 1, 54–177.

Fama, E. F. (1965). "The Behavior of Stock-Market Prices." *Journal of Business* 38, 34–105.

Hansen, L., and K. Singleton (1982). "Generalized Instrumental Variable Estimation of Nonlinear Rational Expectation Models." *Econometrica* 50, 1269–1286.

Ibbotson, R., and Sinquefield, R. (1979). *Stocks. Bonds, Bills and Inflation: Historical Returns (1926–1978).* Charlottesville, VA: Financial Analysts Research Foundation.

Lee, C. F. (1976). "Investment Horizon and the Functional Form of the Capital Asset Pricing Model." *Review of Economics and Statistics* 58 (August), 356–363.

Levhari, D., and H. Levy (1977). "The Capital Asset Pricing Model and the Investment Horizon." *Review of Economics and Statistics* 59, 92–104.

Levy, H. (1972). "Portfolio Performance and the Investment Horizon." *Management Science* 12 (August), B645–B653.

Lintner, J. (1983). "The Lognormality of Security Returns, Portfolio Selection and Market Equilibrium." Unpublished manuscript, Harvard University.

Rubin, M. (1976). "The Valuation of Uncertain Income Streams and the Pricing of Options." *Bell Journal of Economics* 7, 407–425.

RATIONALITY OF NO-CHANGE FORECASTS OF U.S. TREASURY INTEREST RATES

William Reichenstein and Shekar Shetty

ABSTRACT

Financial theory and empirical evidence indicate that interest rate forecasts from the no-change model should better approximate a rational expectation or rational forecast the longer is the maturity of the interest rate being forecast. For 1975.2 through 1989.4, a rigorous series of tests consistently supports at the 5% level the rationality of one-quarter-ahead no-change forecasts of five-year and longer U.S. Treasury interest rates. These no-change forecasts are not "naive forecasts." Rather, they are indistinguishable from rational expectations in Muth's sense. Financial planners can use no-change predictions of long-term interest rates with confidence.

I. INTRODUCTION

Pesando (1979) shows that if the market for fixed-income securities is efficient and expectations of future short-term interest rates are embedded in current longer-term

Advances in Quantitative Analysis of Finance and Accounting,
Volume 2, Part A, pages 93–103.

ISBN: 1-55938-564-2

interest rates, then longer-term rates should follow approximately a martingale sequence.[1] Pesando and Plourde (1988) estimate that the predictable one-quarter-ahead change in long-term Government of Canada bond interest rates has been less than 1% of the actual change. In this environment, the no-change model produces near-term forecasts of longer-term rates that are indistinguishable from the rational expectation forecast. This paper extends their analysis in two directions. First, we use U.S. interest rates and, second, we estimate the shortest maturity for which one-quarter-ahead no-change model forecasts of U.S. Treasury interest rates pass a rigorous series of rational expectations tests at the 5% level of significance.

For U.S. Treasury interest rates ranging from the three-month to the twenty-year rate, we test the rationality or market efficiency of one-quarter-ahead no-change model forecasts using tests of orthogonality of errors to available information, tests of unbiasedness, and estimation of autoregressive moving average models. No-change model forecasts are considered rational expectations in Muth's (1961) sense only if the results from all the tests support the rationality argument. For 1975.2 (second quarter 1975) through 1989.4, the tests support at the 5% level the efficiency of no-change forecasts of five-year and longer U. S. Treasury rates. That is, these no-change forecasts are indistinguishable from rational expectations.

II. THEORETICAL BACKGROUND

Pesando (1979) shows that an efficient markets forecast of a one-period-ahead long-term interest rate, in the absence of time-varying term premiums, is approximately today's rate. Today's interest rate on a pure discount twenty-year (80-quarter) bond, for example, can be expressed as the geometric average of today's one-quarter spot rate and 79 one-quarter forward rates:

$$r_{80,t} = [(1 + r_{1,t})(1 + {}_{t+1}f_{1,t}) \ldots (1 + {}_{t+79}f_{1,t})]^{1/80} - 1, \quad (1)$$

where $r_{i,t}$ is today's i-quarter spot rate and ${}_{t+i}f_{1,t}$ is today's one-quarter forward rate beginning at time $t + i$.

To illustrate the key insight, we use the arithmetic approximation to the geometric mean and assume that the term structure is determined by the pure expectations theory; thus ${}_{t+1}f_{1,t}$ is the market's expectation at time t of the one-quarter spot rate at time t+1. The expectation at time t of the one-quarter-ahead change in the twenty-year spot rate, $E_t[r_{80,t+1} - r_{80,t}]$, is

$$E_t[r_{80,t+1} - r_{80,t}] = 1/80\ [({}_{t+80}f_{1,t} - r_{1,t}) + \sum_{i=1}^{79} (E_t[{}_{t+i}f_{1,t+1} - {}_{t+i}f_{1,t}])]. \quad (2)$$

Let δ_t represent the information available to the market at time t. If the pure expectations theory is valid and the bond market is efficient, then the conditional expectation of ${}_{t+i}f_{1,t+1}$ given information at time t is ${}_{t+i}f_{1,t}$.

$$E_t[_{t+i}f_{1,t+1} \mid \delta_t] = {}_{t+i}f_{1,t} \quad \text{for } i = 1, 2, \ldots, 79. \tag{3}$$

Equations (2) and (3) imply that the expected one-quarter-ahead change in the twenty-year zero-coupon spot rate is (1/80)th the difference between the expected one-quarter rate in 20 years and today's one-quarter rate:

$$E_t[r_{80,t+1} - r_{80,t}] = 1/80[_{t+80}f_{1,t} - r_{1,t}]. \tag{4}$$

Equation (4) clearly implies that the expected near-term change in a long-term zero-coupon interest rate is approximately zero.

The presence of time-invariant term premiums (or, more generally, term premiums whose expected values equal current term premiums) would add a constant to Eq. (1), which would be eliminated in the difference equation (4). That is, the existence of term premiums need not complicate the analysis.

Coupon payments, however, complicate the theoretical analysis of the predicted change in coupon-bearing bond interest rates. Pesando and Plourde (1988) estimate that the predictable one-quarter-ahead change in long-term coupon-bearing Government of Canada bond rates, both before and after the October 1979 change in Federal Reserve operating procedures, has been less than 1% of the actual change.

It follows from these and related studies by Pesando (1978 and 1981) that "the no-change prediction remains a close approximation to the rational-expectations model, at least over quarterly forecasts horizons" (1988, p. 238). Thus the no-change model should produce one-quarter-ahead forecasts of a long-term interest rate that are indistinguishable from rational expectations forecasts. It should also be clear from Eq. (4) that the no-change forecast is a closer approximation to the rational expectations forecast the longer the interest rate's maturity. This suggests an empirical search for the minimum maturity for which no-change forecasts pass a series of rationality tests at the 5% level of significance, the primary significance level used in this study.

III. DATA AND TIME PERIOD

Data for the study come from the Board of Governors of the Federal Reserve System, the Federal Reserve Bank of Dallas, and the Wall Street Journal. Working (1960) has shown that the use of interest rate data averaged over a time period can produce misleading results, so we tried to minimize this potential problem. Interest rates in this study are the average rates for the last week of the quarter, for example, March, June, and so on.

Treasury security rate series for the following maturities are examined: three-month, six-month, one-year, two-year, three-year, five-year, ten-year, and twenty-year.[2] The time period reported in this study is 1975.2 (June 1975) through 1989.4~ Reichenstein (1987) found evidence of a shift in the structure of interest rates at about the time the Federal Reserve began announcing twelve-month target growth ranges for the monetary aggregates in April 1975.

IV. TESTS OF ORTHOGONALITY OF ERRORS TO COSTLESSLY AVAILABLE INFORMATION

A key property of a rational expectation or a rational forecast is that it must fully reflect all costlessly available information. If the no-change model produces rational forecasts, the prediction errors from that model should be unrelated to costlessly available information.

Two sets of errors' orthogonality tests are performed. The first is to regress changes in interest rates (i.e., no-change prediction errors) on a costlessly available information set according to

$$\blacktriangle r_t = b_0 + \sum_{i=1}^{n} b_i X_{t-i} + e_t, \tag{5}$$

where $\blacktriangle r_t$ is the change in r from time $t-1$ to t and X_{t-i} is information available at time $t-i$. The null hypothesis is $H{:}b_0 = b_1 = \ldots = b_n = 0$. Abel and Mishkin (1983) show that the test is valid regardless of the completeness of the right-hand side information set.

The information set X could be any costless economic series. It is represented in this study by all the economic variables considered by Friedman (1980), and by other series. These variables include the unemployment rate (*UN*), the growth in industrial production (*IP*), the inflation rate as measured by the Consumer Price Index (*INF*), the change in inflation rate ($\blacktriangle$*INF*), the growth in M1 money supply (*MG*), the growth in monetary base (*BG*), the national income accounts federal government budget deficit (*GOV*), the change in the three-month Treasury bill rate ($\blacktriangle$*T3M*), and lagged values of the dependent variable (*DEP*). Four lagged values of the independent variable are considered in each test. The tests are designed so that the first right-hand side variable X_{t-1} corresponds to the most recent publicly available observation as of the end of the quarter. To this end, the observations from the second month of a quarter are used for the following series: unemployment rate, Industrial Production Index, CPI, M1, and monetary base. The value of the government deficit from the previous quarter is used as the most recently available observation. Table 1 presents F-statistics for the null hypothesis.

The regression results summarized in Table 1 reject the efficiency of no-change model forecast of the three-month and six-month Treasury bill rates at the 5% level; changes in these rates show a significant negative association with the group of four prior changes in the three-month bill rate. These tests support the hypothesis

Table 1. *F*-Statistics for Errors' Orthogonality Regressions: June 1975 through December 1989

$$\blacktriangle r_t = b_0 + \sum_{i=1}^{4} b_i X_{t-i} + e_t;\ Ho{:}b_0 = b_1 = b_2 = b_3 = b_4 = 0$$

	Independent Variables								
Dependent Variable	*UN*	*IP*	*INF*	▲*INF*	*MG*	*BG*	*GOV*	▲*r3m*	*DEP*
▲*r3m*	1.25	0.67	2.13[b]	2.20[b]	0.23	0.17	0.19	3.48[a]	3.48[a]
▲*r6m*	1.34	0.58	2.11[b]	2.11[b]	0.17	0.16	0.23	2.72[a]	2.70[a]
▲*r*1	1.10	0.50	1.73	1.69	0.56	0.35	0.21	1.47	1.63
▲*r*2	0.78	0.38	1.49	1.31	1.10	0.61	0.55	0.61	0.85
▲*r*3	0.89	0.50	1.69	1.58	0.74	0.45	0.29	.0.98	1.16
▲*r*5	0.73	0.36	1.46	1.20	1.03	0.70	0.35	0.62	0.72
▲*r*10	0.68	0.45	1.52	1.19	0.83	0.95	0.48	0.54	0.32
▲*r*20	0.57	0.36	1.30	0.97	0.76	1.01	0.50	0.60	0.52

Notes: [a,b]Indicates rejection of the null hypothesis at the 5 and 10% levels, respectively. The dependent variables are the quarterly change in the three-month, six-month, one-year, two-year, three-year, five-year, ten-year, and twenty-year Treasury security rates. The independent variables are lagged values of the unemployment rate, growth in Industrial Production Index, inflation rate as measured by the Consumer Price Index, change in inflation rate, M1 money growth rate, growth in monetary base, level of government deficit, change in three-month Treasury bill rate, and the dependent variable.

that the no-change model produces rational one-quarter-ahead forecasts of one-year and longer interest rates.

The second set of errors' orthogonality tests is provided by the correlations between quarterly changes in interest rates and the prior quarter's value of economic variables. If the no-change model produces rational forecasts, the prediction errors from that model should be uncorrelated with prior changes in the same interest rate, prior changes in other interest rates, and prior changes in the macroeconomic variables. Table 2 presents the correlations.

The correlation tests proved to be more difficult hurdles for the rationality hypotheses. They support the theoretical expectation that the no-change forecast better approximates the rational expectations forecast the longer the maturity is. The correlations reject the efficiency of no-change forecasts of three-month through three-year interest rates. Changes in the three-month through one-year interest rates are each correlated at the 5% level with seven lagged variables. Changes in the two-year and three-year interest rates exhibit significant correlations a combined six times. On the positive side, the correlations support the rationality of no-change forecasts of the five-year and longer interest rates.

Table 2. Correlations between Changes in Interest Rates and Prior Publicly Available Economic Series

	$\Delta r3m_t$	$\Delta r6m_t$	$\Delta r1_t$	$\Delta r2_t$	$\Delta r3_t$	$\Delta r5_t$	$\Delta r10_t$	$\Delta r20_t$
$\Delta r3m_{t-1}$	−0.31[a]	−0.32[a]	−0.27[a]	−0.16	−0.23[b]	−0.15	−0.08	−0.08
$\Delta r6m_{t-1}$	−0.28[a]	−0.30[a]	−0.28[a]	−0.19	−0.25[b]	−0.19	−0.12	−0.12
$\Delta r1_{t-1}$	−0.29[a]	−0.31[a]	−0.31[a]	−0.21	−0.28[a]	−0.23[b]	−0.17	−0.18
$\Delta r2_{t-1}$	−0.27[a]	−0.29[a]	−0.31[a]	−0.26[a]	−0.28[a]	−0.25[b]	−0.19	−0.15
$\Delta r3_{t-1}$	−0.27[a]	−0.28[a]	−0.29[a]	−0.19	−0.27[a]	−0.22[b]	−0.16	−0.16
$\Delta r5_{t-1}$	−0.26[a]	−0.27[a]	−0.28[a]	−0.18	−0.26[a]	−0.22[b]	−0.16	−0.17
$\Delta r10_{t-1}$	−0.23[b]	−0.22[b]	−0.23[b]	−0.13	−0.21	−0.17	−0.12	−0.13
$\Delta r20_{t-1}$	−0.22[b]	−0.21	−0.22[b]	−0.09	−0.20	−0.16	−0.11	−0.15
UN_{t-1}	−0.07	−0.08	−0.08	−0.07	−0.08	−0.07	−0.07	−0.05
IP_{t-1}	−0.03	−0.03	−0.04	−0.06	−0.05	−0.06	−0.07	−0.07
INF_{t-1}	−0.04	−0.02	0.02	0.08	0.05	0.10	0.12	0.14
ΔINF_{t-1}	−0.34[a]	−0.33[a]	−0.28[a]	−0.22[b]	−0.26[a]	−0.21	−0.19	−0.14
MG_{t-1}	0.07	0.01	−0.04	−0.07	−0.05	−0.06	−0.06	−0.01
BG_{t-1}	0.04	0.05	0.10	0.10	0.13	0.17	0.19	0.21
GOV_{t-1}	0.07	0.08	0.10	0.07	0.12	0.14	0.16	0.19

Notes: [a,b]Indicates statistical significance at the 5 and 10% levels, respectively. The variables by row are the quarterly changes in the three-month, six-month, one-year, two-year, three-year, five-year, ten-year, and twenty-year Treasury security rates, unemployment rate, growth in Industrial Production Index, inflation rate as measured by the Consumer Price Index, change in inflation rate, M1 growth rate, growth in monetary base, and level of government deficit. The subscripts denote the time period.

V. TESTS OF UNBIASEDNESS

Unbiasedness is a key property of rational expectations in Muth's (1961) sense. Rational interest rate forecasts must be unbiased. That is,

$$r_t = {}_{t-1}r_t^e + u_t, \tag{6}$$

where r_t is the observed rate at time t, ${}_{t-1}r_t^e$ is the expectation of r_t, held at time $t-1$, and u_t is the zero mean forecast error made at time $t-1$ and observed at time t.

Following Theil (1966) and Friedman, among others, we regress each actual interest rate on its one-quarter lagged value to test the unbiasedness of no-change forecasts:

$$r_t = b_0 + b_1 r_{t-1} + u_t. \tag{7}$$

Table 3. Single Equation Unbiasedness Tests
($r_t = b_0 + b_1 r_{t-1}$)

r_t	b_0	b_1	χ^2	*h-stat*
r3m	1.95	0.76	6.37	−1.72[c]
	(0.085)[b]	(0.133)	(0.041)[a]	
r6m	1.76	0.79	5.61	−1.75[c]
	(0.098)[b]	(0.147)	(0.061)[b]	
r1	1.68	0.82	5.23	−1.85[c]
	(0.092)[b]	(0.139)	(0.073)[b]	
r2	1.48	0.85	5.98	−1.50
	(0.041)[a]	(0.070)	(0.050)[b]	
r3	1.48	0.84	5.09	−1.58
	(0.082)[b]	(0.126)	(0.078)[b]	
r5	1.20	0.88	4.54	−1.32
	(0.078)b	(0.114)	(0.103)	
r10	0.94	0.90	3.38	−0.53
	(0.115)	(0.153)	(0.184)	
r20	0.95	0.90	3.42	−0.48
	(0.106)	(0.139)	(0.181)	

Notes: [a,b]Indicates rejection of the null hypothesis at the 5 and 10% levels, respectively. Parameters are estimated with White's (1980) heteroskedasticity-consistent matrix estimator. The numbers in parentheses below b_0 and b_1 are the significance levels for the hypotheses $b_0 = 0$ and $b_1 = 1$, respectively. The χ^2-statistic tests the joint hypothesis $H{:}(b_0, b_1) = (0, 1)$ with its significance level in parentheses. The dependent variables are the three-month, six-month, and one-year through twenty-year Treasury security rates.

[c] The Durbin h-statistic rejects the null hypothesis of no serial correlation at the 10% level.

The null hypothesis of unbiasedness is examined by the following null hypotheses:

$$H_1\colon b_0 = 0;\ H_2\colon b_1 = 1;\ \text{and } H_3\colon (b_0, b_1) = (0, 1). \tag{8}$$

In addition, the Durbin (1970) h-statistic must be consistent with the lack of serial correlation. Table 3 presents the results of these four tests.

The unbiasedness results support Pesando and Plourde's conclusion that no-change forecasts better approximate rational expectations the longer the interest rate's maturity. As maturity lengthens, parameter estimates trend toward the hypothesized values. These tests tell essentially the same economic story as prior tests. Five-year and longer interest rates pass all unbiasedness tests, while we reject the unbiasedness of some of the shorter-term interest rates.

VI. ESTIMATES OF AUTOREGRESSIVE MOVING AVERAGE MODELS

A final test of the rationality of no-change model forecasts is provided by the estimation of autoregressive moving average (ARMA) models. The no-change forecast is a rational forecast if the interest rate follows a random walk. In a random walk, the interest rate is characterized by a first-order autoregressive model AR(1) with the autoregressive term insignificantly different from one. The moving average term in an ARMA(1,1) should be insignificant. Table 4 presents the results from the ARMA models.

The Schwartz (1978) Bayesian criterion indicates that the three-month, six-month, and one-year Treasury bill rates are best characterized by an ARMA(1,1). The significant moving average terms for these interest rates are consistent with the significant negative correlation between consecutive quarterly changes in the bills rates discussed earlier. These results imply that the no-change model does not produce efficient forecasts of the one-year and shorter interest rates.

Table 4. ARMA Models of Treasury Rates: 1975.2–1989.4

Rate	*Model*	Ø	θ	*SBC*
r3m	AR(1)	0.770 (0.007)		245.4
	ARMA(1,1)[a]	0.942 (0.289)	0.421 (0.003)	243.6
r6m	AR(1)	0.802 (0.014)		232.4
	ARMA(1,1)[a]	0.942 (0.280)	0.381 (0.007)	232.1
r1	AR(1)	0.834 (0.027)		232.2
	ARMA(1,1)[a]	0.934 (0.242)	0.309 (0.033)	231.9
r2	AR(1)[a]	0.876 (0.064)		211.0
	ARMA(1,1)	0.935 (0.298)	0.226 (0.121)	212.4
r3	AR(1)[a]	0.868 (0.054)		216.1
	ARMA(1,1)	0.937 (0.242)	0.250 (0.085)	217.1
r5	AR(1)[a]	0.902 (0.099)		193.9
	ARMA(1,1)	0.938 (0.238)	0.175 (0.226)	196.2
r10	AR(1)[a]	0.933 (0.174)	0.080 (0.575)	171.2
	ARMA(1,1)	0.944 (0.250)	0.075 (0.624)	174.9
r20	AR(1)[a]	0.936 (0.167)		164.3
	ARMA(1,1)	0.950 (0.271)	0.100 (0.484)	167.7

Notes: [a]Best fitting model according to the Schwartz (1978) Bayesian criterion (SBC). The first-order autoregressive term is Ø. The moving average term is θ. The numbers to the right of Ø and θ are, respectively, the significance levels for the hypotheses Ø = 1 and θ = 0. The interest rates are, in order, the three-month, six-month, one-year, two-year, three-year, five-year, ten-year, and twenty-year Treasury rates.

The Schwartz Bayesian criterion indicates that the two-year and three-year rates are best represented by an AR(1) with an autoregressive term of about 0.87. The autoregressive terms are barely consistent at the 5% level with the random walk model, which raises suspicion about the quality of these no-change forecasts.

The results provide stronger support for the argument that the five-year interest rate, and especially longer-term interest rates, follow a random walk. Consistent with prior tests, the results support the hypothesis that no-change predictions are rational forecasts of five-year and longer interest rates.

VII. SUMMARY AND CONCLUSIONS

Financial theory and empirical evidence indicate that long-term interest rates follow approximately a martingale sequence. For near-term forecasts, it follows that the no-change prediction better approximates the rational expectations forecast the longer the maturity of the interest rate being forecast. For 1975.2 through 1989.4 we empirically estimate the shortest maturity for which one-quarter-ahead no-change forecasts of U.S. Treasury rates pass, at the 5% level, a rigorous series of rational expectations tests; that is, we estimate the shortest maturity for which the no-change prediction is indistinguishable from a rational expectation in Muth's sense. To be considered indistinguishable from a rational expectation, no-change forecasts must (1) be insignificantly associated with the four lagged values of each of several macroeconomic variables, (2) be uncorrelated with the immediately prior quarter's change in each interest rate and the last publicly available value of the macrovariables, (3) pass four tests of unbiasedness, and (4) be characterized by a first-order autoregressive model with the autoregressive term insignificantly different from one—the random walk model.

The empirical results support the null hypothesis that the no-change model produces efficient one-quarter-ahead forecasts of the five-year and longer U.S. Treasury interest rates. These results imply that no-change forecasts of five-year and longer interest rates are indistinguishable from rational expectations and should be difficult, if not impossible, to beat. A forecast which deviates substantially from this forecast should be considered at odds with the requirements of a rational expectation. This position receives further support from the failure of economists and econometric forecasting services to consistently improve upon no-change forecasts of long-term interest rates.

Pesando and Plourde summarize comparisons between the accuracy of no-change forecasts versus either mean forecasts of a survey of economists or forecasts from econometric forecasting services. Among the one- or two-quarter-ahead forecasts of longer-than-one-year interest rates summarized in their Table II, the no-change model produced more accurate forecasts in 22 of 24 test periods, and forecasts of comparable accuracy in the other two. Similarly, this paper's authors found two-quarters-ahead no-change forecasts of the thirty-year Treasury bond rate to be more accurate, on average, than the mean or median forecasts from the economists in the semiannual *Wall Street Journal* survey.[4]

In summary, if the frequent 5% significance level is adopted, the results consistently support the rationality of one-quarter-ahead no-change forecasts of all Treasury interest rates of at least five years maturity. The results consistently support the argument that five-year and longer interest rates cannot be predicted. Financial planners should adopt with confidence these no-change forecasts. They are not "naive forecasts," as many studies refer to them. Rather, for quarterly forecast horizons, they are indistinguishable from rational expectations.

ACKNOWLEDGMENTS

The authors thank James Pesando for valuable comments on an earlier draft.

NOTES

1. In a martingale, $X_t = X_{t-1} + e_t$, where the lagged variable X_{t-1} is also the expectation at time $t-1$ of the value of variable X_t, and e_t is a zero mean error term. If e_t is independently and identically distributed over time, the martingale is the familiar random walk model.
2. Twenty-year interest rates since 1987 were taken from the *Wall Street Journal*.
3. The period since the October 1979 change in the Federal Reserve's operating procedure was also examined. The results were similar to those reported here.
4. The mean absolute error for no-change model forecasts for the six-month periods ending June 1982 through December 1989 is 1.02%. The comparable errors for the mean and median forecasts are 1.18 and 1.27%.

REFERENCES

Abel, A. B., and Mishkin, F. S. (1983). "An Integrated View of Tests of Rationality, Market Efficiency and the Short-Run Neutrality of Monetary Policy." *Journal of Monetary Economics* 11 (January), 3–24.

Durbin, J. (1970). "Testing for Serial Correlation in Least-Squares Regressions When Some of the Regressors Are Lagged Dependent Variables." *Econometrica* 38, 410–421.

Friedman, B. M. (1980). "Survey Evidence on the 'Rationality' of Interest Rate Expectations." *Journal of Monetary Economics* 6 (October), 453–465.

Muth, J. F. (1961). "Rational Expectations and the Theory of Price Movements." *Econometrica* 29 (July), 315–335.

Pesando, J. E. (1978). "On the Efficiency of the Bond Market: Some Canadian Evidence." *Journal of Political Economy* 86 (December), 1057–1076.

Pesando, J. E. (1979). "On the Random Walk Characteristics of Short- and Long-Term Interest Rates in an Efficient Market." *Journal of Money, Credit, and Banking* 11 (November), 457–466.

Pesando, J. E. (1981). "On Forecasting Interest Rates: An Efficient Markets Perspective." *Journal of Monetary Economics* 8 (November), 305–318.

Pesando, J. E. and Plourde, A. (1988). "The October 1979 Change in the U.S. Monetary Regime: Its Impact on the Forecastability of Canadian Interest Rates." *Journal of Finance* 43 (March), 217–239.

Reichenstein, W. (1987). "The Impact of Money on Short-Term Interest Rates." *Economic Inquiry* 25 (January), 67–82.

Schwartz, G. (1978). "Estimating the Dimension of a Model." *Annals of Statistics* 6 (March), 461–464.

Theil, H. (1966). *Applied Economic Forecasting*. Amsterdam: North Holland, 1966.

White, H. (1980). "A Heteroscedasticity-Consistent Matrix Estimator and a Direct Test for Heteroscedasticity." *Econometrica* 48 (May), 817–838.

Working, H. (1960). "Note on the Correlation of First Differences of Averages in a Random Chain." *Econometrica* 28 (October) 916–918.

THE UNBIASED EXPECTATIONS HYPOTHESIS AND ERROR LEARNING

Robert Brooks, Myung J. Kim, and Miles Livingston

ABSTRACT

A simultaneous test of the unbiased expectations hypothesis and the error learning model of Meiselman are presented in this paper using generalized autoregressive conditional heteroskedasticity in mean. Although significant error learning is found, the evidence simultaneously rejects the unbiased expectations hypothesis.

I. INTRODUCTION

According to the unbiased expectations hypothesis, the implied forward interest rate should be an unbiased predictor of the subsequently observed spot interest rate. Several authors test this hypothesis by examining the difference between the implied forward rate today and the future observed spot rate. These prediction errors are found to be positive on average and increasing with maturity (see Fama 1976, and McCallum, 1975), leading investigators to reject the unbiased expectations hypothesis. For example, Startz (1982) concludes: "A planner interested in future

Advances in Quantitative Analysis of Finance and Accounting,
Volume 2, Part A, pages 105–113.

ISBN: 1-55938-564-2

short rates would be well advised not to take today's implied forward rate as an estimator" (p. 327).

Meiselman (1962) presents error learning as another way of testing the unbiased expectations hypothesis. The Meiselman approach correlates prediction errors between the nearest forward rate and the subsequently observed spot rate with revisions in distant forward rates. The prediction errors are found to be highly correlated with revisions of distant forward rates, with these correlations decreasing as distance into the future increases. The Meiselman results are regarded as strong support for the unbiased expectations hypothesis. According to Wood (1963), after Meiselman, the burden of proof must lie with those who question the unbiased expectations hypothesis. The Meiselman model is still widely referenced in current textbooks. (See Campbell, 1988, Rose, 1989, and Van Horne, 1987.)

In this paper, a test that combines these approaches is presented to show that changes in forward rates over time can be related not only to the anticipated change in the spot rate (contradicting the unbiased expectations hypothesis) but also to the unanticipated change in the spot rate (supporting Meiselman's error learning hypothesis). In this case, the hypothesis that forward rates are unbiased predictors of future spot rates is rejected. However, the hypothesis that forward rates of different maturities are correlated (error learning) is accepted. Thus, Meiselman's error learning model is not, by itself, a valid test of the unbiased expectations hypothesis.

In this paper, empirical tests conducted on Treasury bill data from the CRSP Government Bond tape are reported. Some significant positive correlations between future changes in forward rates and anticipated changes in spot rates are found, as well as strong positive correlations between forward rates and unanticipated changes in spot rates. These results provide some support for expectations having an impact but contradict the pure form of the unbiased expectations hypothesis.[1]

II. TESTING EFFICIENCY AND ERROR LEARNING

The notation used here is the same as that used by Fama (1984a,b). Thus,

$f\tau_t$ = one-month forward rate for month $t + \tau$ observed at t; and

R_{t+1} = one-month spot rate of interest observed at t and earned from t to $t + 1$.

The unbiased expectations hypothesis implies that

$$f2_t = E_t[R_{t+2}] \tag{1}$$

$$f\tau_t = E_t[f\tau_{t+1}] \quad \text{for } \tau = 3, 4, \ldots, n \tag{2}$$

where E_t is the standard expectations operator denoting the expectation at t.

Meiselman reasons that the forward rate forecasts in Eqs. (1) and (2) would not be perfect. Errors in the forecast in Eq. (1) are the result of new information arriving. This new information should affect the forecast errors in Eq. (2) as well. Therefore, an appropriate test of the unbiased expectations hypothesis in Eqs. (1) and (2) is to examine the covariation of the forecast errors. Consequently, the Meiselman error learning model estimates the following regressions for $t = 3$ through n:

$$f\tau_{t+1} - f\tau_t = a_j + b_j[R_{t+2} - f2_t] + \varepsilon. \tag{3}$$

Meiselman (1962) argues that the intercepts a_j should be zero. Otherwise, forward rates are biased predictors of future spot rates. Kessel (1977) pointed out that zero intercepts are necessary but not sufficient conditions for the unbiased expectations hypothesis. He showed that zero intercepts are possible when liquidity premiums exist.

Meiselman, using the Durand data, finds the intercepts (a_j) to be close to zero and the slopes (b_j) significantly positive (see Table 1). He interprets his finding that

Table 1. Error Learning Model for Durand Data, Used by Meiselman (Annual Periods)

	Coefficients[a]		
Period	*a*	b_1	R^2
$t+3$	0.000005	0.70	0.91
	(0.9831)	(0.0001)	
$t+4$	−0.00023	0.52	0.75
	(0.9412)	(0.0001)	
$t+5$	0.000069	0.40	0.59
	(0.8462)	(0.0001)	
$t+6$	−0.000303	0.33	0.46
	(0.4127)	(0.0001)	
$t+7$	−0.000146	0.28	0.41
	(0.6750)	(0.0001)	
$t+8$	−0.000060	0.23	0.39
	(0.8452)	(0.0001)	
$t+9$	−0.000147	0.24	0.40
	(0.6382)	(0.0001)	
$t+10$	0.000058	0.21	0.35
	(0.8441)	(0.0001)	

Notes: [a]Numbers below coefficients are probabilities that the coefficients are zero.

changes in forecast errors are positively related to be consistent with the unbiased expectations hypothesis. The major point of our paper is that it is perfectly plausible that the unbiased expectations hypothesis is not true and that the Meiselman error learning model finds forward interest rate changes to be positively correlated.

An implication of the unbiased expectations hypothesis and market efficiency is that forecasted changes in spot and forward rates should be reflected in current security prices at time t. The forecasted change in spot interest rates (if the unbiased expectations hypothesis is true) is $f2_t - R_{t+1}$. To eliminate opportunities for excess profits in an efficient market, this expected change should be reflected in security prices at time t, and therefore be uncorrelated with changes in forward interest rates from t until time $t + 1$. Thus, the appropriate test to examine the joint hypotheses of efficient markets, error learning, and the unbiased expectations hypothesis is to run the following regressions for $t = 3$ through n (Δ denotes change).

$$\Delta \text{ forward rate} = a + b_1 \cdot [\text{unanticipated } \Delta] + b_2 \cdot [\text{anticipated } \Delta] + \varepsilon \quad (4)$$

$$f\tau_{t+1} - f\tau_t = a_\tau + b_{1,\tau}[R_{t+2} - f2_t] + b_2 + [f2_t - R_{t+1}] + \varepsilon_{r,t}. \quad (5)$$

Inferences based on the least squares estimation of Eq. (5) and on the resulting standard deviations would be biased if the forecasted change in forward rate (the LHS of Eq. [5]) is heteroskedastic and/or serially correlated. A voluminous literature reports the time-varying risk premia in the mean present in this type of regression and conditional heteroskedastic disturbance terms ε_t (see Engle, Lilien, and Robins [1987] and, more recently, an extensive survey by Bollerslev, Chou, and Kroner [1990]). This literature suggests that statistically significant values of a_τ and $b_{2,\tau}$, which should be zero if forward rates are unbiased predictors, would arise if one does not consider the time variation in risk premium. Stated differently, the part of the variation in the forecasted change in forward rate may be predictable using currently available information.

One way of handling the regression with serially dependent and/or conditionally heteroskedastic disturbances would be to employ the generalized method of moments (GMM) method (Hansen, 1982) to obtain robust standard deviations. This paper, however, also estimates the GARCH-M (generalized autoregressive conditional heteroskedasticity in mean) type model directly (Bollerslev, 1986; Engle, Lilien, and Robins, 1987). The Lagrange multiplier test for the presence of ARCH effects indeed suggests strong persistence of the squared residuals in Eq. (5). Since the GARCH (1,1) model specification for the disturbance terms is one way of parsimonious modeling of such persistence and is often found to be sufficient in the earlier empirical term structure literature, we may rewrite the Eq. (5) as

$$f\tau_{t+1} - f\tau_t = a_{0,\tau} + a_{1,\tau}h_t^{1/2} + b_{1,\tau}[R_{t+2} - f2_t] + b_{2,\tau}[f2_t - R_{t+1}] + \varepsilon_{\tau,t}, \tau = 3, \ldots n (6)$$

Table 2. Possible Results of Joint Tests of Error Learning and the Unbiased Expectations Hypothesis

Unbiased Expectations Hypothesis	*Error Learning* True $b_1 > 0$	*Error Learning* Not True $b_1 < 0$
True		
$a = 0$	$a = 0$	$a = 0$
	$b_1 > 0$	$b_1 \leq 0$
$b_2 = 0$	$b_2 = 0$	$b_2 = 0$
Not True		
$a \neq 0$	$a \neq 0$	$a \neq 0$
	$b_1 > 0$	$b_1 \leq 0$
$b_2 \neq 0$	$b_2 \neq 0$	$b_2 \neq 0$

$$\varepsilon_{\tau,t} \,|\, \Omega_{t-1} \sim N(0, h_{\tau,t})$$

$$h_{\tau,t} = \gamma_{0,\tau} + \gamma_{1,\tau}\varepsilon^2_{\tau,t-1} + \gamma_{2,\tau}h_{\tau,t-1},$$

where Ω_{t-1} is a currently available information set. The log likelihood function of this model and the maximum likelihood estimation procedure are described in detail in Bollerslev (1986) and Engle, Lilien, and Robins (1987).

If forward rates are unbiased predictors, the coefficients $b_{2,\tau}$ should be zero. If $b_{2,\tau}$ is nonzero, the unbiased expectations hypothesis is contradicted. If error learning is supported, $b_{1,\tau}$ is positive.

The various possible signs are shown in Table 2. It is plausible that $b_1 > 0$ (as Meiselman found) and $b_2 \neq 0$, meaning that error learning exists but the unbiased expectations hypothesis is not supported by the data. Alternatively, if $b_2 = 0$ and $b_1 > 0$, both error learning and the unbiased expectations hypothesis occur. Finally, if error learning is not found ($b_1 = 0$), this approach would still provide a test of the unbiased expectations hypothesis.

III. EMPIRICAL RESULTS

The model is tested on monthly Treasury bill data from August 1964 through December 1990. Table 3 shows the regression results for Eq. (5) applied to Treasury bill data. The data are taken from the 1991 CRSP Government Bond Tape, specifically the TBILLAVE file, which contains monthly forward rates from August 1964 through December 1990. To obtain a robust standard deviation, we use a heteroskedasticity and autocorrelation consistent covariance estimator of Newey and West (1987) with lag length equal to $2 \cdot (\tau - 3)$. The t-statistics from the Newey and West procedure are denoted as *NWt* in Table 3. Table 3 also reports the t-statistics based on least squares as well as regression R^2.

Table 3. Parameter Estimates for Equation (5)[a]

Period $(t + \tau)$		α	b_1	b_2	R^2
$t + 3$		−0.00011	0.68	0.17	0.45
	OLSt	(−3.54)	(15.81)	(3.00)	
	NWt	(−3.01)	(9.12)	(1.98)	
$t + 4$		0.00014	0.65	0.14	0.36
	OLSt	(3.78)	(12.96)	(2.10)	
	NWt	(3.23)	(7.94)	(1.64)	
$t + 5$		0.00000	0.64	0.10	0.33
	OLSt	(0.00)	(12.15)	(1.44)	
	NWt	(0.00)	(6.38)	(0.99)	
$t + 6$		0.00010	0.56	0.12	0.30
	OlSt	(2.79)	(11.34)	(1.73)	
	NWt	(2.79)	(7.36)	(1.01)	
$t + 7$		0.00015	0.47	0.11	0.18
	OLSt	(3.40)	(8.04)	(1.42)	
	NWt	(2.77)	(4.12)	(0.96)	
$t + 8$		−0.00004	0.53	0.06	0.22
	OLSt	(−0.84)	(9.18)	(0.81)	
	NWt	(−0.94)	(8.87)	(0.73)	
$t + 9$		0.00006	0.64	0.25	0.26
	OLSt	(1.36)	(10.52)	(3.04)	
	NWt	(1.35)	(4.14)	(1.71)	

Notes: [a] $f\tau_{t+1} - f\tau_t = a_\tau + b_{1,\tau}[R_{t+2} - f2_t] + b_{2,,\tau}[f2_t - R_{t+1}] + \varepsilon_{r,t}, \tau = 3, ..., n.$

Data we use are Treasury bill rates from the CRSP tape for the 1964:08–1990:12 period. t-statistics based on a heteroskedasticity and autocorrelation consistent covariance estimator of Newey and West (1987) with lag length equal to $2 \cdot (\tau - 3)$, denoted as *NWt*, are reported along with OLS t-statistics.

Table 4. Parameter Estimates for Equation (6)[a]

Period $(t+\tau)$	$a_{0,\tau}$	$a_{1,\tau}$	$b_{1,\tau}$	$b_{2,\tau}$	$\gamma_{0,\tau}$	$\gamma_{1,\tau}$	$\gamma_{0,\tau}$	*Lik*
$t+3$	−0.037	−0.254	0.561	0.160	0.010	0.292	0.687	−153.65
	(−0.70)	(−1.69)	(11.95)	(2.40)	(2.03)	(4.32)	(10.14)	
$t+4$	0.090	−0.004	0.580	0.108	0.014	0.182	0.784	−216.46
	(1.04)	(−0.02)	(10.46)	(1.62)	(1.97)	(3.65)	(13.09)	
$t+5$	0.137	−0.405	0.565	0.170	0.015	0.192	0.773	−220.50
	(1.91)	(−2.42)	(10.04)	(2.54)	(2.05)	(3.70)	(11.09)	
$t+6$	0.126	−0.102	0.537	0.118	0.040	0.155	0.715	−241.00
	(0.90)	(−0.36)	(8.97)	(1.49)	(1.84)	(2.72)	(6.10)	
$t+7$	0.327	−0.302	0.447	0.085	0.057	0.282	0.591	−276.49
	(2.59)	(−1.33)	(6.08)	(0.98)	(2.02)	(3.12)	(4.90)	
$t+8$	0.024	−0.233	0.405	0.035	0.084	0.572	0.367	−282.06
	(0.29)	(−1.52)	(7.03)	(0.49)	(3.19)	(3.03)	(3.36)	
$t+9$	0.140	−0.207	0.437	0.179	0.073	0.326	0.543	−285.49
	(1.12)	(−0.93)	(6.58)	(2.12)	(2.01)	(2.54)	(3.68)	

Notes: $f\tau_{t+1} - f\tau_t = a_{0,\tau} + a_{1,\tau}h_t^{1/2} + b_{1,\tau}[R_{t+2} - f2_t] + b_{2,\tau}[f2_t - R_{t+1}] + \varepsilon_{\tau,t}$, $\tau = 3, \ldots, n$.

$$\varepsilon_{\tau,t} \mid \Omega_{t-1} \sim N(0, h_{\tau,t})$$

$$h_{\tau,t} = \gamma_{0,\tau} + \gamma_{1,\tau}\varepsilon^2_{\tau,t-1} + \gamma_{2,\tau}h_{\tau,t-1}.$$

Data we use are Treasury bill rates from the CRSP tape for the 1964:08–1990:12 period. It is multiplied by 1,000 before the GARCH (1,1)-M model estimation. Asymptotic t-statistics are in parentheses.

The significant b_1 terms indicate error learning, or at least the change in forward rates is positively correlated with unanticipated changes in the spot rate. The evidence for the unbiased expectations hypothesis is mixed. Although none of the slope coefficients, b_2, is highly significant, a few of the intercepts are. There will be more on this result when we see the results of GARCH.

Table 4 presents the results from the ML estimation of the GARCH(1,1) in mean specification, Eq. (6). Data are multiplied by 1,000 before the estimation. Conditional heteroskedasticity appears to be significant (significant γ's) and strongly persistent ($\gamma_1 + \gamma_2$ close to one). On the other hand, a_1 coefficients are all insignificant, except at $\tau + 4$ with negative value, implying that the effects of changing risk in mean may be trivial. Results from different specification such as use of $\ln h_t$ or h_t, instead of $h_t^{1/2}$, were very similar. The b_1 coefficients are positive and statistically significant at the 1% level for every maturity, indicating evidence of error learning. The coefficient for the anticipated change (b_2) is found to be statistically different from zero at the 5% level for 3 out of 7 periods across the term structure. Two intercepts (a_j) are statistically different from zero at the 5% level. In

4 out of 7 cases, the a_j and/or the b_2 coefficients are different from zero at the 5% level.

These results provide evidence supporting error learning and contradicting the unbiased expectations hypothesis. The evidence against the unbiased expectations hypothesis is statistically significant but not overwhelming. First, although a number of intercepts are statistically significant, their absolute size is small. Second, the explanatory power of the b_2 coefficients is small. The evidence supports error learning but raises doubts about the validity of the unbiased expectations hypothesis.

IV. CONCLUSIONS

In this paper, a simultaneous test of the unbiased expectations hypothesis and error learning is presented. Although error learning is found, there is some evidence inconsistent with the unbiased expectations hypothesis. The error learning model is not a valid test of the unbiased expectations hypothesis. Based on the empirical evidence, expectations affect the term structure, but not in the way suggested by the pure unbiased expectations hypothesis.

NOTE

1. The results found in this paper are in some ways similar to Fama (1984a), although Fama uses different variables. First, Fama (1984a, Eq. [7]) finds that realized risk premiums are positively related to predicted changes in spot rates, contradicting the unbiased expectations hypothesis. Second, actual changes in spot rates (1984a, Eq. [8]) are positively, but not perfectly, related to predicted changes in spot rates. Thus, Fama does not present a joint test of error learning and the unbiased expectations hypothesis.

REFERENCES

Bollerslev, T. (1986). "Generalized Autoregressive Conditional Heteroskedasticity." *Journal of Econometrics* 31, 307–327.

Bollerslev, T., Chou, R. Y., and Kroner, K. F. (1990). "ARCH Modeling in Finance: A Review of the Theory and Empirical Evidence." Working Paper, Northwestern University.

Campbell, T. S. (1988). *Money and Capital Markets.* Glenview, IL: Scott, Foresman.

Engle, R. F., Lilien, D. M., and Robins, R. P. (1987). "Estimating Time Varying Risk Premia in the Term Structure: the ARCH-M Model." *Econometrica* 55, 391–407.

Fama, E. F. (1976). "Forward Rates as Predictors of Future Spot Rates." *Journal of Financial Economics* 3, 361–377.

Fama, E. F. (1984a). "The Information in the Term Structure." *Journal of Financial Economics* 13, 509–528.

Fama, E. F. (1984b). "Term Premiums in Bond Returns." *Journal of Financial Economics* 13, 529–546.

Hansen, L. P. (1982). "Large Sample Properties of Generalized Method of Moments Estimators." *Econometrica* 50, 1029–1054.

Kessel, R. A. (1977). "The Cyclical Behavior of the Term Structure of Interest Rates." In Jack M. Guttentag, ed., *Essays in Interest Rates*, vol. 2. New York: National Bureau of Economics Research.

McCallum, J. S. (1975). "The Expected Holding Period Return, Uncertainty and the Term Structure of Interest Rates." *Journal of Finance* 30, 307–323.

Meiselman, D. (1962). *The Term Structure of Interest Rates*. Englewood Cliffs, NJ: Prentice Hall.

Newey, W. K., and West, K. D. (1987). "A Simple Positive Semi-Definite, Heteroskedasticity and Autocorrelation Consistent Covariance Matrix." *Econometrica* 55, 703–708.

Rose, P. S. (1989). *Money and Capital Markets*, 3d ed. Homewood, IL: Richard D. Irwin.

Startz, R. (1982). "Do Forecast Errors or Term Premia Really Make the Difference Between Long and Short Rates?" *Journal of Financial Economics* 10, 323–329.

Van Horne, J. (1987). *Financial Markets: Rates and Flows*, 2d ed. Englewood Cliffs, NJ: Prentice Hall.

Wood, J. H. (1963). "Expectations, Error, and the Term Structure of Interest Rates." *Journal of Political Economy* 71, 160–171.

MONDAYS, FRIDAYS, AND FRIDAY THE THIRTEENTH

Ramon P. DeGennaro

ABSTRACT

Previous research has established that stock returns tend to be low on Mondays and high on Fridays and suggests that stock returns on Friday the thirteenth may be less than on other Fridays. We find that in a longer time series than previously studied, this difference is no longer significant at conventional levels. More important, we find significantly *positive* returns in six-month Treasury bills and in three different maturities of government bonds. The magnitude of this effect increases with maturity. We uncover no statistically reliable evidence of differences between Friday the Thirteenths and other Fridays in three-month Treasury bills, three different futures contracts or in federal funds.

I. INTRODUCTION AND PREVIOUS RESEARCH

The Efficient Market Hypothesis implies that no trading rule can earn abnormal returns without correspondingly higher risk. In its simplest form, it implies that no

Advances in Quantitative Analysis of Finance and Accounting,
Volume 2, Part A, pages 115–137.

ISBN: 1-55938-564-2

calendar effects can exist. Many researchers, however, have documented several such anomalies. These include the well-known turn-of-the-year effect, size effect, and day-of-the-week effect.

Cross (1973) provides the first evidence that mean returns on Mondays and Fridays differ. He compares 844 paired Monday and Friday observations on the Standard and Poor's Composite Index from January 2, 1953, through December 21, 1970. The results are astonishing. The index rises 62% of the Fridays but only 39.5% of the Mondays. For each of the 18 years, the mean Friday return exceeds the mean Monday return, and the difference is significant in 17 of those years. Cross gives no explanation for this anomaly.

In retrospect, it is perhaps equally astonishing that Cross's paper should generate no further attention for seven years. French (1980) is the first of many papers since to appear that documents the existence of what has come to be regarded as the day-of-the-week effect or the Monday effect. Using the Standard and Poor's Composite Index from 1953 through 1977, French formally tests two models of the stock-return generating process, the trading-time model, and the calendar-time model. The former asserts that returns are generated only when markets are open. Monday's average return should equal Friday's average return if this model is true. The latter model argues that the return-generating model operates continuously, so that Monday's return should be three times that of the other days of the week because investors expect returns to be earned for Saturday and Sunday as well as for Monday. In fact, French shows that neither model holds. Consistent with Cross (1973), Monday's returns are on average negative, whereas Friday's returns are on average positive. French also develops a Bayesian argument to show that the negative returns on Mondays have been so persistently negative that investors must actually expect such results.

Gibbons and Hess (1981) extend the day-of-the-week effect to the stocks comprising the Dow Jones Industrial Average (DJIA) and to Treasury bills. All thirty stocks in the DJIA show negative returns on Mondays during the sample, which extends from July 3, 1962, through December 28, 1978. For bills, the sample period is from December 28, 1962, through December 27, 1968. The results reveal that Mondays offer low returns, but neither Monday's nor Friday's return is best or worst: Thursday's return is the highest and Tuesday's is the lowest. Gibbons and Hess test and reject several possible explanations for their results. For example, they correct for nonstationarity and heteroskedasticity. Neither of these affects the results. They also reject that measurement error or settlement effects are important.

In contrast, Oldfield and Rogalski (1980) claim that common stock returns do not differ according to the day of the week. Using the Kruskal–Wallis test on returns data on five stocks from October 1, 1974, through December 31, 1977, they are unable to reject the hypothesis of no day-of-the-week effects at the 1% level of significance. Further, they are unable to reject, also at the 1% level of significance, that overnight returns on all periods except Friday to Monday are drawn from the same distribution. However, these results are not conclusive because of the limited sample of firms. Also, although Oldfield and Rogalski cannot establish significance at the 1% level, some of their tests are indeed significant at the 5% level.

Lakonishok and Levi (1982) take a different approach. Rather than presuming that stock returns should be equal across days of the week, they argue that *observed* returns should be higher on Fridays and lower on Mondays because of the delivery and payment procedures in the stock markets. Lakonishok and Levi explain that delivery in the United States takes five business days, and that a check presented at settlement requires an additional day to clear, for a total of six. Until delivery, the buyer need not put up funds, and the seller cannot use the proceeds of the sale. They argue that rational investors recognize this and bid up prices to compensate sellers for the lost opportunity cost on the sale. Counting the check-clearing day and ignoring holidays, this delay is eight calendar days on all days except Fridays, when it is ten.

This suggests that Friday's price includes ten days' worth of interest, while the rest of the days of the week contain only eight. Therefore, Friday's price is higher than the other days of the week by two days' worth of interest. It follows that Friday's return should be higher than average. Further, since Monday's price contains only eight days' worth of interest compared to Friday's ten, Monday's return should be lower. Holidays alter the pattern of interest adjustments in a predictable manner. Most important, measured stock returns are affected by holidays more than a week before the holiday.

To test their conjecture, Lakonishok and Levi add two days' worth of interest (based on the prime rate) to Friday's return and subtract two days' worth of interest from Monday's return, taking care to treat holidays correctly. They find this greatly reduces the day-of-the-week effect. The returns on Fridays are considerably reduced, and Monday's returns are larger. However, the conjecture that returns are equal on all days of the week after controlling for delays is rejected.

Dyl and Martin (1985) conclude that the Lakonishok and Levi story cannot explain why Monday's average return is low and Friday's average return is high. They argue that if delays do explain the weekly pattern, then an abrupt change in this pattern should have been observed on February 9, 1968. Until then, the official settlement delay was only four business days rather than five. Check-clearing delays would have made the total delay five business days before February 9, 1968, and six thereafter. Dyl and Martin provide evidence that no substantial change in the weekly pattern occurred on that date. However, Lakonishok and Levi (1985) reply that the distinction between settlement regimes might not have been as abrupt as officially stated. They point out that the primary reason for the change in delivery procedures was that heavy trading often made settlement unreliable. If buyers could not be sure of the total delay, they might have bid prices to a different premium than that predicted by the official delivery schedules. A weekly pattern could have remained. Lakonishok and Levi also point to a major omission in Dyl and Martin's work: the empirical tests drop weeks with holidays. Since the payment-delay story implies investors bid up returns *in advance* of the holiday, simply dropping the week with the holiday is insufficient. For example, consider a Monday holiday. Trades made the previous Monday do not settle on the holiday but rather on the Tuesday after the holiday. Prices on the previous Monday are bid up not by eight business days' worth of interest but rather by nine. Further, all trades during that week would be affected by the holiday in the next week. Lakonishok and Levi argue that dropping the week with the holiday does not test the model on its own ground.

DeGennaro (1990) explicitly tests whether investors consider the six-business-day payment delay in the equities markets. His results fall midway between Lakonishok and Levi (1982, 1985) and Dyl and Martin (1985). Although he finds that investors do consider the delay in pricing assets, he also shows that the delays are unable to explain the weekly pricing pattern.

Baillie and DeGennaro (1989) show that payment delays are an important determinant of stock-return volatility. They show that the reduction in volatility when markets are closed is even more extreme than suggested by French and Roll (1986). After controlling for the disruption of the delivery schedules due to weekends and holidays, the volatility-generating function is virtually inactive when the stock markets are closed.

Rogalski (1984) decomposes daily stock returns into close-to-open and open-to-close components. He finds that the negative returns on Monday occur between Friday's closing price and Monday's opening price. He cannot reject the hypothesis that open-to-close returns are equal across all days of the week. Rogalski also reports that during the month of January, returns from Friday's close to Monday's close, as well as from Friday's close to Monday's open, are positive. Rogalski also uses the CRSP daily stock file from January 1963 through December 1982 to form portfolios based on market value of equity, reporting that portfolios of all sizes do well on Friday. However, smaller portfolios perform best. In fact, mean returns are monotonically decreasing in firm size, and Friday is the only day of the week to demonstrate this relationship.

Keim and Stambaugh (1984) extend the sample period to 55 years. They find a significant day-of-the-week effect exists during their sample period. They examine several possible explanations, including measurement errors and specialist-related bias, but conclude none is satisfactory. Their longer sample period also permits tests of the day-of-the-week effect during periods when the stock market was open on Saturdays. During these times, Friday's mean return was not better than average; Saturday's was. Monday's average returns are not affected by Saturday trading: they remain well below average. Interestingly, small firms offer better Friday returns than large firms but only equally poor Monday returns. This is consistent with the well-known size effect of Banz (1981) and Reinganum (1981). Keim and Stambaugh also document that the weekly seasonal return pattern is not substantially different for stocks traded over the counter.

Harris (1986) examines data from individual transactions during the period December 1, 1981, through January 31, 1983. He finds that the negative returns on Mondays tend to occur between Friday's close and Monday's open for large firms, but from Monday's open to Monday's close for small firms. Surprisingly, prices typically drop for all firms during the first 45 minutes of trading on Monday but tend to rise during that period on all other days of the week. Fridays have the largest mean close-to-close return, while Mondays have the smallest.

Smirlock and Starks (1986) use hourly data from 1963 through 1983 on the DJIA. They report that the weekend effect has been "moving up" in time. For example, from January 1, 1963, through February 9, 1968, the negative returns occur during trading on Monday; the mean return from Friday's close to Monday's open is positive. From February 10, 1968, through September 30, 1974, however, returns from both Friday's close to Monday's open and during trading on Monday are negative. In their most recent sample period, from October 1, 1974, through December 31, 1983, the mean return from Friday's close to Monday's open is negative, whereas during trading on Monday, mean returns are positive. Regardless of the return measure (close to close, close to open, or open to close), Monday's mean return is the smallest. Friday's mean return is the second largest according to all three measures, behind Wednesday, Thursday, and Wednesday, respectively.

Lakonishok and Smidt (1988) extend the time series on the DJIA to encompass the 90 years from 1897 through 1986. They report that Monday's mean return is the lowest, while the last trading day of the week—typically Friday, but Saturday during portions of the sample—has the highest mean returns. During the entire sample, the annualized Monday return is on average minus 30%. In other words, a 250-day year consisting of only Mondays would result in a 30% loss of wealth! In contrast, Fridays have a relatively high return during the full 90-year sample.

II. FRIDAY THE THIRTEENTH

Kolb and Rodriguez (1987) uncover yet another effect, the Friday the thirteenth effect. They report that on this unlucky day, stock returns as measured by a wide variety of indexes are significantly lower than on other Fridays. For value weighted indexes, average returns are in fact negative. They interpret these results—perhaps facetiously—as supporting the hypothesis that the market may be affected by superstition.

But whether Kolb and Rodriguez's intent is to identify a possible market inefficiency or simply to make sport of a profession obsessed with documenting such inefficiencies, their results are curious. Indeed, since the value of a theory lies in the predictions it makes and not in how reasonable it appears, Kolb and Rodriguez raise some interesting questions. Suppose the superstition hypothesis is true. What other predictions does it make? Does it extend to other assets? If so, is some pattern identifiable? What do the answers to these questions mean for the Friday the thirteenth effect in the stock market?

This paper addresses these questions. First, it shows that the results of Kolb and Rodriguez do not necessarily hold given the most recent stock return data. Although returns on Friday the thirteenth remain substantially less than on other Fridays, the difference is no longer statistically reliable at the 5% level. This is consistent with Dyl and Maberly (1988). Also, the predictions of the superstition hypothesis do not extend to two other important markets, the futures market and the federal funds market. However, the negative stock returns on Friday the thirteenth are still significant at the 10% level. In addition, the price change in Treasury bill futures is at least *fifty times* larger than on other Fridays, and for stock-index futures, the Friday the thirteenth price change is at least *one hundred times* larger; however, the small sample sizes prevent establishing statistical significance.

Perhaps most interesting, the holding period returns on Treasury bills and government bonds on Friday the thirteenth are significantly *greater* than on other Fridays, and the disparity increases with maturity. For thirty-year bonds, the returns on Friday the thirteenth are more than thirty-seven times larger than on other Fridays. These results suggest that although it may (or may not) be appropriate to argue that the stock market is affected by superstition, at least one scenario cannot be rejected given the data: we cannot reject that new money flowing to the financial markets on Friday the thirteenth tends to be directed to the bond markets rather than the stock markets.

If the bond market becomes more volatile on Friday the thirteenth, the positive returns could be consistent with market efficiency. However, we develop evidence that suggests the bond market may actually become less volatile as Friday the thirteenth approaches and more volatile after the day has passed. This argues against explanations for the higher returns based on risk. In addition, the variance of returns on Friday the thirteenth itself is the same as other Fridays for all assets studied.

The surprising result that a predictable event such as Friday the thirteenth generates unusual returns without any substantial change in risk is clearly inconsistent with market efficiency. No rational investor would purchase stocks at the close of trading on Thursday the twelfth and bear the loss on Friday the thirteenth. Further, barring an urgent demand for cash that could not be met in a less costly way, none would sell bills or bonds at the close of trading on Thursday the twelfth and forego the gain on Friday the thirteenth. We conclude, therefore, that although the evidence in favor of such an effect in the stock market is less substantial than it first appeared, the superstition hypothesis cannot yet be dismissed as a mere statistical artifact.

III. DATA

Our sample consists of stock returns, federal funds rates, United States Government Treasury bill and bond holding-period returns, and three futures prices: on the New York Stock Exchange Composite Index, the Value Line Index, and Treasury bills. Stock returns are measured by the four CRSP indexes: equal- and value-weighted, with and without dividends. These data extend from July 3, 1962, through December 31, 1987. Federal funds rates and government bill and bond rates are from the Federal Reserve Board. For comparison with stocks, these also extend from July 3, 1962, through December 31, 1987, but since trading days do not precisely match, the number of observations varies slightly across assets. Twenty- and thirty-year bond rates are available from December 29, 1969, through December 31, 1986, and from February 15, 1977, through December 31, 1987, respectively.

Bid yields for next-day delivery are available for both three-month and six-month bills. To obtain the holding-period return, we compute prices based on the usual formula,

$$P = 100[1 - (d * m)/360],$$

where P is the price, d is the quoted discount, and m is the number of days till maturity at delivery. Because quotations are collected too late in the day for same-day delivery, we assume delivery is on the next business day, which is the usual procedure. We compute holding-period returns on day $t + 1$ as $(P_{t+1}/P_t) - 1$.

Government bond yield data are available for ten, twenty, and thirty-year maturities. For the ten-year bonds, observations from the full sample are available. For twenty- and thirty-year bonds, seventeen and eleven years' worth of data are available, respectively. The yields are the Federal Reserve's constant-maturity series. Since the Fed's stated goal in collecting these data is to estimate yields required to sell new securities at par, we compute prices as follows. For each day t, we assume that the bond sells at par and carries a coupon equal to that day's yield. At $t + 1$, we compute the price of this security by discounting all cash flows from the bond at the yield applicable to day $t + 1$. Returns on day $t + 1$ are computed as $(P_{t+1}/1{,}000) - 1$. This procedure ignores accrued interest and the effects of any favored tax treatment for capital gains. We justify this since price changes over one trading day are small and are unlikely to be affected by this. Further, there is no reason to expect this procedure to bias returns on either Friday or Friday the thirteenth.

Futures contracts on financial assets did not exist until relatively recently, so data are not available for the same time period as for the other assets. Nevertheless, it is useful to study them since investors view these instruments as alternatives to holding the assets themselves. We use both stock index futures and Treasury bill futures. The stock index futures are on the Value Line Index, traded on the Kansas City Futures Exchange, and on the New York Stock Exchange Composite (NYSE) Index, traded on the New York Futures Exchange. The Value Line series extends from March 30, 1982, through December 31, 1987, and the NYSE series extends from May 6, 1982, through December 31, 1987. Data for the Treasury bill futures, traded on the Chicago Mercantile Exchange, extend from December 1, 1977, through December 31, 1987.[1] Since futures contracts require no investment, we simply measure returns as price changes.

IV. RESULTS

A. Stocks

Our method is similar to that of Kolb and Rodriguez (1987). We compute t-statistics to test the hypothesis that the returns on Friday the thirteenth differ from the returns on other Fridays. For stocks, our sample contains 1,279 Fridays, of which 43 are Friday the thirteenths. This represents 99 more Fridays and 3 more Friday the thirteenths than in Kolb and Rodriguez (1987).

Table 1 presents the results. Compared to Kolb and Rodriguez, we find that in our longer time series, Friday the thirteenths are no longer worse than other Fridays at the 5% level. For example, for their value-weighted index with dividends, they report a mean Friday the thirteenth return of –0.001. We obtain –0.0005. Their corresponding t-statistic is –1.91, while ours is only –1.45. However, the result is not decisive: Kolb and Rodriguez justify using a one-tailed test since the null hypothesis is that Friday the thirteenths are worse than other Fridays. Using a one-tailed test, we reject the null for all four indexes at the 10% level. The negative mean is not due to outliers: on the value-weighted indexes, for example, 22 of the 43 Friday the thirteenth returns in our sample are negative and 21 are positive. The results using all four indexes are similar. Although some evidence of a low return on Friday the thirteenth remains, our t-statistics are always less significant and the estimated mean return for Friday the thirteenth is always higher than Kolb and Rodriguez report.

The similarity across all indexes extends to the second moment. While certain seasonal effects in variance have been reported (see, for example, French and Roll, 1986), F-tests fail to reject the null hypothesis of equal variances for Friday the thirteenth and other Fridays. Although not reported here for reasons of space, we replicated Kolb and Rodriguez's results and found this is also true during their sample period.

Table 1. Comparison of Means: Friday the Thirteenth and Other Fridays: Stocks

Sample period: July 3, 1962, to December 31, 1987	*Friday the Thirteenth*		*Other Fridays*		*t-Statistic for Equal Mean Returns*
	n	*Mean*	*n*	*Mean*	
Stock Index					
CRSP VW with dividends	43	–0.00051	1,236	0.00113	–1.45*
CRSP VW without dividends	43	–0.00057	1,236	0.00099	–1.38*
CRSP EW with dividends	43	0.00077	1,236	0.00228	–1.36*
CRSP EW without dividends	43	0.00071	1,236	0.00217	–1.32*

Notes: *Significant at the 10% level.

T-tests are one-tailed. The table is constructed such that a positive t-statistic indicates the return on Friday the thirteenth is larger than on other Fridays.

Risk during the Event Period

Although our results suggest that the Friday the thirteenth effect has diminished, it is worth examining the risk of equities during the period surrounding Friday the thirteenth in an attempt to explain the unusual pattern of returns. To do this, we draw on the results of Lockwood and Kadiyala (1988).[2] They test whether the systematic and unsystematic risk of holding equities changes during and after stock splits. They find little evidence that systematic risk changes during the event period, but report that unsystematic risk is concave during the period surrounding the stock split.

If the superstition hypothesis is true, it is reasonable to suspect that investors may perceive risk to be concave during the period surrounding Friday the thirteenth. To study this, we estimate an augmented market model:

$$R_{it} = \alpha_i + \beta_{i1}R_{mt} + \beta_{i2}[(T1 - t)(t - T2)D1_t]R_{mt}$$

$$+ \beta_{i3}[(T2 - T1)D2_t + (t - T1)D1_t]R_{mt} + \varepsilon_t, \qquad (1)$$

where

R_{it}	=	the return on stock i at time t,
R_{mt}	=	the return on the CRSP value-weighted index, including dividends, at time t,
$T1$	=	the first day of the event period (21 trading days before Friday the thirteenth),
$T2$	=	the last day of the event period (21 trading days after Friday the thirteenth),
$D1_t$	=	unity during the event period and zero otherwise,
$D2_t$	=	unity after the event period ends and zero otherwise.

The quadratic term $(T1-t)(t-T2)D1_t$ is zero until time $T1$, the beginning of the event period. It increases at a decreasing rate, peaking on the event date, and then declines at an increasing rate, reaching zero at time $T2$ and remaining zero thereafter. According to Lockwood and Kadiyala, if the estimate of β_2 is positive (negative), systematic risk is concave (convex) during the event period. The term in the last explanatory variable, $(T2-T1)D2_t + (t-T1)D1_t$, is also zero until the beginning of the event period. It then increases linearly during the event period and remains constant after the event period. Therefore, if the estimate of β_3 is positive (negative), systematic risk is greater (less) after the event than before.

Lockwood and Kadiyala (1988) use this approach to study stock splits. To avoid mixing the effects of more than one event, they eliminate stocks that undergo more than one spilt from their sample. This is not possible for our purposes because all stocks experience more than one event (Friday the thirteenth) during our sample.

Table 2. Summary Statistics for the Estimates Obtained by Regressing Individual Stock Returns (100 Randomly Selected) on the CRSP Value-Weighted Index, with Dividends, and Terms Controlling for the Convexity of and Permanent Changes in Market Risk[a]

		Positive Values		*Negative Values*	
Parameter	*Mean (t-Statistic)*	*Total*	*Significant*	*Total*	*Significant*
First sample: May 4, 1965–November 12, 1965: 127 Observations per stock					
α	6.45×10^{-4} (3.32) ***	64	1	36	1
β_1	0.942 (10.61)***	93	49	7	0
β_2	-3.63×10^{-4} (–0.95)	54	1	46	0
β_3	-2.80×10^{-4} (–0.08)	50	2	50	3
Second sample: July 17, 1967–January 16, 1968: 127 observations per stock					
α	1.56×10^{-3} (5.97) ***	75	5	25	0
β_1	1.16 (11.06)***	87	27	13	0
β_2	1.13×10^{-4} (0.32)	51	5	49	3
β_3	1.12×10^{-3} (0.38)	55	0	45	2
Third sample: May 14, 1971–November 11, 1971: 127 observations per stock					
α	-3.61×10^{-4} (–1.95) *	42	2	58	0
β_1	1.18 (12.52)***	92	54	8	0
β_2	2.28×10^{-4} (1.10)	52	9	48	5
β_3	-5.41×10^{-3} (–2.68)	40	2	60	7

(continued)

Table 2. (continued)

Parameter	Mean (t-Statistic)	Positive Values Total	Positive Values Significant	Negative Values Total	Negative Values Significant
Fourth sample: May 14, 1982–November 11, 1982: 127 observations per stock					
α	7.84×10^{-4} (4.15) ***	71	3	29	0
β_1	0.876 (11.60)***	89	42	11	0
β_2	-1.48×10^{-4} (−1.47)	40	3	60	2
β_3	-1.93×10^{-3} (−1.38)	46	1	54	4

Notes: [a]$R_{it} = \alpha_i + \beta_{i1}R_{mt} + \beta_{i2}[(T1 - t)(t - T2)D1_t]R_{mt} + \beta_{i3}[(T2 - T1)D2_t + (t - T1)D1_t]R_{mt} + \varepsilon_{it}$. (1)

R_{it} = return on stock i at time t.

R_{mt} = return on the CRSP value weighted index, with dividends, at time t,

$T1$ = first day of the event period (21 trading days before Friday the thirteenth),

$T2$ = last day of the event period (21 trading days after Friday the thirteenth),

$D1_t$ = unity during the event period and zero otherwise,

$D2_t$ = unity after the event period ends and zero otherwise.

*Significant at the 10% level.

***Significant at the 1% level.

To minimize any possible interaction effects caused by overlapping event periods, we use the Friday the thirteenths that are most isolated from other Friday the thirteenths. Four of these dates occur at least nine months before and after the nearest other Friday the thirteenth. These are August 13, 1965, October 13, 1967, August 13, 1971, and August 13, 1982. This permits us to define an event period two months long, centered on Friday the thirteenth, with pre- and postevent periods each two months long while still keeping the samples distinct from other Friday the thirteenths.[3]

We estimate Eq. (1) for 100 randomly selected stocks in each sample. The stocks used need not be the same in each subperiod.[4] Summary statistics of the results are reported in Table 2. The estimated constant, α, is sometimes positive and sometimes negative. This is not surprising, since in the market model α estimates $(1 - \beta)$. Therefore, it may be positive or negative, depending on the systematic risk of the stock. The interpretation of the coefficient β_1 is more complex than in the usual market model, which restricts β_2 and β_3 to be zero. In that case, β_1 simply estimates systematic risk during the event period. If, however, β_2 is zero and β_3 is not, β_1 estimates systematic risk before and during the event period. If β_3 is zero and β_2 is not, β_1 estimates systematic risk before and after the event period. In all cases, however, risk-aversion suggests that β_1 should be positive.[5] The results are quite consistent with this: the smallest number of positive estimates occurs in the second sample period; even then, 87 estimates of β_1 are positive. The average β_1 ranges from a low of 0.876 in the fourth sample to a high of 1.18 in the third sample. Despite the relatively small number of observations on each stock, almost half the positive estimates are statistically significant, and the sample means are significantly different from zero in all four subperiods.[6]

Positive estimates of β_2 imply systematic risk is concave during the period surrounding Friday the thirteenth. We find relatively little evidence of this. For 100 stocks, we would expect sampling variation to cause about five t-statistics to exceed the 5% critical value in each subperiod. The actual values range from a low of 1 in the first sample to a high of 14 in the third (9 positive and 5 negative). For all four subperiods, we would expect a total of 10 significantly positive estimates and 10 significantly negative estimates. We obtain 18 and 10, respectively. We conclude that there is no substantial evidence of either concave or convex systematic risk during the period surrounding Friday the thirteenth.

Nonzero estimates of β_3 imply that systematic risk exits the event period at a different level than it entered. Again, we find little evidence of this. Estimates are almost equally divided between positive and negative values, and very few individual estimates are significant.

To study possible changes in unsystematic risk, we proceed as follows. For each of the four samples, we estimate the market model for each of the 100 securities:

$$R_{it} = a_i + b_{i1}R_{mt} + e_{it}. \tag{2}$$

We then regress the squared residuals from this regression on a constant, $(T1-t)(t-T2)D1_t$, and $[(T2-T1)D2_t + (t-T1)D1_t]$:

$$e_{it}^2 = \alpha_i + \beta_{i1}(T1-t)(t-T2)D1_t + \beta_{i2}[(T2-T1)D2_t + (t-T1)D1_t] + \varepsilon_{it}. \tag{3}$$

We expect α_i to be positive, while the interpretations of β_1 and β_2 are the same as for β_2 and β_3 in Eq. (1).

Sample statistics for the results are contained in Table 3. As expected, α is positive in all 400 cases. The estimate is significant 338 times, and the sample mean for the estimate of α is significant at the 1% level in all subperiods. For β_1, which tests for concavity of unsystematic risk, the results are less definitive. In each of the four sample periods, we would expect sampling variation to account for five significant estimates. Therefore, we would expect a total of 20 in all, which should be equally distributed between positive and negative values. In fact, we obtain substantially more: 28 positive estimates and 11 negative estimates are significant. However, other evidence suggests unsystematic risk may not be concave. First, although the number of significantly positive estimates is considerably greater than the number

Table 3. Summary Statistics for the Estimates Obtained by Regressing the Variance of Stock Returns on Terms Controlling for the Convexity of and Permanent Changes in Volatility[a]

		Positive Values		Negative Values	
Parameter	*Mean (t-Statistic)*	*Total*	*Significant*	*Total*	*Significant*
First sample: May 4, 1965–November 12, 1965: 127 observations per stock					
α	5.29×10^{-4} (6.84) ***	100	84	0	0
β_1	-6.0×10^{-8} (−0.41)	42	4	58	4
β_2	5.36×10^{-6} (3.03) ***	63	11	37	7
Second sample: July 17, 1967–January 16, 1968: 127 observations per stock					
α	6.74×10^{-3} (7.87) ***	100	85	0	0
β_1	-3.4×10^{-7} (−2.96)***	30	2	70	4
β_2	1.14×10^{-6} (0.84)	66	11	34	4
Third sample: May 14, 1971–November 11, 1971: 127 observations per stock					
α	5.72×10^{-4} (10.09) ***	100	87	0	0
β_1	2.8×10^{-7} (2.72)***	63	11	37	1
β_2	7.0×10^{-8} (0.08)	51	7	49	6
Fourth sample: May 14, 1982–November 11, 1982: 127 observations per stock					
α	4.91×10^{-4} (10.29) ***	100	82	0	0
β_1	4.9×10^{-7} (2.51)**	52	11	48	2
β_2	5.19×10^{-6} (4.33) ***	74	20	26	1

Notes: [a] $e_{it}^2 = \alpha_i + \beta_{i1}(T1 - t)(t - T2)D1_t + \beta_{i2}[(T2 - T1)D2_t + (t - T1)D1_t] + \varepsilon_{it}$.

$$e_{it}^2 = (R_{it} - \overline{R}_i)^2, \tag{3}$$

R_{it} = return on stock i at time t.
$\overline{R}_i = a_i + b_{i1}R_{mt}$, the conditional mean return on stock i,
$T1$ = the first day of the event period (21 trading days before Friday the thirteenth),
$T2$ = the last day of the event period (21 trading days after Friday the thirteenth),
$D1_t$ = unity during the event period and zero otherwise,
$D2_t$ = unity after the event period ends and zero otherwise.
*Significant at the 5% level.
***Significant at the 1% level.

of significant negative values, the number of negative estimates (213) is actually larger than the number of positive values (187). Second, although the mean estimate is significantly positive in the third and fourth samples, it is negative in the first sample and significantly negative in the second.

The most unusual results are for β_2. The number of positive estimates exceeds the number of negative estimates by 254 to 146, and the number of significant positive values is 49 compared to 18 negative values. This implies that the unsystematic risk of the firms after the event period is higher than before the period. However, it is unlikely that this is due to the event itself. It is more reasonable to suspect that the result is due to sampling variation or to a secular increase in volatility, especially during subperiod four, which has almost double the number of significantly positive estimates as any other subperiod.

To ensure that the results in Table 3 are not due to the behavior of the market proxy, we replace the market model (2) with

$$R_{it} = a_i + e_{it}, \tag{4}$$

and repeat the tests. Although not reported for reasons of space, the results are substantially the same as in Table 3.

B. Debt Securities

Kolb and Rodriguez justify using a one-tailed test for stocks since Friday the thirteenth is considered an unlucky day. However, this is not possible for other assets: either of two results could be interpreted as being consistent with the superstition hypothesis. First, one might argue that all assets should suffer lower than average returns on Friday the thirteenth. However, one might also claim that investors are less risk tolerant or perceive risk to be greater on Friday the thirteenth. If so, they may purchase fewer stocks and more lower-risk assets on Friday the thirteenth, thereby causing higher than average returns on assets such as government securities. Therefore, a two-tailed test must be used. Regardless of the sign of the return, though, without a corresponding change in risk, the returns on Friday the thirteenth should not differ from other Fridays in an efficient market. The t-ratio should not differ significantly from zero.

Federal Funds

Federal funds sometimes trade when stocks do not, so our sample of Fed funds rates is slightly larger; it contains 1,309 Fridays, of which 44 are Friday the thirteenths. Table 4 contains the results. In contrast to stock returns, we find no evidence of any Friday the thirteenth effect in federal funds. Fed funds rates on Friday the thirteenth are trivially lower than on other Fridays, but the difference is not statistically significant. On Friday the thirteenth, the average daily Fed funds rate is 0.000203, or 7.41% annually, while on other Fridays it is 0.000205, or 7.47%. The *t*-ratio is only –0.12. The variance of the Fed funds rate is slightly higher on other Fridays but not sufficiently so to establish statistical significance.

Treasury Bills

The abundant evidence that Monday's average stock return is low makes it difficult to argue that stocks earn returns when markets are closed for holidays and weekends. However, interest-bearing securities do earn interest during these times. This creates problems in computing holding-period returns on debt securities. In particular, 4 Friday the thirteenths and 45 other Fridays are influenced by holidays when the government securities market was closed on the previous Thursday. Including these returns in our tests might bias them. To circumvent this problem, therefore, we simply eliminate all returns that might be affected by holidays. The sample tested, then, includes 1,226 observations, including 39 Friday the thirteenths. To ensure this does not bias our comparisons with stock returns, we repeat those tests after discarding multiday returns. This has only a very minimal effect: all the *t*-ratios are slightly lower, but Friday the thirteenths remain substantially worse than other Fridays.

Table 4 shows that for three-month bills, returns on Friday the thirteenth are actually higher than on other Fridays, but the difference is not reliably different from zero. The average Friday the thirteenth return, reflecting a three-day cash investment from Friday the thirteenth to Monday the sixteenth, is 0.000635,

Table 4. Comparison of Means: Friday the Thirteenth and Other Fridays: Federal Funds and Government Debt Securities

Sample Periods Are from July 3, 1962, to December 31, 1987, except as Noted	*Friday the Thirteenth*		*Other Fridays*		*t-Statistic for Equal Mean Returns*
	n	*Mean*	*n*	*Mean*	
Federal funds	44	0.000203	1,265	0.000205	–0.12
Treasury bills					
Three-month	39	0.000635	1,187	0.000576	0.86
Six-month	39	0.000828	1,187	0.000602	2.02 **
Government bonds					
Ten Year	39	0.00218	1,186	0.00014	2.65 ***
Twenty Year Dec. 29, 1969–Dec. 31, 1986	25	0.00368	797	0.00033	2.53 **
Thirty Year Feb. 15, 1977–Dec. 31, 1987	18	0.00474	507	0.00013	2.39 **

Notes: ** Significant at the 5% level.
*** Significant at the 1% level.
T-tests are two-tailed. The table is constructed such that a positive *t*-statistic indicates that the return on Friday the thirteenth is larger than on other Fridays. Since bills and bonds are for next-day delivery, Friday's return reflects a three-day cash investment for those assets.

whereas for other Fridays it is 0.000576. The t-ratio is 0.86. However, for six-month bills, the effect is much more pronounced and indeed is statistically significant. The average Friday the thirteenth return is 0.000828; for other Fridays it is only 0.000602. These rates imply annualized returns of more than 10% on Friday the thirteenth and only about 7.3% on other Fridays. The t-statistic is 2.02, which is significant at the 5% level. Further, this increase does not come at the expense of higher risk: the variance of returns on Friday the thirteenth is only slightly higher than on other Fridays (4.95×10^{-7} compared to 4.72×10^{-7}), and the difference does not approach conventional significance levels.

Government Bonds

The ten-year government bond sample spans the same period as the Treasury bill sample, but since the Federal Reserve does not report yields for July 3, 1964, it contains one fewer observation.[7] We obtain 1,225 observations of which 39 are Friday the thirteenths. The surprising result that Treasury bills earn more on Friday the thirteenth than other Fridays is even more pronounced in the ten-year government bond market. In Table 4 we see that the average holding-period return on Friday the thirteenth is 0.00218, while for other Fridays it is only 0.00014. Given the three-day holding period, this is an annualized rate of 26.6% on Friday the thirteenth.[8] The difference is reliably different from zero, with a t-statistic of 2.65. As is true for Treasury bills, this larger return is not due to a substantially larger variance. On Friday the Thirteenth, the variance of return is 2.70×10^{-5}, while on other Fridays it is 2.24×10^{-5}. The difference is not statistically significant.

Furthermore, this difference in returns is not due to outliers. For example, repeating the test after deleting the two largest and two smallest Friday the thirteenth returns still obtains a significant difference. The t-statistic is –3.11. In addition, the nonparametric Mann–Whitney U-test rejects that the means are equal. The Z-score for the test is 2.89, which is significant at the 1% level. The van der Waerden test described by Lehmann (1975) rejects the null of equal means with a Z-score of 2.86.

The results using twenty- and thirty-year bonds are similar to those from the ten-year bonds. The sample period for twenty-year bonds is from December 29, 1969, through December 31, 1986, containing 822 Fridays including 25 Friday the thirteenths. Friday the thirteenth returns are more than eleven times larger than on other Fridays, and the t-statistic is 2.53. The sample for thirty-year bonds is from February 15, 1977, through December 31, 1987, containing 525 Fridays including 18 Friday the thirteenths. Mean returns on Friday the thirteenths are more than thirty-seven times larger than on other Fridays, and the t-statistic is 2.39.

As is true for ten-year bonds, these results are not due to outliers. The Z-scores for the Mann–Whitney U-tests for twenty- and thirty-year bonds are 2.45 and 2.66, respectively, while for the van der Waerden test the Z-scores are 2.50 for both maturities.

We know of no theoretical reason that returns on government securities on Friday the thirteenth are greater than on other Fridays. If this result is due to some state variable, the response to that factor appears to be an increasing function of maturity or duration.[9] The ratios of Friday the thirteenth returns to those on other Fridays increase almost monotonically with maturity. For three-month bills the ratio is 1.1, while for six-month bills it is 1.38. For ten-year bonds it is 15.7. The sample periods for the longer-term bonds do not match that of the shorter-term assets, but for twenty- and thirty-year bonds the ratios are 11.2 and 37.2, respectively. If we limit the sample period to when all three bonds traded, the ratios are 11.6, 19.3, and 35.7 for the ten-, twenty-, and thirty-year bonds, respectively.

Flannery and Protopapadakis (1988) also report an unexplained market phenomenon which is a function of duration: using seven different maturities of Treasury securities, they find evidence of a systematic negative relation between duration and returns on Monday. Their results and ours suggest that studying the relation between duration and other market anomalies might prove useful.

Risk during the Event Period

To determine if risk varies during the event period, we estimate:

$$e_{bt}^2 = \alpha_b + \beta_{b1}(T1 - t)(t - T2)D1_t + \beta_{b2}[(T2 - T1)D2_t + (t - T1)D1_t] + \varepsilon_{bt}. \quad (5)$$

$$e_{bt}^2 = (R_{bt} - \overline{R}_b)^2, \quad (6)$$

where

R_{bt} = the return on bond b at time t,
$\overline{R}_b$ = the mean return on bond b,
$T1$ = the first day of the event period (21 trading days before Friday the thirteenth),
$T2$ = the last day of the event period (21 trading days after Friday the thirteenth),
$D1_t$ = unity during the event period and zero otherwise,
$D2_t$ = unity after the event period ends and zero otherwise.

Ten-year bonds traded during all four of the event periods used for stocks in Section IV.A. Twenty-year bonds are available during the third and fourth periods, while thirty-year bonds are available only during the fourth. We again delete multiple-day returns. The results, contained in Table 5, are inconsistent with the high returns on bonds during the event periods. The only estimate of β_1 that is not significantly negative is for the ten-year bond in the third subperiod. This suggests that volatility was convex during the event periods: bond volatility decreases as Friday the thirteenth approaches and increases after it passes. This adds to the

Table 5. Estimates Obtained by Regressing the Variance of Bond Returns on Terms Controlling for the Convexity of and Permanent Changes in Volatility[a]

Ten-Year Bonds

First Sample Period: May 4, 1965–November 12, 1965: 124 Observations		*Second Sample Period: July 17, 1967–January 16, 1968: 125 Observations*	
Parameter	*Mean (t-Statistic)*	*Parameter*	*Mean (t-Statistic)*
α	0.00385 (3.88) ***	α	0.0488 (10.98) ***
β_1	-1.470×10^{-5} (–4.01)***	β_1	-9.23×10^{-5} (–5.53) ***
β_2	1.26×10^{-4} (3.87) ***	β_2	1.63×10^{-4} (1.13)

Third Sample Period: May 14, 1971–November 11, 1971: 123 Observations		*Fourth Sample Period: May 14, 1982–November 11, 1982: 123 Observations*	
Parameter	*Mean (t-Statistic)*	*Parameter*	*Mean (t-Statistic)*
α	0.0777 (5.12) ***	α	1.71 (8.03) ***
β_1	3.53×10^{-5} (0.63)	β_1	–0.0052 (–6.57) ***
β_2	0.00172 (3.44) ***	β_2	0.0277 (3.95)***

Twenty-Year Bonds

Third Sample Period: May 14, 1971–November 11, 1971: 123 Observations		*Fourth Sample Period: May 14, 1982–November 11, 1982: 123 Observations*	
Parameter	*Mean (t-Statistic)*	*Parameter*	*Mean (t-Statistic)*
α	0.0431 (7.88) ***	α	1.57 (8.92) ***
β_1	-6.14×10^{-5} (–3.03)***	β_1	–0.0046 (–7.04) ***
β_2	5.59×10^{-4} (3.10) ***	β_2	0.0219 (3.76) ***

(continued)

Table 5. (continued)

Thirty-Year Bonds	
Fourth Sample Period: May 14, 1982–November 11, 1982: 123 Observations	
Parameter	*Mean (t-Statistic)*
α	1.24 (8.72) ***
β_1	−0.0035 (−6.61) ***
β_2	0.0154 (3.28) ***

Notes: [a] $e^2_{bt} = \alpha_b + \beta_{b1}(T1 - t)(t - T2)D1_t + \beta_{b2}[(T2 - T1)D2_t + (t - T1)D1_t] + \varepsilon_{bt}$. (5)

$e^2_{bt} = (R_{bt} - \overline{R}_b)^2$, (6)

R_{bt} = the return on bond b at time t.

$\overline{R}_{bm}$ = the average return on bond b,

$T1$ = the first day of the event period (21 trading days before Friday the thirteenth),
$T2$ = the last day of the event period (21 trading days after Friday the thirteenth),

$D1_t$ = unity during the event period and zero otherwise,

$D2_t$ = unity after the event period ends and zero otherwise.

***Significant at the 1% level.

perplexing result that bond returns are large on Friday the thirteenth. If volatility is generally low, investors would likely accept lower expected returns during the period.

The positive estimates of β_2 imply volatility exits the period at a higher level than at the beginning of the period. One should not interpret this result to mean that the event itself permanently increases the unsystematic risk of the bonds. Causality is not implied. The result may be due to sampling variation or to a secular increase in volatility. This interpretation is plausible because estimates of α and β_2 increase in each subperiod for all bonds.

C. Futures Contracts

Since futures contracts have not existed long enough to have traded on more than a few Friday the thirteenths, they cannot reasonably be expected to show a significant Friday the thirteenth effect. However, they are worth studying because they are more volatile than the other nonequity assets we study. As such, they might better serve as alternative investments for equity investors than, say, government securities.

Table 6. Comparison of Means: Friday the Thirteenth and Other Fridays. Futures Contracts

Contract and Sample Period	Friday the Thirteenth *n*	Friday the Thirteenth Mean	Other Fridays *n*	Other Fridays Mean	*t*-Statistic for Equal Mean Returns
Stock Indexes:					
Value Line					
March 30, 1982– Dec. 31, 1987	11	0.418	278	0.004	0.63
NYSE					
May 6, 1982– Dec. 31, 1987	11	0.523	274	–0.048	1.38
Treasury Bills:					
Dec. 1, 1977– Dec. 31, 1987	18	0.0772	486	0.0014	1.61

Notes: *T*-tests are two tailed. The table is constructed such that a positive *t*-statistic indicates that the return on Friday the thirteenth is larger than on other Fridays.

Stock Index Futures

The Value Line series extends from March 30, 1982, through December 31, 1987. This obtains 289 Fridays, including 11 Friday the thirteenths. The NYSE series extends from May 6, 1982, through December 31, 1987, yielding 285 Fridays, also including 11 Friday the thirteenths.

Table 6 shows that although the limited sample prevents establishing a reliable statistical relationship between Friday the thirteenth and other Fridays, the difference in the magnitude of price changes is hard to ignore. Use of the Value Line Index, for example, shows that the average Friday the thirteenth price change is 0.418, while for other Fridays the price change averages only 0.004. Although the *t*-statistic is an insignificant 0.63, a difference in magnitude of more than one hundred times is difficult to attribute solely to trading procedures, such as those that require futures traders to invest only a fraction of the contract value in a margin account. The NYSE Index is even more extreme. The average Friday the thirteenth price change is 0.523, whereas on other Fridays it is a *negative* value: –0.048. Even with only eleven Friday the thirteenths, the *t*-ratio is 1.38, about as large in magnitude as the Friday the thirteenth effect in the stock market sample but opposite in sign.

However, much of this apparent reversal from the results using stock returns is due to the different sample periods. Limiting the sample period for stocks to match that for futures, we find that returns on Friday the thirteenth are larger in the equity market, much as in the futures markets. For example, when we use the value-weighted index with dividends, Friday the thirteenth's average return is 0.00395, while for other Fridays it is 0.0009. The other indexes offer similar results. Since the cash and futures markets behave comparably, we cannot conclude that Friday the thirteenth provides arbitrage opportunities between these markets during periods when both assets are available for trading. Consistent with this interpretation, the variances of price changes on both stock index futures contracts are statistically the same on Friday the thirteenth and on other Fridays.

It would be incorrect to conclude that the introduction of futures trading is the cause of the decrease or even reversal of a Friday the thirteenth effect. If it reversed, it did so earlier. Ten of the first twelve Friday the thirteenth returns are positive. Beginning with February 13, 1970, nine consecutive observations are negative. Since June 13, 1975, the 22 Friday the thirteenths are evenly divided; stock index futures were introduced midway through this period. Since then, five of the eleven Friday the thirteenth returns are negative.

Treasury Bill Futures

For our sample of 504 Fridays, including 18 Friday the thirteenths, the results using Treasury bill futures contracts are similar to those using stock index futures; we find large positive price changes on Friday the thirteenths relative to other Fridays. Since the sample size is somewhat larger, the t-ratio of 1.61 approaches significance. This is also consistent with the results of the cash market for bills and bonds. Limiting the Treasury bill sample period to match our bill futures sample, we find that Friday the thirteenths still offer higher returns than other Fridays, but the t-statistics are not significant. For six-month bills, for example, the ratio is 1.40. The variance of the price change is the same on Friday the thirteenths as on other Fridays. Again, we cannot conclude that Friday the thirteenth offers arbitrage opportunities between the cash market and Treasury bill futures markets during periods when futures are traded.

V. DISCUSSION

Even if transactions costs were zero on normal trades, differing settlement and delivery procedures preclude generating trading profits using rules based on Friday the thirteenth.[10] If settlement and payment were immediate, for example, our results suggest that investors might wish to sell stocks on Thursday the twelfth and purchase six-month Treasury bills or long-term government bonds. To do this, however, would require special delivery arrangements because settlement for the stock sale would otherwise be made in five business days—usually Thursday the nineteenth. The sale would generate no cash before then. This would be too late to capitalize on the positive bill return. Some families of mutual funds do permit switching from stock funds to money funds on the same day, despite the difference in delivery procedures, but it is hard to imagine enough traders would use this route on Thursday the twelfth to eliminate the negative stock return on Friday the thirteenth.

Our results, however, remain puzzling. Though they might be interpreted as laying one apparent market anomaly to rest by demonstrating that the Friday the thirteenth effect in stock returns is spurious, they raise the equally troublesome question regarding the significantly positive returns on six-month bills and long-term bonds on the same dates. We know of no explanation for these results, nor why the positive returns are an increasing function of maturity. Our finding that bond-return volatility is convex around Friday the thirteenth only adds to the puzzle. Unless and until these results are shown to be spurious, though, they suggest that investors planning to purchase Treasury bills or bonds on Friday the thirteenth might wish to make the transaction on Thursday the twelfth, instead.

ACKNOWLEDGMENTS

This research was begun while the author was a visiting scholar at the Federal Reserve Bank of Cleveland; this paper would not have been possible without its support. He thanks Nan-Ting Chou, Alahassane Diallo, and James T. Moser for helpful comments on earlier versions of this paper. Any remaining errors are the author's responsibility. The views stated herein are those of the author and not necessarily those of the Federal Reserve Bank of Cleveland or the Board of Governors of the Federal Reserve System.

NOTES

1. We thank Joan Junkus for supplying the bulk of these data. A small number of observations from the end of 1987 are from the *Wall Street Journal*.
2. We thank Larry Lockwood for suggesting the approach this paper uses.
3. For computational ease, the event period is actually 21 trading days on either side of Friday the thirteenth rather than one month, while the pre- and postevent periods are 42 trading days each. Therefore, there are 127 observations in each subperiod.
4. The names of the securities are available from the author on request.
5. In principle, a stock could be negatively correlated with the market, but this is at best a very rare security.
6. This significance test must be interpreted with caution because the observations are not independent.
7. On July 3, 1964, government securities dealers operated with only skeleton staffs.
8. Government bonds are also for next-day delivery, so buying on Thursday and selling on Friday represents a three-day cash investment.
9. The data are also consistent with the result being an increasing function of duration as well as maturity. This is because the durations of the bonds increase monotonically with maturity. Using the average yield for each maturity to compute Macaulay's duration, we obtain 7.02, 9.69, and 10.79 years for the ten-, twenty-, and thirty-year bonds, respectively.
10. See Lakonishok and Levi (1982) for a discussion of these procedures.

REFERENCES

Baillie, R. T., and DeGennaro, R. P. (1989). "The Impact of Delivery Terms on Stock Return Volatility." *Journal of Financial Services Research* 3 (December), 55–76.

Banz, R. (1981). "The Relationship between Return and Market Value of Common Stocks." *Journal of Financial Economics* 9 (June), 3–18.

Cross, F. (1973). "The Behavior of Stock Prices on Fridays and Mondays." *Financial Analysts Journal* 29 (November–December), 67–69.

DeGennaro, R. P. (1990). "The Effect of Payment Delays on Stock Prices." *Journal of Financial Research* 13, No. 2 (Summer), 133–145.

Dyl, E. A., and Maberly, E. D. (1988). "The Anomaly That Isn't There: A Comment on Friday the Thirteenth." *Journal of Finance* 43 (December), 1285–1286.

Dyl, E. A., and Martin, S. A. Jr. (1985). "Weekend Effects on Stock Returns: A Comment." *Journal of Finance* 40 (March), 347–349.

Flannery, M. J., and Protopapadakis, A. (1988). "From T-Bills to Common Stocks: Investigating the Generality of Intraweek Return Seasonality." *Journal of Finance* 43 (June) 431–450.

French, K. (1980). "Stock Returns and the Weekend Effect." *Journal of Financial Economics* 8 (March), 55–69.

French, K. and Roll, R. (1986). "Stock Return Variances: The Arrival of Information and the Reaction of Traders." *Journal of Financial Economics* 17 (September), 5–26.

Gibbons, M. and Hess, P. (1981). "Day of the Week Effects and Asset Returns." *Journal of Business* 54 (December), 579–596.

Harris, L. (1986). "A Transaction Data Study of Weekly and Intraday Patterns in Stock Returns." *Journal of Financial Economics* 16 (May), 99–117.

Keim, D. B., and Stambaugh, R. F. (1984). "A Further Investigation of the Weekend Effect in Stock Returns." *Journal of Finance* 39 (July), 819–834.

Kolb, R. W., and Rodriguez, R. J. (1987). "Friday the Thirteenth: 'Part VII'—A Note." *Journal of Finance* 42 (December), 1385–1387.

Lakonishok, J. and Levi, M. (1982). "Weekend Effects on Stock Returns: A Note." *Journal of Finance* 37 (June), 883–889.

Lakonishok, J. and Levi, M. (1985). "Weekend Effects on Stock Returns: A Reply." *Journal of Finance* 40 (March), 351–352.

Lakonishok, J., and Smidt, S. (1988). "Are Seasonal Anomalies Real? A Ninety-Year Perspective." *Review of Financial Studies* 1 (Winter), 403–425.

Lohmann, F. I. (1975). *Nonparametrics: Statistical Methods Based on Ranks*, San Francisco: Holden-Day.

Lockwood, L. J., and Kadiyala, K. R. (1988). "Risk Measurement for Event-Dependent Security Returns." *Journal of Business and Economic Statistics* 6 (January), 43–49.

Oldfield, G. S., and Rogalski, R. J. (1980). "A Theory of Stock Returns Over Trading and Non-Trading Periods." *Journal of Finance* 35 (June), 729–753.

Reinganum, M. R. (1981). "Misspecification of Capital Asset Pricing: Empirical Anomalies Based on Earnings' Yield and Market Values." *Journal of Financial Economics* 3 (June), 19–46.

Rogalski, R. J. (1984). "New Findings Regarding Day-of-the-Week Returns over Trading and Non-Trading Periods: A Note." *Journal of Finance* 39 (December), 1603–1614.

Smirlock, M., and Starks, L. (1986). "Day-of-the-Week and Intraday Effects in Stock Returns." *Journal of Financial Economics* 17 (September), 197–210.

CAPITAL GAINS AND TURN-OF-THE-YEAR STOCK PRICE PRESSURES

Dan S. Dhaliwal and Robert Trezevant

ABSTRACT

Prior research into a tax-related explanation of the January effect has focused on a tax-loss explanation. Our research tests a tax-effects explanation of the January effect that is more general than the tax-loss hypothesis. This tax-effects hypothesis is based on the theoretical work of Constantinides and our detailed analysis of changing tax laws. Consistent with the prediction of Constantinides' theory, we find that January returns are greater for long-term gain stocks following up-market years than following down-market years and that January returns are greater for loss stocks following down-market years than following up-market years. Further, these patterns are related to return variance and risk-free interest rates as predicted by theory. This suggests that the tax-induced component of the January effect is more complicated than the traditional tax-loss explanation implies.

Advances in Quantitative Analysis of Finance and Accounting,
Volume 2, Part A, pages 139–154.

ISBN: 1-55938-564-2

I. INTRODUCTION

A great deal of research effort has been devoted to testing the tax-loss explanation of the January effect. This explanation is based on the assumption that stocks that are eligible for capital loss sales in December of a given year are subject to excessive selling pressure and, hence, experience depressed prices in December. The selling pressure is caused by investors' desire to recognize a tax loss in the current year so as to maximize the present value of cash flows. This selling pressure subsides in January. The stocks whose prices were depressed in December by tax-loss selling show positive returns in early January, since they had been driven to artificially low price levels in the prior month.

Our research tests a tax-effects explanation of the January effect that is more general than the tax-loss explanation. This tax-effects hypothesis is based on the theoretical work of Constantinides (1984) and our detailed analysis of the tax laws. Constantinides (1984) shows that investors can often increase their cash flows if they sell long-term gain stocks at the tax-advantaged long-term tax rate and replace these stocks with similar securities in order to reestablish the potential for a fully deductible short-term capital loss. Taking into account this consideration and the tax laws, our tax-effects hypothesis predicts that long-term gain stocks are sold in the last five trading days of up-market years, and that loss stocks are sold near the end of down-market years.

Consistent with Constantinides' theory, we find that January returns are greater for long-term gain stocks following up-market than following down-market years, and that January returns are greater for loss stocks following down-market than following up-market years. Further, as predicted, January returns are stronger for stocks with larger price variance, and these returns are related to the risk-free interest rate in the expected direction. However, Constantinides' theory predicts that January returns should be stronger for long-term gain stocks in years with a lower ratio of long-term capital gain tax rates to short-term capital loss tax rates; this prediction is not supported in this study. These results suggest that the tax-induced component of the January effect is more complicated than the traditional tax-loss explanation implies.

This research can be regarded as a test of a price pressure hypothesis, if the tax-effects hypothesis is accepted as a maintained assumption. Any tax-loss explanation of the January effect is regarded by many researchers as naive in that it ignores the fact that a January effect would be arbitraged away by counterbalancing purchases of those stocks sold for tax purposes in December (Constantinides, 1984; Roll, 1983). Thus, the results of this research can be interpreted either as support for a price pressure hypothesis predicting that tax-motivated sales of stocks (a maintained assumption) temporarily depress the prices of those stocks sold for tax purposes (a testable hypothesis), or as support for the tax-effects explanation of the January effect (a testable hypothesis) with the price pressure hypothesis considered a maintained assumption.

The rest of this paper is organized as follows. Section II describes the prior theoretical research. Section III describes the relevant features of the Internal

Revenue Code. Section IV develops the hypotheses to be tested, while Section V reports results of tests of these hypotheses. Section VI offers a summary.

II. PRIOR THEORETICAL RESEARCH

The phenomenon that certain common stocks exhibit abnormally positive returns on the last trading day of December and in January is well documented. Prior research on the relationship between tax laws and this January effect has almost exclusively focused on a tax-loss explanation (e.g., Reinganum, 1983; Rozeff, 1985). This explanation is based on the assumption that (1) stocks eligible for tax-loss sales in December of a given year are subject to excessive selling pressure, and (2) these stocks experience downward pricing pressure in December. The selling pressure is caused by investors' desire to recognize tax losses in the current year in order to maximize the present value of cash flows. This selling pressure subsides in January, leading to a price rebound in early January for tax-loss sales candidates of the prior December.

Constantinides (1984) offers a more complete theory of the relationship between tax laws and the January effect: his theory offers a tax-effects explanation rather than a tax-loss explanation of the January effect. Constantinides demonstrates that in addition to recognizing losses to maximize cash flows, investors can often increase cash flows if they recognize long-term capital gains at the tax-advantaged long-term capital gains tax rate and replace these stocks with similar or identical securities in order to reestablish the potential for a short-term capital loss. Constantinides' simulation results are consistent with his proposition that in many situations investors are better off by following this strategy.

Constantinides offers five factors determining the extent to which his predicted sales of long-term gain stocks will hold: relative long-term versus short-term tax rates, the netting procedure for capital gains and losses, the return variance of individual stocks, interest rates, and transaction costs. Lower tax rates on long-term gains relative to short-term losses enhance the benefit of selling long-term gain stocks to reestablish the potential for short-term loss. The netting procedure for capital gains and losses complicates Constantinides' theory. Short-term losses offset long-term gains dollar for dollar. Without this provision, Constantinides shows that investors should sell their short-term loss stocks and certain long-term gain stocks in the same year. With this provision, traditional tax planning dictates that short-term loss sales and long-term gain sales should be segregated into separate years (see Section III).

With respect to the sales of long-term gain stocks, Constantinides shows that those with a higher variance of returns are better tax-sales candidates since the value of a timing option to realize gains long term and losses short term is increasing in return variance. The sales of long-term gain stocks would be accelerated in Constantinides' theory if interest rates are low, due to the increased present value of the potential short-term tax loss in the future. Finally, the sales of long-term gain stocks to reestablish the potential for short-term loss would be more beneficial the lower transaction costs are. However, Constantinides shows that the potential tax benefits of following his strategy are large relative to reasonable transaction costs.

The tax netting procedure would affect the sales of short-term loss stocks as it affects the sales of long-term gain stocks. That is, long-term gains and short-term losses would be recognized in separate years. High variance loss stocks would also be subject to more December selling pressure because these stocks are more likely to have large losses at the end of the year. Interest rates would affect the sales of loss stocks in a manner opposite to their affect on the sales of long-term gain stocks. A low interest rate would decrease the sales of tax-loss stocks since the present value of recognizing the tax loss now rather than later would be relatively smaller.[1] Last, high transaction costs would decrease the sales of loss stocks for tax purposes.

III. RELEVANT TAX LAWS

Our data span the years 1963–1983. The holding period rules determine if a gain or loss on the sale of a stock is defined as long term or short term. The definition of a short-term holding period from 1963 to 1976 was less than or equal to six-months. In the transition year 1977, the definition of short term was extended to less than or equal to nine months. From 1978 through 1983, short term was defined as less than or equal to one year.

With respect to the allowed write-off of long-term and short-term losses, from 1963 to 1969 100% of both long-term and short-term losses could be used to reduce taxable income with a limit of $1,000 per year. From 1970 until 1983, 100% of short-term losses and only 50% of long-term losses could be used to reduce taxable income. Since 1963, unused losses could be carried forward indefinitely but retained their long-term or short-term characterization. The maximum annual loss allowed rose to $2,000 per year in 1977 and $3,000 per year in 1978. Schultz (1988) shows that these annual limits on capital losses were probably nonbinding for most investors during the period examined in this study.[2]

Fifty percent of long-term gains were taxable from 1963 to 1978, whereas only 40% of long-term gains were taxable following 1978. One hundred percent of short-term gains were included in taxable income for the entire period. These rules can be summarized as follows.

Years	*Cutoff ST/LT*	*Percent ST Loss Allowed*	*Percent LT Loss Allowed*	*Percent LT Gain Taxable*	*Maximum Annual Loss*
pre-1970	6 mos.	100	100	50	1,000
1970–1976	6 mos.	100	50	50	1,000
1977	9 mos.	100	50	50	2,000
1978	1 year	100	50	50	3,000
1979–1983	1 year	100	50	40	3,000

There are two additional provisions of the tax code relevant to this study. First, each year a taxpayer determined his/her short-term (ST) and long-term (LT) gain or loss position in two steps. Long-term gains and losses and short-term gains and losses were initially pooled separately to yield a net LT gain or loss and a net ST gain or loss. If both net LT and ST positions were gains or losses, the above rules were applied immediately. If the net positions were such that one was a loss and the other was a gain, they were netted against each other before the above provisions were applied. An important result of this netting process was that the partial taxation benefit of LT gains taken in a given year would be lost if losses were taken in the same year. For this reason, effective tax planning dictated that recognition of LT gains and ST losses be segregated into separate tax years.[3]

Second, prior to the 1986 Tax Reform Act cash-basis taxpayers could use the installment method for capital gains sales executed in the last five trading days of the year. The result was that a capital gain taken on these five days could be recognized in the year of sale or in the year following sale. The decision as to year of gain inclusion did not have to be declared until the tax return for the year of sale was filed.

IV. HYPOTHESIS DEVELOPMENT AND PRIOR EMPIRICAL RESEARCH

Constantinides' work and the tax laws described previously lead to several testable tax-effects hypotheses that are discussed in this section. As described in Section II, Constantinides shows that investors can increase cash flows by following a strategy of taking long-term gains taxed at a low rate in order to reestablish short-term positions with a higher cost basis.

The tax laws in effect from 1963 to 1983 have several implications for the implementation of this strategy. The provisions that (1) long-term gains must be netted against long-term losses and (2) net long-term gains must be netted against net short-term losses would have dictated that investors segregate long-term gains into a tax year during which no losses were taken. Furthermore, in any year that long-term gains were realized, optimal tax planning would have required that they be taken during the last five trading days of the year. This would have allowed the taxpayer to decide on April 15 of the following year if the gains should be reported in the year of sale or the year following sale.

The above considerations, and the assumption of prior research that price pressure on tax sales candidates in December suddenly abates in January, leading to positive January returns for last year's tax sales candidates, result in the first two testable hypotheses of the tax-effects explanation of the January effect:

H1: If the tax-effects explanation holds, then long-term gain stocks following up-market years will have more positive early January returns than long-term gain stocks following down-market years.

H2: If the tax-effects explanation holds, then loss stocks following down-market years will have more positive early January returns than loss stocks following up-market years.

Individuals would realize only LT gains during some years so that LT gains would not be offset by losses. Further, they would tend to realize gains in those years during which they do not have many losses—up-market years. Thus, hypothesis 1 assumes that investors (1) have a preponderance of gain stocks in their portfolios near the end of up-market years, (2) sell their long-term gain stocks during the last five trading days of up-market years in order to reestablish the potential for 100% deductible losses, and (3) sell long-term gain stocks but not loss stocks near the end of up-market years in order to allow the segregation of years with long-term gains and any losses.

In an analogous manner, near the end of down-market years, investors would have a preponderance of loss stocks in their portfolios. They would sell these loss stocks near the end of the down-market year to maximize the present value of taxes saved. At the same time, long-term gain stocks would not be sold near the end of down-market years to allow the segregation of years with losses and long-term gains.[4] Further, based on the findings of Chan (1986) and Dhaliwal, Guo, and Trezevant (1990), both long-term and short-term loss stocks exhibit the January effect. Thus, all hypotheses and empirical tests involving loss stocks include both long-term and short-term loss stocks.

High variance long-term gain stocks should have stronger tax-motivated sales in the last five trading days of December and thus a stronger January effect because the value of the option to realize a short-term loss would be greater for high variance stocks (Constantinides, 1984). High variance loss stocks should have stronger December selling pressure and thus a stronger January effect because they would be those stocks most likely to have experienced large losses during the year (Reinganum, 1983). Thus:

H3: If the tax-effects explanation holds, then there will be a positive relationship between return variance and January returns for both long-term gain stocks following up markets and loss stocks following down markets.

Since investors are more likely to execute tax-motivated sales of long-term gain stocks as the spread between tax rates on long-term gains and short-term losses increases, the following relationship is expected:

H4: If the tax-effects explanation holds, then there will be a negative relationship between the ratio of long-term capital gain tax rates to short-term capital loss tax rates and January returns for long-term gain stocks following up markets.

Finally, interest rate is predicted to systematically affect the sales of loss and long-term gain stocks. With respect to the sales of long-term gain stocks in December of up markets, a lower interest rate should encourage the sales of these gain stocks in December (Constantinides, 1984). On the other hand, a higher interest rate should encourage the sales of loss stocks in December of down markets, since the present value of receiving the tax savings now rather than one year hence would be relatively greater. Thus:

H5: If the tax-effects explanation holds, then there will be a negative relationship between interest rates and January returns for long-term gain stocks following up markets and a positive relationship between interest rates and January returns for loss stocks following down markets.

Prior empirical research related to the above hypotheses has concentrated on the predictions regarding the sales of loss stocks. Further, only control variables for market return and security return variance have been examined by this previous research. Rozeff (1985) and DeBondt and Thaler (1987) control for prior year's market performance. Although their objective was not to examine the generalized tax-effects hypothesis, both papers provide strong empirical evidence that loss stocks have more December selling pressure and a much stronger January effect following down-market years than following up-market years. For example, Rozeff (1985) finds that, based on monthly data from July 1926 to January 1983, the quartile of largest loss stocks has an average monthly January return of 0.1157 following down-market years and 0.0281 following up-market years. Further, DeBondt and Thaler (1987) find that "following down years, long-term losers [perform] better than they do following years in which the market has risen. For losers, the December–January reversals [of price] are significantly more pronounced following years of market declines" (DeBondt and Thaler, 1987, p. 564). Finally, Reinganum (1983) reports evidence that high-variance loss stocks have the largest January returns. His explanation is that these high-variance stocks are most likely to have experienced the largest price declines over the year preceding January.

V. EMPIRICAL VARIABLES, SAMPLE SELECTION, AND TEST RESULTS

A. Empirical Variables and Sample Selection

Empirical surrogates for six variables are necessary to implement tests of hypotheses H1–H5. These variables are annual capital loss or long-term capital gain sale potential of individual stocks, January raw and abnormal returns of individual stocks, return variance of individual stocks, the classification of the stock market as exhibiting an up year or a down year, the annual ratio of long-term to short-term tax rates, and the annual risk-free interest rate.

Long-term gain or loss status of individual securities is measured using price behavior in each of the years 1963–1983. Long-term gain stocks are classified as those stocks that rose in price during both the second half of the year and for the year as a whole. Loss stocks are classified as those stocks that declined in price during both the second half of the year and for the year as a whole. Stocks that fell (rose) in price for the second half of the year and rose (fell) in price for the year as a whole are excluded, since they would simultaneously represent loss and long-term gain stocks in most tax regimes.[5]

Abnormal returns are computed using the market model. For each stock, estimates of alpha and beta are calculated using ordinary least squares over the trading year before the test period described below. These market model abnormal returns and raw returns are calculated for the last trading day of December and the first five trading days of January to capture any January effect. The December/January days are chosen based on prior research findings that identify these days as having abnormally high returns (Roll, 1983).

Variance of return is measured for each stock as the variance of daily price returns for the trading year preceding the January effect test period described previously.

The next step is to determine a measure to classify each sample year as an up-market or down-market year. The change in the level of the Standard and Poor's (S & P) 500 Composite Index for a given year is chosen. An up-year (down-year) is defined as a year in which the S & P Index rose (fell) by at least 10% percent. Table 1 reports the results of this classification.

Market years preceding the January return test period must also be described by their annual risk-free rate and their annual ratio of long-term tax rates to short-term tax rates. Annual risk-free rates are average three-month Treasury bill yields reported in the *Economic Report of the President* (1988). Maximum long-term capital gain tax rates are drawn from Congressional Budget Office (1988) and maximum capital loss rates are drawn from Pechman (1983). The resulting annual data are shown in Table 1. The ratio of tax rates reported is computed as the current year's maximum long-term capital gain tax rate divided by the following year's maximum short-term capital loss tax rate, since Constantinides' theory predicts sales of long-term gain stocks in the current year to allow potential sales of short-term loss stocks in the following year.

For each security in each of the years 1963–1983, a cumulative abnormal return (CAR) and a cumulative raw return (CRR) are calculated by cumulating the six-day January test period abnormal and raw returns. The only sample screen applied in these calculations is to remove firm-year cumulative January returns greater than 200% (a "triple") or less than –99%.

Table 1. Descriptive Annual Data

Year	*Market Return*[a]	*Ratio of Long-Term to Short-Term Loss Tax Rates*[b]	*Risk-free Rate*[c]
		Up Market	
1963	0.1889	0.3247	0.0316
1964	0.1296	0.3571	0.0355
1967	0.2009	0.3322	0.0432
1971	0.1079	0.4643	0.0435
1972	0.1563	0.50	0.0407
1975	0.3155	0.50	0.0584
1976	0.1915	0.50	0.0499
1979	0.1231	0.40	0.1004
1980	0.2577	0.4051	0.1151
1982	0.1476	0.40	0.1069
1983	0.1727	0.40	0.0863
		Down Markets	
1966	−0.1309		0.0488
1969	−0.1136		0.0668
1973	−0.1737		0.0704
1974	−0.2972		0.0789
1977	−0.1150		0.0527

Notes: [a]Return on Standard and Poor's 500 Index for the year. Only years with an increase of greater than 10% or a decrease of less than −10% are included in the sample.

[b]Source for maximum long-term capital gain (loss) tax rates is Table 7 on p. 36 of Congressional Budget Office (1988). Source for maximum tax rate applying to short-term capital losses is from Pechman (1983). The ratio is of the current year's maximum long-term capital gain tax rate divided by the following year's maximum short-term capital loss tax rates.

[c]Annual average three-month Treasury-bill rate as reported in *Economic Report of the President* (1988).

B. Statistical Tests and Results

Table 2 reports descriptive statistics for all firm-year observations. Long-term gain and loss stocks are reported in columns (1) and (2), respectively. For long-term gain stocks, the percentage of stocks with a positive January return is far greater following up-market years than following down-market years. This supports hypothesis H1. For loss stocks, however, there is no significant difference in the percentage of stocks with a positive January return as a function of the preceding year's market return.

Table 2. Descriptive Statistics: Mean Cumulative Abnormal Returns and Mean Cumulative Raw Returns in Up Markets and Down Markets: 1963–1983[a]

	Long-Term Gain Stocks	*Loss Stocks*
Sample Size		
Up Markets	13,115	4,605
Down Markets	2,192	6,782
Mean CAR		
Up Markets	0.032	0.314
Down Markets	−0.016	0.344
Percentage of stocks with positive CAR		
Up Markets	0.484	0.797
Down Markets	0.374	0.797
Mean CRR		
Up Markets	0.099	0.365
Down Markets	0.035	0.461
Percentage of stocks with positive CRR		
Up Markets	0.636	0.836
Down Markets	0.448	0.847
Percentage of stocks:		
z-score of difference	9.55	0.02
in proportions:* CAR	(0.0001)[†]	(0.984)
z-score of difference	16.69	−1.58
in proportions: CRR	(0.0001)	(0.104)

Notes: [a]Cumulative abnormal return for each stock is its cumulated abnormal return for the last trading day of December and the first five trading days of January. Abnormal returns are computed using market model estimates computed over the trading year preceding the last trading day of December. Cumulative raw return for each stock is its cumulated raw return for the last trading day of December and the first five trading days of January. Up or down market is classified by return on Standard and Poor's 500 Index for the year. Only years with an increase of greater than 10% or a decrease of less than −10% are included in the sample. Long-term gain stocks are stocks that went up in price during both the second half of the year and for the year as a whole. Loss stocks are stocks that went down in price during both the second half of the year and for the year as a whole.

*The test is of the difference in the percentage of stocks with positive returns between up markets and down markets divided by a pooled standard error. The pooled standard error is the square root of (p * (1 − p) * (1/number of observations in up markets plus 1/ number of observations in down markets)), p being equal to the percentage of stocks with positive returns in both up and down markets.

[†]P-values (two tailed) are reported in parentheses.

The 26,694 individual firm-year observations are not independent. Therefore, to conduct further statistical analysis, the firm-year observations of long-term gain stocks and the firm-year observations of loss stocks are formed into sixteen annual portfolios each. The mean portfolio cumulative raw return, the mean portfolio cumulative abnormal return, and the mean portfolio variance are then calculated for each annual portfolio of stocks.

Table 3. Comparison of Mean Portfolio Cumulative Abnormal Returns and Mean Portfolio Cumulative Raw Returns between Various Subpartitions: 1963–1983[a]

	Mean CAR	*Mean CRR*	*Upper Minus Lower Variance Stocks*[b]	*Low Minus High Risk-Free Rate*[c]
Panel A: Difference in Mean Portfolio Returns: Long-Term Gain Stocks following Up Markets				
Upper variance	0.0761	0.2072		
Lower variance	0.0208	0.0873		
Low risk-free rate	0.0380	0.1298		
High risk-Free rate	0.0160	0.0670		
t-test of difference in mean CAR*			3.21 (0.001)†	1.84 (0.099)
t-test of difference in mean CRR			3.84 (0.001)	1.76 (0.116)
Panel B: Difference in Mean Portfolio Returns: Loss Stocks following Down Markets				
Upper variance	0.4481	0.5925		
Lower variance	0.2606	0.3219		
Low risk-free rate	0.1821	0.1604		
High risk-free rate	0.4037	0.5657		
t-test of difference in mean CAR			2.39 (0.046)	–4.02 (0.064)
t-test of difference in mean CRR			1.78 (0.117)	–2.84 (0.071)

Notes:[a]See Table 2, note a. Cumulative abnormal returns are formed into annual portfolios, with the mean cumulative abnormal return of each portfolio used to conduct the tests reported in the table.

[b]Upper variance stocks are those whose annual price return variance is in the upper quartile of the annual price return variance distribution for all relevant stocks. Lower variance stocks are those in the lower three quarters of the annual price return variance distribution for all relevant stocks.

[c]Risk-free rate is annual average three-month Treasury-bill rate. High (low) risk-free rates are defined as those above (below) the mean of all annual average Treasury bill rates (6.43%).

*The test is of the difference in mean returns between relevant subsamples divided by the pooled standard error of the subsamples. The pooled standard error is the square root of (the variance of subsample one/ number of observations in subsample one, plus the variance of subsample two/ number of observations in subsample two).

†*P*-values (two tailed) are reported in parentheses.

Table 3 compares differences in mean portfolio January returns between the relevant sample partitions. Results for long-term gain stocks following up markets are reported in panel A, and results for loss stocks following down markets are reported in panel B. Upper variance stocks are those in the upper 25% of their return variance distribution, and lower variance stocks are those in the lower 75% of their return variance distribution.[6]

The results shown in column 3 of Table 3 are supportive of hypothesis H3. Following up markets, upper-variance long-term gain stocks have a larger mean portfolio six-day CAR (0.001 significance[7]) and a larger mean portfolio six-day CRR (0.001 significance) than lower-variance long-term gain stocks. This result supports the contention that following up markets, investors sell their higher-variance long-term gain stocks in the last five trading days of the year in order to reestablish the potential for short-term capital loss.

Following down markets, upper-variance loss stocks have a larger mean portfolio six-day CAR (0.046 significance) and a larger mean portfolio six-day CRR (0.117 significance) than lower-variance loss stocks. This finding confirms prior research results (e.g., Reinganum [1983]) and is consistent with the explanation that high-variance stocks are more likely to be tax-loss sales candidates at the end of the year.

The test results comparing January returns conditioned on Treasury bill yields are reported in column 4 of Table 3. Average Treasury bill yields in the year preceding the January return test period are classified as high or low based on whether they fell above or below the mean of the distribution of annual average Treasury bill yields. The results in Table 3 are of January returns following years with low Treasury bill yields minus January returns following years with high Treasury bill yields. For long-term gain stocks following up markets, Constantinides (1984) and hypothesis H5 predict that this difference should be positive, since the present value of a potential short-term tax loss one year hence would be greater in years of low interest rates. Test results in panel A of Table 3 support this contention (0.116 or better significance).

For loss stocks following down markets, column 4 of panel B reports January returns following low interest rate years minus January returns following high interest rate years. Hypothesis H5 predicts that this difference should be negative because the spread between the present value of a tax loss recognized one year hence and a tax loss recognized currently would be greater in years of high interest rates. The results reported support hypothesis H5 (0.071 or better significance).

Table 4 reports additional results obtained from multiple regression analysis using the following model for loss sales candidates following down markets:

$$CRR_{i,t} = a_0 + B_1 * \text{rate}_t + B_2 * \text{var}_{i,t} + B_3 * \text{mktret}_t + e, \tag{1}$$

where $CRR_{i,t}$ is the mean six-day January cumulative raw return[8] for a portfolio of stocks in variance classification i (i = high [upper 25%], i = low [lower 75%]) following year t, $\text{var}_{i,t}$ is the mean return variance for a portfolio of stocks in variance classification i (i = high [upper 25%], i = low [lower 75%]) during year t, rate_t is the annual average three-month Treasury bill yield during year t, and mktret_t is the annual return on the Standard and Poor's 500 Index for year t. mktret is included as an independent variable based on evidence in other studies that the January effect is stronger following down-market years.

The results of the regression estimates reported in Table 4 lend further support to hypotheses H3 and H5. The estimated interest rate coefficient B_1 is positive at the 0.063 level, indicating that loss stocks following down markets have a larger

Table 4. Regression Results for Mean Portfolio Cumulative Raw Returns: 1963–1983: Loss Stocks following Down Markets[a]

Model $CRR_{i,t}$ =		
a_0:	Intercept	−0.756 (0.070)*
B_1:	Treasury-bill rate[†]	16.26 (0.063)
B_2:	Variance[‡]	134.35 (0.069)
B_3:	Market return[§]	−0.046 (0.970)
Adj. R^2		0.638

Notes: [a]Cumulative raw return for each stock is its cumulated raw return for the last trading day of December and the first five trading days of January. Cumulative raw returns are formed into annual portfolios for stocks in variance classification i (i = high [upper 25%, i = low (lower 75%)], with the mean cumulative raw return of each portfolio used as the dependent variable. Loss stocks are stocks that went down in price during both the second half of the year and for the year as a whole. Down market is classified by return on Standard and Poor's 500 Index for the year. A down market is one in which the S & P Index declined by more than 10%.

*Estimated coefficient values are reported outside parentheses. P-values (two tailed) associated with the coefficient t-statistic are reported in parentheses.

[†]The independent variable is the annual average three-month Treasury-bill rate.

[‡]Variance is the mean variance of the daily price returns of the stocks in an annual portfolio (see note a). A stock's variance of daily price returns is calculated for the year preceding the January return test period defined in note a.

[§]Market return is the percentage decrease in the Standard and Poor's 500 Index in the year preceding the January return test period defined in note a.

January CRR, the higher the risk-free interest rate in the down-market year. The estimated coefficient B_2 is positive at the 0.069 significance level, indicating a positive relationship between return variance and the January effect return for loss stocks following down markets. The estimated coefficient B_3 is insignificant. This last result is probably due to the fact that only five market return observations are available to estimate Eq. (1).

Table 5 reports results of regression estimates for long-term gain stocks following up markets of the models represented by Eqs. (1) and (2):

$$CRR_{i,t} = a_0 + a_1 * D + B_1 * \text{rate}_t + B_2 * \text{var}_{i,t} + B_3 * \text{mktret}_t + e, \quad (2)$$

where $CRR_{i,t}$ $\text{var}_{i,t}$, mktret_t, and rate_t are defined following Eq. (1). D is a dummy variable coded $D = 1$ for years with a high ratio (a ratio greater than 40%) of maximum long-term capital gain tax rates in the current year to maximum short-term capital loss tax rates in the following year and $D = 0$ otherwise. The 40% ratio is chosen as a cutoff to match the results reported in Tables 1 and 2 of Constantinides (1984).

Table 5. Regression Results for Mean Portfolio Cumulative Raw Returns: 1963–1983: Long-Term Gain Stocks[2] following Up Markets[a]

Model $CRR_{i,t}$ =		
a_0: Intercept	0.049	0.048
	(0.333)	(0.339)
B_1: Treasury-bill rate$_t$	−1.27	−1.20
	(0.007)	(0.012)
a_1: Dummy intercept*	—	0.031
		(0.271)
B_2: Variance$_{i,t}$[†]	71.26	72.42
	(0.0002)	(0.0002)
B_3: Market return$_t$[‡]	0.536	0.428
	(0.023)	(0.084)
Adj. R^2	0.615	0.621

Notes: [a]See Table 4, note a. Up market is classified by return on Standard and Poor's 500 Index for the year. An up market is one in which the S&P Index rose by more than 10%.

*DUMMY is set equal to one if the ratio of end-of-current-year maximum long-term capital gain tax rate to the end-of-following-year maximum short-term capital loss tax rate is greater than 40% and set equal to zero otherwise.

[†]Variance is the mean variance of the daily price returns of the stocks in an annual portfolio (see note a). A stock's variance of daily price returns is calculated for the year preceding the January return test period defined in note a.

[‡]Market return is the percentage increase in the Standard and Poor's 500 Index in the year preceding the January return test period defined in note a.

The results of the regressions estimating Eq. (1) are reported in column 1 of Table 5. These results confirm those reported in panel A of Table 3 and support hypotheses H3 and H5. The estimated interest rate coefficient B_1 is negative at the 0.007 significance level, indicating that the January CRR is larger the smaller the risk-free interest rate in the up-market year. This is as predicted since the present value of a potential short-term tax loss recognized in the future would be greatest in years of low risk-free interest rates (Constantinides [1984]). The estimated coefficient B_2 is positive at the 0.0002 significance level, indicating that, following up markets, higher-variance long-term gain stocks have a larger January CRR than lower-variance long-term gain stocks. The estimated coefficient on the annual return on the Standard and Poor's 500 Index in the year preceding the January return test period is significantly positive at the 0.023 level. Our explanation of this result is that investors have more long-term gain stocks available for sale in their portfolios the larger the market return.

Column 2 of Table 5 reports the results when a dummy variable for the ratio of maximum long-term capital gain to maximum short-term capital loss tax rates is added to Eq. (1) (i.e., when Eq. [2] is tested). The magnitude and significance on the estimated coefficients B_1, B_2, and B_3 remain virtually identical. The estimated dummy intercept on the ratio of tax rates variable is insignificantly positive (0.271 significance). This last result is not consistent with the prediction of hypothesis H4 and Constantinides' theory that years with the lowest ratio of long-term to short-term tax rates should have the largest January effect. A possible explanation for this result is that the ratio of maximum long-term capital gain to maximum short-term capital loss tax rates is never large enough to discourage the tax-motivated sales of long-term gain stocks.

VI. CONCLUSION

Prior research into tax-related explanations of the January effect has focused on tax-loss hypotheses. Our study expands this prior research by taking into account the theory of Constantinides (1984) and a detailed analysis of the tax laws to develop a generalized tax-effects explanation of the January effect. This explanation predicts that long-term gain stocks will be sold in the last five days of up-market years in order to reestablish the potential for short-term capital loss, whereas loss stocks will be sold near the end of down-market years in order to maximize the present value of tax savings. This leads to the testable hypothesis that long-term gain stocks (loss stocks) will exhibit a larger January effect following up-market (down-market) years.

Empirical tests of the preceding hypothesis support the tax-effects explanation of the January effect and the theory of Constantinides (1984). In addition, variance of price return for stocks and risk-free rate is related to January abnormal returns as predicted by theory. However, the ratio of long-term capital gain tax rates to short-term capital loss tax rates is not related to January abnormal returns of long-term gain stocks as predicted by theory.

This research indicates that the relation between tax rules and the January effect is more complicated than a simple tax-loss explanation. A fruitful area for future research could involve volume tests of the tax-effects hypothesis.

NOTES

1. Simulations demonstrating that low interest rates should decrease the sales of tax-loss stocks are available from the authors.

2. See Schultz (1988, pp. 6–8). Schultz first shows how investors could avoid the loss limits by converting income into capital gains. He then argues that many investors have long-term gains from assets other than stock that allow the use of all losses on stock investments to be taken. Calculations based on 1982 U. S. Treasury Tax Model data reported in Poterba (1987) support Schultz's argument.

3. This planning strategy is striking. For example, assume a 20% tax rate on long-term gains and a 50% tax rate on short-term losses. Further assume a long-term gain of $700 and a short-term loss of $900. With no taxes the investor loses $200; with taxes and the gain and loss taken in the same year the investor loses $100 of after-tax cash flows; with taxes and the gain and loss segregated into separate

years the investor *gains* $110 of after-tax cash flows. We see that the before-tax loss has become an after-tax gain.

4. Constantinides does not actually predict that investors will segregate sales of long-term gain stocks and loss stocks into separate years. His theory predicts that short-term losses will be recognized as soon as they occur and long-term gains, if they are recognized, will be taken when the gain turns long-term.

5. Stocks that followed the pattern of rise-fall-rise would be short-term loss stocks and long-term gain stocks in all sample years. Stocks that followed the pattern of fall-rise-fall would be long-term loss stocks and long-term gain stocks from 1963 to 1976 and long-term loss stocks and short-term gain stocks from 1977 to 1983. Thus, these price patterns are inappropriate for testing the theory of this study.

6. This cutoff is arbitrary. Test results using a 10%/90% cutoff are similar.

7. Two-tailed significance levels are reported throughout.

8. Raw returns are used in the regression tests because it is the rebound of a stock's price from depressed levels, regardless of market return, that is being tested.

REFERENCES

Chan, K. C. (1986). "Can Tax Loss Selling Explain the January Seasonal in Stock Returns?" *Journal of Finance* 41 (December), 1115–1128.

Congressional Budget Office (1988). "How Capital Gains Tax Rates Affect Revenues: The Historical Evidence." (Washington, DC).

Constantinides, G. M. (1984). "Optimal Stock Trading with Personal Taxes: Implications for Prices and the Abnormal January Returns." *Journal of Financial Economics* 13 (March), 65–89.

DeBondt, W. F. M., and Thaler, R. M. (1987). "Further Evidence on Investor Overreaction and Stock Market Seasonality," *Journal of Finance* 52 (July), 557–581.

Dhaliwal, D S., Guo, M. H., and Trezevant, R. (1990). "Tax Rules and Year-End Stock Price Behavior: Evidence from Tax-Rule Regimes During 1963–1985." Working Paper, University of Arizona, Tucson.

Economic Report of the President. (1988). (Washington, DC).

Pechman, J. A. (1983). "Federal Tax Policy." Washington, DC: Brookings Institution.

Poterba, J. M. (1987). "How Burdensome Are Capital Gains Taxes? Evidence from the United States." *Journal of Public Economics* 33, 157–172.

Reinganum, M. R. (1983). "The Anomalous Stock Market Behavior of Small Firms in January: Empirical Tests for Tax-loss Selling Effects." *Journal of Financial Economics* 12 (June), 89–104.

Roll, R. (1983). "Vas Ist Das? The Turn of the Year Effect and the Return Premium of Small Firms." *Journal of Portfolio Management* 9 (Winter), 18–28.

Rozeff, M. S. (1985). "Tax-loss Selling: Evidence from December Stock Returns and Share Shifts." Working Paper, University of Iowa, Iowa City.

Schultz, P. (1988). "Tax Loss Realization in Common Stocks." Working Paper, University of Illinois, Chicago.

AN EMPIRICAL ANALYSIS BY INDUSTRY OF THE STOCK MARKET EFFECTS OF DEFERRED TAXES

Debra C. Jeter

ABSTRACT

The association between the deferred tax component of earnings and security returns is demonstrated to be stronger for firms whose deferred tax items are less "predictably recurring" and for firms whose growth in deferred taxes on the balance sheet has been slower. These findings are consistent with a view that the market places little confidence in deferred taxes which appear unlikely to "reverse out" in the foreseeable future and are thus unlikely to directly affect future cash flows. For financial analysts and other groups using and analyzing financial statements, the results suggest that a portion of the deferred tax liability reported on the balance sheet might be better treated as equity, while a portion of the deferred tax expense included in net income should, perhaps, be disregarded (or added back) in computing profitability ratios. These results lend some support for changing current reporting practices from comprehensive tax allocation (reporting all deferred tax items) to partial tax allocation (reporting only deferred items expected to reverse in the near future). Consequently, the relative merits of partial versus comprehensive tax allocation merit further consideration.

Advances in Quantitative Analysis of Finance and Accounting,
Volume 2, Part A, pages 155–170.

ISBN: 1-55938-564-2

I. INTRODUCTION

Analysts, investors, and creditors are continually evaluating firms on the basis of profitability, leverage, and short-term and long-term liquidity. Deferred tax expense, as reported on the income statement, directly affects the profitability measures, while the deferred tax liability reported on the balance sheet directly affects certain leverage ratios. However, the analyst (or other user) may opt to treat deferred taxes as equity rather than debt, or as part debt and part equity. A careful analysis of deferred taxes by industry group should lead to an enhanced understanding of the financial statements. In the interpretation of ratios and other tools of financial analysis in the decision-making process, industry averages are commonly used as guidelines for comparison. Therefore, an examination of deferred taxes by industry should provide information helpful for financial statement analysis while expanding the body of knowledge on the subject of deferred taxes.

The topic of accounting for income taxes was controversial long before the issuance of Financial Accounting Standards Board (FASB) Standard No. 96 in 1987, and the controversy has been renewed and intensified since its issuance.[1] One of the criticisms leveled at deferred taxes relates to a lack of relevance of the onerously produced numbers in decision making. Further, from a conceptual viewpoint, it has been argued by some that deferred taxes, as computed under comprehensive tax allocation, do not conform to the definition of a liability laid out in the FASB's conceptual framework (Huss, 1983; Rosenfeld and Dent, 1983). Nonetheless, after examining the arguments, the FASB in Statements No. 96 and No. 109 has chosen not only to keep deferred taxes on the balance sheet but to label them as a liability rather than a deferred credit. Like Accounting Principles Board (APB) Opinion No. 11, the new pronouncements do not permit discounting of the deferred tax account. The issue of discounting alone is sufficient to raise questions about the implication that the deferred tax number has for predicting future cash flows of the firm; in addition, considerable uncertainty exists as to whether timing differences of a recurring nature ever "reverse" in the sense of affecting cash outlays or are merely offset by equal or larger originating differences.

However, prior research suggests that the market is using the information conveyed by the deferred tax computation, as indicated by a negative association between the deferred tax component of earnings and security returns. Among the recent researchers who have examined subcomponents of earnings and have attempted to measure the impact of such disclosures on stock prices are Rayburn (1986), Lipe (1986), Bowen, Burgstahler, and Daley (1987), Wilson (1986, 1987), Bernard and Stober (1988), and Chaney and Jeter (1991).

Noncurrent deferred taxes was one of several variables included in Rayburn's (1986) analysis of subcomponents of earnings, which was repeated over two models and two time periods. The coefficient on deferred taxes was consistently negative, though not statistically significant in every model. Chaney and Jeter (1991) examine the association between the deferred tax coefficient of earnings and security returns and present evidence that a negative association exists between deferred taxes and security returns after controlling for pseudo-net income (net income computed without the deferred tax component); the analysis also indicates that the association is more negative and/or more consistent for some subsets of firms than others.

Although neither Bowen et al. nor Wilson looked at deferred taxes specifically, both drew some inferences about accruals in general. Wilson found that while current accruals have incremental information content beyond cash from operations, noncurrent accruals either do not have incremental information content beyond working capital from operations or they are known prior to the earnings announcement. In contrast to Wilson, who used very short event windows centered on the earnings announcement and the receipt of the annual report, Bowen et al. (1987) examined the association between security returns and components of earnings measured over an annual event window; they obtained results similar to Wilson's. Bernard and Stober (1988) extended the work of Wilson and were unable to confirm that the price reaction to accruals was weaker than that to cash flows except in Wilson's brief test period (the fourth quarters of 1981 and 1982). Bernard and Stober introduced a model which relates the impacts of specific current accruals to what they reveal about management's expectations, but they found no empirical support for the model.

Beaver and Dukes (1972) addressed the interperiod tax allocation controversy by contrasting the association between security prices and earnings measured three ways: reported earnings (called deferral earnings), earnings without deferred taxes, and "cash flow" (computed by adding depreciation, depletion, and amortization to earnings without deferred taxes). They found that the association was the strongest for the first of these three measures (and the weakest for the third).

In this paper, the strength of the association between deferred taxes and security returns is examined by industry group, as well as the extent to which the strength of the association is affected by (1) the composition of deferred taxes and (2) the growth of the deferred tax account over time. By relating the association metric to the probability that the deferred tax is truly a liability for firms within a particular industry, this framework provides the potential for more powerful tests and increased explanatory power.

II. SAMPLE DESCRIPTION

This study examines the effect of deferred taxes on security returns over the period 1969–1985 by industry classification. Firms were required to use comprehensive interperiod tax allocation throughout this period. In contrast, Rayburn's study (1986) extended over the period 1963–1982, which included several years prior to the issuance of APB Opinion No. 11 and hence before comprehensive allocation was required.

Table 1. Descriptive Statistics by Industry

SIC	*Variable*	*Industry*	*BS DTAX*	*Beta*	*Persistence*	*Oper. Vol.*	*Growth (Assets)*	*Size*	*Average Sample Size*
1000–1999	SIC10	Mining, oil, and construction	0.059	1.17	9.55	0.097	2.84	589	54.5
2000–2199	SIC20	Food and beverage producers	0.059	0.93	26.16	0.056	2.48	763	52.4
2200–2399	SIC22	Textile products	0.027	1.17	4.35	0.072	0.89	149	34.2
2400–2799	SIC24	Forest, paper products, publishing	0.063	1.26	14.85	0.049	1.99	582	54.6
2800–2899	SIC28	Chemicals	0.038	1.12	19.60	0.067	2.23	1127	63.6
2900–2999	SIC29	Petroleum products	0.128	1.10	n.a.	0.131	3.13	3916	29.5
3000–3299	SIC30	Rubber, plastics, glass, concrete	0.110	1.19	23.46	0.082	0.96	255	45.0
3300–3499	SIC33	Steel and metal products	0.076	1.22	1.78	0.073	1.13	283	64.6
3500–3599	SIC35	Machinery	0.049	1.23	12.07	0.085	1.41	301	62.4
3600–3699	SIC36	Appliances	0.020	1.44	18.08	0.080	2.40	1118	78.3
3700–3799	SIC37	Aircraft and motor vehicles	0.056	1.30	17.47	0.075	1.64	908	49.0
3800–3999	SIC38	Instruments, sporting goods, toys	0.024	1.37	38.68	0.097	1.82	496	37.0
4000–4999	SIC40	Communication, transportation	0.175	1.24	16.54	0.083	2.09	1117	58.7
5000–5299	SIC50	Wholesalers	0.018	1.22	8.78	0.078	2.35	193	32.5
5300–5999	SIC53	Retailers	0.025	1.19	30.29	0.064	3.74	464	77.5
7000–7999	SIC70	Services	0.055	1.46	16.67	0.069	4.73	337	44.4

Notes: n.a.: sample too small to compute.

Definitions: BS DTAX is the average balance sheet deferred taxes divided by the market value of equity for 1971–1985. Beta is the average systematic risk of firms in each industry. Persistence is the average persistence measure on the deferred tax component, computed as in Lipe (1986). Oper. Vol. is the median standard deviation of the first difference in annual earnings deflated by total assets. Growth is the compound growth rate of net plant assets for the years 1971–1985. Size is the average market value of equity in millions of dollars.

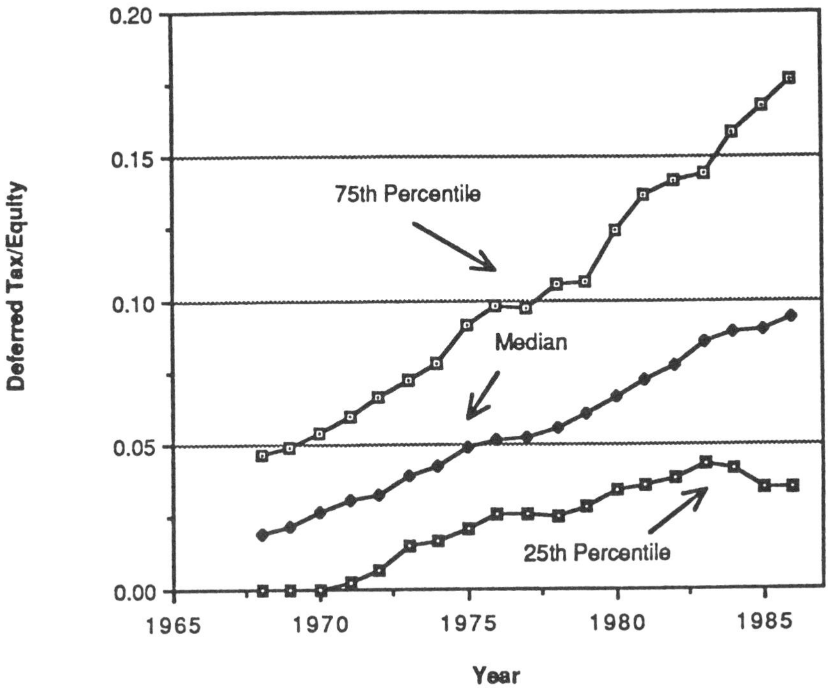

Figure 1. Balance Sheet Deferred Tax Deflated by the Book Value of Equity

Firms were selected in each year for which both Center for Research in Security Prices (CRSP) monthly return and COMPUSTAT data were available for each variable in the study. The average yearly number of firms was 838. Since banks and utilities are regulated industries, they are excluded from the sample. In addition, annual reports were examined manually for the detailed notes regarding the composition of deferred taxes for the years 1981–1983 for those firms for which these data were available; the average yearly number of firms examined was 516.

Firms are divided into sixteen categories based upon their two-digit Standard Industrial Classification (SIC) codes. A summary of the average distribution of firms in each category, the variable names for SIC code used in the analysis, and descriptive statistics is included in Table 1. The communications and transportation industries show the largest average deferred taxes, followed by petroleum products, rubber and plastics, and steel and metal products, in that order.

An examination of Figure 1 reveals that deferred taxes as a percentage of book-value equity have grown steadily since the late 1960s, with a slight leveling off in the 1980s. Figure 2 shows that deferred taxes as a percentage of market-value equity increased until 1975 (particularly soaring during the economic recession of 1974 and 1975), after which they dropped briefly and then leveled off.

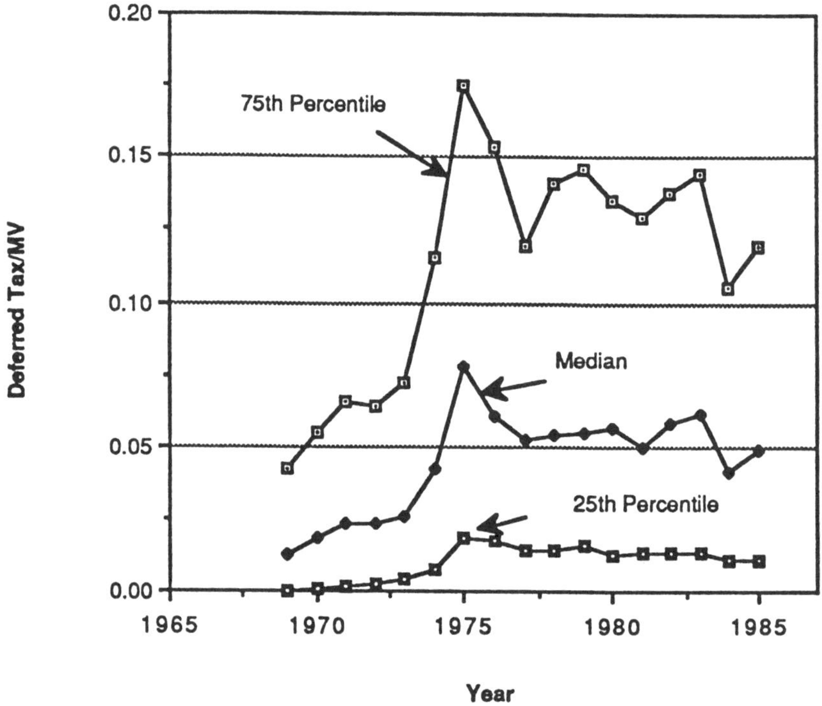

Figure 2. Balance Sheet Deferred Tax Deflated by the Market Value of Equity (*MV*)

III. ASSOCIATION BETWEEN DEFERRED TAXES AND SECURITY RETURNS

If the deferred tax component of earnings is more informative for some firms than for others, the strength of the association between the deferred tax component and security returns may vary by industry group. The FASB's decision via Statement No. 96 to change from the deferral method to the liability method of comprehensive tax allocation suggests that deferred taxes represent a liability to the firm. On the other hand, Bernstein (1989) states that the decision of financial analysts to treat deferred taxes as liability, equity, or part debt and part equity hinges upon the nature of the deferral, the likelihood of future reversal, and whether the account has been constantly growing. Thus one might expect the association between deferred taxes and security returns to be related to the likelihood that individual reversing differences will be offset by future originating differences. This line of reasoning suggests two potential tests for discriminating among firms in the strength of the association: (1) composition of deferred taxes, or nature of the deferral, and (2) growth in deferred taxes over time.

A. Composition of Deferred Taxes

Industry classification is a reasonable proxy for discriminating among firms in terms of the composition of deferred taxes. Most firms in an industry will have similar types of timing differences (and hence a similar makeup of deferred taxes). For instance, deferred taxes in mining companies are apt to result from intangible development and exploration costs deducted in tax returns but capitalized and amortized for financial reporting purposes. An analysis of the detailed composition of deferred taxes included in the notes to the 1983 financial statements reveals, for example, that depreciation is the single largest component of deferred taxes for virtually every firm in the petroleum industry but for only about 30% of the firms in the aircraft and motor vehicles industries, while deferred taxes related to long-term contracts are more prevalent in the aircraft and motor vehicles industries.

If the degree of likelihood that individual reversing differences will be offset by future originating differences is influential in the market's perception of the meaningfulness of deferred taxes, the category of timing differences where this likelihood is perhaps greatest is that of differences in the method used for depreciation or amortization for book and tax purposes. So long as the company is growing, or at least maintaining its operating capacity, future originating differences in depreciation and amortization should be equal to or larger than the reversing differences. A similar argument may be made for differences due to the use of the installment sales method for tax purposes.

For those firms for which predictably recurring items (such as depreciation and amortization differences) represent a relatively large portion of the deferred tax account, the market may perceive the deferred tax component of earnings to be less meaningful in terms of the implications about future cash flows than for industry groups whose deferred taxes include a relatively greater portion of nonrecurring items (or items whose recurring nature is less predictable).

B. Growth of Deferred Taxes over Time

Figure 3 shows that industries have differed in the growth rate in the deferred tax account over time. This rate is calculated as the average annual growth rate in deferred taxes beginning in 1970 and ending in 1985. If the account has been constantly growing, future reversal (affecting cash flows) may be only a remote possibility; that is, deferred taxes are being deferred indefinitely for these firms. Thus, the market might be expected to respond more strongly when deferred taxes have *not* been constantly growing (or for industries with slower growth rates in deferred taxes).

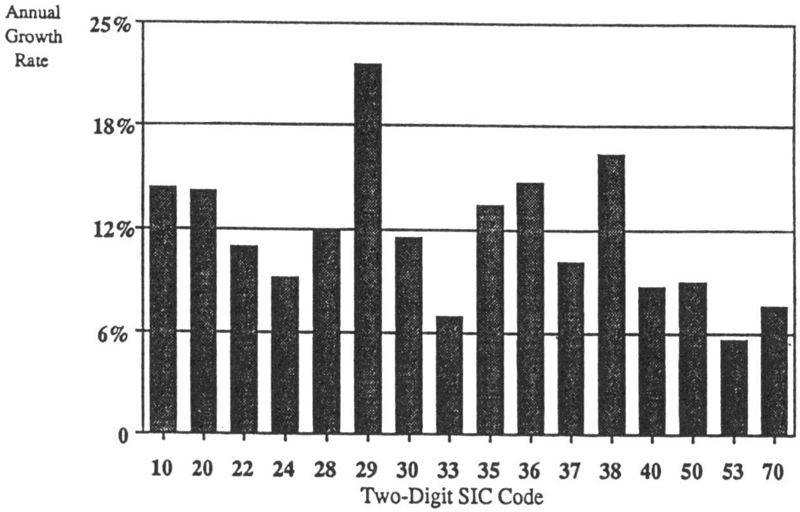

Figure 3. Average Annual Growth in Deferred Taxes by Two-Digit SIC Code from 1969 to 1985

IV. METHODOLOGY AND RESULTS

In an effort to measure the strength of the association between deferred taxes and security returns, the following regression was repeated for each two-digit SIC code:

$$AR_{it} = B_0 + B_1 PNI_{it} + B_2 R_{mt} + B_3 uDTAX_{it} + u_{it}, \tag{1}$$

where

AR_{it} = the rate of return for firm i for year t computed as follows:

$$AR_{it} = \left[\prod_{k=1}^{12} (1 + r_{ik}) \right] - 1,$$

where r_{ik} = the rate of return for firm i for month k.

R_{mt} = the market rate of return for year t computed as follows:[2]

$$R_{mt} = \left[\prod_{k=1}^{12} (1 + r_{mk}) \right] - 1,$$

where

r_{mk} = the CRSP value-weighted market rate of return for month k.

$MV_{i,t-1}$ = the market value of equity at the beginning of year t;

PNI_{it} = pseudo-net income of firm i in year t, or earnings of firm i in year t excluding the deferred tax component of earnings;

$DTAX_{it}$ = change in noncurrent deferred taxes on the balance sheet of firm i from year $t-1$ to year t;

$uPNI_{it}$ = unexpected PNI_{it}, or $[PNI_{it} - E(PNI_{it})]/MV_{i,t-1}$,

where $E(PNI_{it})$ = the market's expectation of PNI_{it} measured at the beginning of year t, or $PNI_{i,t-1}$;

$$uDTAX_{it} = \text{unexpected } DTAX_{it}, \text{ or } [DTAX_{it} - E(DTAX_{it})]/MV_{i,t-1},$$

where $E(DTAX_{it})$ = the market's expectation of $DTAX_{it}$ measured at the beginning of year t, or $DTAX_{i,t-1}$.

The variable PNI_{it}, or pseudo-net income, represents what earnings would be without deferred taxes; that is, if income tax expense were allowed to follow the tax return. A random walk expectations model is used for both pseudo-net income and the deferred tax component of earnings. The result that this model performs well when compared to other earnings expectations models has been well documented in the literature (Albrecht, Lookabill, and McKeown, 1977; Bowen, Burgstahler, and Daley, 1987; Watts and Leftwich, 1977). While analyst forecasts are believed by many to be a superior measure of expectations (Brown and Rozeff, 1978; Elgers, Callahan, and Strock, 1987), such forecasts are not regularly available for deferred taxes.[3]

The results from estimating Eq. (1) are presented in Table 2, columns A1–A3. The t-statistic reported in column A3 is the time-series t-test on the average coefficient from the annual regressions. Those industry groups showing the most statistically significant coefficients on deferred taxes are rubber and plastics (SIC30), steel and metal products (SIC33), and machinery (SIC35).[4] For each of these three groups, the coefficient on deferred taxes was negative and significant at the 5% level in six of the years between 1969 and 1985. These coefficients do not appear to be merely mimicking the coefficients on pseudo income for the various industries; in contrast to the coefficients on $uDATX$, the largest mean coefficients on $uPNI$ are for Sic28, 29, 30, and 50. However, the real test is whether the strength of the association for a particular industry can be explained based upon (1) the recurring/nonrecurring nature of deferred tax items in that particular industry or (2) the growth of the deferred tax account on the balance sheet.

A. Composition of Deferred Tax: Results

Columns B1 and B2 of Table 2 relate to the composition of deferred taxes. Two separate tests were designed using the sample period 1981–1983. To carry out these tests I examined the notes to the financial statements included in the annual reports for the detailed composition of deferred taxes in these years. The purpose of each

Table 2. SIC Code Results[a]

SIC	*Variable*	*Industry*	*A1*	*A2*	*A3*	*A4*	*B1*	*B2*	*C1*
1000–1999	SIC10	Mining, oil, and construction	0.72*	1.87	0.86	4†	0.409	1.141	0.149
2000–2199	SIC20	Food and beverage producers	1.23*	–1.29	–1.71‡	5†	0.330	0.834	0.146
2200–2399	SIC22	Textile products	1.04*	0.94	1.32	3	0.992	1.824	0.113
2400–2799	SIC24	Forest, paper products, publishing	1.59*	–1.19	–1.52‡	5†	1.390	1.650	0.095
2800–2899	SIC28	Chemicals	2.15*	–2.39	–1.85*	4†	0.645	1.418	0.123
2900–2999	SIC29	Petroleum products	2.77*	–0.75	–1.12	4†	1.568	1.930	0.225
3000–3299	SIC30	Rubber, plastics, glass, concrete	2.15*	–2.42	–2.97*	6†	0.583	1.386	0.120
3300–3499	SIC33	Steel and metal products	1.12*	–1.44	–2.89*	6†	0.258	0.934	0.072
3500–3599	SIC35	Machinery	1.61*	–1.38	–2.57*	6†	–0.018	1.027	0.139
3600–3699	SIC36	Appliances	0.90	0.66	0.82	1	0.478	1.321	0.153
3700–3799	SIC37	Aircraft and motor vehicles	0.89*	–0.66	–2.06*	2	1.317	1.108	0.105
3800–3999	SIC38	Instruments, sporting goods, toys	1.23	1.98	1.45	1	0.491	2.577	0.170
4000–4999	SIC40	Communication and transportation	0.93*	–0.42	–1.47‡	5†	1.890	1.032	0.090
5000–5299	SIC50	Wholesalers	3.96‡	–4.42	–1.35‡	4†	–0.462	0.509	0.093
5300–5999	SIC53	Retailers	1.17*	–0.77	–1.36‡	3	0.850	0.782	0.058
7000–7999	SIC70	Services	1.91	–2.84	–1.42‡	2	0.329	0.715	0.078

Notes: [a] $AR_{it} = \beta_0 + \beta_1 uPNI_{it} + \beta_2 R_{mt} + \beta_3 uDTAX_{it} + u_{it}$

Column definitions:

A. Coefficients:

(1) Mean value of β_1, the *uPNI* coefficient, for 1969–1985.

(2) Mean value of β_3, the *uDTAX* coefficient, for 1969–1985.

(3) *T* value of mean of deferred tax coefficient.

(4) Number of years from 1969 to 1985 the deferred tax coefficient was significant at the 5% level.

B. Tests (1) and (2):

(1) Average percentage of deferred taxes from depreciation measured for sample year 1983.

(2) Average percentage of deferred taxes from predictably recurring items (*PRI*) measured for sample year 1983, excluding outliers and firms with credit balances in the deferred tax expense account.

Percentages in tests 1 and 2 may range from negative values to values greater than one due to credit balances in the deferred tax expense or credit balances in recurring items.

C. Growth Test: (1) Average annual growth rate in deferred taxes from 1970 to 1985.

*Significant at the 0.05 level.

†Significant at the 0.05 level based on a binomial test.

‡Significant at the 0.10 level.

of the two tests was to ascertain the extent to which the deferred tax expense consisted of items which were recurring in nature and consistent in sign from year to year (using 1981–1983). To the extent that such items comprise deferred taxes, it seems reasonable to speculate that reversing differences are likely to be offset by originating differences and thus will not lead to the payment of actual tax dollars.

Test 1: Divide deferred taxes arising from depreciation by the total deferred tax expense for the year for each firm. Here depreciation is assumed to proxy for predictably recurring items. Average the individual firm percentages for each industry.

Test 2: Divide predictably recurring items (*PRI*'s) for each firm for the year 1983 by the total deferred tax expense for the year. Average the firm percentages for each industry.

To select *PRI*'s, three years were examined for each firm, 1981–1983. Those components of deferred tax expense (for example, deferred taxes from installment sales, deferred taxes from depreciation differences, difference between financial and tax expense for inventory obsolescence, excess of tax over financial insurance expense, and warranty differences) that appeared in all three years and were of consistent sign in all three years were selected and labeled *PRI*'s. This definition of predictably recurring items was selected on the grounds that, for those items which change signs, reversing amounts are not being entirely offset by originating items and tax payments may result.

Two groups of firms were excluded, outlier firms and those firms having credit balances in the deferred tax expense account for 1983. Outliers were defined as firms whose individual percentage was more than four standard deviations from the mean. The rationale for excluding firms with credit balances in the expense account is that the argument for examining the predictability of deferred tax items relates primarily to items increasing (rather than decreasing) the balance sheet deferred tax account.

The percentages for each of the two tests are presented in Table 2. The hypothesis suggests that the coefficients on deferred taxes should be less negative for those industries for whom predictably recurring items comprised a relatively large portion of deferred taxes. Support of this hypothesis would imply a positive correlation between the *uDTAX* regression coefficient by industry group and each of the industry percentages computed in tests 1 and 2.

Rank correlations were positive, as expected. Specifically, the rank correlation between the *uDTAX* coefficient by SIC code and the average (*DTAX* from *DEPR*)/*DTAX* was 0.46, with a p value of 0.07. The rank correlation between the coefficient and the average *PRI*/*DTAX* was 0.56, with a p value of 0.02.

To improve the visualization of the relationship, I grouped the industries into four portfolios, ranging from those with the largest ratios (test 2) of recurring items to those with the smallest, and the results are summarized in Table 3. The second column of Table 3 presents the weighted average ratio of predictably recurring items to total deferred tax expense for each portfolio. Most of the ratios are greater than

Table 3. Recurring versus Nonrecurring Timing Differences[a]

Portfolio[b]	*Recurring Ratio*[c]	*Average Coefficient on uDTAX*	*Average Coefficient on uPNI*	*Number of Firms*
Portfolio 1	1.96	0.12	1.61*	155
Portfolio 2	1.32	−0.44	1.42*	241
Portfolio 3	1.02	−1.01*	1.15*	235
Portfolio 4	0.74	−1.92†	1.78*	207

Notes: [a]$AR_{it} = B_0 + B_1 uPNI_{it} + B_2 R_{mt} + B_3 DTAX_{it} + u_{it}$

[b]Portfolio 1 includes SIC22, 24, 29, and 38;
Portfolio 2 includes SIC10, 28, 30, and 36;
Portfolio 3 includes SIC33, 35, 37, and 40;
Portfolio 4 includes SIC20, 50, 53, and 70.

[c]Ratio of deferred tax recurring differences to total deferred tax expense.

*Significant at the 0.05 level for all industries in the portfolio.

†Significant at the 0.10 level for all industries in the portfolio.

one because individual credit items often reduce the deferred tax expense. For example, a firm might show predictably recurring items of $10,000, nonrecurring credit items of $2,000, and a net deferred tax expense of $8,000. The ratio of recurring items to deferred tax expense would be 10:8, or 1.25.

The third column presents the mean value of the coefficient on unexpected deferred taxes for firms in each portfolio. This table demonstrates that the average coefficient is more negative for firms with lower ratios of predictably recurring items. The fourth column presents the mean value of the coefficient on unexpected pseudo-net income for firms in each portfolio and reveals no distinct pattern for those coefficients; thus it is clear that the coefficient on deferred taxes for these portfolios is not mimicking the coefficient on unexpected earnings.

These results support the hypothesis that the association between deferred taxes and security returns is less negative for industries where deferred taxes are composed primarily of predictably recurring timing differences. The evidence suggests that partial interperiod tax allocation might be deemed superior to comprehensive allocation; partial allocation limits deferred taxes to those timing differences that may reasonably be expected to reverse in the foreseeable future and thus result in an actual future payment of taxes.

B. Growth in Deferred Taxes: Results

The rank correlation between the coefficients on deferred taxes by industry and growth rates of deferred taxes by industry was also computed. The growth rate of deferred taxes (presented in Figure 3 and also in Table 2, col. C1) is the average annual growth rate in deferred taxes beginning in 1970 and ending in 1985. The rank correlation between this variable and the coefficient on deferred taxes (presented in Table 2, col. A2) was 0.45, with a *p* value of 0.08.

This result suggests that the association between security returns and the deferred tax component of earnings is more negative for industries with lower levels of growth in the deferred tax account on the balance sheet; similarly, the association is nearer zero for industries with rapidly growing deferred taxes. In other words, the market appears to be deriving less information from the deferred tax component of earnings for those firms whose deferred tax account is growing most rapidly on the balance sheet. This finding is also consistent with a conclusion that partial interperiod tax allocation might be deemed superior to comprehensive allocation.

V. SENSITIVITY ANALYSIS

The possibility that the strength of the association between deferred taxes and security returns for various industries is driven (or affected) by variables other than those hypothesized in this study cannot be ignored. In view of this potentiality, rank correlations between the regression coefficients on *uDTAX* by industry group (from Table 2) and variables for systematic risk, operating volatility, growth in assets, or size (from Table 1) were computed. The correlations were as follows.

	uDTAX Coefficient	
Variable	*Rank Correlation*	*P value*
Beta	0.072	0.79
Operating volatility	0.381	0.15
Growth in assets	0.091	0.74
Size	0.150	0.58
Persistence	0.059	0.83

The persistence of the deferred tax component is presented by industry group in Table 1. The persistence measure is derived based on the autocorrelations and cross correlation of specified earnings components. The persistence measure was computed as in Appendix B of Lipe (1986) using nineteen years of data. The components used for the computation were net income before depreciation and taxes, depreciation, current portion of tax expense, and deferred taxes. Each component was deflated by the average consumer price index for each year and mean adjusted. Only survivor firms were used for the computation of the persistence measures, of which adequate data were available to compute persistence measures for about 400 firms. As shown above, the rank correlation between the coefficient on *uDTAX* by industry group and the persistence measure is insignificant. Thus, there is no evidence that the association by industry is significantly affected by this or the other variables examined.

The possibility also exists that the percentages computed in tests 1 and 2 (designed to relate the recurring nature and predictability of deferred taxes to the association metric) were proxying for other relevant variables, such as persistence or operating volatility. Therefore, rank correlations were also computed between the percentages from tests 1 and 2 and the persistence measure, as well as between the percentages and the average operating volatility by industry. These correlations were as follows.

	Persistence		*Operating Volatility*	
Variable	*Rank Correlation*	*P value*	*Rank Correlation*	*P value*
(*DTAX* from *DEPR*)/*DTAX*	0.047	0.86	−0.009	0.97
PRI/*DTAX*	−0.015	0.96	0.322	0.22

Thus, there is no indication that persistence differences or operating volatility differences were driving or confounding those results.

VI. CONCLUSION

The strength of the association between the deferred tax component of earnings and security returns is examined by industry group. Evidence is presented that the association is stronger for firms whose deferred tax items are less "predictably recurring" and for firms whose growth in deferred taxes on the balance sheet has been slower. These findings are consistent with a view that the market places little confidence in deferred taxes which appear unlikely to "reverse out" in the foreseeable future and are thus unlikely to directly affect future cash flows.

For financial analysts and other groups using and analyzing financial statements, the results suggest that a portion of the deferred tax liability reported on the balance sheet might be better treated as equity, while a portion of the deferred tax expense included in net income should, perhaps, be disregarded (or added back) in computing profitability ratios. To the extent that the analyst has the necessary information to ascertain which timing differences are expected to reverse and which ones are not, then he or she can make adjustments to aid in decision making.

A better solution might be a change from comprehensive tax allocation to partial tax allocation by the preparers of the financial statements, with the sanction of the standard-setting bodies. The burden of categorizing timing differences based upon their likelihood to result in tax payments would thus be shifted from the user to the firm, which should have more complete information for making such classifications. Consequently, the relative merits of partial versus comprehensive tax allocation are worthy of further consideration.

NOTES

1. Changes in the accounting for income taxes from APB Opinion 11 to FASB Statements No. 96 and 109 may be summarized as follows.

The term *temporary* difference is used instead of *timing* difference, the former having been broadened to include differences between the tax bases of assets or liabilities and their reported amounts in financial statements as well as the differences between the amount of taxable income and pretax financial income for a year.

The balance sheet accounts created are now considered to be liabilities (or assets) rather than deferred credits (or charges). Deferred tax assets are subject to a valuation allowance.

Under APB Opinion 11, deferred taxes were based on the tax rates in effect when the differences originated and were not subsequently adjusted; under the new method, deferred taxes will be computed using the rates expected to be in effect in the reversal period and are subject to adjustment as rates change or new taxes are imposed.

2. The market return variable is constant for all firms with the same year-end in any given year but differs for firms with varying year-ends.

3. Recent papers suggest that earnings may be less persistent than a random walk (Lipe and Kormendi, 1991; Easton and Harris, 1990). In view of this possibility, two alternative models for deferred taxes and pseudo-net income were included in Chaney and Jeter (1991) to ensure that the results were robust to alternative forecast models. The first of these models was a pure mean reverting model: $uDTAX_{it} = DTAX_{it}$; the second represented an intermediate case: $uDTAX_{it} = DTAX_{it} - 0.5DTAX_{i,t-1}$. The results were robust to these specifications. Thus, a random walk model is used in this paper: $E(PNI_{it}) = PNI_{i,t-1}$ and $E(DTAX_{it}) = DTAX_{i,t-1}$.

4. Two specification checks were conducted. First, the industry partitioning was repeated using residual returns as the dependent variable; the same industry groups showed the most consistent coefficients on the deferred tax component of earnings as in the original analysis (using raw returns as the dependent variable). Thus the results were robust with respect to this specification.

As an additional specification check, the analysis was repeated without the market return variable; while its inclusion improved the overall explanatory power of the regressions on a yearly basis, it had very little effect on the coefficient on deferred taxes, either on a yearly basis or when pooled over the seventeen years examined. The fact that the coefficient on *uDTAX* was not altered indicates that the association between security returns and the deferred tax component of earnings is not driven by market-wide factors.

REFERENCES

Albrecht, W., Lookabill, L., and McKeown, J. (1977). "The Time Series Properties of Annual Earnings." *Journal of Accounting Research* 15 (Autumn), 226–244.

Beaver, W., and Dukes, R. (1972). "Interperiod Tax Allocation, Earnings Expectations, and the Behavior of Security Prices." *Accounting Review* (April), 320–332.

Bernard, V., and Stober, T. (1988). "The Nature and Amount of Information Reflected in Cash Flows and Accruals." Working Paper, The University of Michigan (January).

Bernstein, L. (1989). *Financial Statement Analysis: Theory. Application. and Interpretation*, 4th ed., 212–213, 573–574.

Bowen, R., Burgstahler, D., and Daley, L. (1987). "The Incremental Information Content of Accrual Versus Cash Flows." *Accounting Review* (October), 723–747.

Brown, L., and Rozeff, M. (1978). "The Superiority of Analyst Forecasts as Measures of Expectations: Evidence from Earnings." *Journal of Finance* (March), 1–16.

Chaney, P., and Jeter, D. (1991). "The Effect of Deferred Taxes on Security Prices." Forthcoming, *Journal of Accounting, Auditing, and Finance.*

Easton, P., and Harris, T. (1990). "Empirical Evidence on the Relevance of Earnings and Book Value of Owner's Equity in Security Valuation." Working Paper, Columbia University (October).

Elgers, E., Callahan, C., and Strock, E. (1987). "The Effect of Earnings Yields Upon the Association Between Unexpected Earnings and Security Returns: A Reexamination." *Accounting Review* (October), 241–273.

Huss, H. (1983). "A Contingency Approach to Accounting for Income Taxes." *Journal of Accounting, Auditing, and Finance* (Spring), 60–66.

Leftwich, R. (1981). "Evidence of the Impact of Mandatory Changes in Accounting Principles on Corporate Loan Agreements." *Journal of Accounting and Economics* (March), 3–36.

Lipe, R. (1986). "The Information Contained in the Components of Earnings." *Journal of Accounting Research* (Supplement), 37–64.

Lipe, R., and Kormendi, R. (1991). "The Long-Horizon Properties of Annual Earnings: An Analysis of Persistence and Valuation." Working Paper, University of Michigan (February).

Rayburn, J. (1986). "The Association of Operating Cash Flow and Accruals with Security Returns." *Journal of Accounting Research* 24 (Supplement), 112–137.

Rosenfeld, P., and Dent, W. (1983). "No More Deferred Taxes." *Journal of Accountancy* (February), 44–55.

Watts, R., and Leftwich, R. (1977). "The Time Series of Annual Accounting Earnings." *Journal of Accounting Research* 15 (Autumn), 253–271.

Wilson, P. (1986). "The Relative Information Content of Accruals and Cash Flows: Combined Evidence at the Earnings Announcement and Annual Report Release Date." *Journal of Accounting Research* (Supplement), 165–203.

Wilson, P. (1987). "The Incremental Information Content of the Accrual and Funds Components of Earnings after Controlling for Earnings." *Accounting Review* (April), 293–321.

ON THE PORTFOLIO MANAGEMENT OF COMMERCIAL BANKS WITH TAIWAN'S BANKS AS CASE STUDY

J. T. Chen, S. L. Chang, and Gili Yen

ABSTRACT

In this paper, we allow for randomness not only in asset returns but in its holdings in the portfolio management of commercial banks. The three theoretical choice variables are net borrowings from banks, total investments, and loan rate. It is found that the testable implications are borne out by empirical findings. Almost all the coefficients relating asset and liability levels to interest rates are in conformity with a priori expectations. If these encouraging results are confirmed in further studies, we believe that the proposed model can shed light on the important issue of portfolio management of commercial banks.

I. INTRODUCTION

Portfolio management is the predominant business activity of commercial banks. Generally speaking, earlier studies in this area fell in two camps. In the first

Advances in Quantitative Analysis of Finance and Accounting,
Volume 2, Part A, pages 171–193.

ISBN: 1-55938-564-2

approach, à la Markowitz, scholars compare an actual portfolio with an efficient portfolio. Francis (1978) is perhaps the best example. In the second approach, which attacks from the empirical perspective, scholars pick up the desired portfolio with the aid of optimizing techniques, such as those described in Cohen and Hammer (1967), Echols and Elliott (1976), and Aghili, Cramer, and Thompson (1975). Yet only recently have scholars begun to investigate complications in financial management caused by possible interactions between assets and liabilities. Among others, Parkin (1970), Ghosh and Parkin (1972), Aigner (1973), Spindt and Tarhan (1980), Berndt, McCurdy, and Rose (1980), Humphrey (1981), and Jahera and Sinkey (1984) are eminent examples of studies on this subject. Most of the studies just mentioned chose a set of explanatory variables such as interest rates on assets and/or liabilities, and the levels of particular assets and liabilities, to determine the optimal portfolio. In models of this kind, although the returns on assets or liabilities are allowed to vary from time to time, the levels of assets or liabilities are regarded as given and hence are determined exogenously. The purpose of this study is twofold. First, on the theoretical front, we allow for randomness not only in asset returns but in its holdings. Second, on the empirical front, the present study attempts to make use of recently developed econometric techniques to obtain better empirical results.

The paper is divided into five sections. In addition to the introductory section, which describes the research motive and objective of the present study, the remaining portion of the paper is organized as follows. Section II derives testable implications from an expected-utility-oriented theoretical framework. Section III specifies an econometric model and establishes testing hypotheses. Empirical results are presented and discussed in Section IV. Section V contains the conclusion.

II. ANALYTIC FRAMEWORK

A. Classification of Assets and Liabilities

To proceed, assets/liabilities of a commercial bank are classified into six mutually exclusive categories on the basis of characteristics regarding the level of assets (liabilities) of each type and its associative yield (cost). The term *liabilities* is used in a broader sense, including external liabilities and internal liabilities (net worth). Let us consider each type in turn.

First, we consider the assets/liabilities of those amounts that can be controlled by the bank; the interest on these, however, is stochastic. Funds due or borrowed from the Central Bank or other banks are eminent examples. Assuming there are k items of such assets/liabilities, we denote the assets/liabilities by a $k \times 1$ vector, A_1, and their interest rates by another $k \times 1$ vector, R_1.

Second, there are assets/liabilities that are demanded by the public. Loans and discounts are examples. Obviously, predicting the optimal amounts of these assets/liabilities is extremely difficult, if not totally impossible. We denote them by an $l \times 1$ vector, A_2, assuming l kinds of such assets/liabilities are present. In practice, the interest rates of these assets/liabilities are established by the bank and are denoted by an $l \times 1$ vector, R_2.

Time and savings deposits can be considered as a third type. The amount of assets/liabilities of this type is primarily determined by the depository behavior of depositors. Hence, from the point of view of the banks, these items are random. Although the interest rates of these assets/liabilities are determined by the banks, they normally vary only within a very small range. For convenience, we will treat these rates as fixed. These assets/liabilities and the corresponding rates are denoted by two $m \times 1$ vectors, A_3 and R_3, respectively.

Fourth, for some assets/liabilities, the banks usually do not pay interest. Cash and excess reserves, among others, belong to this category. Typically, the holding of these assets/liabilities is seen to change in step with the financial market. The vector that represents these p assets/liabilities is A_4.

Fifth, in contrast to the fourth category, there are assets/liabilities that carry implicit interest rates. Capital stocks and bank premises and equipment are two examples. These assets/liabilities usually are maintained at a prespecified level and are denoted by a $q \times 1$ vector, A_5.

In addition, the assets/liabilities holdings in A_2, A_3, and A_4 might be subject to unexpected changes on the demand side. To accommodate such unexpected changes, we need a residual account to absorb them. Assets/liabilities in the residual account are denoted by A_0 and their corresponding interest rates, R_0.

B. Model Building

As stated in the beginning of this paper, we emphasize the important role played by the interaction between assets and liabilities in portfolio management. Viewed from this perspective, the expected net income of a commercial bank is influenced by the amount held as well as the return (rate of interest) charged regarding controllable items. In the following, we will set up a formal model to illuminate the entire decision-making process facing a portfolio manager. To achieve the aforementioned objective, let us start with a discussion on determinants of each variable. Meanwhile, necessary notations will be given in proper places.

Let $i = 0, \ldots, 5$, denote the expected level of A_i as μ_{A_i}, we can write $A_i = \mu_{A_i} + a_i$ due to the randomness of some assets/liabilities, where a_i's are random errors with $E(a_i) = 0$. It is worth pointing out, in accord with our earlier discussions, that a_1 and a_5 are set at zero. Similarly, for $i = 0, 1, 2, 3$, the expected value of R_i is denoted by μ_{R_i}. Since R_2 and R_3 are fixed, we have $\mu_{R_2} = R_2$ and $\mu_{R_3} = R_3$. In contrast, because of the presence of disturbing terms, R_0 and R_1 can be defined as $R_0 = \mu_{R_0} + \gamma_0$ and $R_1 = \mu_{R_1} + \gamma_1$, assuming $E(\gamma_0) = 0$ and $E(\gamma_1) = 0$. The determinants of the amount of assets/liabilities in A_2 through A_4, however, need a little elaboration. In our model, A_i's, $i = 2, 3, 4$, are determined by R_2 and Z, while Z is a vector including intercept (the catchall term), interest rates, a measure of the pace of business activity, and possibly other demand side variables. The interest rates in Z may include rates which may affect demand for the financial claims of the bank but do not show up in the bank's net income function. R_2 is separated from other interest rates since it presumably exerts substantial influences on the holdings of A_2, A_3, and A_4. In formal terms, $\mu_{A_i} = \beta_i \mu_{R_2} + \omega_i \mu_Z$; $i = 2, 3, 4$, for some unknown parameters β_i's and ω_i's.

To save enormous use of notations, liabilities are treated as negative assets. Under such circumstances, the amounts of all assets on the bank's balance sheet must add up to zero. This identity can be written formally as

$$e_1'A_1 + e_2'A_2 + e_3'A_3 + e_4'A_4 + e_5'A_5 + A_0 = e'A + A_0 = 0, \tag{1}$$

where e_i is a vector of ones with the order equal to A_i, $i = 1, \ldots, 5$, $e = (e_i', e_2', e_3', e_4', e_5')'$ and $A = (A_1', A_2', A_3', A_4', A_5')'$. The net income function can then be defined as

$$\pi = R_1'A_1 + R_2'A_2 + R_3'A_3 + R_0 A_0. \tag{2}$$

Evoking the identity in Eq. (1), we can rewrite the net income function as

$$\begin{aligned} \pi &= R_1'A_1 + R_2'A_2 + R_3'A_3 + R_0(-e'A) \\ &= (R_1 - R_0 e_1)'A_1 + (R_2 - R_0 e_2)'A_2 + (R_3 - R_0 e_3)'A_3 - (R_0 e_4)'A_4 - (R_0 e_5)'A_5 \\ &= R'A, \end{aligned} \tag{3}$$

where the interest rate spreads of the corresponding asset categories, R, can be expressed as $[(R_1 - R_0 e_1)', (R_2 - R_0 e_2)', (R_3 - R_0 e_3)', (-R_0 e_4)', (-R_0 e_5)']'$. Similar to what we did above, R can be defined as

$$R = \mu_R + \tilde{\gamma}, \tag{4}$$

where $\mu_R = (\mu_1, \mu_2, \mu_3, \mu_4, \mu_5)'$ denotes arithmetic means of R's; $\tilde{\gamma}$ denotes the error terms and $E(\tilde{\gamma}) = 0$.

Following the usual practice, the interest rates in R_1 are assumed to be uncorrelated with the asset levels in A_2, A_3, and A_4. Furthermore, the interest rate in R_0 is assumed to be independent from the level of each asset, which amounts to assuming $E(\tilde{\gamma} a') = 0$ and $E(\tilde{\gamma}' a) = 0$[1]. Accordingly, we can derive the expected net income and its variance as

$$\mu_\pi = \mu'_R \mu_A \tag{5}$$

and

$$\sigma_\pi^2 = \mu_A' C \mu_A + \mu_R' G \mu_R + tr\, GC, \tag{6}$$

where

$$C = E(\tilde{\gamma}\tilde{\gamma}') = \{C_{ij}\}\ (i, j = 1, \ldots, 5)$$

$$G = E(aa') = \{G_{ij}\}\ (i, j = 1, \ldots, 5)$$

and

$$tr\,GC = E(\tilde{\gamma}'aa'\tilde{\gamma}).$$

In viewing the importance of the variance of the expected net income (hereafter combined risk), a little elaboration is in place. The rationale that we referred to "the variance of the expected net income" as "combined risk" goes as follows. The combined risk is composed of three components, namely, $\mu'_A C \mu_A$, $\mu'_R G \mu_R$, and $tr\,GC = E(\tilde{\gamma}'aa'\tilde{\gamma})$, which in turn are determined by C and G. To start, C corresponding to price or rate risk in the literature represents the covariance matrix of interest rate spreads. As for G, corresponding to quantity risk or volume risk in the literature, it represents the covariance matrix of asset holdings. At this juncture, the components of the covariance matrix can be definitively signed as follows: the covariance between any pairwise asset and liability must always be negative since interest income inflows and interest expense outflows are inverse movements of funds within a bank; as for the covariance terms between any two assets, or for that matter any two liabilities, must be positive simply because associative fund flows are always moving in the same direction. Given the meanings of C and G, we are in a position to define $\mu'_A C \mu_A$, $\mu'_R G \mu_R$ and $tr\,GC$ accordingly. The first risk component, $\mu'_A C \mu_A$, refers to the risk arising from a change in the interest rates spread, given that the levels of asset holdings remain unchanged. The second risk component, $\mu'_R G \mu_R$, in contrast, refers to the risk arising from a change in asset holdings, given that interest spreads remain unchanged. The third risk component, $tr\,GC$, refers to the risk arising from a simultaneous small change in both asset holdings and interest spreads. It turns out that $tr\,GC$ is independent of both μ_{A_1} and μ_{R_2}.[2]

Under the assumption that net income is normally distributed, the portfolio manager is postulated to maximize the expected utility with the real net income, π, as its main argument

$$E(U) = b_0 - b_1[\exp(\frac{-b_2}{2}\mu_\pi + (\frac{b_2}{2^2}\sigma_\pi^2)] , \tag{7}$$

where $b_0 \neq 0$, $b_1 > 0$, and b_2 is some unknown positive constant representing the degree of risk aversion.[3]

With the exponential function increasing monotonically, maximizing the transformed utility function as shown in Eq. (8) guarantees maximization of the original expected utility function

$$W = \mu_\pi - \frac{b_2}{2}\sigma_\pi^2. \tag{8}$$

In order to find the maximizer of Eq. (8), we take the first derivatives with respect to μ_{A_1} and μ_{R_2} and assign them the value of zero. The resulting equations can be simplified to

$$\mu^*_{A_1} = \psi_{11}\mu_{R_1} + \psi_{13}\mu_{R_3} + \psi_{10}\mu_{R_0} + \psi_{15}e'_5\mu_{A_5} + \psi_{1z}\mu_Z \tag{9}$$

and

$$\mu^*_{R_2} = \psi_{21}\mu_{R_1} + \psi_{23}\mu_{R_3} + \psi_{20}\mu_{R_0} + \psi_{25}e'_5\mu_{A_5} + \psi_{2z}\mu_Z\,, \tag{10}$$

where ψ_{ij} represents the coefficient matrix of parameters for Eqs. (9) and (10) (i = 1, 2 and j = 0, 1, 3, 5, Z). (See Appendix A for detailed derivation.) Assuming the solutions obtained from Eqs. (9) and (10) satisfy the second-order conditions, W is maximized at ($\mu^*_{A_1}$, $\mu^*_{R_2}$).

Although the bank cannot control A_0, the bank can influence A_0 indirectly by choosing A_1. Using the identity in Eq. (1) in company with the demand functions in A_2, A_3, A_4, and the asset and interest rate equations in (9) and (10), we can obtain the residual amount

$$\mu^*_{A_0} = \psi_{01}\mu_{R_1} + \psi_{03}\mu_{R_3} + \psi_{00}\mu_{R_0} + \psi_{05}e'_5\mu_{A_5} + \psi_{0z}\mu_Z\,, \tag{11}$$

where $\psi_{0i} = -e'_1\psi_{1i} - \beta\psi_{2i}$, $i = 0, 1, 3, 5$; $\psi_{0z} = -e'_1\psi_{1z} - \beta\psi_{2z} - \omega$, $\beta = e'_2\beta_2 + e'_3\beta_3 + e'_4\beta_4$; and $\omega = e'_2\omega_2 + e'_3\omega_3 + e'_4\omega_4$.

III. EMPIRICAL SPECIFICATION

A. An Econometric Model

An econometric analysis will be conducted in this section. Before we move on, however, a little discussion regarding the choice of empirical variables would be appropriate. As shown at the end of the previous section, three variables—quantities of the assets of the assets μ_{A_0}, μ_{A_1}, and interest rate of asset category A_2, that is, μ_{R_2}—are of importance. It has been further shown that μ_{A_0}, owing to the intrinsic constraint imposed by the accounting identity, can be determined once μ_{A_1} is determined. In viewing their representativeness, net borrowings from banks, investments (i.e., the expected value)[4] and the interest rate on loans are singled out as empirical counterparts in the ensuing regression analysis for μ_{A_1}, μ_{A_0}, and μ_{R_2}, respectively. From Eqs. (9)–(11), each empirical variable is in turn seen to be a function of its own rate, the rates of other choice variables, relevant balance sheet items and their interest rates, and some economic variables.

In this study, seven balance sheet items, four interest rate variables, and one economic variable as shown in Table 1 are considered. The three choice variables are (1) A_0: total investments (I), defined as the sum of Treasury bills and other securities; (2) A_1: net borrowings from banks (B), defined as borrowings from banks

Table 1. Variable Definitions

Asset Categories	Balance-Sheet Items	Interest Rates	Definition
A_0	I	RI	Investments
A_1	B	RB	Net borrowings from banks
A_2	L	RL	Loans and discounts
A_3	T	RT	Time and savings deposits
A_4	D	—	Demand deposits
	E	—	Excess reserves
A_5	F	—	Other assets
Economic variable	IPI	—	Industrial production index

minus due from banks; and (3) R_2: loan rate (RL), defined as interest revenue divided by the combined amount of loans and discounts. The explanatory variables taken from the balance sheet include excess reserves (E), loans and discounts (L), time and savings deposits (T), demand deposits (D), and other assets (F).[5] The term *other assets* represents the total value of those assets contained in A_5. The explanatory variables of interest rates include the investments rate (RI), net borrowings rate (RB), and time and savings deposit rate (RT). Finally, we choose index of industrial production (IPI) as the barometer of the economic climate.[6]

To estimate the model as specified above, the following modifications are necessary. Due to the reserve requirements on deposit liabilities, allocatable funds from time and savings deposits and demand deposits are reduced to $TKT = T(1 - K_T)$ and $DKD = D(1 - K_D)$, where K_T and K_D denote the effective legal reserve requirements on time and savings deposits and on demand deposits, respectively. For the same reason, the nominal rate needs to be adjusted to $RTKT = RT/(1 - K_T)$, where $RTKT$ can be viewed as the effective rate on time and savings deposits after adjusting for K_T. Included in μ_Z in Eqs. (9)–(11) are intercept term, excess reserves (E), loans and discounts (L), allocatable time and savings deposits (TKT), allocatable demand deposits (DKD), and the index of industrial production (IPI).

Based on the above discussions, the econometric model can be accordingly specified as

$$\begin{bmatrix} B \\ I \end{bmatrix} = \Gamma_{10} + \Gamma_{11} \begin{bmatrix} RB \\ RI \end{bmatrix} + \Gamma_{12}\, RTKT + \Gamma_{13} F + \Gamma_{14} E + \Gamma_{15} L + \Gamma_{16}\, TKT + \Gamma_{17}\, DKD + \Gamma_{18}\, IPI + \varepsilon_1 \tag{12}$$

and

$$RL = \Gamma_{20} + \Gamma_{21} \begin{bmatrix} RB \\ RI \end{bmatrix} + \Gamma_{22}\, RTKT + \Gamma_{23} F + \Gamma_{24} E + \Gamma_{25} L + \Gamma_{26}\, TKT + \Gamma_{27}\, DKD + \Gamma_{28}\, IPI + \varepsilon_2, \quad (13)$$

where ε_1 and ε_2 are error terms.

B. Potential Econometric Problems

Following the usual practice, we verify our empirical model by applying ordinary least squares regression to time series data for sample banks. This technique requires that the variances of the error terms in the estimated equations (12) and (13) be invariant across all observations, that is, $\mathrm{var}(\varepsilon_i) = \sigma^2$ for each observation i. When heteroskedasticity and autocorrelated disturbances are present, as is the case here, the assumption of constant variance will be violated. Under such circumstances, standard errors of coefficient estimates will be biased. All t ratios and F statistics will be biased as well. This may lead the researcher to draw incorrect conclusions based on these biased coefficients. Hence, it is important to check the assumption of constant variance.

For financial data of sample banks, $\mathrm{var}(\varepsilon_i)$ may be systematically related to an independent variable such as bank earning assets (EA). Two possible relationships are $\mathrm{var}(\varepsilon_i) = \sigma^2 \cdot EA^2$ and $\mathrm{var}(\varepsilon_i) = \sigma^2 \cdot EA$. Following the procedure suggested by Goldfeld and Quandt (1965), we split the sample into two subsamples to test for heteroskedasticity with respect to a particular independent variable (in this case, earning assets). The first subinterval covers the period from January 1981 to June 1985, the other covers the period from July 1985 to December 1989. Estimates of σ^2 are then obtained from the two subsamples. The estimated variances of the two groups can be tested against each other by applying an F test. Where there is homoskedasticity, the estimated variances will be approximately of the same magnitude, hence the F ratio will not deviate significantly from 1. In the present study, testing the null hypotheses $\mathrm{var}(\varepsilon_i) = \sigma^2$, $\mathrm{var}(\varepsilon_i) = \sigma^2 \cdot EA^2$, and $\mathrm{var}(\varepsilon_i) = \sigma^2 \cdot EA$ yields F ratios of 0.96, 3.17, and 2.55 in equation B; 1.12, 4.24, and 3.21 in equation I; 1.08, 3.27, and 2.45 in equation RL, respectively. The F ratios indicate that only the basic empirical model, in which variances are assumed to be equal to σ^2, can pass the homoskedasticity test. This is the very reason that the econometric model used in our empirical analysis was set up as specified by Eqs. (12) and (13). As a result, when it comes to testing hypotheses, we will rely upon the basic empirical model just mentioned.

When regression is applied to time series data, the error terms may not be independent. In other words, the problem of autocorrelation might exist. To solve this problem, we make use of the Durbin–Watson statistic to test whether or not the autocorrelation coefficient of the error term equals zero. It is found that no matter what specification is adopted, the null hypotheses that autocorrelation exists can be rejected at the 0.05 significance level. (See results below.)

In addition to the two problems, we need to address issues brought in by high influence observations and multicollinearity. To detect potentially high influence observations, we begin by locating the data points that have a large HAT[7] diagonal, a large R-Student value (in magnitude), or both. Whenever R-Student values exceed 2.0 in magnitude, or the HAT diagonal values lying in the neighborhood of 1, these sample points on the raw data set are further checked (see Hocking [1983]). Through this screening procedure, 18 outliers out of the original 648 sample points are dropped from the data set. As for the multicollinearity problem, preliminary analysis indicates that we ran into a severe multicollinearity problem when an attempt was made to estimate *B, I,* and *RL* in Eqs. (12) and (13). For example, the estimate for the own-rate coefficient in the *B* equation was positive, in discordance with the theoretical model with a *t* value reaching statistical significance. Furthermore, multicollinearity among short-term interest rates is widely acknowledged in the literature. The multicollinearity problem here is intensified by the presence of both quantities and rates associated with balance sheet items. Singling out a specific quantity or rate variable, we found that the variable in question exhibits a high degree of simple pairwise and partial correlation with the remaining variables. In viewing the serious multicollinearity problems, the decision was made to eliminate either the interest rates or quantities from Eqs. (12) and (13). Specifically speaking, the quantity or rate variable is deleted when the following three criteria are simultaneously satisfied: (1) the variance inflation factor (*VIF*) exceeds 10; (2) the condition number of the correlation matrix considered is greater than 30; and (3) the variance decomposition proportion, associated with each high condition index, is greater than 0.5 (see SAS Institute [1984, chap. 4, pp. 126–145]). After a tedious and repetitive process of elimination, the following explanatory variables are finally chosen: net borrowings rate (*RB*), investments rate (*RI*), effective rate on time and savings deposits (*RTKT*), excess reserves (*E*), loans and discounts (*L*), allocatable time and savings deposits (*TKT*), allocatable demand deposits (*DKD*), and index of industrial production (*IPI*).

IV. EMPIRICAL ANALYSIS

A. Two Complementary Data Sets

In our judgment, monthly data are preferred to annual data because they contain many more sample points. When we limit ourselves to the monthly data, there are two possible candidates. On the one hand, Economic Research Department, the Central Bank of China, published on an aggregate basis, *Financial Statistics Monthly, Taiwan District, the Republic of China*. On the other hand, the authors have managed to obtain original data for the six leading commercial banks from Department of Monetary Affairs, the Ministry of Finance.[8]

The published aggregate data have two major advantages. First of all, they cover all commercial banks. Therefore, we need not to worry about the issue of representativeness. Additionally, the nonproprietary nature of the published data make it possible to cross-check the reliability of empirical results in follow-up studies. In contrast, the unpublished disaggregate data set has three distinctive features. First, the original data are disaggregate, which are more appropriate in viewing our model is individual bank oriented. Second, in the consolidated financial statements, no distinction has been made between passbook deposits and passbook savings deposits. As a result, there is no way of knowing the exact amount of legal reserves, hence allocatable demand deposits. Similarly, foreign currency time deposits are not separately reported. Put differently, only through the disaggregate data can we effectively identify the amount of required reserves, hence allocatable time and savings deposits. Last, but far from the least, several necessary variables are missing from the published data. Among others, they include the interest rates associated with the following four items: (1) loans and discounts, (2) investments, (3) net borrowings from banks, and (4) time and savings deposits. The other assets cannot be retrieved from the consolidated financial statements either. All considered, the disaggregate data allow us to test more directively and thoroughly the efficacy of the proposed models.

In brief, these two data sets are complementary in nature. Therefore, we run in the first place a multivariate regression based on the published aggregate data and report the results as preliminary findings. We then move on to report and discuss empirical findings on the basis of the disaggregate data set. (See Appendix B for data description of the six sampled commercial banks.)

B. Preliminary Analysis

As mentioned in the preceding paragraph, the loan rate (*RL*) cannot be identified. Therefore, only the remaining two choice variables, B and I, will be used as regressands. As for the right-hand side, because of the absence of several variables, only the following five explanatory variables—excess reserves (*E*), loans and discounts (*L*), allocatable time and savings deposits (*TKT*), allocatable demand deposits (*DKD*), and index of industrial production (*IPI*) are considered. In viewing the ability of selecting independent explanatory variables, the stepwise regression technique is applied to estimate the models. The results so obtained are reported in Table 2.

In Table 2, empirical results show the following. From the equation for *B*, it is found that net borrowings from banks, aside from excess reserves and index of industrial production, are primarily affected by allocatable time and savings deposits and allocatable demand deposits yet are less affected by loans and discounts; from the equation for *I*, it is found that securities purchasing behavior can be

Table 2. Ordinary Least Squares Results from the Aggregate Data

	Response Variables	
Explanatory Variables	*B*	*I*
Intercept	320.04	80.26
	(13.43)	(2.63)
E	2.02*	1.02
	(1.95)	(0.77)
L	0.02	−0.91
	(0.60)	(20.89)
TKT	−0.23	0.84
	(5.13)	(14.71)
DKD	−0.23	1.55
	(4.76)	(25.17)
IPI	−0.023*	1.44
	(0.09)	(4.23)
$\bar{R}^2$	0.88	0.97
DW	0.37	0.32

Notes: All asset (liability) entries are in billions of NT dollars, and IPI is the index of industrial production (1986 = 100). $\bar{R}^2$ is the coefficient of determination corrected for degrees of freedom; *DW* is the Durbin–Watson statistic. Numbers in parentheses beneath regression coefficients are absolute values of corresponding *t* ratios. An asterisk indicates that the estimated coefficient disagrees with the expected sign.

explained by the same set of explanatory variables reasonably well. By and large, these empirical results are in conformity with our expectations. Besides, the high adjusted R^2's also indicate a high degree of fitness of our empirical models. Turning to the other side of the coin, the quite low Durbin–Watson values suggest that serious problems of autocorrelation do exist which in turn may be caused by the missing of important explanatory variables. Next we explore such possibilities.

C. Some Further Empirical Analysis

In the ensuing analysis, the empirical results are obtained from the sample of six leading commercial banks in Taiwan. It can be legitimately argued that six is not a big number, hence our results might not be representative of the whole banking sector. Fortunately, the severity of this problem is mitigated by the simple fact that these six leading financial institutions altogether account for some 75% of the total earning assets held by all commercial banks. Furthermore, from an analytic point of view, the six commercial banks are located within a small and well-defined

Table 3. Ordinary Least Squares Results from the Disaggregate Data

	Response Variables		
Explanatory Variables	*B*	*I*	*RL*
Intercept	−18.34	20.15	3.58
	(3.11)	(2.03)	(3.34)
RB	−1.75*		
	(1.60)		
RI		−5.08*	
		(1.72)	
RTKT			0.68
			(3.27)
E	−2.37	2.18	
	(3.19)	(2.02)	
L	0.42	−1.23	0.031
	(2.97)	(5.02)	(5.20)
TKT		1.38	−0.038
		(4.72)	(3.12)
DKD	0.80*	1.98	−0.023
	(1.42)	(7.35)	(2.45)
IPI	0.24		−0.15
	(1.98)		(3.25)
$\bar{R}^2$	0.83	0.88	0.91
DW	1.629	2.201	2.058
C(P)	5.82	5.59	5.76

Notes: All interest rates are in percentage points per annum, *C*(*P*) is the Mallow statistic, and all other notes are the same as for Table 2.

geographical area; operate in a similar business environment, serving primarily domestic customers; and are subject to the same banking laws and governmental regulations. It is thus to be expected that the six commercial banks should face similar conditions insofar as portfolio selection is concerned. Thus, to simplify the analysis, these six leading commercial banks are treated as a single group. The empirical results obtained from ordinary least squares are reported in Table 3. To facilitate discussion of our empirical findings, let us examine in turn the expected signs of our crucial variables.

Based on conventional assumptions regarding substitutability among financial claims, income or wealth constraints, and the intermediation process (Tobin, 1969; Tobin and Brainard, 1963), the expected signs for variables appearing in Eqs. (12) and (13) can be discussed as follows. In the net borrowings equation, we expect net borrowings from banks to vary positively with loans and discounts and index of industrial production and to vary negatively with the interest rate on borrowings from banks, excess reserves, and allocatable demand deposits. In the investments equation, we expect the sign of the own rate or, for that matter, the allocatable time and demand deposits, to be positive. As for the remaining variables, we expect their coefficients to be negative. Similarly, in the loan rate equation, we expect a positive relationship between the loan rate and the level of loans or between the loan rate and the effective rate on time deposits, and negative relationships between the loan rate and each of the following three variables: index of industrial production, the level of time deposits, and the level of demand deposits.

Excluding intercepts, the three models in Table 3 generate 15 regression coefficient estimates. Among these 15 coefficients, 12 are in conformity with our prior expectations. Moreover, 11 out of the 12 coefficients carry t values exceeding 2 and hence are statistically significant. Among the three discordant regression coefficients, one involves the balance sheet items. The remaining incorrect signs are witnessed on the own rate coefficient in either the net borrowings from banks equation or investments equation. The largest t ratio, however, is only 1.72 and hence fails to achieve statistical significance. The explanatory powers of the equations as measured by $\overline{R}^2$ are good, and each of the three coefficients of determination corrected for degrees of freedom is larger than 0.83. In addition, serious autocorrelation does not appear when the Durbin–Watson statistics are applied to test the degree of first-order serial correlation. Finally, we use the Mallow $C(P)$ statistics to test the predictive power of the econometric model, which is formed by six selected explanatory variables (see Mallows, 1973). Since the values of $C(P)$ for each equation are less than 6, we find that the developed model is satisfactory.

Viewed from the variation of quantities in the balance sheet, when the demand for loans increases or the economic climate improves, net borrowings from banks expand only gradually. However, when there are excess reserves, net borrowings from banks shrink drastically. As allocatable time and demand deposits grow, investments increase accordingly; in contrast, when the demand for loans increases, investments will be lowered. It is worth pointing out that, in terms of magnitude, changes in the former will be slightly higher than in the latter. Although the demand for loans and the allocatable time deposits influence the interest rate on loans in opposite directions, the magnitude of their influence remains roughly the same. Lowering the interest rate on loans, on the one hand, reflects the abundancy of the allocatable demand deposits. On the other hand, the interest rate, once lowered, attracts a large amount of industrial investment and hence stimulates the economy. Concurrent adjustments of the interest rate on loans and the effective rates on time deposits, as seen from Table 3, suggest the reasonableness of financial operation of the commercial banks as a whole.

The monetary sector of Taiwan in the 1980s faced the complicated situation of huge foreign exchange reserves, incomplete liberalization, and excessive flooding of funds, which in turn led to serious distortions in the money and interbank call loans markets. In the presence of distortions, it seems safe to conclude that an adjustment in the position of the banks does not truly reflect the underlying changes in supply or demand. This may help explain why we came up with three "incorrect" signs—expressed differently, three unreasonable relationships between explanatory variables and variables to be explained—in our empirical analysis.

V. CONCLUSION

The aim of this study is to explain the portfolio behavior of commercial banks on the basis of a choice-theoretical framework, in which interaction between assets and liabilities, as well as uncertainty regarding quantity and rate, is allowed.

It is found that the testable implications are borne out by empirical findings. Almost all the coefficients relating asset and liability levels to interest rates are in conformity with a priori expectations. If these encouraging results are confirmed in further studies, we believe that the proposed model can shed some light on the important issue of portfolio management of commercial banks.

APPENDIX A: A PORTFOLIO-MANAGING MODEL OF COMMERCIAL BANKS

This appendix shows the detailed derivation of the main equations, namely, Eqs. (9) and (10).

To Start, from Eq. (4), we have $\mu_j = \mu_{R_j} - \mu_{R_0} e_j$ ($j = 1, \ldots, 5$); $\tilde{\gamma}_1 = \gamma_1 - \gamma_0 e_1$; and $\tilde{\gamma}_j = -\gamma_0 e_j$ ($j = 2, \ldots, 5$) since error terms are independent of all rate vectors except for R_1.

Next we rewrite the submatrices of C and G in Eq. (6) as

$$C_{11} = E(\tilde{\gamma}_1 \tilde{\gamma}_1'); \tag{A1}$$

$$C_{1j} = E[\tilde{\gamma}_1(-\gamma_0 e_j')] = -\sigma_{10} e_j' \quad (j = 2,\ldots,5) \tag{A2}$$

$$C_{ij} = E(\tilde{\gamma}_i \tilde{\gamma}'_j)$$

$$= E[(-\gamma_0 e_i)(-\gamma_0 e_j')] = \sigma_0^2 e_i e_j' \quad (j = 2,\ldots,5) \tag{A3}$$

$$G_{ij} = 0 \quad (i = 1, 5; j = 1, \ldots, 5) \tag{A4}$$

and

$$G_{ij} = E(a_i a_j') \quad (i, j = 2, 3, 4), \tag{A5}$$

where $\sigma_{10} = E(\tilde{\gamma}_1 \gamma_0)$, a $k \times 1$ vector; $\sigma_0^2 = E(\gamma_0^2)$; 0 in Eq. (A4) indicates a zero matrix of the appropriate order.

The expected-utility maximizing problem faced by the commercial bank can be specified as

$$W = \mu_\pi - \frac{b_2}{2}\sigma_\pi^2 , \tag{A6}$$

where W is the expected-utility maximand in Eq. (8), and μ_π and σ_π^2 are defined in Eqs. (5) and (6), respectively.

In order to find the maximizer of (A6), we take the first derivatives with respect to μ_{A_1} and μ_{R_2} and assign them the value of zero:

$$\begin{aligned}\partial W/\partial\mu_{A_1} &= (\partial\mu_A/\partial\mu_{A_1})(\partial\mu_\pi/\partial\mu_A) - (b_2/2)(\partial\mu_A/\partial\mu_{A_1})(\partial\sigma_\pi^2/\partial\mu_A)\\ &= [I, 0, 0, 0, 0]\mu_R - b_2[I, 0, 0, 0, 0]C\mu_A\\ &= 0\end{aligned} \tag{A7}$$

and

$$\begin{aligned}\partial W/\partial\mu_{R_2} &= (\partial\mu_R/\partial\mu_{R_2})(\partial\mu_\pi/\partial\mu_R) + (\partial\mu_A/\partial\mu_{R_2})(\partial\mu_\pi/\partial\mu_A)\\ &\quad - (b_2/2)[(\partial\mu_A/\partial\mu_{R_2})(\partial\sigma_\pi^2/\partial\mu_A) + (\partial\mu_R/\partial\mu_{R_2})(\partial\sigma_\pi^2/\partial\mu_R)]\\ &= [0, I, 0, 0, 0]\mu_A + [0, \beta_2', \beta_3', \beta_4', 0]\mu_R\\ &\quad - b_2[0, \beta_2', \beta_3', \beta_4', 0]C\mu_A - b_2[0, I, 0, 0, 0]G\mu_R\\ &= 0\end{aligned} \tag{A8}$$

where

$\partial\mu_A/\partial\mu_{A_1} = [I, 0, 0, 0, 0]$, a $k \times (k + l + m + p + q)$ matrix;

$\partial\mu_R/\partial\mu_{R_2} = [0, I, 0, 0, 0]$, an $l \times (k + l + m + p + q)$ matrix;

and

$\partial\mu_A/\partial\mu_{R_2} = [0, \beta_2', \beta_3', \beta_4', 0]$, an $l \times (k + l + m + p + q)$ matrix.

The underlying demand relationships in $\mu_{A_i} = \beta_i\mu_{R_2} + \omega_i\mu_Z$ $(i = 2, 3, 4)$ are used to obtain the following partial derivatives as shown in Eq. (A8):

$$\partial\mu_{A_i}/\partial\mu_{R_2} = \beta_i' \quad (i = 2,3,4). \tag{A9}$$

Expanding Eqs. (A7) and (A8), we obtain

$$\mu_1 - b_2(C_{11}\mu_{A_1} + C_{12}\mu_{A_2} + C_{13}\mu_{A_3} + C_{14}\mu_{A_4} + C_{15}\mu_{A_5}) = 0 \tag{A10}$$

and

$$\mu_{A_2} + \beta_2'\mu_2 + \beta_3'\mu_3 + \beta_4'\mu_4 - b_2 \sum_{i=1}^{5} (\beta_2'C_{2i} + \beta_3'C_{3i} + \beta_4'C_{4i})\mu_{A_i}$$

$$-b_2(G_{22}\mu_2 + G_{23}\mu_3 + G_{24}\mu_4) = 0\,. \tag{A11}$$

By substituting the demand relationships in μ_{A_2}, μ_{A_3}, and μ_{A_4} into Eqs. (A10) and (A11) and evoking Eqs. (A1)–(A3), we obtain $(k + l)$ equations, which specify the optimal values for hte K assets in μ_{A_1} and the L interest rates in μ_{R_2}. Spelled out in full, these equaitons are

$$(1/b_2)\mu_{R_1} - (1/b_2)e_1\mu_{R_0} + \sigma_{10}e'_5\mu_{A_5} + \sigma_{10}\omega\mu_Z$$

$$= C_{11}\mu_{A_1} - \sigma_{10}\beta\mu_{R_2} \tag{A12}$$

and

$$[\overline{G} - (\beta'/b_2)]\mu_{R_0} - \sigma_0^2\beta'e'_5\mu_{A_5} + [(\omega_2/b_2) - \sigma_0^2\beta'\omega]\mu_Z + [(\beta'_3/b_2) - G_{23}]\mu_{R_3}$$

$$= - \beta'\sigma'_{10}\mu_{A_1} + \{G_{22} + \sigma_0^2\beta'\beta - [(\beta_2 + \beta'_2/b_2]\}\mu_{R_2}\,, \tag{A13}$$

where

$$\overline{G} = G_{22}e_2 + G_{23}e_3 + G_{24}e_4, \text{ an } l \times 1 \text{ vector;} \tag{A14}$$

$$\beta = e'_2\beta_2 + e'_3\beta_3 + e'_4\beta_4, \text{ a } 1 \times l \text{ vector;} \tag{A15}$$

and

$$\omega = e'_2\omega_2 + e'_3\omega_3 + e'_4\omega_4, \text{ a } 1 \times l \text{ vector.} \tag{16A}$$

Here, β and ω are sums of column sums of coefficients from the demand relationships. In verbal terms, β and ω represent the impact of variables in R_2 and Z on the total amount of asset holdings in A_2, A_3, and A_4. In deriving Eqs. (A12) and (A13), expected interest–rate spreads involving the expected rate on the residual account have been eliminated since this expected rate appears on its own in several terms in Eq. (A11).

The equations in (A12) and (A13), if expressed in the form of matrix, can be written as

$$XT = \theta M, \tag{A17}$$

where

$$X = \begin{bmatrix} X_{11} & X_{12} \\ X_{21} & X_{22} \end{bmatrix} = \begin{bmatrix} C_{11} & -\sigma_{10}\beta \\ -\beta'\sigma'_{10} & G_{22} + \sigma_0^2\beta'\beta - [(\beta_2 + \beta_2')/b_2] \end{bmatrix}, \tag{A18}$$

a symmetric matrix of order $(k + l)$;

$$T = \begin{bmatrix} \mu_{A_1} \\ \mu_{R_2} \end{bmatrix}, \text{ a } \quad (k+l) \times 1 \text{ vector;} \tag{A19}$$

$$\theta = \begin{bmatrix} \theta_{11} & \theta_{12} & \theta_{13} & \theta_{14} & \theta_{15} \\ \theta_{21} & \theta_{22} & \theta_{23} & \theta_{24} & \theta_{25} \end{bmatrix}, \text{ a } \quad (k+l) \times (k+m+2+n) \text{ matrix} \tag{A20}$$

and

$$M = \begin{bmatrix} \mu_{R_1} \\ \mu_{R_3} \\ \mu_{R_0} \\ e'_5\mu_{A_5} \\ \mu_Z \end{bmatrix}. \tag{A21}$$

The submatrices of θ are given by

$$\theta_{11} = (1/b_2)I, \text{ a } k \times k \text{ matrix;} \tag{A22}$$

$$\theta_{12} = 0, \text{ a } k \times m \text{ matrix of zeros;} \tag{A23}$$

$$\theta_{13} = -(1/b_2)e_1, \text{ a } k \times 1 \text{ vector;} \tag{A24}$$

$$\theta_{14} = \sigma_{10}, \text{ a } k \times 1 \text{ vector;} \tag{A25}$$

$$\theta_{15} = \sigma_{10}\omega, \text{ a } k \times n \text{ matrix;} \tag{A26}$$

$$\theta_{21} = 0, \text{ an } l \times k \text{ matrix of zeros;} \tag{A27}$$

$$\theta_{22} = (\beta'_3/b_2) - G_{23}, \text{ an } l \times m \text{ matrix;} \tag{A28}$$

$$\theta_{23} = \overline{G} - (\beta'/b_2), \text{ an } l \times 1 \text{ vector;} \tag{A29}$$

$$\theta_{24} = -\sigma_0^2\beta', \text{ an } l \times 1 \text{ vector;} \tag{A30}$$

and

$$\theta_{25} = (\omega_2/b_2) - \sigma_0^2\beta'\omega, \text{ an } l \times n \text{ matrix.} \tag{A31}$$

Solving (A17) for the choice variables in T, we have

$$\begin{bmatrix}\mu_{A_1}\\ \mu_{R_2}\end{bmatrix} = \begin{bmatrix}X^{11} & X^{12}\\ X^{21} & X^{22}\end{bmatrix}\begin{bmatrix}\theta_{11} & \theta_{12} & \theta_{13} & \theta_{14} & \theta_{15}\\ \theta_{21} & \theta_{22} & \theta_{23} & \theta_{24} & \theta_{25}\end{bmatrix}\begin{bmatrix}\mu_{R_1}\\ \mu_{R_3}\\ \mu_{R_0}\\ e'_5\mu_{A_5}\\ \mu_Z\end{bmatrix}, \tag{A32}$$

where

$$X^{-1} = \begin{bmatrix}X^{11} & X^{12}\\ X^{21} & X^{22}\end{bmatrix}, \text{ the partitioned inverse matrix of } X \tag{A33}$$

The second-order conditions for a maximum require that X (and, therefore, X^{-1}) be positive definite. We assume that the second-order conditions are satisfied.

Finally, the optimal values for μ_{A_1} and μ_{R_2} can be solved from Eq. (A32) by the following two equations:

$$\mu^*_{A_1} = \psi_{11}\mu_{R_1} + \psi_{13}\mu_{R_3} + \psi_{10}\mu_{R_0} + \psi_{15}e'_5\mu_{A_5} + \psi_{1Z}\mu_Z \tag{A34}$$

and

$$\mu^*_{R_2} = \psi_{21}\mu_{R_1} + \psi_{23}\mu_{R_3} + \psi_{20}\mu_{R_0} + \psi_{25}e'_5\mu_{A_5} + \psi_{2Z}\mu_Z \tag{A35}$$

where

$$\psi_{11} = (1/b_2)X^{11}, \text{ a } k \times k \text{ matrix;} \tag{A36}$$

$$\psi_{13} = X^{11}\theta_{12} + X^{12}\theta_{22}, \text{ a } k \times m \text{ matrix;} \tag{A37}$$

$$\psi_{10} = X^{11}\theta_{13} + X^{12}\theta_{23}, \text{ a } k \times 1 \text{ vector;} \tag{A38}$$

$$\psi_{15} = X^{11}\theta_{14} + X^{12}\theta_{24}, \text{ a } k \times 1 \text{ vector;} \tag{A39}$$

$$\psi_{1z} = X^{11}\theta_{15} + X^{12}\theta_{25}, \text{ a } k \times n \text{ matrix;} \tag{A40}$$

$$\psi_{21} = (1/b_2)X^{21}, \text{ an } l \times k \text{ matrix;} \tag{A41}$$

$$\psi_{23} = X^{21}\theta_{12} + X^{22}\theta_{22}, \text{ an } l \times m \text{ matrix;} \tag{A42}$$

$$\psi_{20} = X^{21}\theta_{13} + X^{22}\theta_{23}, \text{ an } l \times 1 \text{ vector;} \tag{A43}$$

$$\psi_{25} = X^{21}\theta_{14} + X^{22}\theta_{24}, \text{ an } l \times 1 \text{ vector;} \tag{A44}$$

and

$$\psi_{2z} = X^{21}\theta_{15} + X^{22}\theta_{25}, \text{ an } l \times n \text{ matrix.} \tag{A45}$$

APPENDIX B: A DESCRIPTION OF OUR SAMPLE

Our sample is composed of Bank of Taiwan, the Co-operative Bank of Taiwan, the First Commercial Bank, Hua-nan Commercial Bank, Chang Hwa Commercial Bank, and the International Commercial Bank of China, the six largest commercial banks in Taiwan. They are required by the statutory code to file monthly financial reports to the Ministry of Finance, from which the authors have managed to obtain the original file for the period from January 1981 to December 1989. In correspondence to our theoretical model, variables are grouped into fourteen categories as follows:

Net borrowings from banks (B): Borrowings from banks minus due from banks.

Total investments (I): Sum of Treasury bills and other securities.

Other assets (F): Residual assets minus residual liabilities, where residual assets can be defined as total assets minus the sum of total investment, loans and discounts, and actual reserves; residual liabilities can be defined as total liabilities minus the sum of net borrowings from banks, time and savings deposits, and demand deposits.

Excess reserves (E): Actual reserves, which is the sum of deposits with Central Bank, deposits with Bank of Taiwan, deposits with the Co-operative Bank of Taiwan, and cash in vaults, minus required reserves.

Loans and discounts (L): Sum of loans to government agencies, government enterprises, private enterprises, and others.

Time and savings deposits (T): Sum of time deposits, time savings deposits, foreign exchange certificates, foreign currency time deposits, negotiable time deposits, and postal savings deposits.

Allocatable time and savings deposits (TKT): The TKT can be defined as $T(1 - K_T)$, where T and K_T denote the "time and savings deposits" and the effective legal reserve requirements on T, respectively.

Demand deposits (D): Sum of checking account, passbook deposits, foreign currency deposits, foreign exchange proceeds deposits, and government deposits.

Allocatable demand deposits (DKD): DKD can be defined as $D(1 - K_D)$, where D and K_D denote the demand deposits and the effective legal reserve requirements on D, respectively.

Loan rate (RL): Defined as interest revenue divided by the combined amount of loans and discounts.

Net borrowings rate (RB): Defined as interest cost divided by the holdings of net borrowings from banks.

Investments rate (RI): Defined as interest revenue divided by the amounts of investments.

Time and savings deposit rate (RT): Defined as interest cost divided by the holdings of time and savings deposit.

Table B1. Annual Data for the Six Leading Banks

Year	*B*	*I*	*F*	*E*	*L*	*TKT*	*DKD*	*RL*	*RB*	*RI*	*RTKT*
Sample Bank 1											
1981	23,055	18,881	9,245	809	73,593	52,612	26,614	15.58	14.80	18.37	15.37
1982	22,359	35,102	4,240	908	82,451	63,356	29,382	12.46	11.89	12.52	11.96
1983	21,863	44,395	8,057	1,089	95,703	78,735	34,617	9.46	8.48	8.35	8.96
1984	22,441	58,999	14,200	1,163	107,996	99,123	38,838	9.16	8.17	7.35	8.66
1985	12,847	62,409	20,767	1,241	117,914	124,944	43,102	8.64	7.85	6.44	8.11
1986	10,628	115,278	17,313	1,456	126,298	145,739	61,792	7.11	6.32	3.29	6.61
1987	5,913	205,070	7,643	1,818	146,266	160,328	95,063	6.88	6.25	3.90	6.38
1988	–7,451	207,020	10,577	2,162	191,439	184,906	125,205	7.04	6.62	4.85	6.54
1989	–11,674	168,486	8,825	2,688	259,471	250,134	139,743	8.95	8.49	8.52	8.33
Sample Bank 2											
1981	18,541	8,323	9,554	581	47,201	40,110	20,397	15.47	14.54	17.51	15.23
1982	14,613	11,645	10,506	687	61,496	48,400	22,642	12.36	11.67	11.98	11.86
1983	10,041	16,001	9,743	870	68,660	60,457	26,946	9.29	8.36	8.17	8.75
1984	5,257	20,092	8,477	948	74,029	76,365	30,382	8.99	8.04	7.24	8.44
1985	–6,071	17,176	7,832	1,022	76,022	96,683	33,967	8.49	7.67	6.35	7.92
1986	–17,151	20,129	9,221	1,232	85,509	112,698	49,166	6.91	6.15	3.35	6.34
1987	–28,139	17,513	23,694	1,585	111,313	124,643	77,187	6.70	6.06	3.75	6.13
1988	–36,107	19,573	23,719	1,787	153,506	142,642	100,802	6.90	6.38	4.68	6.36
1989	–48,598	24,945	23,653	2,041	214,131	186,827	104,597	8.83	8.22	8.12	8.20
Sample Bank 3											
1981	10,147	33,427	8,849	456	158,731	76,606	68,315	15.51	14.43	17.62	15.17
1982	10,373	36,758	10,845	440	163,989	86,175	70,277	12.40	11.56	12.04	12.08
1983	10,413	45,455	10,399	437	170,047	100,077	74,108	9.36	8.18	8.19	8.81
1984	10,771	58,945	12,234	428	176,194	118,379	77,172	9.06	7.86	7.25	8.49
1985	8,708	68,029	12,596	437	179,952	141,731	80,383	8.55	7.49	6.36	8.02
1986	8,772	92,039	10,047	448	184,348	160,477	93,967	6.99	5.89	3.34	6.31
1987	1,642	123,567	8,540	465	194,369	174,533	119,102	6.77	5.80	3.77	6.14
1988	–3,015	121,556	15,500	750	217,132	195,692	140,099	6.96	6.17	4.70	6.46
1989	–10,265	105,155	34,086	1,294	251,122	248,024	143,424	8.88	8.05	8.17	8.48
Sample Bank 4											
1981	34,809	46,374	6,680	551	103,893	50,368	33,026	15.84	14.95	17.56	15.33
1982	35,128	60,343	4,651	602	110,743	58,556	35,433	12.70	12.01	12.01	12.23
1983	34,307	71,233	6,920	478	120,429	70,149	40,155	9.88	8.51	8.18	9.06
1984	33,475	89,391	8,359	634	131,344	84,974	43,739	9.59	8.19	7.24	8.75
1985	20,679	98,766	9,910	2,375	142,866	103,609	47,333	9.04	7.91	6.36	8.26
1986	19,849	149,363	13,982	2,855	149,565	120,477	62,873	7.64	6.35	3.34	6.62
1987	29,608	202,269	14,718	2,574	153,866	132,729	90,447	7.37	6.31	3.76	6.43
1988	22,974	203,267	18,261	2,218	175,202	153,099	114,971	7.43	6.71	4.69	6.69
1989	11,980	165,478	17,730	2,450	206,279	203,574	119,981	9.26	8.63	8.14	8.66

(continued)

Table B1. (continued)

Year	B	I	F	E	L	TKT	DKD	RL	RB	RI	RTKT
					Sample Bank 5						
1981	13,743	12,839	1,998	55	69,968	35,294	23,975	15.49	14.49	17.60	15.23
1982	18,299	25,660	3,327	125	80,629	43,068	26,758	12.38	11.53	12.03	12.13
1983	14,174	30,582	4,058	152	86,888	54,280	31,875	9.32	7.81	8.19	8.90
1984	8,692	41,047	5,129	197	92,298	69,040	35,763	9.01	7.47	7.25	8.58
1985	-7,497	47,421	9,342	215	95,256	87,865	39,674	8.51	7.16	6.36	8.11
1986	-6,148	97,390	11,117	284	103,019	101,280	56,708	6.94	5.31	3.34	6.42
1987	13,424	189,884	12,562	235	125,118	110,299	87,012	6.72	5.28	3.77	6.24
1988	10,377	191,198	15,690	306	159,909	125,667	114,207	6.92	5.84	4.69	6.54
1989	-2,241	150,012	18,949	578	207,662	160,144	119,507	8.85	7.92	8.16	8.54
					Sample Bank 6						
1981	-400	10,139	7,137	137	122,236	79,731	62,833	15.68	14.47	17.71	15.50
1982	-,1029	21,326	11,396	179	135,725	89,871	65,344	12.56	11.50	12.10	12.37
1983	-499	33,385	12,334	219	150,131	104,513	70,118	9.63	7.73	8.21	9.18
1984	-866	46,706	13,551	310	165,715	123,655	73,743	9.34	7.38	7.26	8.87
1985	-18,451	55,101	16,618	355	180,072	147,995	77,383	8.81	7.07	6.37	8.37
1986	-20,806	88,448	16,686	434	190,014	168,252	93,180	7.33	5.18	3.33	6.72
1987	-25,106	136,018	15,405	342	214,527	183,399	121,246	7.08	5.16	3.78	6.52
1988	-32,790	137,922	17,322	326	271,615	206,659	146,317	7.20	5.75	4.72	6.78
1989	-44,869	112,178	22,887	333	357,436	264,485	151,323	9.08	7.87	8.21	8.77

Aggregate Sample Bank

Year	B	I	E	L	TKT	DKD	IPI
1981	230,475	80,087	12,281	737,895	315,676	186,303	59.68
1982	217,108	144,818	11,970	845,800	380,141	205,681	66.36
1983	208,168	181,959	13,729	961,053	472,412	242,326	74.46
1984	210,961	240,280	14,467	1,085,052	594,740	271,873	85.82
1985	130,679	254,012	16,212	1,188,446	749,667	301,720	87.34
1986	106,345	465,596	19,269	1,274,057	874,436	432,547	100.06
1987	61,300	824,936	30,832	1,475,185	961,974	665,444	112.54
1988	-15,873	835,584	30,302	1,930,043	1,109,437	876,441	115.46
1989	-150,098	686,890	34,764	2,613,625	1,500,808	978,203	119.85

Effective rate on time and savings deposits (*RTKT*): *RTKT* can be viewed as the effective rate on *T* after adjusting for K_T.

Appendix B summarizes the original data of the six leading commercial banks in Taiwan. Table B1 is the yearly data of the sample banks, respectively. For yearly data, all assets/liabilities are stated in billions of New Taiwan dollars. Interest rates are stated in percent per annum in Table B1.

Appendix B summarizes the original data of the six leading commercial banks in Taiwan. Table B1 is the yearly data of the sample banks, respectively. For yearly data, all assets/liabilities are stated in billions of New Taiwan dollars. Interest rates are stated in percent per annum in Table B1.

ACKNOWLEDGMENTS

The authors are indebted to M. T. Chen, Division Chief, the Ministry of Finance, for making data available, to P. C. Wang for helpful comments, and to Karen S. Chung for valuable stylistic advice. Finally, the authors would like to express heartfelt thanks to C. F. Lee for his constant encouragement and to Jack Francis for his constructive criticisms.

NOTES

1. These two assumptions are less restrictive than they first might appear. Compared with the independence assumption used in Ghosh and Parkin (1972), in which the authors assumed that the rates of return of assets are independent from the levels of assets, we only required that interest rate spreads be independent from the levels of assets.

2. The independence assumption is used to establish that $\mu'_A E(\tilde{\gamma}\tilde{\gamma}'a) = \mu'_R E(aa'\tilde{\gamma}) = 0$ and that $E(\tilde{\gamma}aa'\tilde{\gamma}) = tr\, E(aa'\widetilde{\gamma\gamma}') = tr\, [E(aa')E(\widetilde{\gamma\gamma}')] = tr\, GC$, a term which does not include the choice variables μ_{A_1} and μ_{R_2}.

3. For utility function of this type, see Parkin (1970, p. 473). As a matter of fact, the normality assumption is not as important as it first might appear. Farrar has written: "[T]he expected utility maximand in *(8)* (italics, ours) is obtainable as an approximation from the mathematical expectation of a Taylor-series expansion about the mean of net income (profit, his usage) for a twice differentiable utility, ignoring all terms of the expansion higher than the second order." See Farrar, 1962, p. 21.

4. Investments of the commercial bank itself, excess reserves, and borrowings from the Central Bank are possible candidates for residual assets, namely, A_0. However, when the monetary flows associated with the latter two accounts change, they usually are considered as temporary and will eventually be reflected in the investment account at the end of the decision period. Thus, the investment account is chosen to represent A_0 in our formal model.

5. It can be argued that the demand deposit should be grouped together with assets/liabilities in A_3 since, in the United States or most other places in the world, demand deposits are paid with interest. In the case of Taiwan, however, commercial banks do not pay interest on their customers' demand deposits. Therefore, when the proposed model is applied to analyze portfolio-managing behavior for commercial banks located in other countries, the set of explanatory variables should be expanded to include an interest variable on demand deposits. Fortunately, the applicability of the proposed model remains intact since the nature of the model is virtually unaffected by such expansion.

6. Monthly data for the index of industrial production were obtained from various issues of the *Industry of Free China Bulletin*.

7. The quantity **H** is defined as the matrix where diagonal elements are the quadratic forms

$$h_{ii} = \mathbf{x}'_i (\mathbf{X}'\mathbf{X})^{-1}\mathbf{x}_i ,$$

where $\mathbf{x}_i$ reflects the model and location for the ith data point. The off-diagonal elements are $h_{ii} = \mathbf{x}'_i (\mathbf{X}'\mathbf{X})^{-1}\mathbf{x}_j$, for $i \neq j$.

8. To spell them out in full, these commercial banks are Bank of Taiwan, the Co-operative Bank of Taiwan, the First Commercial Bank, Hua-nan Commercial Bank, Chang Hwa Commercial Bank, and the International Commercial Bank of China.

REFERENCES

Aghili, P., Cramer, R. H., and Thompson, H. E. (1975). "Small Bank Balance Sheet Management: Applying Two-Stage Programming Models." *Journal of Bank Research* 5, No. 4 (Winter), 246–256.

Aigner, D. J. (1973). "On Estimation of an Econometric Model of Short-Run Bank Behavior." *Journal of Econometrics* 1, 201–228.

Berndt, E. R., McCurdy, T. H., and Rose, D. (1980). "On Testing Theories of Financial Intermediary Portfolio Selection." *Review of Economic Studies* (Fall), 861–873.

Cohen, K. J., and Hammer, F. S. (1967). "Linear Programming and Optimal Bank Asset Management Decisions." *Journal of Finance* 22, No. 2 (May), 147–165.

Echols, M. E., and Elliot, J. W. (1976). "Forecasting vs. Allocational Efficiency in Bank Asset Planning: An Integrated Evaluation." *Journal of Bank Research* 6, No. 4 (Winter), 283–295.

Farrar, D. E. (1962). *The Investment Decision under Uncertainty.* Englewood Cliffs, NJ: Prentice Hall.

Francis, J. C. (1978). "Portfolio Analysis of Asset and Liability Management in Small-, Medium-, and Large-Sized Banks." *Journal of Monetary Economics* 4 (August), 460–480.

Ghosh, D., and Parkin, M. (1972). "A Theoretical and Empirical Analysis of the Portfolio, Debt, and Interest Rate Behavior of Building Societies." *Manchester School XL* (September), 321–344.

Goldfeld, S. M., and Quandt, R. F. (1965). "Some Tests for Homoskedasticity." *Journal of the American Statistical Association* 60 (September), 539–547.

Hocking, R. R. (1983). "Developments in Linear Regression Methodology: 1959–1982." (with discussion), *Technometrics* 25, 219–245.

Humphrey, D. B. (1981). "Intermediation and Cost Determinants of Large Bank Liability Composition." *Journal of Banking and Finance* (June), 167–185.

Jahera, J. S., Jr., and Sinkey, J. F., Jr. (1984). "A Note on the Intacyclical Balance-Sheet Behavior of Large Commercial Banks." *Journal of Banking and Finance* (August), 109–117.

Mallows, C. L. (1970). "Some Comments on C_p." *Technometrics* 15, 661–675.

Parkin, J. M. (1970). "Discount House Portfolio and Debt Selection." *Review of Economic Studies* (October), 469–497.

SAS Institute Inc. (1984). *SAS Views: SAS Principles of Regression Analysis, 1984 Edition.* Cary, NC: SAS Institute Inc.

Spindt, P. A., and Tarhan, V. (1980). "Liquidity Structure Adjustment Behavior of Large Money Center Banks." *Journal of Money, Credit and Banking* (May), 198–208.

Tobin, J. (1969). "A General Equilibrium Approach to Monetary Theory." *Journal of Money, Credit and Banking* (February), 15–29.

Tobin, J., and Brainard, W. C. (1963). "Financial Intermediaries and the Effectiveness of Monetary Controls." *American Economic Review* (May), 383–400.

AN INVESTIGATION OF THE USEFULNESS OF ACCOUNTING AND FINANCIAL DATA IN THE ASSESSMENT OF SECURITY RISK

Kenneth R. Ferris and William Reichenstein

ABSTRACT

This study investigates the usefulness of accounting and financial data in the assessment of security risk. Value Line expectational data are used in conjunction with a multidimensional model of risk to investigate the predictive ability of traditional measures of accounting and financial risk versus updated risk-variable specifications. The analyses are conducted both before and after the imposition of the Tax Reform Act of 1986. The findings indicate that (1) financial statement users can better assess security risk and return using accounting risk measures than using beta alone; (2) with the exception of an ex post measure of earnings variability, the ex ante and/or updated accounting and financial risk measures outperformed the traditional risk surrogates; (3) dividend policy, financial leverage, firm size, and growth prospects were found to be the most important determinants of expected return; (4) predictions of risk premium using a multidimensional model proved more accurate than predictions from

Advances in Quantitative Analysis of Finance and Accounting,
Volume 2, Part A, pages 195–219.

ISBN: 1-55938-564-2

unidimensional risk models; and (5) financial leverage outperformed beta as a measure of expected covariance of return with the market.

I. INTRODUCTION

The Financial Accounting Standards Board (FASB) (1978) states that one goal of financial reporting is to enable investors, creditors, and other financial statement users to assess the uncertainty, or risk, associated with future cash flows and, by extension, the relative riskiness of a security. Similarly, Beaver, Kettler, and Scholes (1970) argue that "we cannot hope to construct an accounting system or evaluate the current system in terms of a decision-making criterion without a knowledge of the interaction between accounting data and market price variables." Thus, a stated goal of accounting standards setters is, and should be, the provision of information that is useful in the formation of risk and return assessments by external users. Whether this goal is currently being attained is the focus of this study.

There have been several major advances in the last decade in securities market research. Evidence now exists, for example, that questions the efficacy of the capital asset pricing model and the ability of beta to adequately represent security risk. Advances have also been made with respect to the specification and measurement of accounting and financial risk variables. Finally, measures of risk on an ex ante basis are now available. Given these advances and the stated goals of the FASB, it is appropriate to readdress the issues raised by Beaver et al. (1970) two decades ago, namely, the relation between security risk as priced by the marketplace and accounting and financial risk variables.

Thus, the purpose of this study is to investigate the usefulness of reported accounting and financial data in the assessment of security risk. The relationship between risk and various risk surrogates is examined using both ex post and ex ante data, as well as updated variable specifications for the accounting and financial risk measures. The study investigates the market's preference for accounting versus market-based measures of risk, and attempts to assess the informational adequacy of traditional accounting risk surrogates as shown by their association with market equilibrium expected returns.

Results from Value Line data on industrial firms for the period 1981–1987 indicate that the use of accounting data permits a better assessment of security risk than the use of beta alone. Further, security prices were found to reflect (directly or indirectly) a firm's dividend policy, financial leverage, growth opportunities, and size; measures of earnings uncertainty and beta were also found to be significant but on an inconsistent basis. Finally, firm liquidity, as reflected by liquidity ratios, was not found to be associated with expected returns.

These findings should be useful to financial statement users in the formation of risk and return assessments, as well as to accounting regulatory officials in the resolution of information disclosure issues. With respect to users, the findings should enable investors to form portfolios that are more closely aligned with their risk preferences and may allow creditors to more accurately estimate the probability distribution of customer default. With respect to accounting standard setters, the results indicate that in at least some areas (e.g., liquidity), current disclosure practices may not be adequate to permit users to fully assess a firm's risk.

II. RESEARCH ISSUES

In financial markets characterized by risk-averse investors, securities will be priced to offer higher expected returns on investments with higher nondiversifiable risk. Until recently, it was widely held that the capital asset pricing model (CAPM) provided an efficient formulation of the relationship between security risk and return, and that beta was an adequate proxy of security risk premium as priced by financial markets (e.g., see Roll, 1977; Ross, 1978).

In recent years, however, there has been a proliferation of market studies indicating that the joint hypothesis of capital market efficiency and CAPM beta as the relevant measure of security risk presents an inadequate description of the market's pricing mechanism. For example, anomalous returns have been reported for portfolios specializing in the securities of small firms (Banz, 1981; Reinganum, 1981), firms neglected by institutional investors (Arbel and Strebel, 1983), low price-earnings ratio securities (Basu, 1977, 1983; Goodman and Peavy, 1983), and for other investment strategies (Copeland and Mayers, 1982; Holloway, 1981). These results are usually interpreted to indicate that financial markets view these variables (or variables correlated with them) as proxies for risk that is not reflected in beta.

Further, psychological studies and studies of individuals' risk perceptions (Alderfer and Bierman, 1970; Cooley, 1977; Coombs and Pruitt, 1960; Farrelly, Ferris, and Reichenstein, 1985; Farrelly and Reichenstein, 1984) confirm this interpretation, suggesting that investors' risk perceptions cannot be adequately represented by a one-dimensional risk measure. These studies have led to a consideration of risk as a multidimensional construct, while maintaining the hypothesis of efficient capital markets. The arbitrage pricing theory (APT) is one example of this revised thinking (e.g., see Dybvig and Ross, 1985; Ross, 1976).

A. Risk

There appears to be little disagreement in the financial community regarding the importance of risk and that investors are averse to risk. Beyond that, however, there is little consensus (e.g., see Tinic and West, 1984). As Blume (1971, p. 1) observed:

> The concept of risk has so permeated the financial community that no one needs to be convinced of the necessity of including risk in investment analysis. Still of controversy is what constitutes risk and how it should be measured.

While "what constitutes risk" remains extremely elusive, a review of the extant literature suggests a number of widely accepted risk-related concepts, such as firm size, dividend policy, financial leverage, growth, liquidity, variability in earnings, and beta.[1] With the exception of the omission of accounting beta, these concepts closely parallel the accounting-determined risk measures initially investigated by Beaver et al. (hereafter BKS).[2] Subsequent research (Beaver and Manegold, 1975) has questioned the stability of accounting beta, in part because the inherent lack of accounting observations (due to the length of the traditional accounting period) prevents the acquisition of sufficiently reliable point estimates of accounting beta. Thus, accounting betas estimated from adjacent time periods tend to be highly independent,[3] indicating that they may be of little use in measuring risk. For these reasons, a further consideration of accounting beta appears unwarranted.

B. Purpose

This study investigates the usefulness of accounting and financial data in the assessment and prediction of risk, and assesses the informational adequacy of traditional accounting-based risk surrogates. It extends the line of inquiry begun by BKS, and that of Eskew (1979) and Elgers (1980). It examines the question of whether financial statements permit a better assessment of security risk than reliance on market-based beta alone. In short, the study investigates whether one of the stated objectives of the FASB's conceptual framework is currently being attained, namely, providing users with information to assess and predict uncertainty.

Using a set of widely accepted accounting and financial risk proxies and assuming that security markets are informationally efficient, we investigate the risk variables priced by the market as an approach to identifying the set of informationally useful risk concepts. The findings indicate that the "best" set of risk surrogates contains some accounting variables, and thus supports the contention that financial statements provide information beyond that embodied in past stock prices.

The findings should be of interest to financial statement users by identifying, among the plethora of available accounting and financial measures, those likely to be most useful in assessing the riskiness of a security. The findings should also be of interest to accounting standard setters in that they reveal, among the variables examined, those accounting measures possessing information on risk and those whose informational value is in question.

This study also attempts to extend prior research in three areas. First, where possible, ex ante measures of risk and expected return are used. With the exception of Ang and Peterson (1985) and Farrelly et al. (1985), prior research has measured risk only on an ex post basis; however, risk is a futuristic construct and hence should be estimated from ex ante data. Second, a multidimensional model of risk is used. Most prior research has been based on the CAPM, which assumes that (the unidimensional) beta is an adequate measure of a security's risk and that a security's risk premium is linearly related to beta. Recent thinking, however, suggests that risk is a multidimensional construct and that a security's risk premium is related to variables besides beta risk. Finally, research by Hamada (1972), Brown, Kleidon, and Marsh (1983), and others suggests specifications of risk measures other than those used by BKS and other accounting researchers; these alternative variable specifications are considered in the current study.

III. RESEARCH METHOD

To investigate the relationship between security risk and return, an extension of the after-tax capital asset pricing model developed by Brennan (1970), and later refined by Litzenberger and Ramaswamy (1979) and Ang and Peterson (1985) is used:

$$RP_i = \alpha_0 + \alpha_1 EY_i + \sum_{j=2}^{n} \alpha_j RM_{ij}, \tag{1}$$

where RP_i, the risk premium, is the before-tax expected return on security i less the risk-free rate; EY_i is the expected dividend yield less the risk-free rate; RM_{ij} is the value of the jth risk factor for security i; and $\alpha_0, \alpha_1, \ldots \alpha_n$ are parameters to be estimated.

The generally higher taxation of dividends as compared to capital gains which existed under the U.S. Tax Code through 1986 implies a positive value for α_1. Recent tax law changes affecting long-term capital gain income realized in 1987 and thereafter, however, reduce the taxation distinction between dividends and capital gains. Although the 60% capital gain exclusion was eliminated, capital gains continue to enjoy two tax advantages: deferral of taxes on unrealized gains and the ability to time the realization of gains for a low tax rate year. We allow for the impact of recent tax code changes by conducting our analyses both before and after the imposition of the Tax Reform Act (TRA) of 1986.

A. Accounting and Financial Risk Measures

It is widely accepted that financial markets price only the nondiversifiable risk of a security and that beta captures some, but not all, of that risk (Ross, 1976, 1978). Although there is uncertainty as to what other aspects of risk are also being priced, the extant literature suggests a number of important risk-related concepts: dividend policy, growth, financial leverage, liquidity, firm size, and variability in earnings.

1. Dividend Policy

Since the 1970 BKS study, there has been substantial evidence indicating that, ceteris paribus, securities with high yields and payouts offer higher before-tax returns (Litzenberger and Ramaswamy, 1979, 1982; Ang and Peterson, 1985). This may be due to the favorable tax treatment enjoyed by long-term capital gains as compared to dividends, and not necessarily to the association of dividend policy with risk.

Another view of a firm's dividend policy maintains that, ceteris paribus, firms with low dividend yields or payout ratios are riskier:

> If firms follow a policy of dividend stabilization (i.e., firms are reluctant to cut back, once a dividend level has been established), and are adverse to paying out more than 100 percent (or X percent) of earnings in any single fiscal period, then firms with greater volatility in earnings will pay out a lower percentage of expected earnings. Thus, the payout ratio can be viewed as a surrogate for management's perception of the uncertainty associated with the firm's earnings. (BKS, 1970, p. 660)

Beaver et al. represented dividend policy by the ex post payout ratio, measured as the sum of common dividends divided by the sum of earnings available to common shareholders for a given period. They note that "difficulties arise because the payout ratio must be computed on observed (ex post) earnings rather than expected (or permanent) earnings. This problem is not unique to the payout ratio and is present to varying degrees in all of the [ex post] risk measures" (p. 660).

In the present study, this limitation was avoided by utilizing ex ante forecasts provided by the *Value Line Investment Survey*. Hence, the target payout ratio, PAYOUT, is measured as the ratio of Value Line's ex ante three-to-five-year dividends-per-share divided by ex ante three-to-five-year earnings-per-share. Following BKS, we also use an ex post payout ratio for the preceding five years, denoted PAYOUTB. Finally, Value Line's ex ante one-year dividend yield is also considered; this variable enters the after-tax CAPM as yield less the risk-free rate, denoted YLD.

2. Growth

An above average expected growth rate may be a function of investment opportunities at rates of return above the firm's cost of capital, retention and investment of earnings at the cost of capital, or both. BKS argue that firms with excess earnings opportunities will have higher risk and expected returns; such firms will tend to have high returns on equity. As previously discussed, firms with high retention, and hence low payout, will tend to be riskier according to BKS.

In the current study, growth is measured two ways: (1) the ex post continuously compounded annual growth rate in total assets over the past five years, GRB, which follows BKS; and (2) the product of Value Line's ex ante three-to-five-year return on common equity and the ex ante three-to-five-year retention ratio, GR.

3. *Financial Leverage*

In general, the higher the degree of financial leverage, the greater the risk borne by common shareholders. Hamada (1972) and others have shown that, for a given level of firm asset risk, a security's nondiversifiable risk is linearly related to the ratio of the market value of debt to the market value of common equity.

In this study, the traditional BKS measure of financial leverage and two updated specifications are considered: (1) the ratio of total senior debt to total assets, LEVB, which follows BKS; (2) the ratio of long-term debt, preferred stock, and unfunded vested pension liability to the market value of the firm's common equity, LEV(1); and (3) the ratio of current debt, long-term debt, preferred stock, and unfunded vested pension liability to the firm's market value of common equity, LEV(2).[4] The latter two measures are expected to benefit from respecification using common equity instead of total assets and from the use of the market value of equity rather than its book value. Whether current liabilities should be considered debt in measures of financial leverage has been a long-standing controversy; however, the method adopted in this study permits an empirical investigation of this issue.

4. *Size*

The impact of firm size on security returns is an important stock market anomaly. Studies by Banz (1981) and Reinganum (1981) were among the first to observe that average returns to small firms' shares were significantly above that predicted by CAPM. Similar findings were obtained by Barry and Brown (1984), Basu (1983), Brown et al. (1983a), Keim (1983), Reinganum (1983), and Stoll and Whaley (1983), among others.

Brown, Kleidon, and Marsh (1983b) report that the security return-firm size relation is best represented when size is measured as the natural logarithm of the market value of a firm's common equity. This measure has a number of advantages over total assets; notably, market value may be determined at any point in the calendar year and is not dependent upon the infrequent availability of accounting data. In addition, a firm's total assets are often affected by significant seasonal fluctuations, which should not affect investor risk perceptions. In the present study, size is measured in two ways: (1) the natural logarithm of total assets, SIZEB, which follows BKS, and (2) the natural logarithm of a firm's market value of common equity, denoted SIZE.

5. *Liquidity*

The sources of firm liquidity have changed dramatically in recent years. Whereas most corporate managers previously relied almost exclusively upon current assets, today they are more prone to use liability accounts to satisfy at least a part of their liquidity needs. Examples of liabilities providing liquidity include commercial paper, accounts payable, and unused bank lines of credit, although this latter source is not reflected in the balance sheet accounts.

Traditional measures of liquidity suffer the limitation that they implicitly assume that liquidity is obtained solely from current assets. Unfortunately, there is no established approach to overcome this limitation. In the current study, two measures of liquidity which share this limitation are investigated: (1) current assets divided by current liabilities, LIQ, as used by BKS, and (2) an updated specification, the natural logarithm of the current ratio, LN(LIQ). The natural logarithm is considered under the assumption that a difference in the current ratio of 1.5 versus 2 is more important than, say, a difference of 9.5 versus 10.

6. *Variability of Earnings*

The variability of corporate earnings has been found to be positively related to expected return. Following BKS, one measure of variability investigated is the standard deviation of annual earnings available to common shareholders divided by the market value of common equity, denoted VARB. A second measure, VAR, was developed by Value Line to reflect a firm's earnings variability and is a modified variance of year-to-year quarterly earnings around trend.[5] Both are ex post measures based on the variability of past earnings.

7. *Beta*

Beta is an ex post measure of the sensitivity of a security's price to overall market fluctuations. It is a measure of security risk based on past stock price data and has come to be recognized as but one aspect of the relative riskiness of a given security. Hence, unlike BKS, who treated beta as the dependent variable in their analysis, in the current study beta is treated as one of several independent risk variables. Value Line's beta, denoted BETA, adjusts ex post beta for its tendency to move toward one; the ex post beta is calculated with weekly data for a five-year period.

B. Expected Return Measures

Strictly speaking, the market's expected return for a given security (or a portfolio of securities) is unobservable, and any surrogate for this measure is subject to potential measurement errors. In the current study, two steps are taken to minimize these measurement problems. First, three measures of expected return (ER) are examined, one based on Gordon's (1959) constant growth model and two based on models of normalized earnings-price ratios. Second, Value Line's assessment of a security's expected short-term performance, denoted RANK, is included as an independent variable in the analyses. The inclusion of this variable is hypothesized to reflect any differences between the Value Line forecasts and the market's equilibrium forecasts of earnings and expected return.[6]

Gordon's (1959) constant growth model is specified as

$$ER_1 = \frac{D_1}{P_0} + g, \tag{2}$$

where D_1/P_0, the ratio of expected dividends to current share price, is the forecast of next year's dividend yield, and g is the projected geometric annual capital gains using Value Line's projected share price three-to-five years out;[7] projected share price is the average of three-to-five-year high and low projected prices as provided by Value Line.

The other two measures define expected return as the ratio of expected normal earnings (NE) to current share price (i.e., $ER = NE/P_0$). Ball (1978), among others, argues that earnings-price models, especially those based on forecasted earnings to current share price, are good proxies for market-expected returns. Moreover, Basu (1977, 1983) and Sorensen and Williamson (1985) have previously utilized an earnings-price ratio as a measure of expected return.

Value Line provides both near-term and long-term earnings projections. Near-term forecasts may differ from normal earnings due to cyclical factors, whereas long-term forecasts may be of limited value for firms with earnings that are particularly difficult to forecast. To reflect this difficulty, a model of normalized earnings is estimated as a weighted average of near-term and long-term earnings forecasts:

$$NE = W_1\ EPS_1 + (1 - W_1)\ EPS_{3\text{-}5}\ , \tag{3}$$

where EPS_1 is the sum of ex ante earnings-per-share for the most recent past two quarters (i.e., actual EPS) *plus* forecasted earnings-per-share for the succeeding two quarters, $EPS_{3\text{-}5}$ is the ex ante three-to-five-year earnings-per-share, and W_1 is a weighting factor. In general, the greater the difficulty of forecasting earnings, the less the weighting placed on long-term earnings forecasts and the greater the emphasis on near-term forecasts. The weighting factor, W_1, reflects this emphasis by setting $W_1 = (2 + \text{DIFF})/10$, where DIFF is the Value Line ranking (1 [easy] to 5 [difficult]) of the difficulty of forecasting a firm's earnings.[8] The corresponding model of expected return then becomes

$$ER_2 = NE/P_0. \tag{4}$$

A final model of expected return, essentially equivalent to Eq. (4) except that actual ex post EPS for the past four quarters is substituted for the ex ante EPS_1 in Eq. (3), is

$$ER_3 = \frac{W_1 EPS_0 + (1 - W_1)EPS_{3\text{-}5}}{P_0}\ . \tag{5}$$

ER_2 is conceptually superior to ER_3 because current share prices should be based on earnings expectations.

The risk premium (RP_{ij}) for security i is thus specified as

$$RP_{ij} = ER_{ij} - R_f, \tag{6}$$

where $j = 1, 2, 3$, and R_f is the risk-free rate of return, that is, the rate of return on three-month U.S. Treasury bills.

C. Data Analysis

Data for the current study were obtained from the *Value Line Investment Survey* data base. In addition to historical financial statement data, the data base contains forecasts (i.e., as of April 1986 and 1987) for such key variables as earnings, dividends, and share price. Complete data sets were available for 553 industrial firms in 1986 and 472 in 1987. Utilities, gas companies, banks, and savings and loans were not considered due to their unique regulatory environment and evidence that investors may interpret dividend policy differently for such firms (e.g., see Baker, Edelman, and Farrelly, 1985).[9]

The use of expectational data is an important attribute of this study. Not only is the extended after-tax CAPM model specified in ex ante form, but interpretation of the model using ex post data suffers from difficulties associated with separating tax and information effects. Miller and Scholes (1982) suggest the use of expectational data in empirical tests to resolve these concerns. Moreover, investors who subscribe to Value Line are likely to adopt the forecasts as their own; and since the *Value Line Investment Survey* is the most widely followed investment advisory service, it follows that its forecasts represent a substantial portion of the market. Prior research has also confirmed the quality of these forecasts. Brown and Rozeff (1978), for example, found Value Line's earnings forecasts to be superior to those generated by various statistical models. And Black (1973), Copeland and Mayers (1982), and Holloway (1981) document the usefulness of Value Line's return (i.e., price) forecasts. Finally, Ang and Peterson (1985) report that Value Line's yield and return forecasts "provide information beyond that contained in historical data" (p. 540).

The relation between risk premium and risk variables was examined using multiple regression analysis. A common problem encountered in cross-sectional research using linear regression analysis is the presence of heteroskedasticity, or nonconstant residual variance. Ordinary least squares (OLS) regression analysis produces consistent parameter estimates in the presence of heteroskedasticity, but inconsistent covariance estimates. As a result, the t-statistic produced by OLS regression analysis will provide faulty inferences in the presence of heteroskedasticity.

The Goldfeld–Quandt (1965) test indicated the presence of multiplicative heteroskedasticity in the current study.[10] To correct for this data problem, the t-statistics reported herein were based on the heteroskedasticity-consistent covariance matrix estimator developed by White (1980).

IV. EMPIRICAL RESULTS

A. Selecting the Optimal Risk Measures

This section reports the performance of the updated risk surrogate specifications versus the traditional BKS specifications and evaluates the optimal specification of each risk concept for subsequent analyses. For our purposes, "optimality" was defined with regard to the contribution to explained variance in otherwise similar regressions.

Table 1. Summary Statistics for Risk Variables

	1986		*1987*	
Variable	*Mean*	*Standard Deviation*	*Mean*	*Standard Deviation*
Dividend policy				
PAYOUTB^2	0.371	0.22	0.405	0.25
PAYOUT^1	0.320	0.18	0.325	0.20
YLD^1	0.028	0.02	0.026	0.02
Growth				
GRB^2	0.096	0.09	0 099	0.09
GR^1	0.104	0.04	0.103	0.04
Financial leverage				
LEVB^3	0.413	0.15	0.416	0.15
LEV(1)^3	0.358	0.49	0.348	0.45
LEV(2)^3	0.644	0.76	0.648	0.86
Size				
SIZEB^3	6.602	1.50	6.673	1.59
SIZE^3	6.579	1.37	6.679	1.50
Liquidity				
LIQ^3	2.193	1.30	2.187	1.34
LN(LIQ)^3	0.586	0.76	0.606	0.64
Earnings uncertainty				
VARB^2	0.018	0.01	0.018	0.01
VAR^2	3.042	5.04	3.396	5.41
Market sensitivity				
BETA^2	0.984	0.24	0.985	0.22

Notes: 1 indicates ex ante measure.
2 indicates ex post measure.
3 indicates measure using data from current financial statements.

Tables 1 and 2 present summary statistics and correlation coefficients, respectively, for the accounting and financial risk measures used in this study. Table 1 distinguishes among ex ante measures, ex post measures (those formed from past data), and current measures (those formed from current financial statement data). Some of the current measures are based on current stock price in addition to accounting data. These are considered to be accounting measures for purposes of this study; restricting the definition to only those measures using exclusively accounting data would bias the analysis against the finding that accounting data are useful.

Table 3 summarizes the 1986 and 1987 regressions of risk premium on the BKS variable specifications (Part I) and on the updated specifications (Part II). With respect to the updated variable specifications in Part II, where alternative updated specifications exist (i.e., dividend policy and financial leverage), multiple analyses were undertaken to identify the variable specification with the highest contribution to explained variance. Thus, the variables reported in Part II represent the empirically "best" set of updated risk variable specifications.[11]

For each year and for each risk premium model, the adjusted coefficient of determination is higher for the updated variable specification regressions. This finding reflects the anticipated advantage of the updated variable specifications *as a group*. This advantage is largely due to the use of the ex ante measures YLD and GR instead of the ex post measures PAYOUTB and GRB. These results also appear to confirm BKS's suspicion that ex post measures suffer from measurement errors.

The coefficient of PAYOUTB is inconsistent in sign, while the coefficient of YLD is consistently positive and significant in all regressions for both 1986 and 1987. These results imply that, in the assessment of security return, a firm's dividend yield is informationally superior to its target payout ratio.

The superiority of the ex ante measure GR accords well with BKS, who suggest that the dominant factor producing an above normal growth rate is the presence of earnings opportunities at rates above the cost of capital. Such firms tend to have high earnings retention and a high return on equity, both components of GR, and tend to be relatively risky. The coefficient of GR was consistently positive and usually significant, whereas the coefficient of the ex post measure GRB was inconsistent in sign and insignificant, leading one to question its ability to capture the concept of growth.

All three financial leverage measures exhibit positive and significant coefficients and are highly correlated ($r \geq 0.58$). This indicates that each has empirical merit and suggests that empirical inferences using LEVB or similar measures would likely remain valid if other measures of leverage were used. LEV(2) performed slightly better than LEV(1) and consistently better than LEVB in terms of explained variance in otherwise similar regressions. This indicates that measures of financial leverage based on the market value of common equity are more closely aligned with security risk. The slight advantage of LEV(2) over LEV(1) suggests a modest

Table 2. 1986/1987 Correlation Coefficient Matrix[a]

	1987																		
	1	*2*	*3*	*4*	*5*	*6*	*7*	*8*	*9*	*10*	*11*	*12*	*13*	*14*	*15*	*16*	*17*	*18*	*19*
	PAYOUTB	*PAYOUT*	*YLD*	*GRB*	*GR*	*LEVB*	*LEV(1)*	*LEV(2)*	*SIZEB*	*SIZE*	*LIQ*	*LN(LIQ)*	*VARB*	*VAR*	*BETA*	*RP1*	*RP2*	*RPB*	*RANK*
1	—	0.77	0.70	–0.52	–0.58	0.21	0.27	0.12	0.26	0.14	–0.29	–0.28	0.18	0.04	–0.04	–0.15	–0.03	–0.04	0.17
2	0.80	—	0.87	–0.42	–0.73	0.16	0.32	0.13	0.29	0.18	–0.30	–0.30	–0.05	–0.17	–0.55	–0.16	0.01	0.06	0.23
3	0.73	0.86	—	–0.40	–0.68	0.21	0.32	0.21	0.23	0.04	–0.30	–0.35	0.02	–0.16	–0.54	0.00	0.20	0.25	0.32
4	–0.48	–0.44	–0.42	—	0.44	0.07	0.01	0.05	–0.29	0.00	0.16	0.26	–0.15	0.04	0.43	0.22	–0.01	0.01	–0.18
5	–0.54	–0.67	–0.65	0.36	—	–0.22	–0.41	–0.29	–0.29	0.00	0.24	0.26	–0.15	0.04	0.43	0.20	–0.07	–0.09	–0.34
6	0.14	0.13	0.18	0.12	–0.14	—	0.62	0.58	0.29	0.01	–0.52	–0.46	0.21	0.12	–0.09	0.09	0.24	0.20	0.17
7	0.20	0.27	0.33	0.10	–0.37	0.60	—	0.59	0.22	–0.09	–0.03	–0.29	0.31	0.06	–0.19	0.08	0.35	0.32	0.24
8	0.16	0.18	0.28	0.09	–0.33	0.65	0.78	—	0.34	–0.01	–0.39	–0.52	0.23	–0.01	–0.04	0.24	0.53	0.49	0.22
1986																			
9	0.29	0.28	0.30	–0.13	–0.28	0.28	0.30	0.38	—	0.88	–0.52	–0.50	–0.01	–0.14	0.11	–0.18	0.08	0.08	–0.01
10	0.17	0.16	0.08	–0.08	0.02	0.00	–0.05	–0.01	0.87	—	–0.34	–0.27	–0.21	–0.18	–0.21	–0.29	–0.20	–0.18	–0.21
11	–0.23	–0.23	–0.25	0.03	–0.17	–0.58	–0.36	–0.44	–0.45	–0.25	—	0.90	–0.03	0.00	0.15	0.06	–0.14	–0.11	–0.08
12	–0.18	–0.19	–0.23	0.01	0.18	–0.49	–0.30	–0.54	–0.43	–0.20	0.80	—	–0.02	0.02	0.18	–0.04	–0.25	–0.23	–0.12
13	0.10	–0.02	0.19	–0.16	–0.20	0.10	0.26	0.23	0.04	–0.17	–0.03	0.00	—	0.37	0.03	0.11	0.27	0.22	0.20
14	0.01	–0.16	–0.09	–0.02	–0.02	–0.00	0.03	0.00	–0.15	–0.21	0.08	0.11	0.29	—	0.16	0.04	–0.06	–0.09	–0.06
15	–0.39	–0.50	–0.45	0.29	0.32	–0.02	–0.09	–0.05	0.10	0.16	0.08	0.10	0.01	0.17	—	0.14	–0.09	–0.10	–0.28
16	–0.10	–0.09	0.11	0.12	0.07	0.14	0.15	0.12	–0.05	–0.16	0.02	0.09	0.25	0.18	0.24	—	0.50	0.51	0.29
17	0.15	0.17	0.38	–0.12	–0.24	0.30	0.46	0.46	0.21	–0.10	–0.23	–0.25	0.36	–0.03	–0.18	0.30	—	0.91	0.28
18	0.11	0.18	0.39	–0.12	–0.28	0.27	0.45	0.45	0.18	–0.13	–0.21	–0.22	0.38	–0.03	–0.18	0.30	0.91	—	0.28
19	0.15	0.21	0.33	–0.18	–0.36	0.04	0.24	0.20	0.06	–0.16	–0.04	0.01	0.27	0.06	–0.05	0.35	0.23	0.32	—

Note: Correlation coefficients for 1986 are presented to the left of the diagonal. Coefficients with values exceeding 0.12 are significant at $p \leq 0.01$.

Table 3. Multiple Regression Analysis: BKS vs. Updated Variable Specifications[a]

	Dependent Variable	Constant	Risk Measures: Dividend Policy	Growth	Financial Leverage	Size	Liquidity	Variable of Earnings	Market Sensitivity		Adjusted R^2	F^*
Part I BKS Variable Specification			**PAYOUTB**	**GRB**	**LEVB**	**SIZEB**	**LIQ**	**VARB**	**BETA**	**RANK**		
	RP_1	–.078	0.033	0.087	0.056	–0.005	0.003	0.577	0.059	0.020	0.26	24.7
			(2.58)	(2.46)	(3.51)	(3.14)	(1.51)	(2.57)	(6.06)	(9.04)		
1986	RP_2	0.080	–0.007	–0.008	0.032	0.002	–0.000	0.467	–0.019	0.003	0.26	25.5
			(1.43)	(0.73)	(4.63)	(3.20)	(0.49)	(4.47)	(4.57)	(3.02)		
	RP_3	0.004	–0.014	–0.007	0.030	0.002	–0.000	0.497	–0.022	0.006	0.29	29.0
			(2.40)	(0.57)	(4.44)	(3.08)	(0.56)	(4.39)	(5.13)	(5.67)		
	RP_1	–0.010	0.000	0.123	0.020	–0.007	–0.003	0.247	0.052	0.020	0.21	17.0
			(0.08)	(3.39)	(0.97)	(4.54)	(1.09)	(1.44)	(4.04)	(7.47)		
1987	RP_2	0.015	–0.022	0.001	0.023	0.001	–0.000	0.486	–0.014	0.005	0.18	13.7
			(3.42)	(0.07)	(2.28)	(1.20)	(0.63)	(2.98)	(2.03)	(4.51)		
	RP_3	0.010	–0.021	0.012	0.017	0.002	–0.000	0.417	–0.017	0.006	0.15	11.4
			(3.20)	(0.60)	(1.80)	(1.62)	(0.32)	(2.42)	(2.27)	(4.87)		

(continued)

Table 3. (continued)

			Risk Measures									
			Dividend Policy	*Growth*	*Financial Leverage*	*Size*	*Liquidity*	*Variable of Earnings*	*Market Sensitivity*		*Adjusted R^2*	*F^**
Part II Updated Variable Specification			**YLD**	**GR**	**LEV(2)**	**SIZE**	**LN(LIQ)**	**VAR**	**BETA**	**RANK**		
	RP_1	−0.047	1.109	0.504	0.011	−0.006	0.009	0.001	0.069	0.018	0.32	33.2
			(5.80)	(4.35)	(3.90)	(3.96)	(3.87)	(2.05)	(6.33)	(7.30)		
1986	RP_2	0.037	0.370	0.083	0.012	−0.002	−0.000	−0.000	−0.003	0.002	0.31	30.8
			(3.44)	(2.29)	(4.29)	(2.74)	(0.24)	(0.43)	(0.57)	(1.96)		
	RP_3	0.032	0.361	0.066	0.012	−0.002	0.000	−0.000	−0.003	0.004	0.32	33.4
			(3.23)	(1.75)	(4.31)	(3.00)	(0.35)	(1.03)	(0.58)	(4.05)		
	RP_1	−0.020	0.963	0.651	0.014	−0.011	−0.003	0.000	0.068	0.017	0.36	34.8
			(6.43)	(8.03)	(5.67)	(7.21)	(0.71)	(0.14)	(5.14)	(7.15)		
1987	RP_2	0.024	0.338	0.177	0.015	−0.003	−0.000	−0.000	0.004	0.004	0.38	36.4
			(3.16)	(4.79)	(4.42)	(3.78)	(0.14)	(1.45)	(0.56)	(3.26)		
	RP_3	0.018	0.455	0.190	0.014	−0.003	0.000	−0.000	0.007	0.004	0.35	33.0
			(4.02)	(5.00)	(4.16)	(3.29)	(0.22)	(1.67)	(0.87)	(3.25)		

Notes: Absolute value of t-statistic is presented in parentheses below regression coefficient. Critical values for t-statistic, 595 degrees of freedom:

P	t-value
0.05	1.96
0.01	2.58

*All F-values are significant at beyond the 0.0001 level.

preference by the market for the inclusion of current liabilities in the definition of financial leverage.

Firm size appears best represented by the logarithm of the market value of common equity (SIZE), which is consistent with research on the size effect (e.g., see Brown et al., 1983b). Only SIZE consistently carries a negative coefficient, which is consistent with the extant literature; this outcome argues for the use of a market-based specification of common equity values.

The results in Table 3 indicate a relative absence of a relationship between expected return and firm liquidity. The sign of the liquidity coefficient is inconsistent among regressions and never exhibits the significant negative coefficient suggested by theory. The negative correlations between the measures of liquidity and RP_2 and RP_3 suggest that these measures may have some merit as stand-alone risk measures. However, the regression analysis suggests that a firm's liquidity is generally insignificant after adjusting for other risk concepts. This finding may be attributable to the inability of the measures used, and hence of traditional accounting measures, to depict a firm's actual liquidity position. It is of interest to note that the correlations between the two measures of firm liquidity and the logarithm of total assets, SIZEB, were approximately –0.50 ($p < 0.001$). This finding may reflect the fact that larger firms usually have greater access to the commercial paper market and larger lines of credit; hence, lower liquidity ratios for large firms may reflect their ability to use liabilities (as opposed to assets) to satisfy liquidity needs.

The volatility of earnings construct is better represented by the traditional ex post variable specification, VARB. The regression coefficient on Value Line's ex post measure of earnings uncertainty (VAR) was inconsistent in sign and significance; hence, VARB is the only BKS specification to outperform an updated specification.

B. Measurement Bias

To capture potential measurement bias associated with the use of Value Line expectational data as a surrogate for the market equilibrium expected return, we included RANK as an independent variable in the set of regressions. RANK is a Value Line assessment of the expected price performance of a security over the next 12 months, measured on a scale of 1 (highest) to 5 (lowest).

Table 3 reveals that the RANK coefficients are positive and significant in each of the regressions. The analyses were also conducted without RANK to assess the impact of this variable on the model results.[12] In general, the findings from Table 3 were relatively unaffected by the inclusion of RANK. The sign and significance of each coefficient were essentially unchanged, and the choice of the optimal risk measures was unaffected.

C. Market-Determined Risk Concepts

A principal objective of this study is to examine whether accounting data permitted a superior assessment of security risk than is possible by using only the information associated with past stock price data (i.e., beta). A second objective is to investigate the dimensionality of risk.

To address these issues, we investigate the risk concepts (directly or indirectly) priced by the marketplace. The "empirically best" set of variable specifications obtained in Table 3 is used for this analysis: YLD, GR, LEV(2), SIZE, VARB, and BETA; a liquidity variable was not included due to the poor performance of both LIQ and LN(LIQ). Estimation of the extended after-tax CAPM was then undertaken, removing one variable at a time until all the remaining variable coefficients were significant at 0.05 or better. The results for 1986 and 1987 are presented in Table 4.

Among the risk measures, the largest, consistent *t*-statistics are observed for the coefficients of YLD, LEV(2), SIZE, and GR. VARB is found to be significant in three of six regressions, while BETA is significant only in the RP_1 regressions.[13] The results, however, are not entirely consistent across both years. For example, in the 1986 RP_1 regression, LEV (2) is insignificant at the 0.05 level and VARB is significant, whereas in 1987 LEV (2) is significant and VARB is insignificant (p = 0.121). Similarly, in the 1986 RP_3 regression, GR is insignificant (p = 0.063) and VARB is significant, whereas in 1987 GR is significant and VARB is not (p = 0.095). Nevertheless, it is encouraging that despite the debate, passage, and implementation of arguably the most important tax overhaul in U.S. history, virtually the same set of variables best reflects risk across both years. At the 0.10 level, the same set of variables is significant in the RP_2 and RP_3 models in both years. Only the insignificance of VARB in 1987 prevents the same statement from being true for RP_1. This suggests that empirical relations are likely to remain sufficiently stable to prove useful to users of financial statements. In this context, the road to superior financial analysis may be to more quickly recognize the slowly changing relations.

The results indicate for both years that security risk can be better assessed using accounting data than past stock price data alone, and that risk is best represented as a multidimensional concept.[14] Finally, the results also suggest that the most important and consistent variables affecting a security's expected return in 1986 and 1987 are the expected dividend yield, the expected covariance of security return with the market, firm size, and growth prospects; and, that expected covariance is best proxied, among the set of variables examined, by LEV(2).

It is well known that the sensitivity of share price to the market should be related to the ratio of the market value of debt-to-equity (Hamada, 1972). The consistently high *t*-statistic observed for LEV(2) and the absence of a consistently significant BETA coefficient suggests that LEV(2) may be a superior proxy for a security's true market sensitivity at the individual security level than BETA itself.[15] It is not particularly surprising that LEV(2) outperformed BETA, since this latter measure

Table 4. Extended After-Tax CAPM Regression Analysis Results: Best Variable Specification[a]

Dependent Variable	Constant	Dividend Policy	Financial Growth	Leverage	Size	Variability of Earnings	Market Sensitivity		Adjusted R^2	F*
			Risk Measures							
Predicted Sign		+/–	+	+	–	+	+			
1986 Regressions										
		YLD	**GR**	**LEV(2)**	**SIZE**	**VARB**	**BETA**	**RANK**		
RP_1	–0.035	1.041	0.460	N.S.	–0.007	0.460	0.075	0.018	0.31	36.5
		(5.55)	(4.29)		(4.61)	(2.24)	(7.20)	(7.02)		
RP_2	0.032	0.377	0.081	0.011	–0.001	0.349	N.S.	N.S	0.35	38.9
		(4.27)	(2.44)	(4.77)	(2.32)	(4.11)				
RP_3	0.029	0.282	N.S.	0.010	–0.002	0.353	N.S.	0.003	0.35	42.4
		(4.31)		(4.36)	(2.33)	(3.82)		(2.70)		
1987 Regressions										
RP_1	–0.023	0.980	0.653	0.015	–0.011	N.S.	0.067	0.017	0.37	46.5
		(6.65)	(8.30)	(8.45)	(7.60)	(5.20)	(5.20)	(7.14)		
RP_2	0.017	0.369	0.200	0.015	–0.003	0.292	N.S.	0.003	0.40	52.5
		(4.31)	(5.40)	(6.98)	(4.20)	(2.42)		(3.01)		
RP_3	0.020	0.430	0.200	0.014	–0.003	N.S.	N.S.	0.004	0.35	51.3
		(4.31)	(4.91)	(6.04)	(4.36)			(3.28)		

Notes: [a]Absolute value of *t*-statistic is presented in parentheses below regression coefficient. N.S. implies "not significant" at the 0.05 level.
*All *F*-values are significant at beyond 0.001 level.

suffers from the ex post measurement problems noted earlier. Moreover, Blume (1971) and others report that historic beta, and even adjusted historic beta as developed by Value Line, are unstable at the individual security level.

The dividend yield coefficient in the after-tax CAPM may be interpreted as an estimate of the marginal tax rate. The positive coefficient implies that high yield stocks must offer higher before-tax expected returns, ceteris paribus, to compensate for the differential tax treatment between dividends and capital gains. The implied tax rates in the RP_1 regressions are approximately 100%, while the implied marginal rates in the earnings-price models appear more reasonable (i.e., 37% in 1987). The similarity of results across the two years suggests that tax reform did not materially impact the risk relations.

D. Forecasts of 1987 Risk Premiums

If risk is best viewed as a multidimensional construct, and if there exists a stable relationship between risk premium and the accounting and financial risk measures, then forecasts of the 1987 risk premium using the 1986 multidimensional models in Table 4 should prove more accurate than forecasts from a one-dimensional model.

Table 5 summarizes the forecast accuracy of several multi- and unidimensional risk models. Forecast errors were calculated as the actual less the forecasted risk premium. The MULTI forecasts reflect the use of the 1986 coefficients from Table 4 and the 1987 values of the independent variables. Several one-dimensional risk

Table 5. Accuracy of Risk Premium Forecasts

	Accuracy Measures			
Forecasts	*ME*	*t(ME)**	*RMSE*	*MAE*
RP1 Forecasts				
MULTI	0.0085	0.19	0.0461	0.0349
F-BETA	0.0037	0.07	0.0504	0.0388
F-LEV	0.0037	0.07	0.0516	0.0394
BETA87	†	†	0.0503	0 0390
RP2 Forecasts				
MULTI	0.0007	0.03	0.0204	0.0144
F-BETA	0.0020	0.08	0.0245	0.0170
F-LEV	0.0020	0.09	0.0212	0.0152
BETA87	†	†	0.0243	0.0172

Notes: †By construction, ME of BETA87 is zero.
‡*t*-statistic for hypothesis that $ME = 0$.

forecast models were considered. F-BETA is the CAPM benchmark of accuracy—it uses 1986 coefficients from the regressions of risk premium on BETA and RANK and the 1987 values of BETA and RANK; RANK is included in the forecast models to capture potential measurement bias. F-LEV reflects the corresponding forecasts using LEV(2). And, BETA87 reflects fitted values from the regression of 1987 risk premium on 1987 values of BETA and RANK. In contrast to F-BETA, BETA87 measures are not true forecasts in that they benefit from information not available to the other models. As such, BETA87 should present a benchmark of forecast accuracy which is difficult to exceed.

All mean errors (ME) are consistent with the null hypothesis of zero mean error, which implies that no forecast appears biased. The root mean squared error (RMSE) and mean absolute error (MAE) are preferable measures of accuracy because, unlike ME, they reflect errors that are opposite in sign but of equal magnitude.

Do accounting data allow superior assessment of security risk to what is possible using beta alone? Based on the RMSE and MAE criteria, the forecast errors are consistently smaller for the multidimensional model than for either F-BETA or BETA87. The MULTI errors of RP_1 and RP_2 average approximately 10 and 20% less, respectively, than the average errors of BETA87 despite the latter advantage.

Do multidimensional models provide more accurate assessment of risk than one-dimensional models? In this test, yes. MULTI proved more accurate than any one-dimensional model. Based on the RMSE and MAE criteria, the MULTI forecasts averaged approximately 10 and 5% better, respectively, than the next best forecasts of RP_1 and RP_2.

Finally, among the one-dimensional risk models, the accuracy of forecasts of RP_1 are similar, but F-LEV produced the most accurate forecasts of RP_2. This supports the earlier finding that LEV(2) may be a more accurate measure of the expected covariance of an individual security's return with the market.[16]

V. DISCUSSION AND CONCLUSIONS

If corporate financial reporting is to be adequately supportive of investment decision making, then it must provide information useful to the formation of risk and return assessments. This study attempts to provide evidence regarding the adequacy of financial reporting in the formation of risk-return assessments by investigating the relation between the market's pricing of security risk and various accounting and financial risk surrogates. Our study examined this association under a variety of variable specifications and measurement approaches. Given the significant resources expended in the production of financial statement data, evidence regarding this relation is important not only to investors and analysts but also to accounting standard setters.

The results of our investigation suggest a number of inferences. First, the study provides evidence that reliance on accounting data in conjunction with other information enables a better assessment of security risk than reliance on market-based data alone. Regressions imply that the four most important and consistent variables affecting security risk are a firm's dividend policy (YLD), financial leverage [LEV(2)], size (SIZE), and growth prospects (GR). LEV(2) and SIZE use accounting data, and a firm's dividend yield can be forecast from historical dividend payments. Among the four variables, three can be accurately forecast from financial statement (and other) data. It is only unclear whether a firm's growth prospects can be accurately forecast from these data.

Second, it is possible to improve upon many traditional risk measures. For example, measures of financial leverage and firm size that use the market value of common equity are informationally superior to their book value counterparts. In general, however, the ex post measure of earnings uncertainty (VARB) is not without merit. Furthermore, traditional measures of liquidity were not found to be associated with security risk in any of the models investigated, which may be indicative of a failure of current accounting disclosure to adequately represent this theoretically important risk construct.

Third, risk appears to be best reflected as a multidimensional construct. Forecasts of risk premium using a multidimensional approach proved more accurate than forecasts using a single risk variable. Finally, the results suggest that financial leverage [LEV(2)] may be a better measure of the expected covariance of return with the market at the individual security level than ex post beta or measures which adjust ex post beta for its tendency to move toward unity (e.g., BETA). Unfortunately, even our best model accounted for little more than one-third of the explained variation in expected return, suggesting the omission of one or more significant risk surrogates.

A discussion of some of the limitations of this study is in order. There can be no guarantee that the set of risk measures that proved optimal for the assessment of security risk in 1986 and 1987 is also the optimal set for other types of risk (e.g., default risk) or for other time periods. Nonetheless, the findings of this study confirm the importance of accounting data, in conjunction with other information, in the formation of risk assessments of publicly traded stocks. These results are, however, of only limited use in addressing valuation issues involving privately held firms. Such valuations must rely on risk measures that use accounting data only. Despite these limitations, the study provides risk modeling and variable specification information of value to financial statement users and accounting standard setters.

ACKNOWLEDGMENTS

The instructive comments of Christopher Barry, Ed Deakin, Robert Kellogg, Raymond King, John W. Peavy, III, David Peterson, and three anonymous reviewers on earlier drafts of this paper are acknowledged. All errors remain the responsibility of the authors.

NOTES

1. The quantity and quality of information available on a firm may also affect a security's perceived risk (Arbel, 1985; Arbel, Carvell, and Strebel, 1983; Arbel and Strebel, 1983; Barry and Brown, 1984); however, measures of the information effect tend to be highly correlated with firm size, and Barry and Brown (1984) and Dowen and Bauman (1986) find that the firm size effect dominates the information effect.

2. A number of studies have investigated these risk-related concepts (e.g., see Bowen, 1981; Derstine and Huefner, 1974; Elgers, 1980; Eskew, 1979; and Farrelly, Ferris, and Reichenstein, 1985).

3. For example, BKS found the rank correlation and product-moment correlation between accounting betas for individual securities in adjacent periods to be only 0.034 and –0.060, respectively.

4. See Dhaliwal (1986) and Landsman (1986) for a discussion of issues regarding the inclusion of unfunded pension obligations in the measurement of financial leverage.

5. The interested reader is referred to Value Line's data base manual for a description of the development of this variable.

6. The inclusion of RANK is intended to reflect any biasing or mispricing in the Value Line earnings forecasts. An alternative approach would involve replacing the Value Line forecasts with expectational data from several sources, such as the Institutional Brokers Estimate Service (IBES), which collects analysts' forecasts of individual firm five-year annual earnings growth. Although analyses using the IBES data bank were attempted, those results are not reported herein. The empirical results using an IBES-based risk premium model were found to be counterintuitive, inconsistent between years, and at odds with the relation between ex post returns and the risk measures. We attribute these counterintuitive findings to at least two factors. First, as O'Brien (1988) observes, the average age of IBES summary forecasts is nearly 100 trading days, due in part to publication lags and the IBES updating process, while the average age of a Value Line forecast is *less* than half that of its IBES counterpart. O'Brien shows that having a *current* earnings forecast is more critical to forecast accuracy than using a mean forecast. Second, the IBES forecast solicitation process is subject to considerable question (e.g. see Harris, 1986).

7. Following Ang and Peterson (1985), we deleted the few firms with ER_1 less than zero. These firms' share prices are usually influenced by merger discussion or merger speculation. Value Line does not adjust projected three-to-five-year prices during these periods. No firm had ER_2 or ER_3 values less than zero.

8. Alternative weightings schemes were considered, including $W_1 = \text{DIFF}/6$ and $W_1 = (1 + \text{DIFF})/8$. A slightly higher coefficient of determination was obtained for the adopted scheme; the regression results were not meaningfully affected by the alternative weighting methods.

9. Minor adjustments to the data were made when considered reasonable or to prevent extreme values from dominating a variable. For example, PAYOUTB was constrained to the range 0 to 1, which follows BKS. LIQ was set at 10 for the few firms with current ratios in excess of that amount; this prevents one extreme value (e.g., LIQ = 281) from dominating a coefficient in a least squares regression. Finally, the risk premiums were constrained to be nonnegative.

10. For example, the 1986 F-statistics for LEV(2) in the RP_1, RP_2, and RP_3 regressions were 1.46, 2.51, and 2.50, respectively; the critical F-value at the 0.01 level is approximately 1.50. Goldfeld–Quandt tests also revealed heteroskedastic errors related to YLD, GR, SIZE, LN(LIQ), VARB, and BETA at the 0.01 level for at least one of the dependent variables.

11. The updated variable specifications not reported in Table 3, namely, PAYOUT and LEV(1), generally outperformed PAYOUTB and LEVB in terms of t-statistics and explained variances in otherwise similar regressions.

12. Results are available upon request from the authors. It is of interest to note that the coefficient and related t-statistic of RANK is substantially larger in the RP_1 regressions, which suggests that the potential for errors in variables may be severer for the constant growth model than for the earnings-price models.

13. The insignificant BETA coefficient in the RP_2 and RP_3 regressions does not necessarily mean that beta is without merit. In both years, BETA is significantly correlated with YLD, GR, and SIZE, and these variables were already in the regressions.

14. The generally low correlation among the independent variables provides evidence that they are not noisy measures of a single risk dimension.

15. In a study using ex post returns, Bhandari (1988) found that "the expected returns on common stocks are positively related to the debt-to-equity ratio, controlling for beta and firm size, both including and excluding January" (p. 527). Further, he found ex post returns to be insignificantly related to beta in regressions that also include financial leverage.

16. Comparable forecast models excluding RANK as an independent variable were also investigated. The most accurate forecasts, by every criterion, were generated by the MULTI model, followed by F-LEV.

REFERENCES

Alderfer, C. P., and Bierman, H. (1970). "Choice with Risk: Beyond the Mean and Variance." *Journal of Business* (July), 200–217.

Ang, J. S., and Peterson, D. R. (1985) "Return, Risk, and Yield: Evidence from Ex Ante Data." *Journal of Finance* (June), 537–548.

Arbel, A. (1985). "Generic Stocks: An Old Product in a New Package." *Journal of Portfolio Management* (Summer), 4–13.

Arbel, A., Carvell, S., and Strebel, P. J. (1983). "Giraffes, Institutions and Neglected Firms." *Financial Analysts Journal* (May/June), 57–63.

Arbel, A., and Strebel, P. J. (1983). "Pay Attention to Neglected Firms!" *Journal of Portfolio Management* (Winter), 37–42.

Baker, H. K., Farrelly, G. E., and Edelman, R. B. (1985). "A Survey of Management Views on Dividend Policy." *Financial Management* (Autumn), 78–84.

Ball, R. (1978). "Anomalies in Relationships Between Securities' Yields and Yield-Surrogates." *Journal of Financial Economics* 103–126.

Banz, R. W. (1981). "The Relationship Between Return and Market Value of Common Stocks." *Journal of Financial Economics* (March), 3–18.

Barry, C., and Brown, S. (1984). "Differentiated Information and the Small Firm Effect." *Journal of Financial Economics* 283–294.

Basu, S. (1977). "Investment Performance of Common Stocks in Relation to their Price-Earnings Ratios: A Test of the Efficient Market Hypothesis." *Journal of Finance* (June), 663–682.

Basu, S. (1983). "The Relationship Between Earnings, Yield, Market Value and Return for NYSE Common Stocks." *Journal of Financial Economics* (June), 129–156.

Beaver, W., Kettler, P., and Scholes, M. (1970). "The Association Between Market Determined and Accounting Determined Risk Measures." *Accounting Review* (October), 654–682.

Beaver, W., and Manegold, J. (1975). "The Association between Market-Determined and Accounting-Determined Measures of Systematic Risk: Some Further Evidence." *Journal of Financial and Quantitative Analysis* (June), 231–284.

Bhandari, R. (1988). "Debt/Equity Ratio and Expected Common Stock Returns." *Journal of Finance* (June), 507–528.

Black, F. (1973). "Yes, Virginia, There is Hope: Tests of the Value Line Ranking Systems." *Financial Analysts Journal* (September), 10–14.

Blume, N. W. (1971). "On the Assessment of Risk." *Journal of Finance* (March), 1–10.

Bowen, R. (1981). "Valuation of Earnings Components in the Electric Utility Industry." *Accounting Review* (January), 1–22.

Brennan, M. J. (1970). "Investor Taxes, Market Equilibrium and Corporate Finance." Ph.D. dissertation (MIT).

Brown, L., and Rozeff, M. (1978). "The Superiority of Analysts' Forecasts as Measures of Expectations: Evidence from Earnings." *Journal of Finance* (March), 1–16.

Brown, P., Keim, D. B., Kleidon, A. W., and Marsh, T. A. (1983a). "Stock Return Seasonalities and the Tax-Loss Selling Hypothesis." *Journal of Financial Economics* (June), 105–128.

Brown, P., Kleidon, A. W., and Marsh, T. A. (1983b). "New Evidence on the Nature of Size-Related Anomalies in Stock Prices." *Journal of Financial Economics* (June), 33–56.

Cooley, P. L. (1977). "A Multidimensional Analysis of Institutional Investor Perception of Risk." *Journal of Finance* (March), 67–78.

Coombs, C. H., and Pruitt, D. G. (1960). "Components of Risk in Decision Making: Probability and Variance Preference." *Journal of Experimental Psychology* (November).

Copeland, T. E., and Mayers, D. (1982). "The Value Line Enigma (1965–1978): A Case Study of Performance Evaluation Issues." *Journal of Financial Economics* (November), 289–231.

Derstine, J. S., and Huefner, R. J. (1974). "LIFO-FIFO, Accounting Ratios and Market Risk." *Journal of Accounting Research* (Fall), 216–234.

Dhaliwal, D. S. (1986). "Measurement of Financial Leverage in the Presence of Unfunded Pension Obligations." *Accounting Review* (October), 651–661.

Dowen, R. J., and Bauman, W. S. (1986). "The Relative Importance of Size, P/E and Neglect." *Journal of Portfolio Management* (Spring), 30–34.

Dybvig, P. H., and Ross, S. A. (1985). "Yes, the APT is Testable." *Journal of Finance* (September), 1173–1188.

Elgers, P. T. (1980). "Accounting-Based Risk Predictions: A Reexamination." *Accounting Review* (July), 389–408.

Eskew, R. K. (1979). "The Forecasting Ability of Accounting Risk Measures: Some Additional Evidence." *Accounting Review* (January), 107–118.

Farrelly, G. E., Ferris, K. R., and Reichenstein, W. (1985), "Perceived Risk, Market Risk, and Accounting Determined Risk Measures." *Accounting Review* (April), 178–188.

Farrelly, G. E., and Reichenstein, W. R. (1984). "Risk Perceptions of Institutional Investors." *Journal of Portfolio Management* (Summer), 5–12.

Financial Accounting Standards Board (1978). "Objectives of Financial Reporting by Business Enterprises." *Statement of Financial Accounting Concepts No. 1* (Stamford, CT).

Goldfeld, S. M., and Quandt, R. F. (1965). "Some Tests for Homoskedasticity." *Journal of the American Statistical Association* (September), 539–547.

Goodman, D. A. and Peavy, J. W., III (1983). "Industry Relative Price-Earnings Ratios as Indicators of Investment Returns." *Financial Analysts Journal* (July–August), 60–66.

Gordon, M. (1959). "Dividends, Earnings and Stock Prices." *Review of Economics and Statistics* (May), 99–105.

Hamada, R. S. (1972). "The Effects of the Firm's Capital Structure on the Systematic Risk of Common Stock." *Journal of Finance* (May), 435–452.

Harris, R. (1986). "Using Analysts' Growth Forecasts to Estimate Shareholder Required Rates of Return." *Financial Management* (Spring), 58–67.

Holloway, C. (1981). "A Note on Testing an Aggressive Investment Strategy Using Value Line Ranks." *Journal of Finance* (June), 711–719.

Keim, D. B. (1983). "Size-Related Anomalies and Stock Return Seasonality." *Journal of Financial Economics* (June), 13–32.

Landsman, W. (1986). "An Empirical Investigation of Pension Fund Property Rights." *Accounting Review* (October), 662–691.

Litzenberger, R., and Ramaswamy, K. (1979). "The Effect of Personal Taxes and Dividends on Capital Asset Prices: Theory and Empirical Evidence." *Journal of Financial Economics* (June), 163–195.

Litzenberger, R., and Ramaswamy, K. (1982). "The Effects of Dividends on Common Stock Prices: Tax Effects or Information Effects?" *Journal of Finance* (May), 429–444.

Miller, M., and Scholes, M. (1982). "Dividends and Taxes: Some Empirical Evidence." *Journal of Political Economy* (December), 1118–1141.

O'Brien, P. (1988). "Analysts' Forecasts as Earnings Expectations." *Journal of Accounting and Economics* (January), 53–88.

Reinganum, M. R. (1981). "Misspecification of Capital Asset Pricing: Empirical Anomalies Based on Earnings Yields and Market Values." *Journal of Financial Economics* (March), 19–46.

Reinganum, M. R. (1983). "The Anomalous Stock Market Behavior of Small Firms in January." *Journal of Financial Economics* (June), 89–104.

Roll, R. (1977). "A Critique of the Asset Pricing Theory's Tests." *Journal of Financial Economics* (March), 129–176.

Ross, S. A. (1976), "The Arbitrage Theory of Capital Asset Pricing." *Journal of Economic Theory* (December), 341–360.

Ross, S. A. (1978). "The Current Status of the Capital Asset Pricing Model." *Journal of Finance* (June), 885–1901.

Sorensen, E. H., and Williamson, D. A. (1985). "Some Evidence on the Value of Dividend Discount Models." *Financial Analysts Journal* (November–December), 60–69.

Stoll, H. R., and Whaley, R. E. (1983). "Transaction Costs and the Small Firm Effect." *Journal of Financial Economics* (June), 57–80.

Tinic, S., and West, R. (1984). "Risk and Return." *Journal of Financial Economics* (December), 561–574.

White, H. (1980). "A Heteroskedasticity-Consistent Covariance Matrix Estimator and a Direct Test for Heteroskedasticity." *Econometrica* (May), 817–838.

THE ASSOCIATION BETWEEN RISK MEASURES AND FINANCIAL LEVERAGE:

A TIME-SERIES ANALYSIS

Patricia M. Fairfield

ABSTRACT

This paper presents the results of comparative time-series tests of the relation between financial leverage and the risk of common equity. The results do not provide strong support for the hypothesized association between equity risk and financial leverage when beta is the measure of risk. Most of the time-series behavior of beta remains unexplained, and the data do not support even a strong monotonic association between beta and financial leverage. In contrast, a pronounced time-series association is observed between total return variance and leverage, at both the individual security level and the portfolio level. The test results are also not consistent with the claim that market measures of leverage are superior to accounting measures in establishing the risk-leverage relation. In most of the time series regressions, accounting leverage yielded results comparable to those using market leverage.

Advances in Quantitative Analysis of Finance and Accounting,
Volume 2, Part A, pages 221–239.

ISBN: 1-55938-564-2

I. INTRODUCTION

The association between accounting-determined and market-determined measures of risk has been an issue of concern to accountants since the early work of Beaver, Kettler, and Scholes (BKS) (1970). In the two decades since the original BKS study, an extensive literature has developed on the specific relation between financial leverage and equity risk. From this literature a consensus has emerged which encompasses two points: (1) a strong empirical association exists between security price betas and financial leverage; and (2) market measures of leverage are theoretically and empirically superior to accounting measures of leverage in establishing this relation (see, for example, Foster, 1986.) The association is now so well accepted that it has provided the foundation for tests of the extent to which particular obligations of the firm (e.g., leases, pensions) are valued as "debt" by investors (Bowman, 1980a; Dhaliwal, 1986).

The evidence supporting this consensus derives almost exclusively from cross-sectional tests of the relation between risk and leverage; a common problem in these tests is the confounding influence of operating risk. Use of various proxies to control for operating risk has not yielded (the consensus notwithstanding) unanimous or unambiguous findings. Rosenberg and McKibben (1973), Bildersee (1974), Ben-Zion and Shalit (1975), Bowman (1980b), Hill and Stone (1980), Chance (1982), Elgers and Murray (1982), Mandelker and Rhee (1984), Dhaliwal (1986), and Lee et al. (1986) presented empirical results pointing to a positive cross-sectional relation between financial leverage and security price betas. In contrast, Logue and Merville (1972), Breen and Lerner (1973), Lev and Kunitzsky (1974), Boness, Chen, and Jatusipitak (1974), Thompson (1976), Eskew (1979), Fairfield (1985), and Ali (1988) failed to find convincing cross-sectional evidence in support of the beta-leverage relation. Bhandari (1988) found the debt-equity ratio to be useful in explaining common stock returns *after* controlling for beta, and argues that the evidence suggests that the premium associated with the debt-equity ratio is not a risk premium. Christie (1982), in a time-series test that introduced no explicit control for operating risk, reported a pronounced linear association between financial leverage and an alternative market risk proxy, total return variance. Schwert (1989) found that financial leverage can explain only a small proportion of the changes in the standard deviation of aggregate stock market returns over time. Taken together, these results raise some questions about the strength and stability of the association between financial leverage and equity risk.

In the cross-sectional tests of the risk-leverage relation, financial leverage has been measured using both market and book values of equity (debt is measured almost exclusively using book values), although the former are more commonly cited as the theoretically "correct" values.[1] Bowman (1980b) and Mulford (1985) present results based on cross-sectional data which suggest that substitution of accounting values for market values in leverage ratios yields weaker empirical evidence of the beta-leverage relation. The original BKS motivation for examining the beta-leverage relation, to determine the association between security price behavior and accounting data, has been largely abandoned in recent years.

This paper presents the results of comparative time-series tests of the relation between the risk of common equity and financial leverage. The study makes three contributions to the extant literature on the association between equity risk and financial leverage. The time-series design represents an alternative approach to controlling for operating risk to those employed in previous tests of the beta-leverage association, thus testing the robustness of prior results against an alternative empirical design. The use of two different measures of market risk, beta and total return variance, as dependent variables in the time-series regressions, and two different procedures for estimating beta reveal the sensitivity of the hypothesized relation to choice of risk proxy. Two measures of leverage, an accounting measure and a market measure, are used to test the claim that the former does not adequately capture the information impounded into the market risk parameter.

The empirical results cast some doubt on both elements of the consensus opinion and in turn on the usefulness of beta risk in financial analysis. The hypothesized linear association between risk and financial leverage is not strongly supported by the evidence when beta is the measure of risk. A pronounced time-series association is observed between total return variance and leverage, at both the individual security level and the portfolio level; in contrast, the data do not reveal even a strong monotonic relation between beta and financial leverage.

The results of the time-series tests are also not consistent with the claim that market measures of equity are superior in establishing empirically the risk-leverage association. Surprisingly, accounting leverage led to slightly stronger results than did market leverage in most of the time series regressions. Different definitions of accounting leverage seemed to affect the results only slightly, with the "traditional" leverage measure (all balance sheet debt plus deferred taxes and preferred stock over common equity) performing better than the other variants. The results using the book value of leverage indicates that pure accounting information may have value not always recognized in the literature. In turn this suggests that further analytical work establishing the valuation function between accounting data and market risk may be warranted (see, for example, Garman and Ohlson [1980]).

II. SAMPLE SELECTION AND VARIABLE DEFINITIONS

For purposes of this study, firms in the sample were required to have

1. 24 years of balance sheet data on the Compustat tape (1959–1982), which resulted in an initial sample size of 563 firms;
2. 28 years of returns data on the Center for Research in Security Prices (CRSP) monthly tape for estimation of the moving window beta (see below), which reduced the sample to 284 firms;

Table 1. Cross-Sectional Means of Population and Two Samples

	Total Sample n = 563	*Moving Window Beta Firms n = 284*	*Ohr Beta Firms n = 150*
Accounting	1.36	1.09	0.94
leverage	(11.9)	(1.17)	(.78)
Market	1.32	1.19	1.11
leverage	(2.0)	(1.7)	(1.6)
Net income	57.4	81.5	104.7
	(153.4)	(199.8)	(246.3)
Moving window		1.05	1.05
beta		(0.42)	(0.39)
OHR beta			1.07
			(0.38)

Note: The figures in parentheses are the cross-sectional standard deviations.

3. 50 years of returns data for estimation of the stochastic parameter regression beta (see below), which resulted in a subsample of 150 firms.

Summary statistics for the initial group of 563 firms and the two subsets (henceforth, the moving window beta [MWB] firms and the stochastic parameter regression [SPR] firms, respectively) are presented in Table 1. The relative sizes of net income for the three samples indicate that the selection criteria bias the samples heavily toward large "survivor" firms, which have slightly lower than average debt-equity ratios. The possibility that the selection criteria may bias against rejection of the null hypothesis is explored in the tests to follow.

The independent variable in the time series tests is the firm's financial leverage, or debt-equity ratio. The book value of debt over the market value of equity (MLEV) as well as its "pure" accounting analog, the book value of debt over the book value of common equity (ALEV), have been used in previous research. To provide insight into the relative explanatory power of the market and book values of leverage, both were used in the firm level and portfolio tests.[2] In addition, since debt and equity can be computed in different ways using balance sheet data, the individual firm tests were repeated using five different definitions of book leverage for the firm level tests. ALEV is the "traditional" debt/equity ratio and classifies as debt current liabilities, long-term debt, deferred taxes, and preferred stock. ALEVDT reclassifies deferred taxes as equity; ALEVCL drops current liabilities from the numerator; and ALEVPS drops preferred stock from the numerator. ALEVTA is "traditional" debt over total assets.

Both total return variance (RETVAR) and beta (MWBETA) were measured using a 48-month moving window capital-asset-pricing model (CAPM) regression of the firm return on the value-weighted market index. The moving window is a time series of parameter estimates created by picking up and dropping a month's observations at either end of the data series used to generate the estimate over the period of interest. To minimize sampling variance in the dependent variable, the annual estimate of beta and total return variance represent the average over the 12 months prior to the balance sheet date on which leverage was measured.[3]

To provide evidence on the robustness of the results with respect to systematic risk, a second beta estimation procedure is used here. The procedure provides a general model of the beta process, allowing for stationary, sequential, and random components of systematic risk. Following Ohlson and Rosenberg (1982) and DeJong and Collins (1985), I estimated betas using a stochastic parameter regression model,[4]

$$\beta_t = \beta + \delta_t + \mu_t,$$

where

$$\delta_t = \theta\delta_{t-1} + \xi_t.$$

The individual parameters were estimated from 600 months of data using an iterative process of generalized least squares and maximum likelihood techniques. The stochastic-parameter regression beta (SPRBETA) has three components: a stationary mean, β, a deviation δ_t obeying a first-order autoregressive process, and a purely temporal error, μ_t. The beta estimates used here do not incorporate the purely temporal component, μ_t.[5] Preliminary tests showed that the sequential beta process accounts for about one-third of the total variation in firm betas; identifying and removing the two-thirds of the beta variance that is noise should make it easier to detect the effect of financial leverage on beta.[6]

Two data modifications were made on the basis of preliminary tests run on a subset of firms. To reduce the problem of autocorrelated residuals in the OLS regressions, the subsequent tests have had a second-order autoregressive transformation applied to the residuals. This transformation eliminated the serious autocorrelation in the regressions, so that the reported t-statistics and R^2's may be taken at their face values.[7] Because there is a secular trend in the leverage variables over time, the regression results reported below use standardized versions of leverage (ALEVSTD and MLEVSTD) as the independent variables in the beta regressions.[8]

III. INDIVIDUAL FIRM RESULTS

Table 2 shows the regression results for the individual firm tests using total return variance, the moving window beta, and the SPR beta as dependent variables, and the traditional accounting leverage and market leverage as independent variables. The equation used in the tests was $Y_t = \alpha + \theta X_t + \mu_t$, where Y was replaced by RETVAR, MWBETA, and SPRBETA, respectively, and X was replaced by ac-

Table 2. Cross-Sectional Averages of Individual Firm Regression Statistics Using 24 Years of Data: Model: $Y_t = \alpha + \theta X_t + \mu$

Y_t	X_t	
RETVAR (n = 284)	**ALEV**	**MLEV**
θ	0.0017	0.0010
t-statistic	1.07	0.95
R^2	0.13	0.11
Percentage positive and significant*	39%	33%
Percentage negative and significant*	5%	5%
MWBETA (n = 284)	**ALEVSTD**	**MLEVSTD**
θ	0.068	−0.005
t-statistic	0.41	−0.12
R^2	0.08	0.07
Percentage positive and significant*	24%	14%
Percentage negative and significant*	10%	19%
SPRBETA (n = 150)	**ALEVSTED**	**MLEVSTED**
θ	0.054	−0.067
t-statistic	0.46	−0.20
R^2	0.08	0.08
Percentage positive and significant*	21%	13%
Percentage negative and significant*	7%	18%

Notes: *These percentages refer to the number of t-statistics which are significant at the 10% confidence level, assuming, for both the positive and negative cases, that a one-tailed test was appropriate. To the extent that a two-tailed test was appropriate, these percentages are overstated.

RETVAR is total return variance; MWBETA is the moving-window beta; SPRBETA is the stochastic parameter beta; ALEV is the book value of leverage; MLEV is the market value of leverage; ALEVSTD is the standardized book leverage; MLEVSTD is the standardized market leverage.

counting leverage (ALEV or ALEVSTD) and market leverage (MLEV or MLEVSTD). Six regressions resulted. For each of the six regressions, the cross-sectional averages of the leverage coefficient θ, the associated t-statistics, and the R^2 are reported, as well as the percentage of the individual firm regressions that resulted in significant positive and negative coefficients.

If we ignore for now possible cross-sectional dependencies in the regressions, the initial results suggest that leverage and risk are positively correlated only when risk is measured as total equity risk rather than systematic risk. For the total return variance equations, 39% of the individual coefficients on accounting leverage and 33% of the coefficients on market leverage are positive and significant at a 10% confidence level. Only 5% of the total return variance equations have negative and significant coefficients on the leverage variables.

Table 3. Cross-Sectional Averages of Correlation Coefficients between Different Measures of Accounting Leverage (Panel A) and Percentages of Significant Positive and Negative Regression Coefficients from Regressions of Risk Variables on Different Measures of Accounting Leverage (Panel B)

Panel A: Correlation

	ALEV	*ALEVDT*	*ALEVCL*	*ALEVPS*	*ALEVTA*
ALEV	1.00	0.92	0.87	0.98	0.97
ALEVDT		1.00	0.80	0.97	0.90
ALEVCL			1.00	0.85	0.84
ALEVPS				1.00	0.95
ALEVTA					1.00

Panel B: Percentages of Significant Regression Coefficients

	Independent Variable				
Dependent Variable	*ALEV*	*ALEVDT*	*ALEVCL*	*ALEVPS*	*ALEVTA*
RETVAR					
Percentage positive and significant	39	33	34	35	34
Percentage negative and significant	5	7	6	6	8
MWBETA					
Percentage positive and significant	24	23	21	23	24
Percentage negative and significant	10	9	10	9	11
SPRBETA					
Percentage positive and significant	21	20	23	19	19
Percentage negative and significant	7	6	7	6	5

Notes: RETVAR is total return variance; MWBETA is the moving-window beta; SPRBETA is the stochastic parameter beta; ALEV is total liabilities, deferred taxes, and preferred stock over common equity; ALEVDT is ALEV with deferred taxes reclassified as common equity; ALEVCL is ALEV with current liabilities dropped from the numerator; ALEVPS is ALEV with preferred stock dropped from the numerator; ALEVTA is total liabilities, deferred taxes, and preferred stock over total assets.

In contrast, 24% of the coefficients on accounting leverage are positive and significant, while 10% are negative and significant; and for the market leverage equations a greater number of the significant coefficients are negative than are positive. Thus, the evidence suggests that even a strong monotonic association between beta and leverage cannot be detected at the individual firm level. The SPRBETA results are comparable to those using the moving window beta. The beta results were not markedly improved by the introduction of a stochastic parameter model to estimate beta, demonstrating that the weak results were not attributable to the estimation procedure.[9]

Table 3 provides evidence on the sensitivity of the results to alternative definitions of accounting leverage. In panel A of Table 3 are the average correlations

Table 4. Cross-Sectional Averages of Individual Firm Regression Statistics for Firms Showing Largest Changes in Leverage, 1959–1982: Model: $Y_t = \alpha + \theta X_t + \mu$

Y_t	X_t	
RETVAR (n = 50)	**ALEV**	**MLEV**
θ	0.0013	0.0004
t-statistic	1.58	1.25
R^2	0.15	0.14
Percentage positive and significant*	50%	36%
Percentage negative and significant*	2%	6%
MWBETA (n = 284)	**ALEVSTD**	**MLEVSTD**
θ	0.123	−0.07
t-statistic	0.81	−0.49
R^2	0.08	0.09
Percentage positive and significant*	26%	12%
Percentage negative and significant*	6%	18%
SPRBETA (n = 150)	**ALEVSTED**	**MLEVSTED**
θ	0.032	−0.008
t-statistic	0.47	−0.34
R^2	0.13	0.12
Percentage positive and significant*	20%	20%
Percentage negative and significant*	15%	20%

Notes: *These percentages refer to the number of t-statistics which are significant at the 10% confidence level, assuming, for both the positive and negative cases, that a one-tailed test was appropriate. To the extent that a two-tailed test was appropriate, these percentages are overstated.

RETVAR is total return variance; MWBETA is the moving-window beta; SPRBETA is the stochastic parameter beta; ALEV is the book value of leverage; MLEV is the market value of leverage; ALEVSTD is the standardized book leverage; MLEVSTD is the standardized market leverage.

between the different measures of accounting leverage for the individual firms. These correlations are quite high, suggesting that the different definitions are linear transformations of one another. It is unlikely that the regression results would be significantly affected by the substitution of one definition for another. The regression summary in panel B bears this out: the percentages of significant positive and negative regression coefficients are stable across the four leverage definitions. The traditional leverage measure, ALEV, performs marginally better than the others, and it is used in all subsequent tests.[10]

The superiority, for both total return variance and beta, of the regression results using accounting leverage over those using market leverage is an unexpected result.

Table 5. Individual Firm Regressions, By Subperiod: Model: $Y_t = \alpha + \theta X_t + \mu$

Y_t	X_t			
	Period One		*Period Two*	
RETVAR (n = 284)	**ALEV**	**MLEV**	**ALEV**	**MLEV**
θ	0.0014	0.0023	–0.007	–0.002
t-statistic	1.08	0.90	–0.02	–0.03
R^2	0.25	0.23	0.19	0.16
Percentage positive and significant*	37%	36%	20%	11%
Percentage negative and significant*	10%	8%	19%	23%
MWBETA (n = 284)	**ALEVSTD**	**MLEVSTD**	**ALEVSTED**	**MLEVSTD**
θ	0.1226	–0.0106	–0.03	–0.14
t-statistic	0.43	0.003	–0.02	–0.22
R^2	0.21	0.22	0.14	0.16
Percentage positive and significant*	27%	21%	13%	13%
Percentage negative and significant*	16%	19%	15%	20%
SPRBETA (n = 150)	**ALEVSTED**	**MLEVSTED**	**ALEVSTED**	**MLEVSTD**
θ	0.1085	0.374	–0.05	–0.24
t-statistic	0.44	0.06	0.07	–0.36
R^2	0.19	0.20	0.15	0.20
Percentage positive and significant*	24%	23%	16%	7%
Percentage negative and significant*	12%	20%	14%	13%

Notes: *These percentages refer to the number of *t*-statistics which are significant at the 10% confidence level, assuming, for both the positive and negative cases, that a one-tailed test was appropriate. To the extent that a two-tailed test was appropriate, these percentages are overstated.

RETVAR is total return variance; MWBETA is the moving-window beta; SPRBETA is the stochastic parameter beta; ALEV is the book value of leverage; MLEV is the market value of leverage; ALEVSTD is the standardized book leverage; MLEVSTD is the standardized market leverage.

It is particularly surprising given the prevailing tendency in the literature to view accounting leverage as a poor substitute for market leverage (see, for example, Bowman [1980b] and DeJong and Collins [1985]). The empirical evidence presented here suggests that investors attribute meaning to the evolution of a firm's accounting leverage over time.

A. Sensitivity of Individual Firm Results to Magnitude of Changes in Leverage

To determine the sensitivity of the regression results to the magnitude of the changes in leverage, and to provide some indirect evidence on the effect of restricting the tests to firms with 28- and 50-year returns histories, the regressions were run on the 50 MWB firms and the 20 SPR firms showing the largest changes in leverage over the 24 years. These two subsets experienced significantly greater changes in their leverage ratios over the period than did the average firm.[11]

Restricting the analysis to this high-change group (Table 4) improved the regression results for the total return variance equations. At the 10% confidence level, 50% of the individual coefficients are significant. For the market leverage equations, the percentage of the coefficients in the sample that are positive and significant has increased slightly, from 33% for the total sample to 36% for this group.

In contrast, the regressions using beta as the dependent variable do not yield markedly better results for this subset of firms. This is true for both the moving window betas and the SPR betas. Thus even in the case of an extreme change in an individual firm's leverage over the period, the tests do not indicate a strong positive correlation between beta and leverage. This is notwithstanding the fact that there is strong evidence of a linear relation between total return variance and leverage for these firms.

B. Tests of Subperiods

To provide evidence on the extent to which the assumption of stability of operating risk over the entire 24-year period might bias the results, the individual firm regressions were run on two 12-year subperiods, 1959–1970 and 1971–1982. The results for the two subperiods, shown in Table 5, are no better than those for the entire 24-year period. In fact, the most notable divergence from the earlier results is the relative inferiority of the second-period regressions.[12]

IV. PORTFOLIO LEVEL RESULTS

Portfolio tests were carried out in another attempt to mitigate the effects of changes in operating risk on the results. Firms were sorted according to the magnitude of total change in leverage over the 24-year period and aggregated to form portfolios.[13] Three sources of a change in operating risk might confound the analysis: a change in the ratio of fixed to variable operating costs, a move by the firm into a new industry, or an external change in the firm's operating environment. There is no obvious reason that any of these should cause operating risk to shift simultaneously in the same direction among the individual firms in a portfolio.[14] The one exception to this would occur if the firms in a portfolio were concentrated in a single industry; this issue is addressed below.

The portfolio results using total return variance as the dependent variable (and still ignoring possible cross-sectional dependence in the results) are striking (Table 6). For all portfolio sizes (5-, 10-, and 20-security portfolios were tested) and both the accounting and market versions of leverage, well over half the regressions yield

Table 6. Cross-Sectional Averages of Regression Statistics for Portfolios of Industrial Firms Sorted by Magnitude of Change in Leverage, 1959–1982: Model: $Y_t = \alpha + \theta X_t + \mu$

Y, X	*Number in Portfolio*	θ	*t-Statistic*	R^2	*Percentage Significant** +	–
RETVAR, ALEV	5	0.0015	2.09	0.23	64	4
	10	0.0017	2.54	0.28	75	4
	20	0.0017	2.94	0.31	85	8
RETVAR, ALEV	5	0.008	2.14	0.21	64	2
	10	0.008	2.29	0.22	79	0
	20	0.009	3.50	0.37	92	0
RETVAR, ALEVSTD	5	0.029	0.24	0.08	19	13
	10	0.077	0.51	0.10	42	8
	20	0.077	0.57	0.13	33	8
MWBETA, ALEVSTD	5	0.057	0.12	0.09	16	16
	10	0.036	0.18	0.05	13	13
	20	0.094	0.51	0.10	33	8
SPRBETA, ALEVSTD	5	0.098	0.82	0.18	46	14
	10	0.133	0.84	0.09	28	0
	20	0.107	1.77	0.15	43	0
SPRBETA, MLEVSTD	5	0.008	0.23	0.07	14	4
	10	0.020	0.13	0.06	7	14
	20	–0.001	–0.21	0.05	14	14

Notes: *These percentages refer to the number of *t*-statistics which are significant at the 10% confidence level, assuming, for both the positive and negative cases, that a one-tailed test was appropriate. To the extent that a two-tailed test was appropriate, these percentages are overstated.

RETVAR is total return variance; MWBETA is the moving-window beta; SPRBETA is the stochastic parameter beta; ALEV is the book value of leverage; MLEV is the market value of leverage; ALEVSTD is the standardized book leverage; MLEVSTD is the standardized market leverage.

positive and significant coefficients, and a negligible number are negative and significant. The cross-sectional average R^2's range from 0.21 to 0.37 for the market leverage equations, and from 0.23 to 0.31 for the accounting leverage equations, indicating that a substantial portion of the portfolio's total risk is explained by financial leverage. The greater the degree of aggregation in the portfolios, the stronger the results, indicating that the individual firm results are likely attributable to changes in financial leverage rather than to contemporaneous changes in operating risk. Contrary to the results from the individual firm regressions, use of market leverage yields slightly better results than does accounting leverage, with 92 and 85%, respectively, of the coefficients significant when portfolios of size 20 are used.

The beta portfolio regressions do not show the dramatic improvements of the total return variance regressions. The results using the accounting version of leverage are again stronger than those using market leverage. The number of portfolios with positive and significant coefficients is greater than the number with negative and significant coefficients for both the moving window beta and the SPR beta, and for all levels of aggregation. The strongest results are those for the 20-security portfolios with the SPR beta as the dependent variable. Forty-three percent of these portfolios (three of seven) had positive and significant coefficients; the average R^2 for the portfolios was 0.15. Thus even when the (SPR) regression procedure removes much of the random variation in systematic risk, leverage explains relatively little of the remaining variance.

The results using market leverage as the dependent variable in the beta portfolio regressions are particularly poor; with the single exception of the 20-security portfolios and the moving window beta, there are as many negative and significant parameters as there are positive and significant ones. The average R^2's are between 0.05 and 0.10—much lower than those from the total return variance equations, and since these averages include equations where the empirical relation is the reverse of that hypothesized, they should be interpreted cautiously. Overall, this evidence is not consistent with the common assertion that market measures of leverage are positively correlated with systematic equity risk.

A. Sensitivity of Portfolio Results to Magnitude of Changes in Leverage

To provide some evidence on the sensitivity of the portfolio results to the magnitude of the change in leverage over the period, the distributions of significant coefficients among the individual 10-security portfolios are shown in Table 7.[15] For the total return variance equations, the distribution of the t-statistics bolsters the conclusion that total return variance and leverage are related. Note in particular in Table 7 that five of the six portfolios which do not show a positive and significant coefficient on leverage for the equations using total return variance and accounting leverage are among the bottom portfolios—that is, among those portfolios in which average leverage does not change very much over the period. Most of the portfolios in this bottom group experienced a negligible change or a slight decrease in leverage over the period.

The distribution of the significant regression coefficients for the beta equations does not reveal the same pattern as the total return variance regression coefficients. Some portfolios with relatively insignificant changes in leverage over the period show a strong relation between beta and leverage while others with large changes show no relation. Failure to observe stronger evidence of the anticipated relation

Table 7. t-Statistics on Regression Coefficients for 10-Stock Portfolios, Sorted by Magnitude of Change in Financial Leverage, 1959–1982

Independent	*Average Leverage*			*Market Leverage*		
Dependent Portfolio	*RETVAR*	*MWBETA*	*SPRBETA*	*RETVAR*	*MWBETA*	*SPRBETA*
1	1.26	1.53*	0.48	1.65*	0.81	−2.59
2	2.97*,†	1.44*	0.28	4.39*,†	0.54	0.82
3	2.89*,†	−0.41	3.08*,†	1.33*	0.60	2.28*,†
4	2.30*,†	2.76*,†	1.58*,†	1.40*	−1.88	0.34
5	8.65*,†	1.32*	0.88	4.28*,†	0.22	−0.26
6	2.58*,†	1.95*,†	2.58*,†	1.47*,†	0.67	1.30
7	5.37*,†	2.89*,†	−0.51	4.34*,†	−1.91	−0.29
8	4.82*,†	0.59	−0.74	2.65*,†	1.25	0.55
9	2.60*,†	1.66*	1.24	3.14*,†	1.76*,†	−1.20
10	2.18*,†	0.27	0.88	1.67*	−0.73	0.82
11	6.42*,†	2.38*,†	0.58	1.04	0.46	0.10
12	3.28*,†	0.18	3.19*,†	3.99*,†	0.18	1.16
13	1.90*,†	−0.08	0.74	2.00*,†	0.66	0.25
14	1.85*,†	−0.62	−1.28	2.45*,†	−0.08	−1.51
15	3.94*,†	1.60*		2.67*,†	−1.14	
16	2.69*,†	−0.30		3.60*,†	1.36*	
17	5.32*	−1.33		1.16	0.41	
18	1.70*	−0.51		4.30*,†	0.52	
19	2.45*,†	0.51		3.04*,†	1.21	
20	0.01	2.07*,†		0.69	1.32*	
21	−0.78	−1.13		−0.03	0.43	
22	−0.18	−3.90		2.51*,†	−1.20	
23	0.11	−0.54		1.44*	0.88	
24	−3.29	−0.13		−0.14	−2.02	

Notes: *Positive and significant at the 10% confidence level, assuming a one-tailed test.
†Positive and significant at the 5% confidence level, assuming a one-tailed test.
RETVAR is total return variance; MWBETA is the moving-window beta; SPRBETA is the stochastic parameter beta; ALEV is the book value of leverage.

between beta and leverage is not obviously attributable to limitations of the research design: the distribution of the coefficients suggests that the more plausible interpretation of the results is that a positive correlation between beta and leverage is not pronounced among the firms in the sample.

B. Evidence on the Stability of Operating Risk within Portfolios

The creation of portfolios constitutes an effective control for changes in operating risk only to the extent that the changes are uncorrelated among the firms in a

Table 8. Number of Distinct 2-Digit SIC Codes Represented in Each 10-Stock Portfolio Sorted by Magnitude of Change in Financial Leverage, 1959–1982

Independent Dependent Portfolio	Accounting Leverage		Market Leverage	
	RETVAR, MWBETA	*SPRBETA*	*RETVAR, MWBETA*	*SPRBETA*
1	5*	7†	6†	7†
2	7†	7†	8	8
3	8	8	8	9
4	9	9	8	7†
5	9	9	8	7†
6	7	8	8	9
7	7	8†	9	9
8	8	10	7†	10
9	7	8†	9	9
10	8	9	6†	8
11	7	9	7	6†
12	8†	8	8	8†
13	6*	6*	7†	8†
14	10	8	7†	10
15	8		8	
16	7		8	
17	10		6†	
18	7		8†	
19	8		5†	
20	6†		7	
21	9		7†	
22	6†		9	
23	7†		7†	
24	10		8	

Notes: *Portfolio has four firms with identical 2-digit SIC codes.
†Portfolio has three firms with identical 2-digit SIC codes.
RETVAR is total return variance; MWBETA is the moving-window beta; SPRBETA is the stochastic parameter beta.

portfolio. The one obvious violation of this would occur if the firms in a portfolio were concentrated in a single industry. Evidence on this issue is presented in Table 8.

For each 10-stock portfolio, the number of distinct industries represented by the firms are shown in the table. Portfolios with three (four) firms in the same industry are shown by a (double) asterisk. Industry membership is broadly defined as the firm's 2-digit SIC code, which makes this a conservative test of industry concentration. For these portfolios,[16] in only two instances do four out of the ten firms belong to the same industry. In roughly 30% of the portfolios (slightly more for those sorted by market leverage, slightly less for those sorted by accounting leverage) three of ten firms belong to the same industry. This degree of concentration is not extreme, making it difficult to attribute the portfolio results to simultaneous changes in operating risk.

V. TESTS FOR CROSS-SECTIONAL CORRELATION AMONG THE REGRESSIONS

Using OLS to estimate the regression parameters implicitly assumes cross-sectional independence among the individual equations. Because all the data come from the same time period, commonalities across firms could cause the residuals to be cross-sectionally correlated. The "seemingly unrelated regression procedure" was applied to the data here to compensate for the loss of efficiency in estimating the regression parameters and the bias in the estimated t-statistics. The results of reestimating the equations for the 20-security MWB portfolios and for the 10- and 20-security SPR portfolios are shown in Table 9.[17]

Of the portfolio regressions using total return variance 92 and 85% show the hypothesized relation using accounting leverage and market leverage, respectively, and none of the portfolios shows negative and significant relations. The tentative conclusion drawn in the previous section, that leverage and total return variance are linearly related over time, is corroborated here. The evidence also indicates that the book value of leverage is not inferior to the market value of leverage in establishing that association.

For the moving window betas a strong positive correlation between beta and market leverage still does not emerge. Although 42% of the regression coefficients are positive and significant at the 10% level, 25% are negative and significantly different from zero at this level. When we use accounting leverage as the independent variable, one-third of the portfolios show a positive and significant relation between beta and leverage, which is equivalent to the results that obtained when OLS was applied to the data. However, more firms show a significant negative association between beta and leverage than in the OLS regressions, 17% as compared to 8%. The fact that these regressions yield on the whole more significant results than those using only the diagonal covariance matrix suggests that certain economy-wide events may have been obscuring the effect of accounting leverage on beta in the OLS regressions.

Qualitatively similar results emerge when the SPR regressions are reestimated using the full variance-covariance matrix. For the regressions using market leverage, nearly equal numbers of positive and negative coefficients appear for both 10- and 20-security portfolios. For the regressions using accounting leverage, for both 10- and 20-security portfolios 28% of the individual coefficients are positive and significant; none is negative and significant. This last result is the strongest

Table 9. Cross-Sectional Averages for Portfolios of Industrial Firms Sorted by Magnitude of Change in Leverage, 1959–1982, Using Seemingly Unrelated Regressions: Model: $Y_t = \alpha + \theta X_t + \mu$

Y, X	*Number in Portfolio*	θ	*t-Statistic*	*Percentage* Positive and Significant*	*Percentage* Negative and Significant*
RETVAR, ALEV	20	0.0013	4.38	92	0
RETVAR, MLEV	20	0.0042	5.28	85	0
MWBETA, ALEVSTD	20	0.0796	1.46	33	17
MWBETA, MLEVSTD	20	0.018	0.60	42	25
SPRBETA,	10	0.12	1.50	28	0
ALEVSTD	20	0.09	2.27	28	0
SPRBETA,	10	0.017	–0.14	36	28
MLEVSTD	20	0.025	0.15	14	14

Notes: *These percentages refer to the number of *t*-statistics which are significant at the 10% confidence level, assuming, for both the positive and negative cases, that a one-tailed test was appropriate. To the extent that a two-tailed test was appropriate, these percentages are overstated.

RETVAR is total return variance; MWBETA is the moving-window beta; SPRBETA is the stochastic parameter beta; ALEV is the book value of leverage; MLEV is the market value of leverage; ALEVSTD is the standardized book leverage; MLEVSTD is the standardized market leverage.

evidence to emerge from any of the tests that the hypothesized relation does exist between accounting leverage and systematic risk.

VI. CONCLUDING REMARKS

The results reported here raise some questions about the extent to which the widely accepted association between the systematic risk of a firm and its financial leverage is supported by the evidence. A pronounced time-series relation between financial leverage and equity risk is strongly evidenced only when risk is measured by total return variance; most of the time-series behavior of beta is unaccounted for and even a strong monotonic association between beta and leverage does not emerge from the data. This result is consistent with the mounting evidence that beta is an inadequate measure of the risk of common stock returns (see, for example, Bhandari [1988]). Also contrary to widely held beliefs, use of book values in the leverage ratios did not lead to inferior empirical results in the time-series regressions. This result was unexpected and suggests that investors, when assessing the financial risk of a firm, may put more emphasis on balance sheet data than is commonly appreciated.

ACKNOWLEDGMENTS

I would like to express my appreciation to Ashiq Ali, William Baber, In-Mu Haw, James Ohlson, Victor Pastena, Richard Sweeney, Thomas Verghese, the members of my dissertation committee at Columbia University, and two anonymous reviewers for their comments and suggestions.

NOTES

1. Hamada (1972) develops the theoretical relation between beta and market leverage using the CAPM framework; Bowman (1979) and Fairfield (1985) argue that a theoretical link could also be established between beta and accounting measures of leverage.

2. Bowman (1980b) reports the results of cross-sectional tests using book and market values for both the numerator and denominator of leverage. He cites significant improvements over pure book values by using the market value of equity, and very slight deterioration in results when the market value of debt is introduced. Obtaining 24 years of market data for debt would be prohibitively costly, so only the "quasi-market" leverage ratio is used here.

3. The tests were originally conducted on a small sample using a returns window that spanned the balance sheet date. Surprisingly, the results were not as strong as those using returns data preceding the balance sheet date and are not reported here.

4. Details of the estimation procedure may be found in Ohlson and Rosenberg (1982) and Collins, Ledolter, and Rayburn (1984).

5. If μ_t is a true shock to beta it could theoretically be predicted with reference to exogenous variables. If, on the other hand, μ_t is the result of heteroskedasticity, it could not be predicted; it is known only that its absolute value will be correlated with the market return.

6. Collins et al. (1984), using 500 weeks of return data, concluded that at the portfolio level the stochastic parameter model was clearly superior to a stationary and a random-coefficients beta as a model of the beta process. Fairfield (1985), using 600 months of data, found that the SPR beta outperformed the OLS beta, the random coefficients beta, and the autoregressive-only beta (in which there is no purely random error) for both individual firms and for portfolios of firms.

7. Individual runs tests on the residuals from regressions with a first-order autocorrelation correction indicated that about 20% of all the regressions still exhibited statistically significant autocorrelation. After the correction for second-order autocorrelation, these percentages were below 5%. The coefficients on leverage were reasonably stable across the three regression variations (OLS, first-order correction, second-order correction). The t-statistics on leverage declined significantly after the correction for first-order autocorrelation but were little changed after the second-order correction.

8. The standardization procedure divides individual firm leverage by the cross-sectional mean for that year. The regressions were also run on a sample of firms using leverage after subtracting mean leverage for each year and after normalizing firm leverage for each year. The procedure used here, which emphasizes leverage changes in high leverage firms, led to slightly more significant results than the other two.

9. Although the SPR process provides a "better" estimate of the beta series for the individual firms, its introduction also restricts the analysis to a subset of firms with relatively more stable leverage ratios over the time period. Evidence on the marginal effects of using the SPR beta as the dependent variable and of restricting the sample to these "survivor" firms suggested that the SPR estimation procedure created little advantage, at least at the individual firm level, and that the sample bias created by restricting the SPR analysis to the subset of 150 firms was negligible.

10. The numerator was also varied (by removing deferred taxes, current liabilities, and preferred stock, alternately) in the market leverage equations, with negligible effect on the results.

11. When change in leverage was measured as the difference between the debt-equity ratios at the beginning and end of the periods, each high-change sample had an average change over three times that of the entire sample. The tests were also conducted on a sample of firms which had high variance in leverage over the period. With the exception of the OHRBETA, ALEVSTD regressions, which showed a slight improvement, the results were comparable to those reported here.

12. Ali (1988) argues that greater volatility in the debt markets reduced the correlation between financial leverage and equity betas in the 1980s. This effect may be in part responsible for the weaker results in the later period.

13. Firms with the largest increases in leverage over the period were grouped together in the top portfolio, and firms with the largest decreases were in the bottom portfolio. Firms were weighted equally in forming the portfolios. Betas were reestimated for the portfolios using both the moving window technique and the stochastic parameter regression technique, and average leverage for each portfolio was calculated for each year. Separate portfolios were created for industrial firms and for utilities. Because the results are similar, only the industrial firm portfolio results are presented in this paper.

14. Mandelker and Rhee (1984) provide evidence that financial leverage and operating leverage have a negative correlation of 0.30 for a cross section of firms. For each firm a single estimate of financial leverage and operating leverage was calculated from a 20-year time series of data. Although the authors suggest that a management strategy of trading off operating leverage against financial leverage could be inferred from their result, they were unable to reject the hypothesis of stability of operating leverage and financial leverage over a 20-year period for 90% of their sample.

15. Similar results were observed for the 5- and 20-security portfolios.

16. The data were also examined for the 5-stock and 20-stock portfolios. Industry concentration was slightly more pronounced in the 5-stock portfolios and less so in the 20-stock portfolios.

17. Zellner (1962) proposed that the full variance-covariance matrix of residuals be estimated by applying OLS to the individual regressions, and the computed residuals used to estimate the elements of the matrix. Generalized least squares is then applied to estimate the individual regression parameters. One limitation of the Zellner approach is that the number of observations must be greater than the number of equations so that the variance-covariance matrix may be estimated; thus its application here is limited to fewer than 24 portfolios.

REFERENCES

Ali, A. (1988). "Pension Assets and the Systematic Risk of Equity." Working paper, New York University Schools of Business.

Beaver, W., Kettler, P., and Scholes, M. (1970). "The Association Between Market-Determined and Accounting-Determined Risk Measures." *Accounting Review* (October), 654–682.

Ben-Zion, U., and Shalit, S. S. (1975). "Size, Leverage, and Dividend Record as Determinants of Equity Risk." *Journal of Finance* (September) 1015–1026.

Bhandari, L. C. (1988). "Debt-Equity Ratios and Expected Common Stock Returns: Empirical Evidence." *Journal of Finance* (June), 597–528.

Bildersee, J. (1974). "The Association Between a Market-Determined Measure of Risk and Alternative Measures of Risk." *Accounting Review* (April), 81–98.

Boness, A. J., Chen, A., and Jatuspitak, S. (1974). "Investigations of Non-Stationarity in Prices." *Journal of Business* (October), 519–537.

Bowman, R. C. (1979). "The Theoretical Relationship Between Systematic Risk and Financial (Accounting) Variables. *Journal of Finance* (June), 617–630.

Bowman, R. C. (1980a). "The Debt Equivalence of Leases: An Empirical Investigation." *Accounting Review* (April), 237–253.

Bowman, R. C. (1980b). "The Importance of a Market-Value Measurement of Debt in Assessing Leverage." *Journal of Accounting Research* (Spring), 617–630.

Breen, W. J. and Lerner, E. M. (1973). "Corporate Financial Strategies and Market Measures of Risk and Return." *Journal of Finance* (May), 339–352.

Chance, D. M. (1982). "Evidence on a Simplified Model of Systematic Risk." *Financial Management* (Autumn), 53–63.

Christie, A. A. (1982). "The Stochastic Behavior of Common Stock Variances." *Journal of Financial Economics* (December), 407–432.

Collins, D. W., Ledolter, J., and Rayburn, J. (1984). "Some Further Evidence on the Stochastic Properties of Systematic Risk." Working paper, University of Iowa, (October).

DeJong, D., and Collins, D. (1985). "Explanations for the Instability of Equity Beta, Risk-Free Rate Changes and Leverage Effects." *Journal of Financial and Quantitative Analysis* (September), 595–637.

Dhaliwal, D. (1986). "Measurement of Financial Leverage in the Presence of Unfunded Pension Obligations." *Accounting Review* (October), 651–661.

Elgers, P., and Murray, D. (1982). "The Impact of Choice of Market Index on the Evaluation of Accounting Risk Measures." *Accounting Review* (April), 358–373.

Eskew, R. (1979). "The Forecasting Ability of Accounting Risk Measures: Some Additional Evidence." *Accounting Review* (January), 107–118.

Fairfield, P. M. (1985). "The Information Content of Leverage, A Time-Series Analysis." Ph.D. dissertation, Columbia University.

Foster, C. (1986). *Financial Statement Analysis*. Englewood Cliffs, NJ: Prentice-Hall.

Garman, M., and Ohlson, J. (1980). "Information and the Sequential Valuation of Assets in Arbitrage-Free Economies." *Journal of Accounting Research* (Autumn), 420–440.

Hamada, R. S. (1972). "The Effects of a Firm's Capital Structure on the Systematic Risk of Common Stocks." *Journal of Finance* (May), 435–452.

Hill, N. C., and Stone, B. K. (1980). "Accounting Betas, Systematic Operating Risk, and Financial Leverage: A Risk-Composition Approach to the Determinants of Systematic Risk." *Journal of Financial and Quantitative Analysis* (September), 595–637.

Lee, C. F., Newbold, P., Finnerty, J., and Chu, C. (1986). "On Accounting-Based, Market-Based, and Composite-Based Beta Predictions: Methods and Implications." *Financial Review* (February), 51–68.

Lev, B., and Kunitzsky, S. (1974). "On the Association Between Smoothing Measures and the Risk of Common Stocks." *Accounting Review* (April), 259–270.

Logue, D. E., and Merville, L. J. (1972). "Financial Policy and Market Expectations." *Financial Management* (Summer), 37–44.

Mandelker, G. N., and Rhee, S. C. (1984). "The Impact of Degrees of Operating and Financial Leverage on Systematic Risk of Common Stock." *Journal of Financial and Quantitative Analysis* (March), 45–57.

Mulford, C. (1985). "The Importance of a Market Value Measurement of Debt in Leverage Ratios: Replication and Extensions." *Journal of Accounting Research* (Autumn), 897–906.

Ohlson, J., and Rosenberg, B. (1982). "Systematic Risk of the CRSP Equal-Weighted Common Stock Index: A History Estimated by Stochastic-Parameter Regression." *Journal of Business* (January), 121–145.

Rosenberg, B., and McKibben, W. (1973). "The Prediction of Systematic and Specific Risk in Common Stocks." *Journal of Financial and Quantitative Analysis* (March), 317–333.

Schwert, G. W. (1989). "Why Does Stock Market Volatility Change Over Time?" *Journal of Finance* (December), 1115–1153.

Thompson, D. J. (1976). "Sources of Systematic Risk to Common Stocks." *Journal of Business* (April), 173–188.

Zellner, A. (1962). "An Efficient Method of Estimating Seemingly Unrelated Regressions and Tests for Aggregation Bias." *Journal of the American Statistical Association* (June), 348–368.

ON THE USE OF MAGNITUDE SCALING IN ACCOUNTING RESEARCH

Roger W. Bartlett

ABSTRACT

For decades, researchers in accounting have attempted to measure attitudes, perceptions, and other social science phenomena using Likert-type categorical scales. Recent advances in the application of sensory psychophysics in the social sciences have led to the development of magnitude estimation which is theorized to produce ratio level data. This study utilizes magnitude estimation techniques to investigate the perceived levels of assurance provided by different types of financial statement reports. Questionnaires were mailed to a sample of 455 CPAs and bankers, with usable responses being received from 223 individuals. Results indicate that logarithmic interval scales were produced which compare favorably with results obtained in other studies. These scales are compared with data collected using 5-point summated rating scales. Implications of this study for future research are discussed.

I. INTRODUCTION

For decades, accounting researchers have attempted to measure social science phenomena such as attitudes and perceptions using Likert-type summated rating

Advances in Quantitative Analysis of Finance and Accounting,
Volume 2, Part A, pages 241–260.

ISBN: 1-55938-564-2

scales. Use of these scales has subjected accounting research to criticism regarding the nature of data collected by categorical scales and the limitations on statistical analysis which can be legitimately performed on such data.

In recent years, social scientists interested in measuring the intensity of attitudes, perceptions, and opinions have extended the pioneering work of Stevens (1957) and others in the development and use of practical, highly reliable ratio scales of subjective magnitude.

The goal of this paper is to extend the accounting literature related to magnitude estimation by reporting research findings on the development and validation of a scale for measuring the perceived level of assurance provided by various types of financial statement reports. This study differs from prior research in that it incorporates the "cross-modality matching paradigm" (Lodge, 1981, pp. 24–30) to validate the ratio scales produced.

The results of the study[1] presented in this paper are strong evidence for the use of magnitude scaling in the measurement of the strength of opinions about accounting topics. Consistent with research in the social sciences, these techniques applied in an accounting context successfully produce logarithmic interval scales, a significant improvement over the level of measurement obtained from traditional, Likert-type scaling methods.

II. AN OVERVIEW OF MAGNITUDE SCALING

Lodge (1981) provides a straightforward introduction to the methodology of magnitude estimation, and much of the discussion in this section is based on his work.

Beginning in the late 1950s, S. S. Stevens and his associates produced a considerable body of research on the numeric estimation of a variety of physical stimuli. What initially resulted from this research was the observation that human judges are capable of using numbers to evaluate the stimulus levels of most aspects of the five senses. Further, the research showed that when these numeric estimates were logged, averaged, and plotted against the actual value of the physical stimuli, the points fell on a straight line. This observed linear relationship has been reduced to the status of a law: **equal stimulus ratios produce equal subjective ratios.** This law may be represented as

$$Y = kX^n,$$

where Y is the respondent's impression of stimulus magnitude, X is the actual magnitude of the stimulus, n is the exponent that characterizes the power relationship, and k is a constant of proportionality. When transformed into logarithms, the equation becomes linear:

$$\log Y = b \log X + \log k.$$

This geometric relationship has been observed to hold for many physical stimuli.

Psychophysicists next observed that, if these power relations hold true when subjects use numbers to estimate physical intensity, then one physical stimulus may serve to measure the intensity of another physical stimulus. This "cross-modality matching paradigm" (Lodge, 1981, p. 24) provides a validation of the power law and the magnitude estimation methodology by demonstrating that, when respondents indicate their subjective estimation of one physical stimulus using another (for example, using a hand grip to indicate the intensity of light), the slope of the line produced by plotting the actual stimuli and the response stimuli will be close to the ratio of the measured exponents. Lodge (1981, p. 28) states:

> The logic of the cross-modality matching paradigm is straightforward: If the power law is valid and if the exponents derived from magnitude estimation are truly characteristic, then any **two** quantitative response measures with established exponents could be used to judge a sensory continuum and the validity of the derived ratio scale confirmed by obtaining a close match between the theoretical and empirically obtained ratios **between the two response measures**. (emphasis in original)

To utilize the cross-modality matching paradigm in the validation of research results, the researcher must double the basic matching task, requiring respondents to make magnitude estimates using two response mediums, each of which grows at a known rate. Using this paradigm, a magnitude scale of impression is validated when the slope obtained from the matches to a common set of stimuli produces the approximate ratio between the psychophysical response modes.

In recent years, this method of scaling has been successfully taken outside the laboratory by the utilization of number estimation and line drawing as response modalities, which have known exponents of 1.0 and which do not require sophisticated apparatus to administer and measure.

In the last two decades, a considerable body of research utilizing magnitude estimation has been created. Stevens (1966, 1972) provides a review of the early efforts in psychophysical scaling of social variables while Lodge (1981) reviews the literature in political science. Generally, the conclusion of this research is that magnitude scaling is appropriate in situations where no physical scale exists. "As such, these scaling techniques appear to be applicable to any attitudinal domain that varies in magnitude or intensity" (Miethe, 1985, p. 96).

Recently, Wegener (1983) conducted research which indicates that category-rating scales generally produce interval scales while cross-modality matching scales produce logarithmic interval scales. Miethe (1986) studied magnitude scaling procedures in terms of convergent validity and reliability; he found that, for the sample used, magnitude estimation scales were slightly less reliable and had slightly less discriminatory power.

III. MAGNITUDE ESTIMATION IN ACCOUNTING RESEARCH

Research using ratio scale measurements has investigated issues of current value/constant dollar accounting (Abdel-Magid, 1979a,b; Vickery, 1976), whistle-blowing (Johnson, 1979), and human resource accounting (Tomassini, 1979). Howard (1981) introduced the work of Stevens (1966) into the accounting literature. Following Howard (1981), recent accounting research utilizing magnitude estimation has focused on the measurement of the perceived quality of academic journals (Cargile and Bublitz, 1986; Howard and Nikolai, 1983; Hull and Wright, 1990; Nobes, 1985; Schroeder, Payne, and Harris, 1988).

The applications of the magnitude estimation technique by accounting researchers to date have used an abbreviated method asking respondents to compare the *relative* strength of attitude compared to a predetermined base but have not used the "cross-modality matching paradigm" (Lodge, 1981, pp. 24–30). Lodge (1981, p. 30) considers the power of this paradigm to validate the ratio estimates developed as an essential feature of the use of magnitude estimation techniques.

Howard (1981) suggests the evaluation of the seriousness of conflict-of-interest situations and the importance of disclosure items as two accounting contexts where magnitude estimation techniques might be fruitfully employed to tap attitudes and opinions. Two additional areas which show promise are the seriousness of internal control weaknesses and the relative importance of various factors in audit judgment process. This study focuses on perceptions of levels of assurance provided by various types of reports on financial statements.

IV. MEASUREMENT OF PERCEIVED LEVEL OF ASSURANCE

Considerable journal space has been devoted to studying the messages conveyed by different types of reports on financial statements with which an auditor/accountant may associated. The Cohen Commission (AICPA, 1978) set the seed of limited assurance engagements when it noted:

> The assurance provided by different forms of association is difficult for users to understand and for auditors to describe because it is now not possible to quantify or evaluate the difference in assurance provided by audits, reviews, or other forms of association. However, a simple ranking can be made. That is, an audit provides more assurance than a review, and a review more than other forms of association with unaudited information. Eventually, after experience is gained, it may be possible to determine the probabilities that the procedures in each form of assurance will detect various errors, omissions, or misrepresentations. (p. 66)

To date research conducted on this issue (Bailey, Bylinski, and Shields, 1984; Bartlett, 1991; Holt and Moizer, 1990; Libby, 1979; Nair and Rittenberg, 1987; Pany and Smith, 1982; Pillsbury, 1985; and Yardley, 1989) has generally confirmed the observations of the Cohen Commission.

Libby (1979) and Libby and Short (1980) studied the message conveyed by ten different types of audit reports ranging from an unqualified opinion to an unaudited disclaimer. They conclude that there is considerable similarity between bankers' and auditors' perceptions of the messages intended by audit reports (Libby and Short, 1980, p. 62). Pany and Smith (1982) studied the perceived reliability of financial information with one of four forms of auditor association: full audit, disclaimer of opinion, unaudited footnote in year-end audit, and no association. Their subjects generally were not able to distinguish different levels of association. The authors conclude: "The results are unlikely to allay the fears of those who question user ability to differentiate between the likely effects of varying forms of auditor association" (p. 479).

Bailey et al. (1984) extended previous research by including the recently introduced (AICPA, 1978) compilations and reviews in a survey of bankers and CPAs. The authors found that the auditors and bankers perceived different messages. Pillsbury (1985) extended the work of Pany and Smith (1982) by expanding the number of potential associations to include compilations and other limited assurance engagements. She noted that the reports seemed to group themselves into three categories based on the level of assurance dimension but was not able to make comparisons within or between those levels.

Nair and Rittenberg (1987) sampled bankers and CPAs from large and small entities. They found that bankers place less responsibility on management and more on the CPA than do the CPAs themselves. They conclude that "the responsibilities assumed by the auditor, the nature of the procedures performed, and the degree of assurance communicated is far from clear" (p. 35). Yardley (1989) studied perceptions of assurance provided by the performance of limited procedures performed in negative assurance reports. His results indicate that significant differences in perception exist between users and CPAs.

Holt and Moizer (1990) studied differences in interpretation of the message provided by various audit reports using a sample of users and accountants in the United Kingdom. The authors found differences in the meanings attached to the various reports. Bartlett (1991) found significant differences in the levels of assurance perceived to be provided by various audit and nonaudit reports. His results, developed using ratio-level data, indicate the magnitude of differences both within and among the various respondent groups.

The research conducted to date has established that CPAs and the user groups sampled are in relative agreement about the **ranking** of assurance provided by various reports. However, with the exception of Bartlett (1991), the methodologies employed to date have not allowed the researchers to determine or even speculate about the relative level of assurance provided by the different reporting formats.

V. THE STUDY

A. Participants

This study utilizes a combination of convenience and random samples in an effort to acquire responses from people with diverse backgrounds within the target populations. Certified public accountant participants were selected from staff listings of the Sacramento offices of nine national firms and one local firm. In addition, a random sample was made of 100 CPAs listed as members of the California Society of CPAs. The sample of bankers was developed in two ways also. First, the presidents of 125 local banks were mailed two copies of a questionnaire to forward to commercial loan officers. In addition, senior vice presidents in several major banks in the Sacramento area were contacted and asked to participate in the study by providing lists of their commercial loan officers.

In total, 455 questionnaires were mailed to CPA firm employees and bank loan officers working in northern California. I received a total of 231 responses. Of those, 8 where not usable because of the extent of missing data. As a test for nonresponse bias, early and late responses were compared; no significant differences were found. Further, no significant differences were found between the convenience and random samples. Table 1 shows some characteristics of the 223 respondents.

B. Questionnaire Development

The questionnaire was developed following the steps suggested in Lodge (1981). Parts I, IV, and V are scales asking respondents to evaluate the level of assurance that they feel each of ten different reports which auditors and accountants can issue on financial statements provides. Parts II and III are exercises in the use of magnitude estimation techniques.

For the purposes of this study, level of assurance is defined as "how much credence the user should be willing to place on the financial statements covered by the report." This differs from the version offered by the American Accounting Association Committee on Basic Auditing Concepts, which defined assurance as "degrees of credibility—the probability that a given assertion is true or valid" (1973). This distinction is made in order to utilize the unconstrained upper limits of magnitude estimation. If assurance was defined as a probability, the range of assurance would be from 0 to 1.00, which creates another form of Likert scale.

The ten report types were selected to represent the diversity of situations where the CPA may be associated with financial information. Reports included not only the three levels of assurance discussed in the professional literature—audit, review, and compilation (including clean opinion, except for, and disclaimer audits and compilations with and without footnotes)—but also some situations where information is included in tax returns and prescribed forms. An instance where the CPA is known to be associated with the information but no report attached is included. These associations occur frequently in the environment in which the respondent groups work.

Part I is a five-point Likert-type scale asking respondents to indicate their opinions about the level of assurance provided by each of ten different reports (see

Table 1. Response Statistics and Demographics

	CPAs	*Bankers*	*Total*
Response Statistics			
Responses			
Returned usable	118	105	223
Returned not usable	6	2	8
	124	107	231
Nonresponses			
Returned letter	15	7	22
No response	90	112	202
Total mailed	229	226	455
Demographics			
CPA firm employees (n = 118)			
CPAs	92		
Size of firm			
Big-8	75		
Other	43		
Years of experience			
Average	8.7 years		
Range	1–39 years		
Level of responsibility			
Partners	44		
Managers	20		
Supervisors	11		
Seniors	21		
Staff	22		
Pecent of time preparing (averages)			
Audits	45%		
Reviews	8		
Compilations	10		
Specialization			
Audit	55		
Tax	44		
Other	19		
Bankers (n = 105)			
Size of bank:			
Greater than 1,000 million	73		
Less than 1,000 million	32		
Years of experience			
Average	15 years		
Range	1–32 years		
Percent commercial clients:			
Average	75%		
Personal unsecured loan limit			
Average	50,000		
Range	0–1 million		
Courses in accounting			
Average	4		

Appendix A). Part I and its placement were designed to accomplish two objectives: first, to introduce the respondent to the purpose of the questionnaire and get them to think in terms of "levels of assurance"; second, to compare the responses to this scale to the magnitude estimation as a measure of construct validity.

Parts II and III (see Appendix B) provided the respondent with exercise in making magnitude estimations. Part II presented a reference line with a preestablished number and a series of line lengths and asked the participant to make numerical estimations of the relative magnitude of each line length in comparison to the reference line. Part III presented the opposite task: respondents were presented with a reference number corresponding to a preestablished line and a series of numbers with space to draw lines. They were asked to draw a line which they felt represented the magnitude of that number in relation to the reference line. The results of these two exercises were also used to check the calibration of the respondents (i.e., how good are they at making magnitude estimations).

Part IV of the questionnaire asked the respondent to use numeric estimation to indicate the level of assurance provided by the various forms of financial reports listed (see Appendix C). The report type "reviewed financial statements" was given a score of 200 as a reference point to be used in assigning scores. "Reviewed financial statements" was selected as a reference point because it stands as a middle point between the highest level of assurance provided by an audit and the lower levels of assurance provided by compilations and other forms of reports that CPAs can issue. The score of 200 was assigned because in the pretests, some respondents indicated that the original value of 100 did not allow enough room downward to scale the lower reports.

Part V (see Appendix D) presented the ten financial reports in random order. The respondents are asked to draw a line which they feel indicates the level of assurance provided. Again, "reviewed financial statements" is provided as a reference with a 40-mm line as the base. Care was taken to ensure that the respondents have sufficient room to answer, and a blank page was inserted after each list.

Part VI asked respondents their opinions about some statements describing the auditor or audits. The analysis of these responses is not part of this study. Last, part VII asks for demographic information. Forms of the questionnaire distributed to bankers and CPAs differed only in the demographic questions asked.

The instructions for the respondents to follow were based on those reported by Lodge (1981, pp. 50–51), modified for the questionnaire format being used (see Appendixes C and D). Short phrase descriptions of the financial statement reports were employed rather than the actual reports for dummy companies as in prior research (Libby, 1979; Nair and Rittenberg, 1987; Pillsbury, 1985). Based on the results of pretests of the questionnaire, CPAs, bankers, students, and university professors reported no difficulty working with the shorter phrases. The questionnaires together with a letter describing the research project were mailed to the sample of CPAs and bankers.

VI. RESULTS

A. Reliability

The various scales included in the questionnaire were analyzed separately for reliability. The categorical scale of ten Likert statements in part 1 showed reasonable reliability with an equal-length Spearman–Brown coefficient of 0.800, while parts IV and V, the magnitude estimation scales, produced a coefficient of 0.835. These values are consistent with reliability coefficients reported by Miethe (1985, p. 199) and considerably higher than Nair and Rittenberg (1987, p. 201).

B. Calibration Analysis

Lodge (1981, pp. 8–12, 45–46) describes the use of the practice sessions as a calibration of the respondent's ability to utilize magnitude estimation techniques. First, responses to numeric or line length stimuli are reduced to common logarithms (base 10). Next, the arithmetic mean of these logs is calculated, and the means of the logs is exponentiated to obtain the geometric mean of the responses. This calculation is performed because "the geometric mean is the standard measure of central tendency with magnitude data" (Lodge, 1981, p. 46). These geomeans are then plotted against the actual stimulus values on log-log paper. If the resulting distribution can be reasonably explained by a straight line, we can assume that the respondents are properly making ratio-level estimations of stimuli.

As observed in Figure 1 below, plots of the two sets of response data indicate that the function is approximately linear. The slopes of the two lines, 1.925 for numeric estimation (NE) and 0.338 for line production (LP), indicate that respondents consistently overestimate the relationship between numbers and lines by assigning numbers that are approximately twice what they should be to lines and by assigning lines that are approximately one-third of what they should be to numbers. These results were expected. As Lodge (1981, p. 48) notes, "LP is sometimes found to be regressive and will warrant the application of a correction factor when computing social scale values if, as expected, the same regressive tendency is found for the LP matches to the social stimuli." However, in both cases, the linear relationship is an extremely accurate estimate of the respondent's perceptions as evidenced by the very small standard deviations for the regression (± 0.023 for NE and ± 0.005 for LP) and very high correlation coefficients between predicted and actual values ($r^2 = 0.989$ for NE and $r^2 = 0.999$ for LP).

The results indicate that respondents are capable of making extremely consistent magnitude estimates, but they demonstrate a significant regressive tendency in assigning numbers to lines or vice versa.

C. Scales of Assurance

The analysis of the actual scaling of perceived levels of assurance (parts IV and V of the questionnaire) proceeds in similar fashion. First, the magnitude data are reduced to common logarithms (base 10). Next, the arithmetic average of these logs

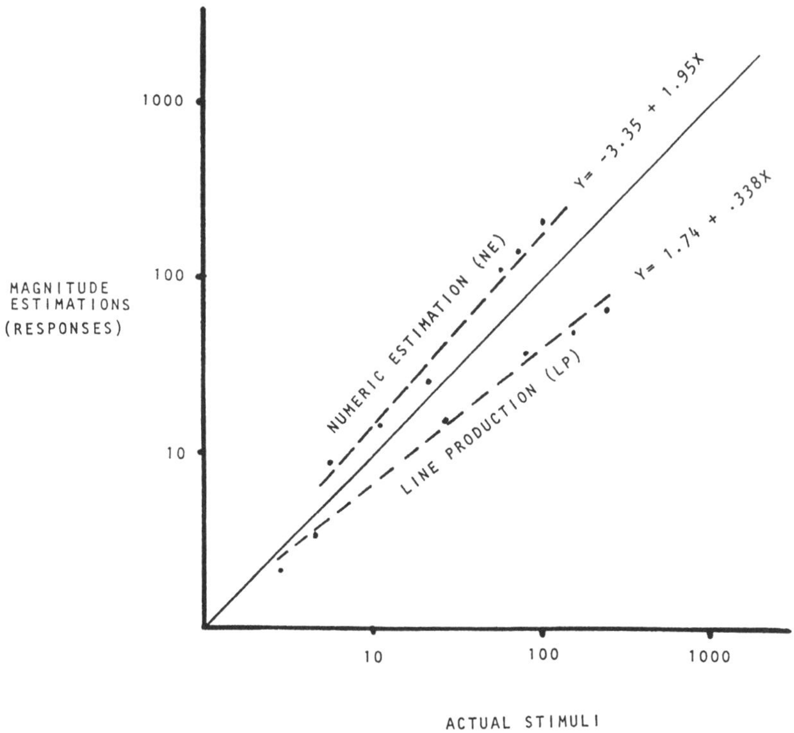

Figure 1. Plot of Calibration Lines

is calculated and exponentiated to derive the geometric means. Statistics for these geometric means are presented in Appendixes C and D.

Figure 2 shows the cross-modal match between the geometric means of the NE and LP response measures for the different reports which served as stimuli (the dotted line) adjusted for the difference in base measures (i.e., the base for line drawing is ⅕ of the base for numeric estimation). The linear relationship is described by the equation

$$Y = -5.18 + 1.102X.$$

This relationship is highly linear with a very high correlation between the responses ($r^2 = 0.995$). These results indicate that respondents were able to utilize magnitude estimation techniques to report their perceived levels of assurance.

D. A Ratio Scale of Levels of Assurance

Since the responses to parts II and III of the questionnaire indicate that respondents are capable of using magnitude estimation to make open-ended judgments

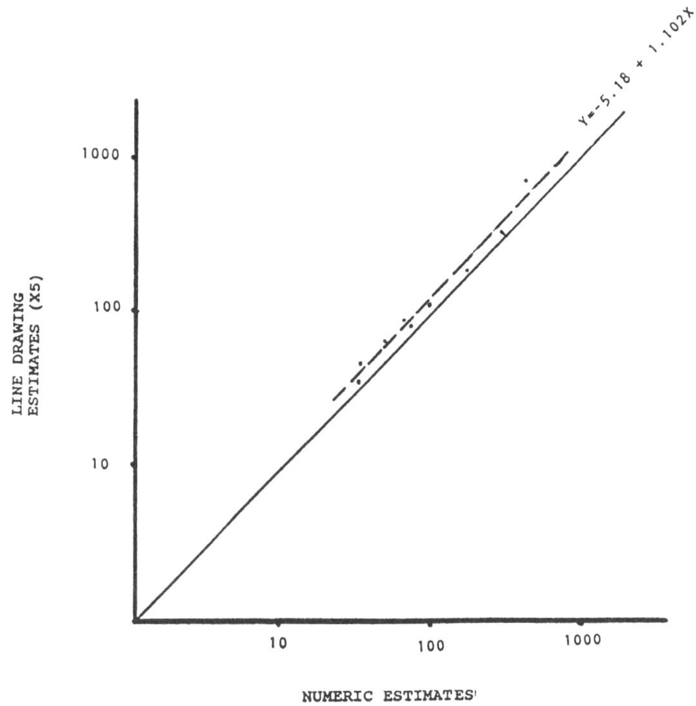

Figure 2. Plot of Geometric Means for Response Modes

using number estimation and line production, a ratio scale of the levels of assurance can be constructed using the magnitude responses from the appendixes. Each magnitude estimation was made using "reviewed financial statements" with a base magnitude of 200 for numeric estimation and a line of 40 mm for line production. The ratio scale developed in Table 2 is the average of the ratios obtained by dividing the geometric means of the responses for each report by the base magnitudes [i.e., for "audited financial statements with a 'clean' opinion" the ratios would be as follows: (417.8/200 = 2.089) + (92.9/40 = 2.323)/2 = 2.206].

This ratio scale shows that, on average, respondents perceive than an audited financial statement with a clean opinion would provide about 2.2 times as much assurance as a "reviewed financial statement" whereas compiled financial statements without footnote disclosures provides only about one half the assurance of a review. Because the scale is ratio in nature, comparisons can be made between any of the items, that is, a compilation with footnotes provides approximately 20% of the assurance of a clean opinion audit. Figure 3 shows the ratio-scale data in graphic form.

Table 2. Average Ratio-Scale Values

	Appendix C		*Appendix D*		
	Geometric Mean	*Ratio (/200)*	*Geometric Mean*	*Ratio (/40 mm)*	*Average Ratio*
Audited financial statements with a "clean" opinion	417.8	2.089	92.9	2.323	2.206
Audited financial statements with "except for" opinion	293.8	1.469	62.2	1.555	1.512
Reviewed financial statements (base)	200.0	1.000	40.0	1.000	1.000
Audited financial statements with a disclaimer of opinion	106.4	0.532	31.1	0.778	0.665
Compiled financial statements with footnotes disclosures	67.0	0.335	19.6	0.490	0.413
Financial information in "prescribed forms"	54.2	0.271	15.5	0.388	0.330
Balance sheet information in tax returns prepared by CPA	42.2	0.211	15.7	0.393	0.302
Unaudited financial statements of interim periods	39.6	0.198	13.2	0.330	0.264
Compiled financial statements without footnote disclosures	26.6	0.133	10.6	0.265	0.199
Financial statements with no report attached but CPA known to be associated	18.0	0.090	8.9	0.223	0.157

E. Comparison with Categorical Scale

In the questionnaire, respondents first indicated their perceived level of assurance for the various reports using a five-point Likert-type summated rating scale with response categories ranging from "high level of assurance" (5) to "no assurance" (1). Respondents could indicate "no opinion" as an option (0). Appendix A presents statistics for these categorical responses.

Comparing Appendix A with Table 2, we find that the ranking of the reports using either magnitude or categorical data is exactly the same. One error in the construction of the questionnaire should be noted. In the categorical scaling task, respondents evaluated the level of assurance provided by "financial statements with a disclaimer of opinion" about 0.6 lower than a review. In magnitude scaling, "audited financial statements with a disclaimer of opinion" were evaluated as providing 66% of the assurance of a review. This mistake in construction provides evidence that respondents were consistent in the overall evaluation of the levels of assurance provided in each case.

From all appearances, this application of magnitude estimation techniques has been successful at producing log-interval or ratio-level data which are internally

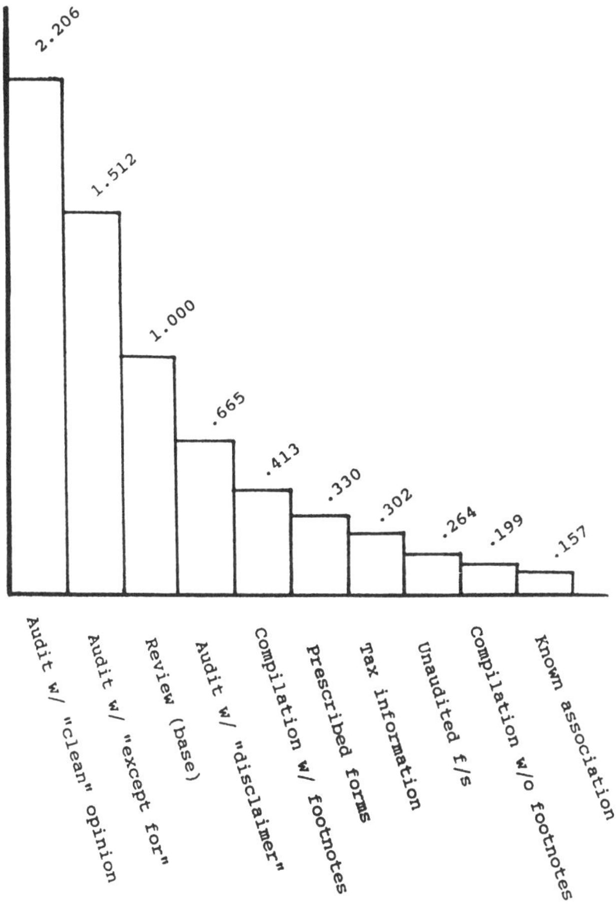

Figure 3. Graph of Levels of Assurance Expressed as Ratios

consistent and reliable and demonstrate a high degree of construct validity when compared to categorical data. Ratio-level data provide the researcher with the ability to make valid comparisons between and within groups of respondent data. Lodge (1981) notes:

> Categorical scaling does not produce regression coefficients which can be meaningfully interpreted as quantitative expressions of the relationship between variables. Regression coefficients are arbitrary when produced by variables measured categorically because of the arbitrariness of the categorical measure—first, in the number of categories imposed by the format of the scale and, second, in the numbers assigned to the categories. (p. 69)

And later:

> The central problem is of course that category scaling is oblivious to the true range of stimuli and the subjective range of opinion. Because the range of response is fixed, category scales cannot adjust to changes in the true range of stimuli or track the magnitude of opinion strength. (p. 70)

VII. SUMMARY AND CONCLUSIONS

The objectives of this study are twofold: first, to demonstrate that magnitude estimation techniques as validated by the cross-modality matching paradigm can be applied to measure attitudes and perceptions in an accounting context; and second, to present a study of the perceived levels of assurance provided by types of financial statement reports as an illustration of the application of this measurement technique to an accounting issue.

This research provides considerable support for the conclusion that respondents are able to use magnitude estimation techniques to make consistent, highly reliable estimates of their perceptions in accounting contexts. Further, when compared to a traditional categorical rating scale, the ratio scale produced highly consistent results at comparable levels of reliability. Because of the ratio nature of the magnitude scale, it is possible to compare relational rather than ranked concepts.

These results should be of interest to both academic researchers and accounting practitioners. If, as indicated by the results of this study, magnitude scaling techniques are successful at developing ratio or log-interval scales of attitude or belief, the resultant measurements can be meaningfully analyzed using the most powerful statistical tools available. As Lodge (1981) observes:

> No one, of course, favors weak, crude measurement, so the basic issue between category and magnitude scaling ultimately turns on the question of utility—the relative worth of the two scaling methods in the description, prediction, and explanation of social phenomena. The reliance on category scaling appears to compromise the full range of social science research activity from the simple description of opinion distributions to the formal modeling of preferences and behavior.
>
> Perhaps the most serious consequence of crude measurement is weak theory. Given ordinal-level measurement, one is unable to test quantitative hypotheses: One can state only that Y "depends on" X to some extent. The magnitude of effect of X on Y cannot be specified. What is lost is a sensitive, quantitatively meaningful measure of the relationship between variables. What is lost is the capacity to determine the form of functional relationships or measure the impact of change on relationships. (p. 76)

Academic accounting researchers should welcome the opportunity to develop measurements which will enable them to determine the strength of association between variables. The resulting analyses of the type "How much does X increase for a change in Y?" should produce stronger theory.

In the current environment of change, accounting practitioners should welcome the results of research that would provide more reliable answers to issues such as the "expectation gap" (Auditing Standards Board, 1986), the relationship between management consulting services and auditor independence (for example, Burton, 1980) and auditor judgment (for example, Gibbons, 1984). Each of these issues has an extensive body of research producing inconsistent or inconclusive results. Of course, the extent to which the inconsistencies are related to the quality of measurement is a matter of debate, but research that can provide more sensitive measurements would seemingly be worth the increased effort.

APPENDIX A: INSTRUCTIONS, REPORT TYPES, AND STATISTICS FOR PART I: LIKERT-TYPE CATEGORICAL RESPONSE MODE

Instructions:

Part I

The purpose of this part of the survey is to determine your opinions regarding the levels of assurance being provided, either explicitly or implicitly, by the various report formats which CPAs can be associated with. A "Level of Assurance" refers to how much credence the user should be willing to place on the statements covered by the report.

Below is a list of some of the reports which CPAs can be associated with. Indicate the level of assurance which you feel is being provided to users of those reports by circling the appropriate response. If you don't have an opinion about a report, please mark the "O" option.

Level of Assurance

High *None* *No Opinion*

5 4 3 2 1 0

* * * * *

Report Type and Statistics	*Average*	*Standard Deviation*	*Modal Response*
Compiled financial statements without footnote disclosures	1.785	0.772	2.00
Unaudited financial statements of interim periods	1.958	0.896	2.00
Balance sheet information in tax returns prepared by CPA	2.386	1.116	2.00
Audited financial statements with a "clean" opinion	4.685	0.547	5.00
Financial statements with a disclaimer of opinion	2.491	1.258	2.00
Reviewed financial statements	3.059	0.857	3.00
Financial statements with no report attached but CPA known to be associated	1.735	0.830	1.00
Financial statements contained in "prescribed forms" signed by CPA	2.422	1.222	2.00
Compiled financial statements with footnote disclosure	2.473	0.929	2.00
Audited financial statements with "except for" opinion based on GAAP departure involving the use of current values for equipment	4.064	0.988	4.00

APPENDIX B: INSTRUCTIONS AND FORMAT FOR PARTS II AND III CALIBRATION EXERCISES

Part II

This part of the survey contains a series of line lengths. Your task is to tell how much longer or shorter they are compared to the first line. The first line is your reference and it has been given the number 100.

Please write a number in the box below each line given. The longer a line appears in comparison to the reference line, the larger the number you will write. As examples, if one of the lines seems about twice as long as the reference line, you would write in the number 200. If the line appears to be 10 times shorter, you would write the number 10.

Once you begin, please do not look back to any of the numbers or lines other than the reference line. PLEASE DO NOT USE A RULER OR OTHER MEASURING DEVICE. WE ARE INTERESTED IN YOUR IMPRESSIONS OF RELATIVE MAGNITUDE ONLY.

REFERENCE LINE: ____________________

(100)

Five additional line lengths of 70, 28, 110, 6, and 85 mm provided.

* * * * *

Part III

This part of the survey contains a series of numbers. Your task is to indicate the magnitude of a particular number by drawing a line to represent that number in relation to the reference number and line. The reference number is 100 with an assigned line length as indicated.

For each of the numbers given below, please draw a line which you feel represents the magnitude of that number in comparison to the reference line. For example, if the number given is 300, draw a line which you think is 3 times the length of the reference line. If the number given is 25, draw a line which you think is 1/4 the length of the reference line.

PLEASE DO NOT USE A RULER OR OTHER MEASURING DEVICE. WE ARE INTERESTED IN YOUR IMPRESSIONS OF RELATIVE MAGNITUDE ONLY.

REFERENCE NUMBER: (100)

Reference line: ____________________

Five additional numbers of 35, 100 6, 200 and 3 were provided.

APPENDIX C: INSTRUCTIONS, REPORT TYPES, AND STATISTICS FOR PART IV: MAGNITUDE ESTIMATION RESPONSE MODE: NUMERIC ESTIMATION

Part IV

In this part of the survey, we are going to ask you to use the tasks that you just completed to tell us about the Levels of Assurance which you feel are being provided, either explicitly or implicitly, by the various forms of financial reports which CPAs can be associated with.

Below is a list of some of these reports. The first report, "reviewed financial statements," is provided as a reference point and has been assigned a score of "200" to indicate a level of assurance. Please use it as the basis for indicating what levels of assurance you feel are being provided by the other reports listed. For example, if you feel that by a given report the CPA is providing TWO AND ONE HALF TIMES more assurance than with a review, you should assign that report a number around 500. If you feel that a CPA provides no assurance, you should give that report a zero.

Report On	*Level of Assurance*
REFERENCE:	
Reviewed financial statements	*200*

* * * * *

Report Type and Statistics

	Raw Data		
	Average	*Range*	*Geometric Mean*
Compiled financial statements without footnote disclosures	64	0–500	26.6
Audited financial statements with a disclaimer of opinion	215	0–800	106.4
Unaudited financial statements of interim periods	87	0–450	39.6
Audited financial statements with a "clean" opinion	453	100–2,000	417.8
Compiled financial statements with footnote disclosures	116	0–500	67.0
Financial statements with no report attached but CPA known to be associated	57	0–300	18.0
Balance sheet information in tax returns signed by CPA	99	0–450	42.2
Financial information contained in "prescribed forms" signed by CPA	121	0–750	54.2
Audited financial statements with "except for" opinion based on GAAP departure involving the use of current values for equipment	353	0–2,000	293.8

APPENDIX D: INSTRUCTIONS, REPORT TYPES, AND STATISTICS FOR PART V: MAGNITUDE ESTIMATION RESPONSE MODE: LINE PRODUCTION

Instructions:

Part V

Below is the same list of reports as provided in Part IV. Without looking back, please use your line drawing judgment to indicate the Level of Assurance which you feel is being provided by each report. Again, the report "reviewed financial statements" is provided to you with a line already drawn for reference. For example, if you feel that in a given situation, the CPA is providing TWO TIMES as much assurance as in reviewed financial statements, then you should draw a line which is twice as long as the reference line. PLEASE DO NOT USE RULERS OR OTHER MEASURING DEVICES. WE ARE INTERESTED IN YOUR IMPRESSIONS OF RELATIVE ASSURANCE.

RERFERENCE CASE:

Reviewed financial statements:

Line: ______________________

Report Types and Statistics

	Raw Data		
	Average	*Range*	*Geometric Mean*
Audited financial statements with a "clean" opinion	101.2	10–355	92.9
Compiled financial statements without footnote disclosures	17.5	0–66	10.6
Audited financial statements with "except for" opinion based on GAAP departure involving the use of current values for equipment	76.8	0–300	62.2
Financial statements with no report attached but CPA known to be associated	19.3	0–73	8.9
Financial statements contained in "prescribed forms" signed by CPA	29.4	0–210	15.5
Audited financial statements with a disclaimer of opinion	51.6	0–210	31.1
Compiled financial statements with footnote disclosures	28.9	0–175	19.6
Balance sheet information in tax returns prepared by CPA	29.4	0–116	15.7
Unaudited financial statements of interim periods	21.8	0~100	13.2

ACKNOWLEDGMENTS

The author is a professor in the Accounting Department at California State University, Sacramento. He would like to acknowledge the generous support of the School of Business and Public Administration Dean's Fund and the Sacramento, California, office of Price Waterhouse. The research has benefited greatly from the helpful comments of Professor Milton Lodge; however, any mistakes or weaknesses are the sole responsibility of the author.

NOTE

1. This paper presents the development and validation of the measurement methodology. An earlier paper (Bartlett, 1991) discusses comparisons between respondent groups using the ratio-level data created by this methodology.

REFERENCES

Abdel-Magid, M. F. (1979a). "Toward a Better Understanding of the Role of Measurement in Accounting." *Accounting Review* (April), 346–357.

———. (1979b). "General-Price-Level-Adjusted Historical-Cost Statements and the Ratio-Scale View: A Comment." *Accounting Review* (October), 825–829.

American Accounting Association, Committee on Basic Auditing Concepts. (1973). *A Statement of Basic Auditing Concepts: Studies in Accounting Research* 6 (Sarasota, FL: AAA).

American Institute of Certified Public Accountants, Commission on Auditor's Responsibilities. (1978). *Report, Conclusions, and Recommendations* (New York: AICPA).

Auditing Standards Board. (1986). "The Auditing Standards Board Responds to Public Expectations." Exposure Draft No. 2575, (October 10), mimeographed 19 pp.

Bailey, K., Bylinski, J., and Shields, M. (1984). "The Comparative Perceived Messages of Audit, Review, and Compilation Reports." *Papers and Proceedings of the American Accounting Association Annual Meeting.*

Bartlett, R. W. (1991). "Perceived Levels of Assurance of Bankers and CPAs: A Comparison." *Advances in Accounting* 9, 205–225.

Burton, J. C. (1980). "A Critical Look at Professionalism and Scope of Services." *Journal of Accountancy* (April), 48–56.

Cargile, B. R., and Bublitz, B. (1986), "Factors Contributing to Published Research by Accounting Faculties." *Accounting Review* (January), 158–178.

Gibbons, M. (1984). "Propositions about the Psychology of Professional Judgment in Public Accounting." *Journal of Accounting Research* (Spring), 103–125.

Holt, G., and Moizer, P. (1990). "The Meaning of Audit Reports." *Accounting and Business Research* (Spring), 111–121.

Howard, T. P. (1981). "Attitude Measurement: Some Further Considerations." *Accounting Review* (July), 613–621.

Howard, T. P., and Nikolai, L. A. (1983). "Attitude Measurement and Perceptions of Accounting Faculty Publication Outlets." *Accounting Review* (October), 765–776.

Hull, R. P., and Wright, G. B. (1990). "Faculty Perceptions of Journal Quality: An Update." *Accounting Horizons* (March), 77–87.

Johnson, D. A. (1979). "To Blow the Whistle or Not: An Employee's Dilemma with Internal Control Implications." *Symposium on Auditing Research III* (University of Illinois), pp. 239–256.

Libby, R. (1979). "Bankers' and Auditors' Perceptions of the Message Communicated by the Audit Report." *Journal of Accounting Research* 17, 99–122.

Libby, R., and Short, D. (1980). "A Review and Test of the Meaning of Audit Reports from the Perspective of Bankers," *Journal of Commercial Bank Lending* (August), 48–62.

Lodge, M. (1981). *Magnitude Scaling: Quantitative Measurement of Opinions*, (Beverly Hills, CA: Sage).

Miethe, T. (1986). "Social Psychological Measurement: A Comparison the Measurement Properties of Magnitude and Categorical Scaling of Social Perceptions." *Social Science Quarterly* 67, 195–204.

Nair, R., and Rittenberg, L. (1987). "Messages Perceived from Audit, Review, and Compilation Reports: Extension to More Diverse Groups." *Auditing: A Journal of Practice & Theory*, 7, 15–38.

Nobes, C. W. (1985). "International Variations in Perceptions of Accounting Journals." *Accounting Review* (October), 702–705.

Pany, K., and Smith, C. (1982). "Auditor Associations with Quarterly Financial Information: An Empirical Test." *Journal of Accounting Research* 20, 472–481.

Pillsbury, C. (1985). "Limited Assurance Engagements." *Auditing: A Journal of Practice & Theory* 4, 63–79.

Schroeder, R. G., Payne, D. D., and Harris, D. G. (1988). "Perceptions of Accounting Publications Outlets: A Further Analysis." *Accounting Educators' Journal* (Fall), 1–17.

Stevens, S. S. (1957). "On the Psychophysical Law." *Psychological Review* 64, 153–181.

———. (1966). "A Metric for the Social Consensus." *Science* 151, 530–541.

———. (1972). *Psychophysics: Introduction to Its Perceptual, Neural, and Social Prospects* (New York: John Wiley).

Tomassini, L. A. (1977). "Assessing the Impact of Human Resource Accounting: An Experimental Study of Managerial Decision Preferences." *Accounting Review* (October) 904–914.

Vickery, D. W. (1976). "General-Price-Level-Adjusted Historical-Cost Statements and the Ratio-Scale View." *Accounting Review* (January), 31–40.

Wegener, B. (1983). "Category-Rating and Magnitude Estimation Scaling Techniques." *Sociological Methods & Research* 12, 31–75.

Yardley. J. A. (1989). "Lenders' and CPAs' Perceptions of the Assurance Provided by Prescribed Procedures." *Auditing: A Journal of Practice and Theory* (Fall) 58–79.

Advances in Quantative Analysis of Finance and Accounting

Edited by **Cheng-Few Lee,** *Department of Finance, School of Business, Rutgers University.*

Associate Editors: **Thomas J. Frecka,** *Department of Accountancy, University of Notre Dame* and **Louis O. Scott,** *Department Banking and Finance, The University of Georgia*

Volume 1, 1991, 2 Volume Set
Set ISBN 1-55938-026-8 $157.50

Volume 1, Part A
1991, 249 pp.
ISBN 1-55938-026-8 (A) $78.75

CONTENTS: On the Stochastic Nature of the Stock Price Variance Rate and Strike Price Bias in Option Pricing, *Larry J. Merville and Dan R. Pieptea.* **Arbitrage Pricing Theory Factors and their Relationship to Macro-Economic Variables,** *Carl B. McGowan and Jack Clark Francis.* **Stock Prices and Market Fundamentals in a Consumption-Based Capital Asset Pricing Model,** *Louis O. Scott.* **Divided Behavior, Claim Dilution, and Warrants at Maturity: An Empirical Examination of the Implied Variability of Stock Prices,** *Stephan E. Sefcik.* **Geometric Mean Approximations and Risk Policy in Long-Term Investment,** *David C. Cheng and Marvin J. Karson.* **An Empirical Analysis of Japanese Direct Investment in Taiwan: A Neoclassical Approach,** *De-Min Wu.* **Normative Portfolio Theory and the Stable-Pareto Distribution,** *George M. Frankfurter and Christopher G. Lamouureux,.* **Estimation Issues in Bond Rating Models,** *Sara Ann Reiter and Douglas R. Emery.* **Optimal Portfolio Choices of Commodity Options in Incomplete Markets: A Simulation Analysis,** *Avner Wolf, Jack Clark Francis.*

Volume 1, Part B
1991, 214 pp.
ISBN 1-55938-138-8 (B) $78.75

CONTENTS: Stock Splits: Price per Share and Trading Volume, *Victor J. Defeo and Prem C. Jain.* **The Specialized Common Carrier Decision and the Systematic Risk of AT&T,** *Randolph P. Beatty and William N. Lanen.* **Seasonal Adjustment at the Corporate Level Using X-II Procedures,** *Thomas J. Frecka, Paul Newbold, Peter A. Silhan.* **The Incremental**

J A I

P R E S S

Information Content of Historical Cost and Current Cost Income: Cross-Sectional Analyses for 1962-1980, *Victor L. Bernard and Robert G. Ruland.* **An Examination of the Difference Between Allowed Set Rates of Return and Realized Rates of Return for Utilities,** *Scott Besley, Steven E. Bolten and Samuel B. Bulmash.* **Improving the Effectiveness of Offshore Production Agreements in Dynamic Product Markets,** *Daniel Blakley, Barry Doyle, L. and William Murray.* **An Analysis of the Use of Arps Funds in Corporate Cash Management,** *John D. Martin, Laurence E. Blose and J. William Petty.* **Investment Cutoff Rates, Cash Flow Uncertainty and the Theory of the Firm,** *Paul S. Peyser.* **Empirical Option Price Bands on the CBOE and the Redundancy of Options,** *David M. Chen and Robert L. Welch.* **Mean-Semivariance CAPM and International Portfolio Diversification: The Case of U.S.-Based International Mutual Funds,** *Musa Essayyad and H.K. Wu.* **An Application of a Multiple Time Series Forecasting Technique in Finance: The Case of Stock Prices,** *James S. Ang and Jess H. Chua.*